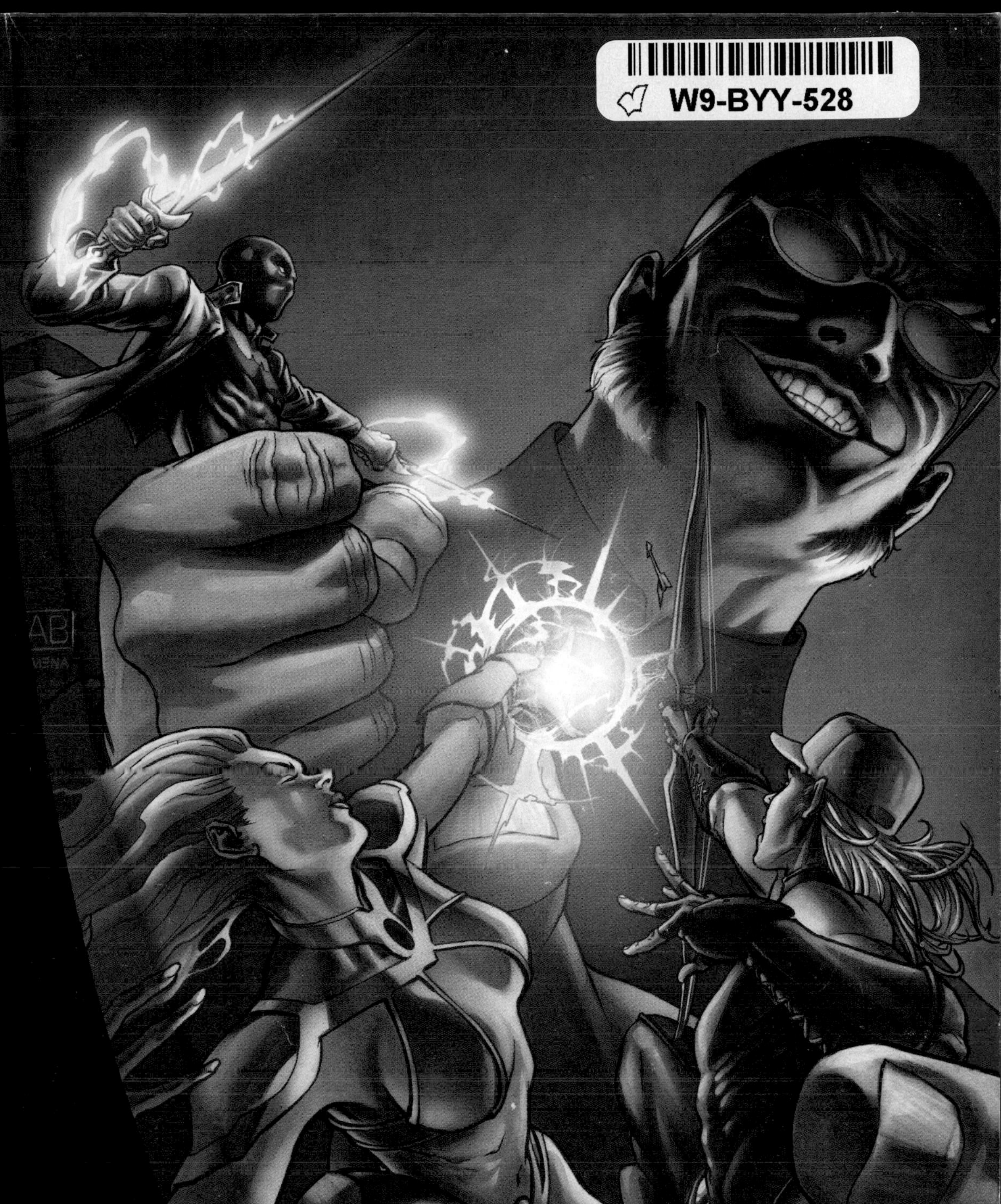

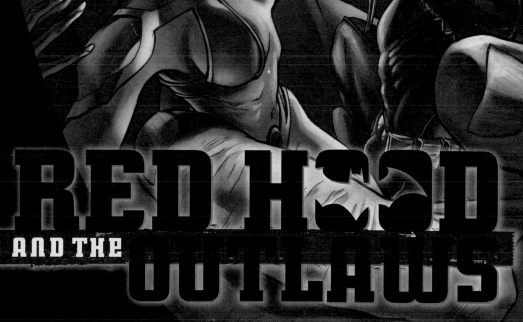

RED HOOD AND THE OUTLAWS

VOLUME 4 LEAGUE OF ASSASSINS

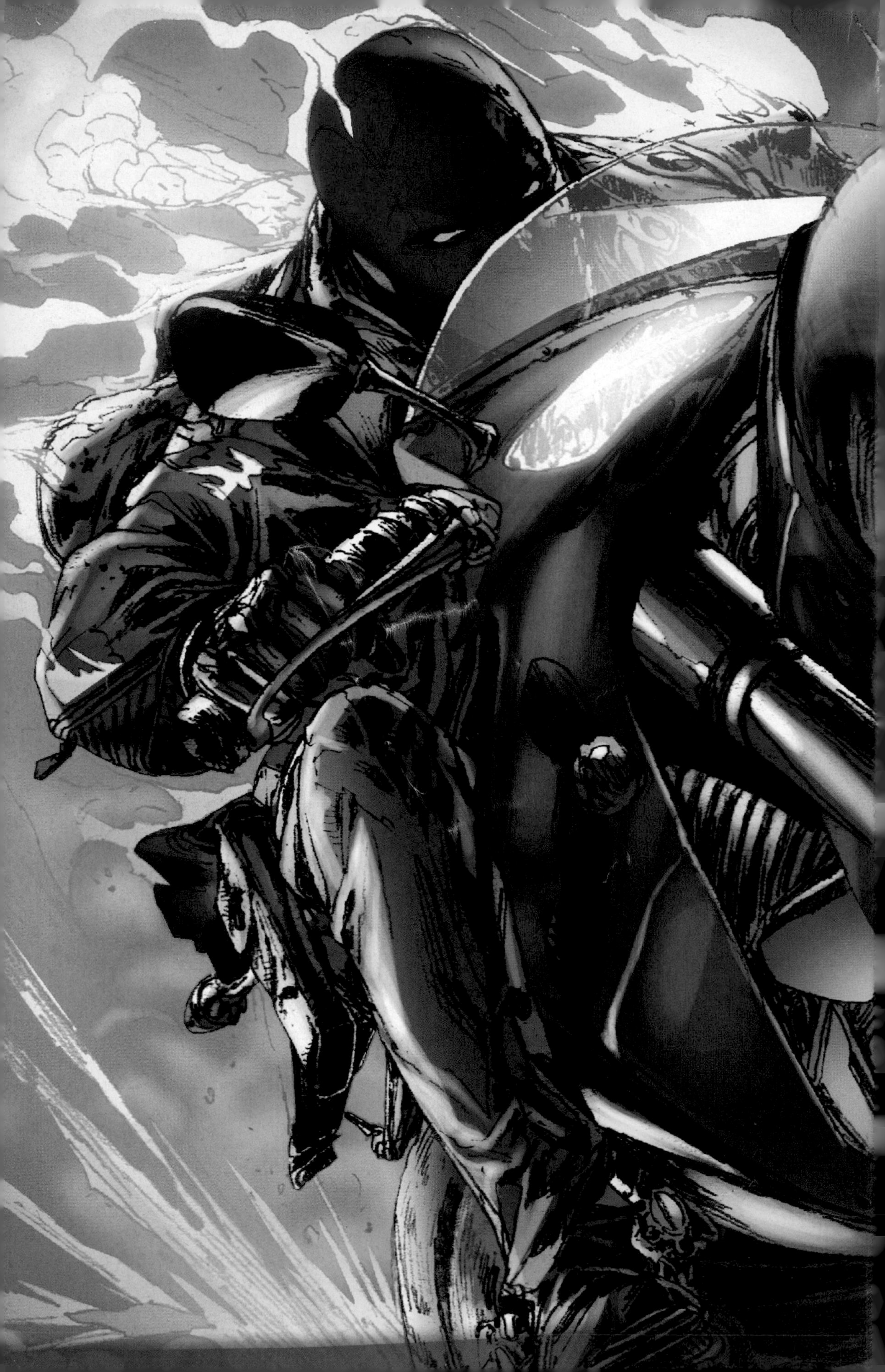

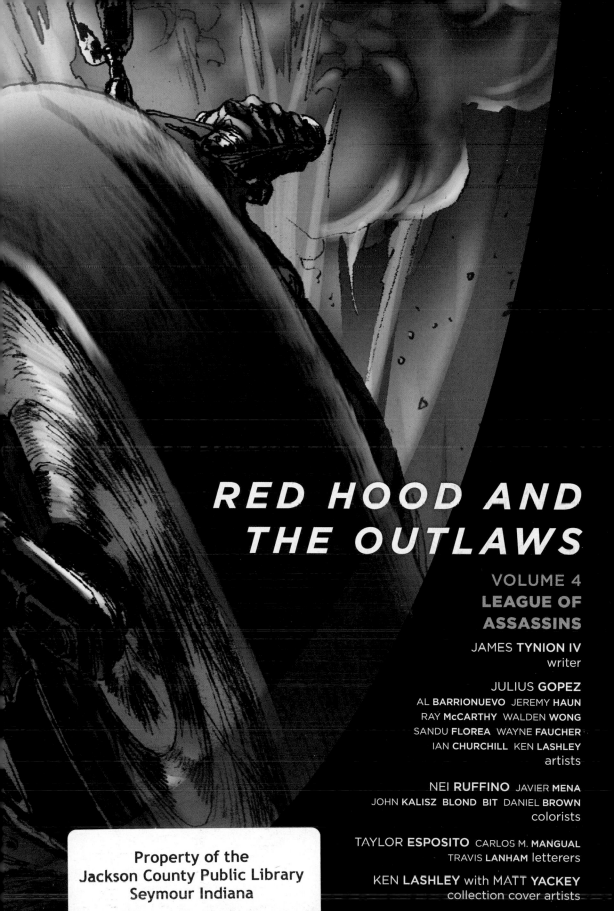

RED HOOD AND THE OUTLAWS

VOLUME 4
LEAGUE OF ASSASSINS

JAMES **TYNION IV**
writer

JULIUS **GOPEZ**
AL **BARRIONUEVO** JEREMY **HAUN**
RAY **McCARTHY** WALDEN **WONG**
SANDU **FLOREA** WAYNE **FAUCHER**
IAN **CHURCHILL** KEN **LASHLEY**
artists

NEI **RUFFINO** JAVIER **MENA**
JOHN **KALISZ** BLOND BIT DANIEL **BROWN**
colorists

TAYLOR **ESPOSITO** CARLOS M. **MANGUAL**
TRAVIS **LANHAM** letterers

KEN **LASHLEY** with MATT **YACKEY**
collection cover artists

**Property of the
Jackson County Public Library
Seymour Indiana**

EDDIE BERGANZA Editor – Original Series RICKEY PURDIN Associate Editor – Original Series
ROBIN WILDMAN Editor ROBBIN BROSTERMAN Design Director – Books ROBBIE BIEDERMAN Publication Design

BOB HARRAS Senior VP – Editor-in-Chief, DC Comics

DIANE NELSON President DAN DIDIO and JIM LEE Co-Publishers
GEOFF JOHNS Chief Creative Officer
JOHN ROOD Executive VP – Sales, Marketing and Business Development
AMY GENKINS Senior VP – Business and Legal Affairs NAIRI GARDINER Senior VP – Finance
JEFF BOISON VP – Publishing Planning MARK CHIARELLO VP – Art Direction and Design
JOHN CUNNINGHAM VP – Marketing TERRI CUNNINGHAM VP – Editorial Administration
ALISON GILL Senior VP – Manufacturing and Operations HANK KANALZ Senior VP – Vertigo and Integrated Publishing
JAY KOGAN VP – Business and Legal Affairs, Publishing JACK MAHAN VP – Business Affairs, Talent
NICK NAPOLITANO VP – Manufacturing Administration SUE POHJA VP – Book Sales
COURTNEY SIMMONS Senior VP – Publicity BOB WAYNE Senior VP – Sales

RED HOOD AND THE OUTLAWS VOLUME 4: LEAGUE OF ASSASSINS

Published by DC Comics. Copyright © 2014 DC Comics. All Rights Reserved.

Originally published in single magazine form as RED HOOD AND THE OUTLAWS 19-26,
RED HOOD AND THE OUTLAWS ANNUAL 1 © 2013, 2014 DC Comics. All Rights Reserved.
All characters, their distinctive likenesses and related elements featured in this publication are trademarks of DC Comics.
The stories, characters and incidents featured in this publication are entirely fictional.
DC Comics does not read or accept unsolicited ideas, stories or artwork.

DC Comics, 1700 Broadway, New York, NY 10019
A Warner Bros. Entertainment Company.
Printed by RR Donnelley, Salem, VA, USA. 5/9/14. First Printing.

ISBN: 978-1-4012-4636-5

SUSTAINABLE
FORESTRY
INITIATIVE

Certified Chain of Custody
At Least 20% Certified Forest Content
www.sfiprogram.org
SFI-01042
APPLIES TO TEXT STOCK ONLY

Library of Congress Cataloging-in-Publication Data

Tynion, James, IV, author.
Red Hood and the Outlaws. Vol. 4, League of Assassins / James Tynion IV ; illustrated by Julius Gopez ; illustrated by Al Barrionuevo.
pages cm. — (The New 52!)
Summary: "A new era begins for Red Hood and the Outlaws! Following the Joker's horrifying attack on the Bat-family,
Jason Todd finds himself lost in his own past. Kori and Arsenal set out on a treacherous journey to the far reaches of the globe
to rescue him, but when they come face to face with the All Caste, Hugo Strange, and the League of Assassins, the Outlaws might
reach their breaking point. Collects Red Hood and the Outlaws 19-24 and Red Hood and the Outlaws Annual 1"— Provided by publisher.
ISBN 978-1-4012-4636-5 (paperback)
1. Graphic novels. I. Gopez, Julius M., illustrator. II. Title. III. Title: League of Assassins.
PN6728.R4385T96 2014
741.5'973—dc23
2014008599

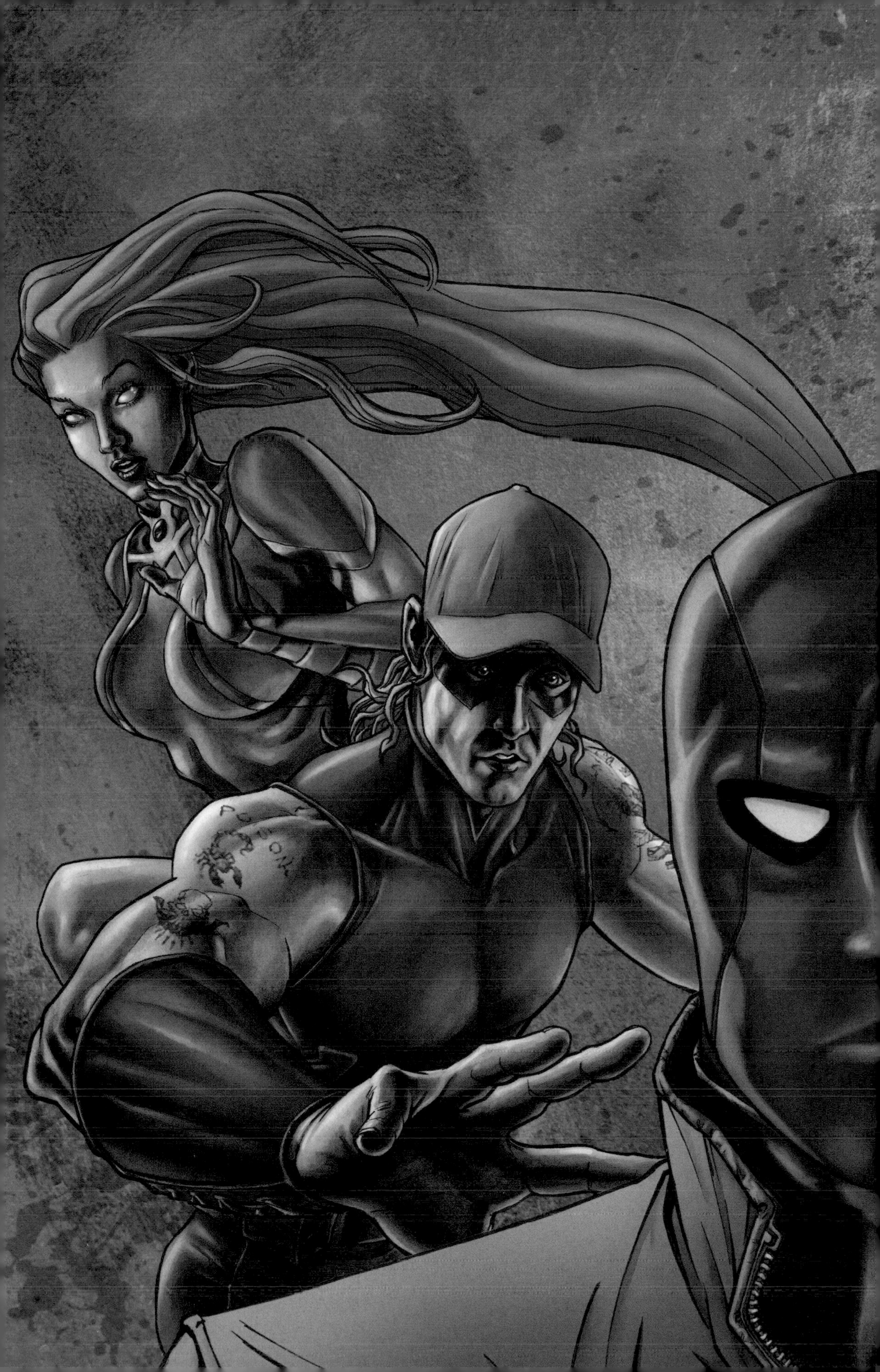

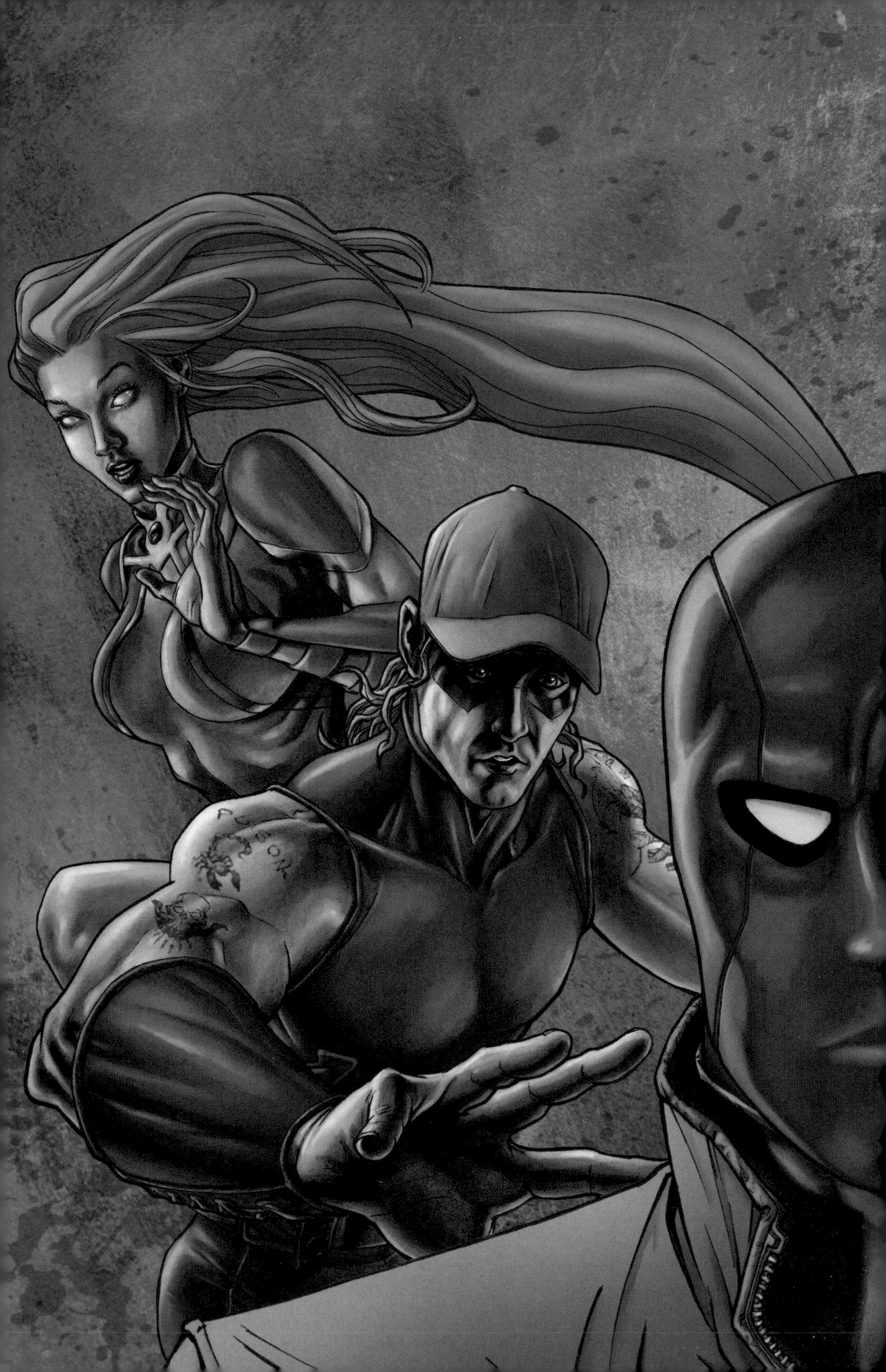

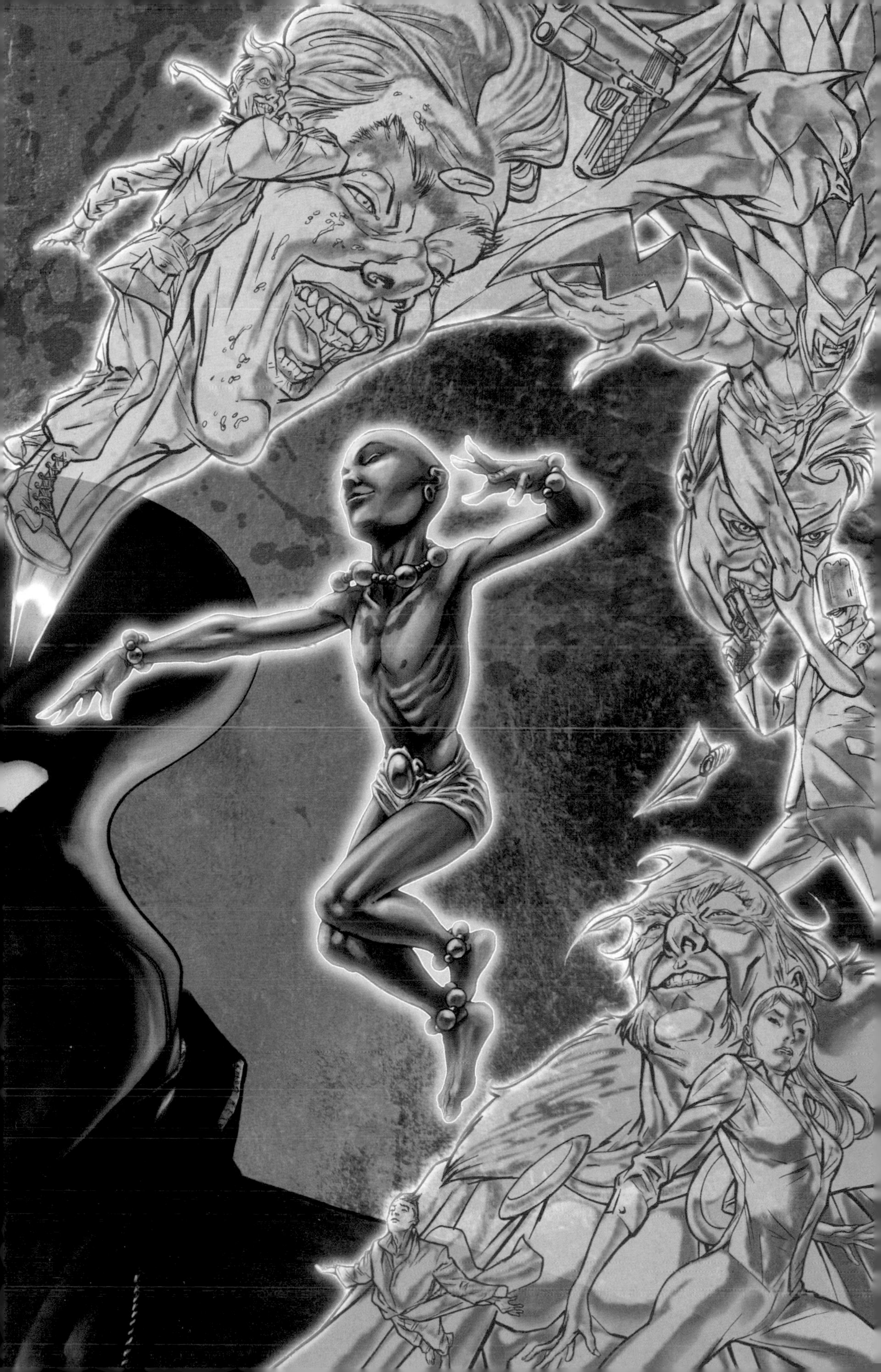

JAMES TYNION IV writer **JULIUS GOPEZ** artist **NEI RUFFINO** colorist **AL BARRIONUEVO** with **JAVIER MENA** cover artists

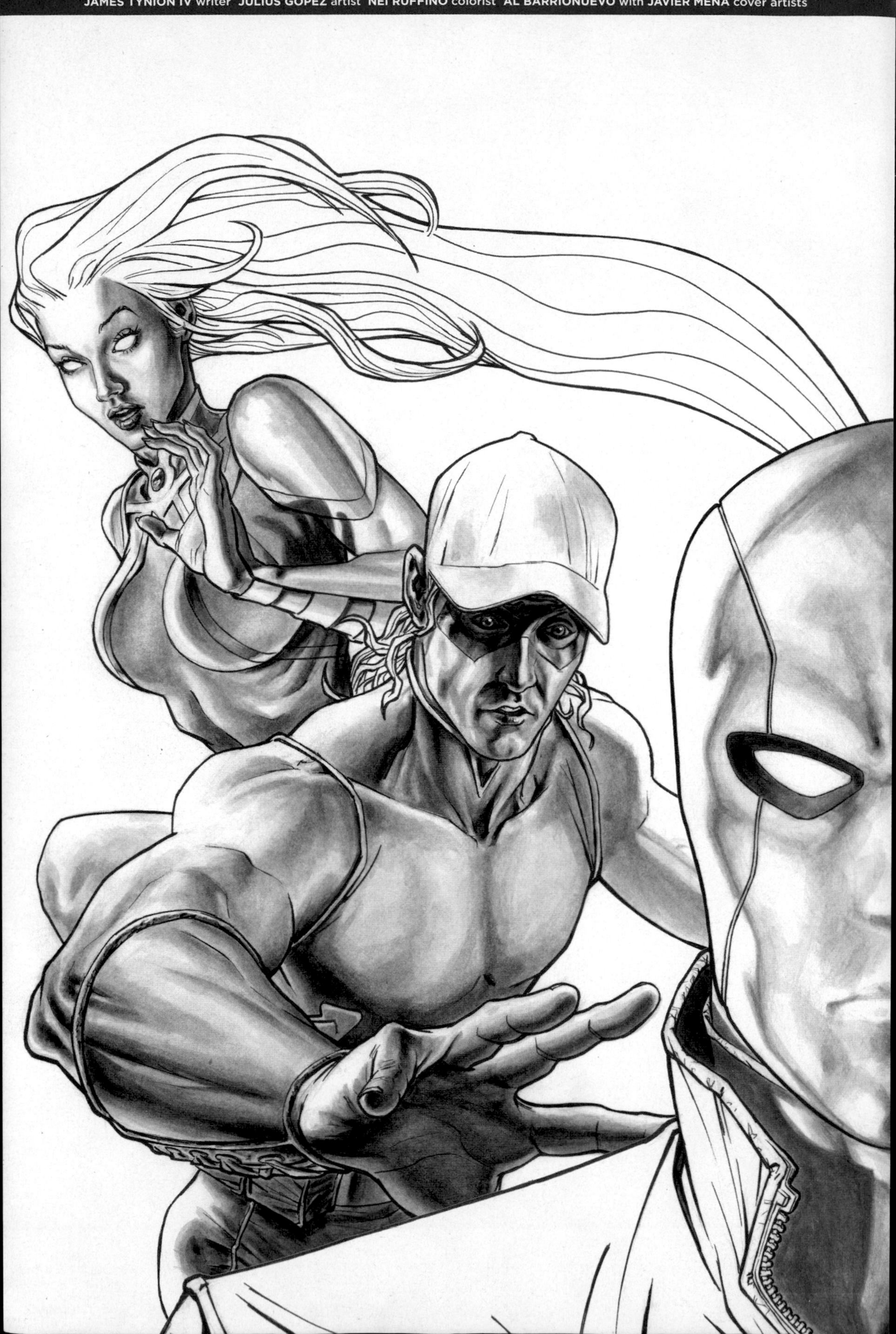

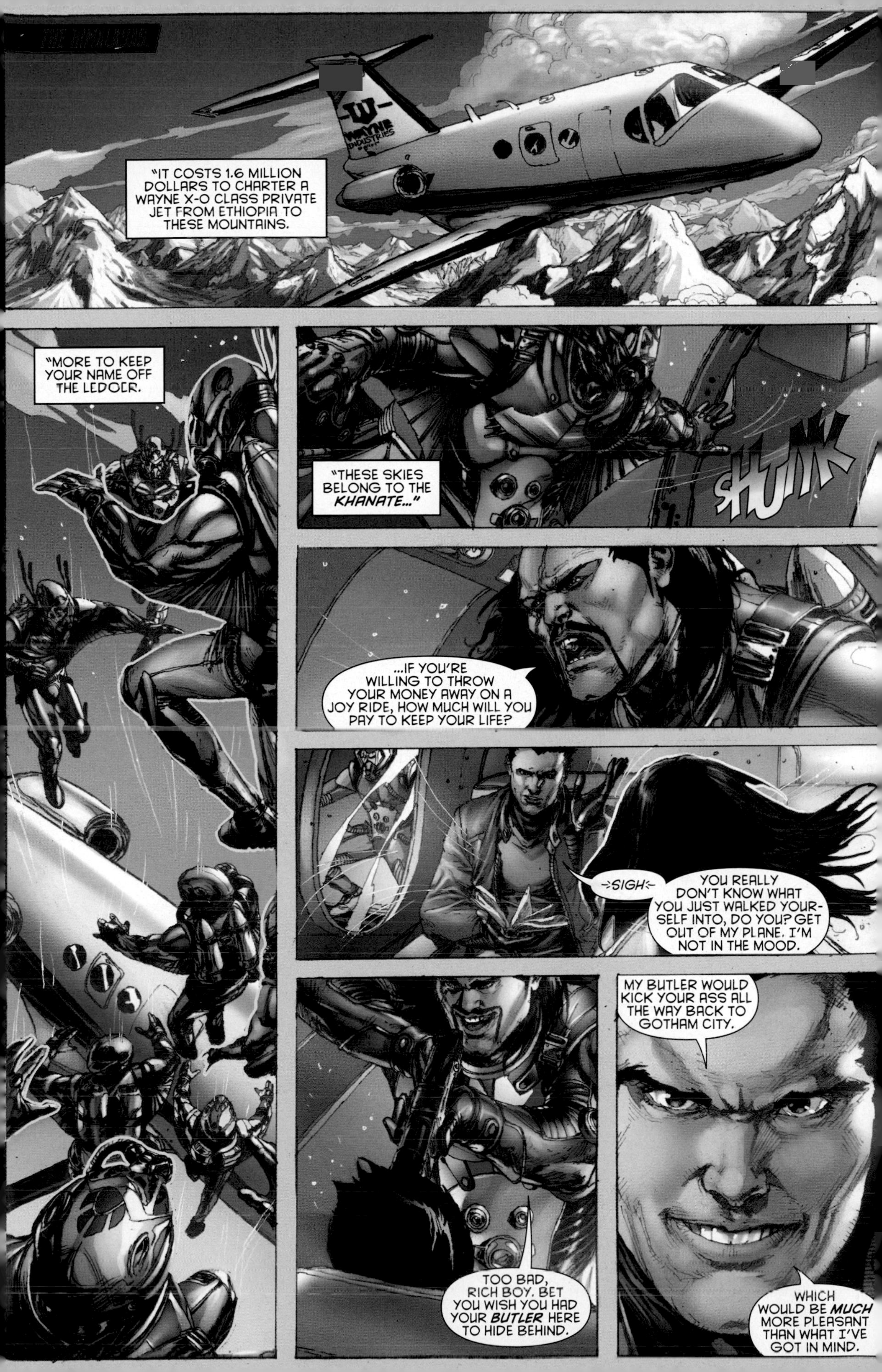
"IT COSTS 1.6 MILLION DOLLARS TO CHARTER A WAYNE X-O CLASS PRIVATE JET FROM ETHIOPIA TO THESE MOUNTAINS.
"MORE TO KEEP YOUR NAME OFF THE LEDGER.
"THESE SKIES BELONG TO THE KHANATE..."
SHUNK
...IF YOU'RE WILLING TO THROW YOUR MONEY AWAY ON A JOY RIDE, HOW MUCH WILL YOU PAY TO KEEP YOUR LIFE?
SIGH
YOU REALLY DON'T KNOW WHAT YOU JUST WALKED YOURSELF INTO, DO YOU? GET OUT OF MY PLANE. I'M NOT IN THE MOOD.
TOO BAD, RICH BOY. BET YOU WISH YOU HAD YOUR BUTLER HERE TO HIDE BEHIND.
MY BUTLER WOULD KICK YOUR ASS ALL THE WAY BACK TO GOTHAM CITY.
WHICH WOULD BE MUCH MORE PLEASANT THAN WHAT I'VE GOT IN MIND.

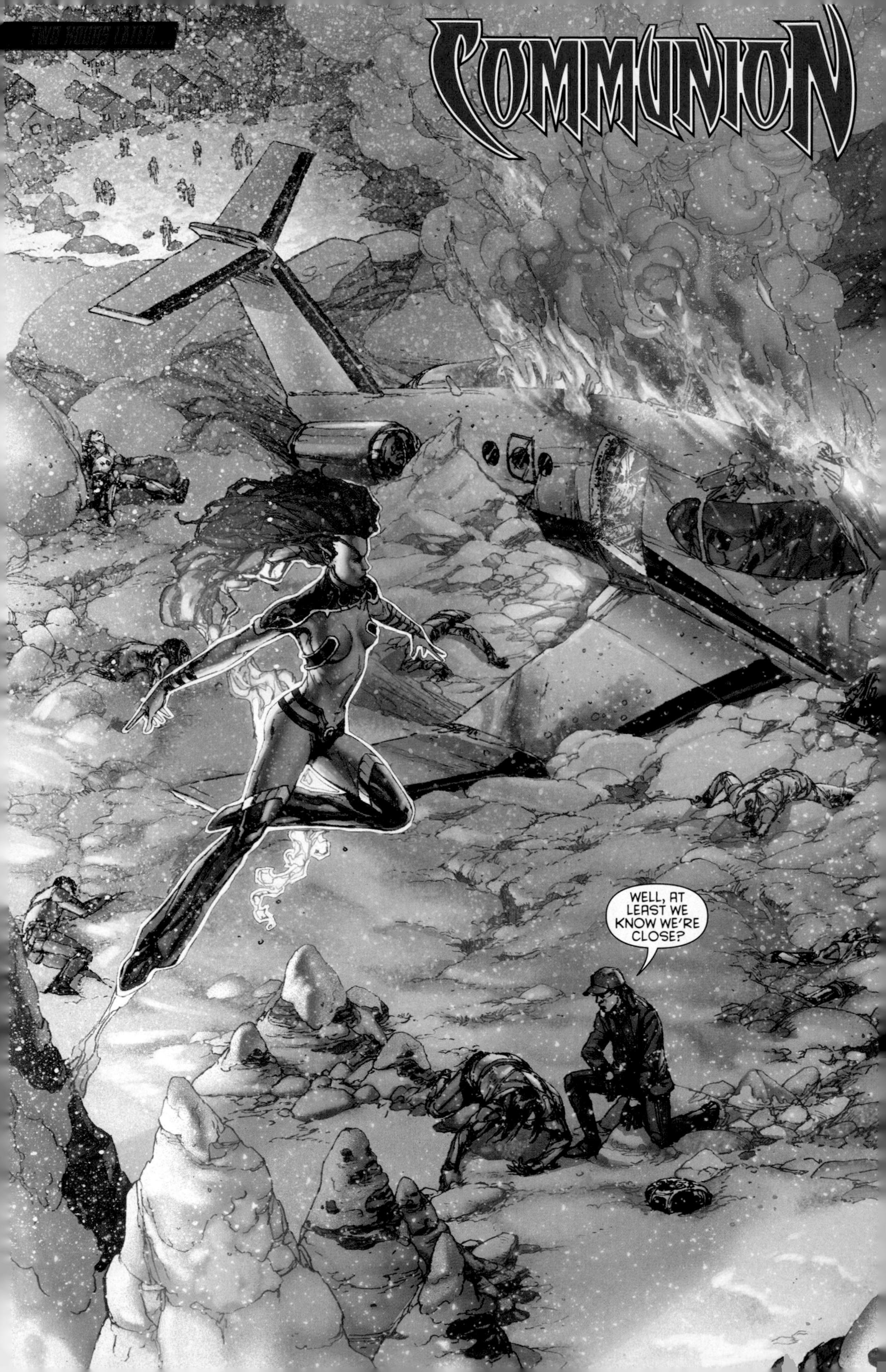
TWO HOURS LATER...
COMMUNION
WELL, AT LEAST WE KNOW WE'RE CLOSE?

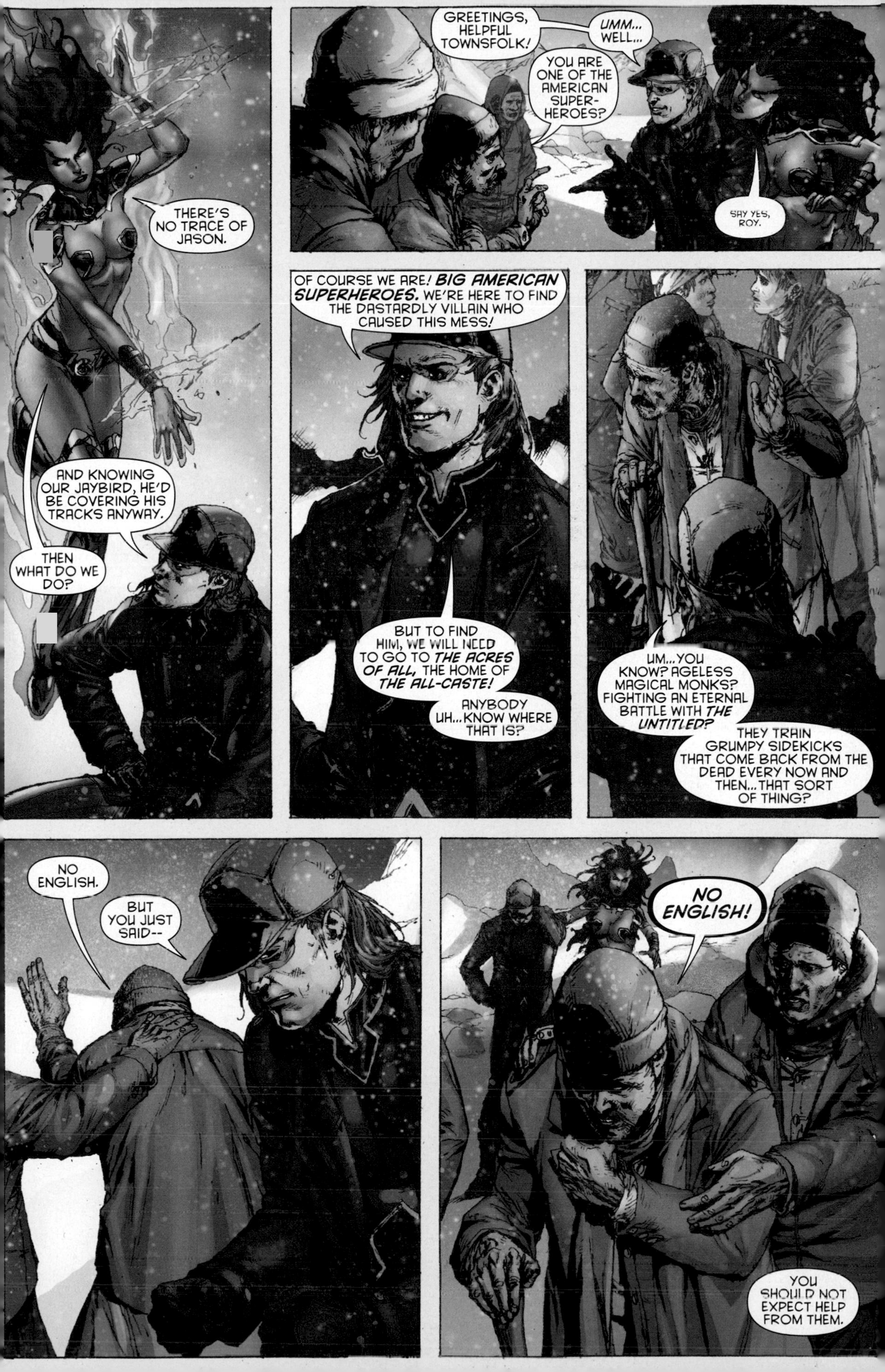
THERE'S NO TRACE OF JASON.
AND KNOWING OUR JAYBIRD, HE'D BE COVERING HIS TRACKS ANYWAY.
THEN WHAT DO WE DO?
GREETINGS, HELPFUL TOWNSFOLK!
UMM... WELL...
YOU ARE ONE OF THE AMERICAN SUPER-HEROES?
SAY YES, ROY.
OF COURSE WE ARE! BIG AMERICAN SUPERHEROES. WE'RE HERE TO FIND THE DASTARDLY VILLAIN WHO CAUSED THIS MESS!
BUT TO FIND HIM, WE WILL NEED TO GO TO THE ACRES OF ALL, THE HOME OF THE ALL-CASTE!
ANYBODY UH...KNOW WHERE THAT IS?
UM...YOU KNOW? AGELESS MAGICAL MONKS? FIGHTING AN ETERNAL BATTLE WITH THE UNTITLED?
THEY TRAIN GRUMPY SIDEKICKS THAT COME BACK FROM THE DEAD EVERY NOW AND THEN...THAT SORT OF THING?
NO ENGLISH.
BUT YOU JUST SAID--
NO ENGLISH!
YOU SHOULD NOT EXPECT HELP FROM THEM.

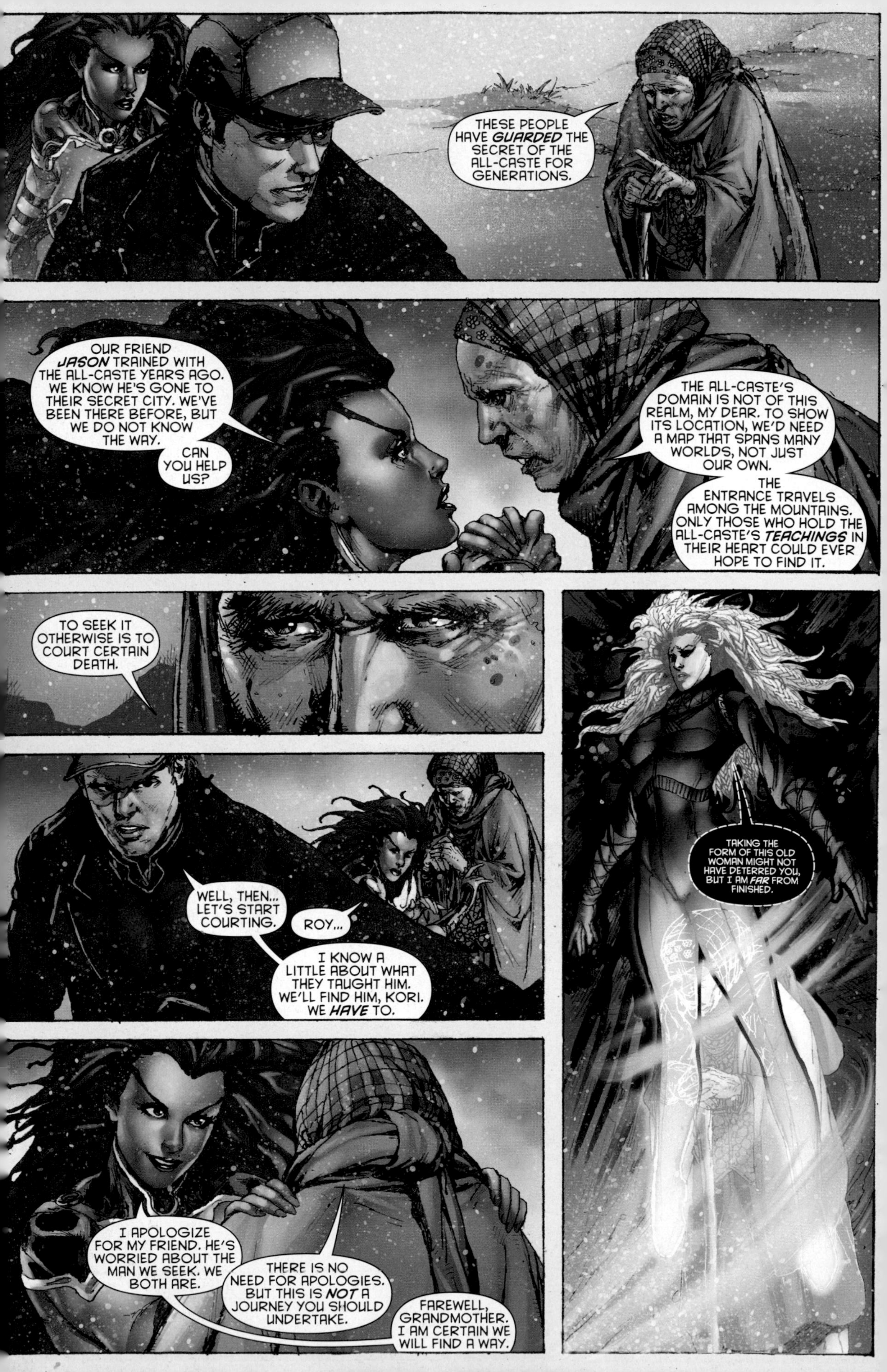
THESE PEOPLE HAVE GUARDED THE SECRET OF THE ALL-CASTE FOR GENERATIONS.
OUR FRIEND JASON TRAINED WITH THE ALL-CASTE YEARS AGO. WE KNOW HE'S GONE TO THEIR SECRET CITY. WE'VE BEEN THERE BEFORE, BUT WE DO NOT KNOW THE WAY.
CAN YOU HELP US?
THE ALL-CASTE'S DOMAIN IS NOT OF THIS REALM, MY DEAR. TO SHOW ITS LOCATION, WE'D NEED A MAP THAT SPANS MANY WORLDS, NOT JUST OUR OWN.
THE ENTRANCE TRAVELS AMONG THE MOUNTAINS. ONLY THOSE WHO HOLD THE ALL-CASTE'S TEACHINGS IN THEIR HEART COULD EVER HOPE TO FIND IT.
TO SEEK IT OTHERWISE IS TO COURT CERTAIN DEATH.
WELL, THEN... LET'S START COURTING.
ROY...
I KNOW A LITTLE ABOUT WHAT THEY TAUGHT HIM. WE'LL FIND HIM, KORI. WE HAVE TO.
I APOLOGIZE FOR MY FRIEND. HE'S WORRIED ABOUT THE MAN WE SEEK. WE BOTH ARE.
THERE IS NO NEED FOR APOLOGIES. BUT THIS IS NOT A JOURNEY YOU SHOULD UNDERTAKE.
FAREWELL, GRANDMOTHER. I AM CERTAIN WE WILL FIND A WAY.
TAKING THE FORM OF THIS OLD WOMAN MIGHT NOT HAVE DETERRED YOU, BUT I AM FAR FROM FINISHED.

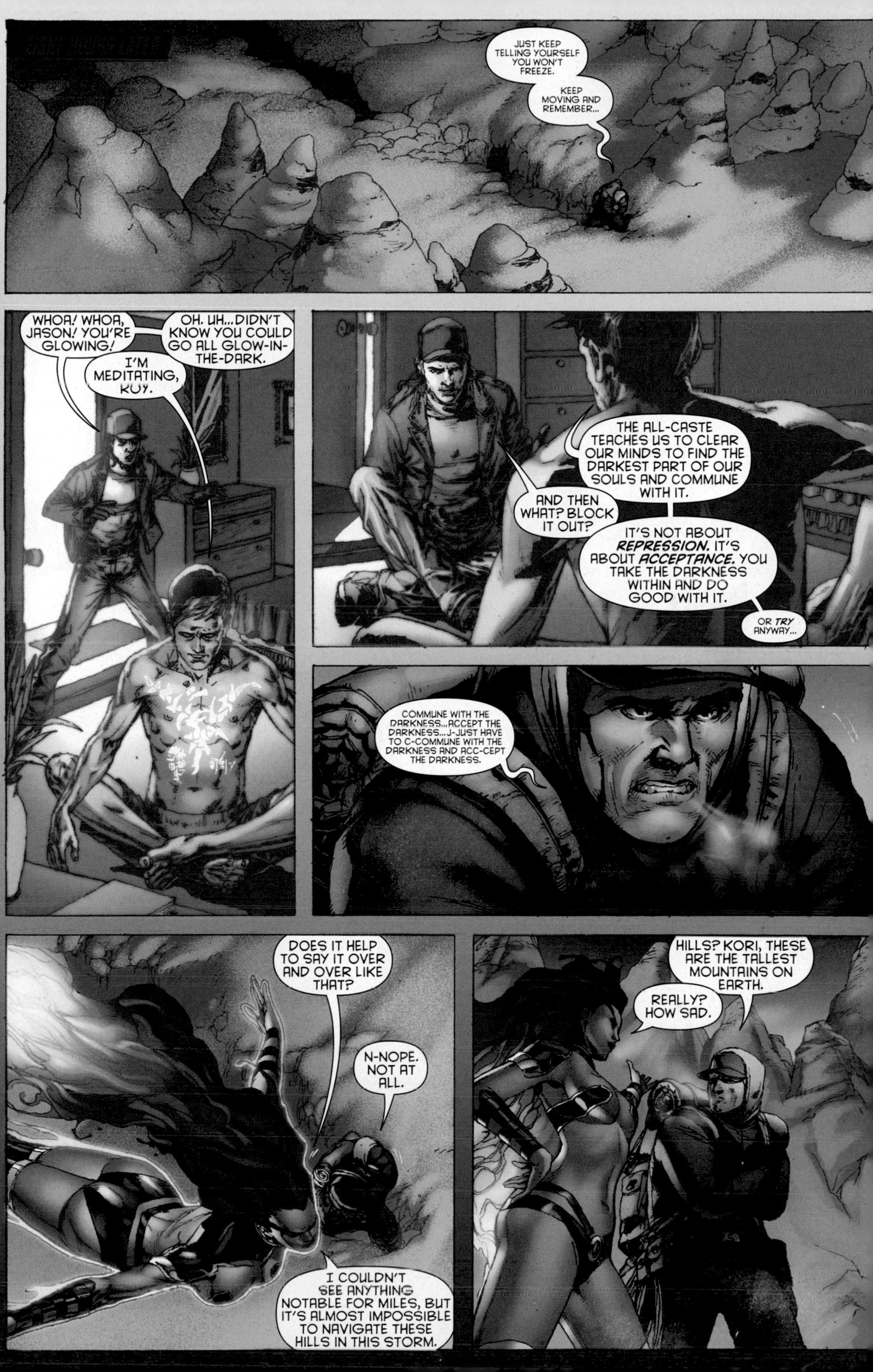
JUST KEEP TELLING YOURSELF YOU WON'T FREEZE.
KEEP MOVING AND REMEMBER...
WHOA! WHOA, JASON! YOU'RE GLOWING!
OH. UH...DIDN'T KNOW YOU COULD GO ALL GLOW-IN-THE-DARK.
I'M MEDITATING, ROY.
THE ALL-CASTE TEACHES US TO CLEAR OUR MINDS TO FIND THE DARKEST PART OF OUR SOULS AND COMMUNE WITH IT.
AND THEN WHAT? BLOCK IT OUT?
IT'S NOT ABOUT REPRESSION. IT'S ABOUT ACCEPTANCE. YOU TAKE THE DARKNESS WITHIN AND DO GOOD WITH IT.
OR TRY ANYWAY...
COMMUNE WITH THE DARKNESS...ACCEPT THE DARKNESS...J-JUST HAVE TO C-COMMUNE WITH THE DARKNESS AND ACC-CEPT THE DARKNESS.
DOES IT HELP TO SAY IT OVER AND OVER LIKE THAT?
N-NOPE. NOT AT ALL.
I COULDN'T SEE ANYTHING NOTABLE FOR MILES, BUT IT'S ALMOST IMPOSSIBLE TO NAVIGATE THESE HILLS IN THIS STORM.
HILLS? KORI, THESE ARE THE TALLEST MOUNTAINS ON EARTH.
REALLY? HOW SAD.

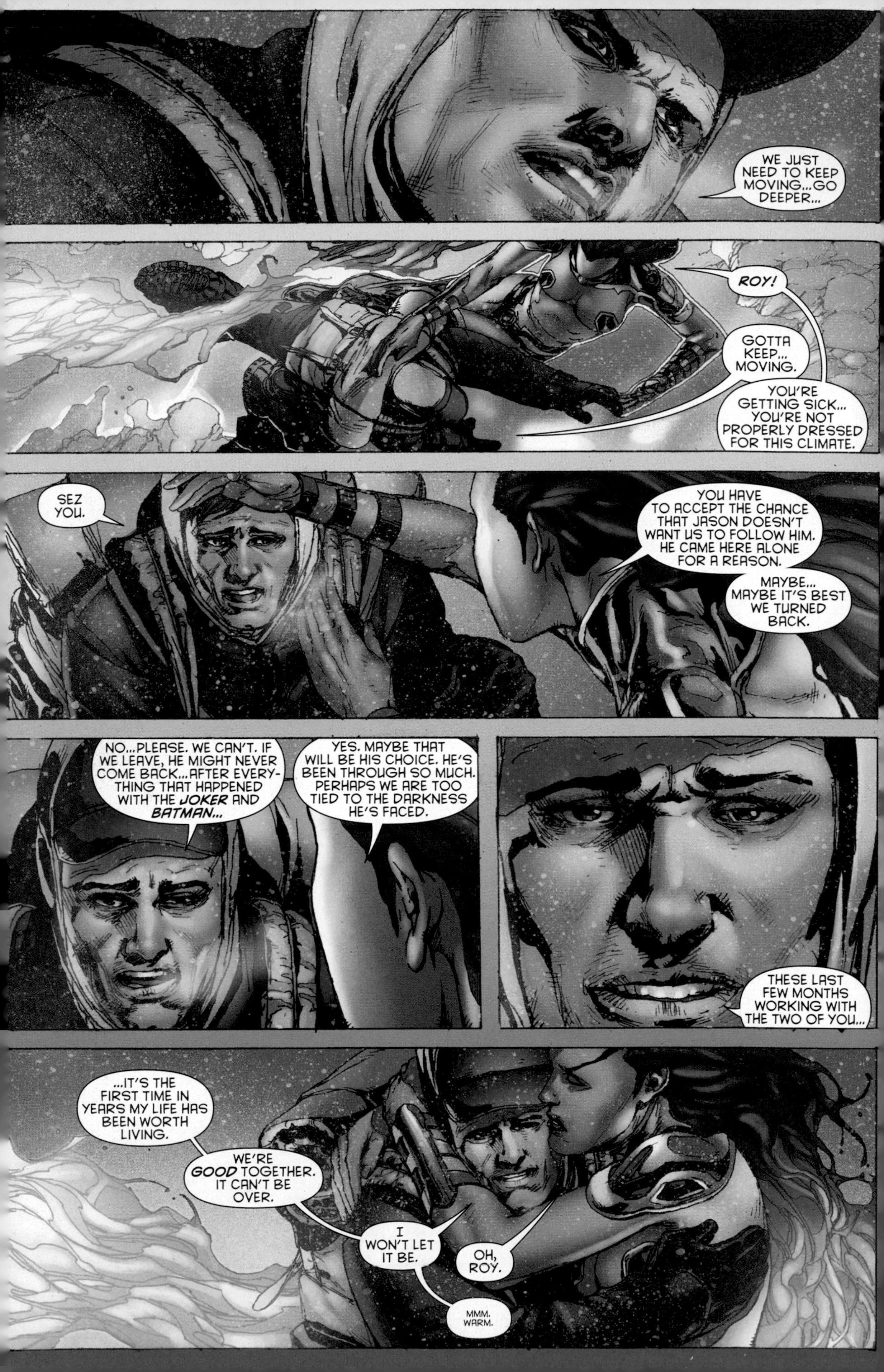
WE JUST NEED TO KEEP MOVING...GO DEEPER...
ROY!
GOTTA KEEP... MOVING.
YOU'RE GETTING SICK... YOU'RE NOT PROPERLY DRESSED FOR THIS CLIMATE.
SEZ YOU.
YOU HAVE TO ACCEPT THE CHANCE THAT JASON DOESN'T WANT US TO FOLLOW HIM. HE CAME HERE ALONE FOR A REASON.
MAYBE... MAYBE IT'S BEST WE TURNED BACK.
NO...PLEASE. WE CAN'T. IF WE LEAVE, HE MIGHT NEVER COME BACK...AFTER EVERY-THING THAT HAPPENED WITH THE JOKER AND BATMAN...
YES. MAYBE THAT WILL BE HIS CHOICE. HE'S BEEN THROUGH SO MUCH. PERHAPS WE ARE TOO TIED TO THE DARKNESS HE'S FACED.
THESE LAST FEW MONTHS WORKING WITH THE TWO OF YOU...
...IT'S THE FIRST TIME IN YEARS MY LIFE HAS BEEN WORTH LIVING.
WE'RE GOOD TOGETHER. IT CAN'T BE OVER.
I WON'T LET IT BE.
OH, ROY.
MMM. WARM.

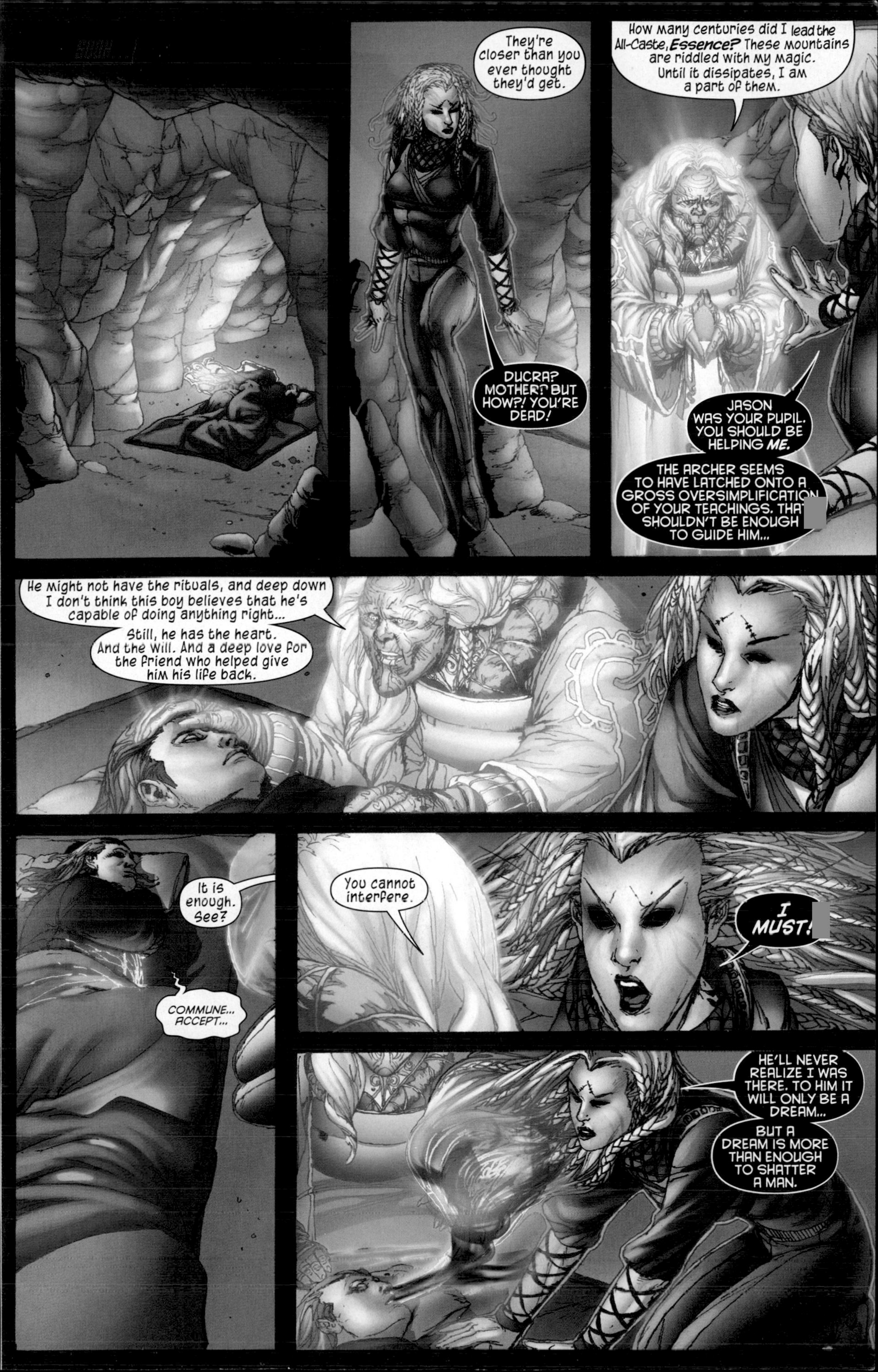

They're closer than you ever thought they'd get.
DUCRA? MOTHER?! BUT HOW?! YOU'RE DEAD!
How many centuries did I lead the All-Caste, *Essence?* These mountains are riddled with my magic. Until it dissipates, I am a part of them.
JASON WAS YOUR PUPIL. YOU SHOULD BE HELPING *ME.*
THE ARCHER SEEMS TO HAVE LATCHED ONTO A GROSS OVERSIMPLIFICATION OF YOUR TEACHINGS. THA SHOULDN'T BE ENOUGH TO GUIDE HIM...
He might not have the rituals, and deep down I don't think this boy believes that he's capable of doing anything right...
Still, he has the heart. And the will. And a deep love for the friend who helped give him his life back.
It is enough. See?
COMMUNE... ACCEPT...
You cannot interfere.
I MUST!
HE'LL NEVER REALIZE I WAS THERE. TO HIM IT WILL ONLY BE A DREAM...
BUT A DREAM IS MORE THAN ENOUGH TO SHATTER A MAN.

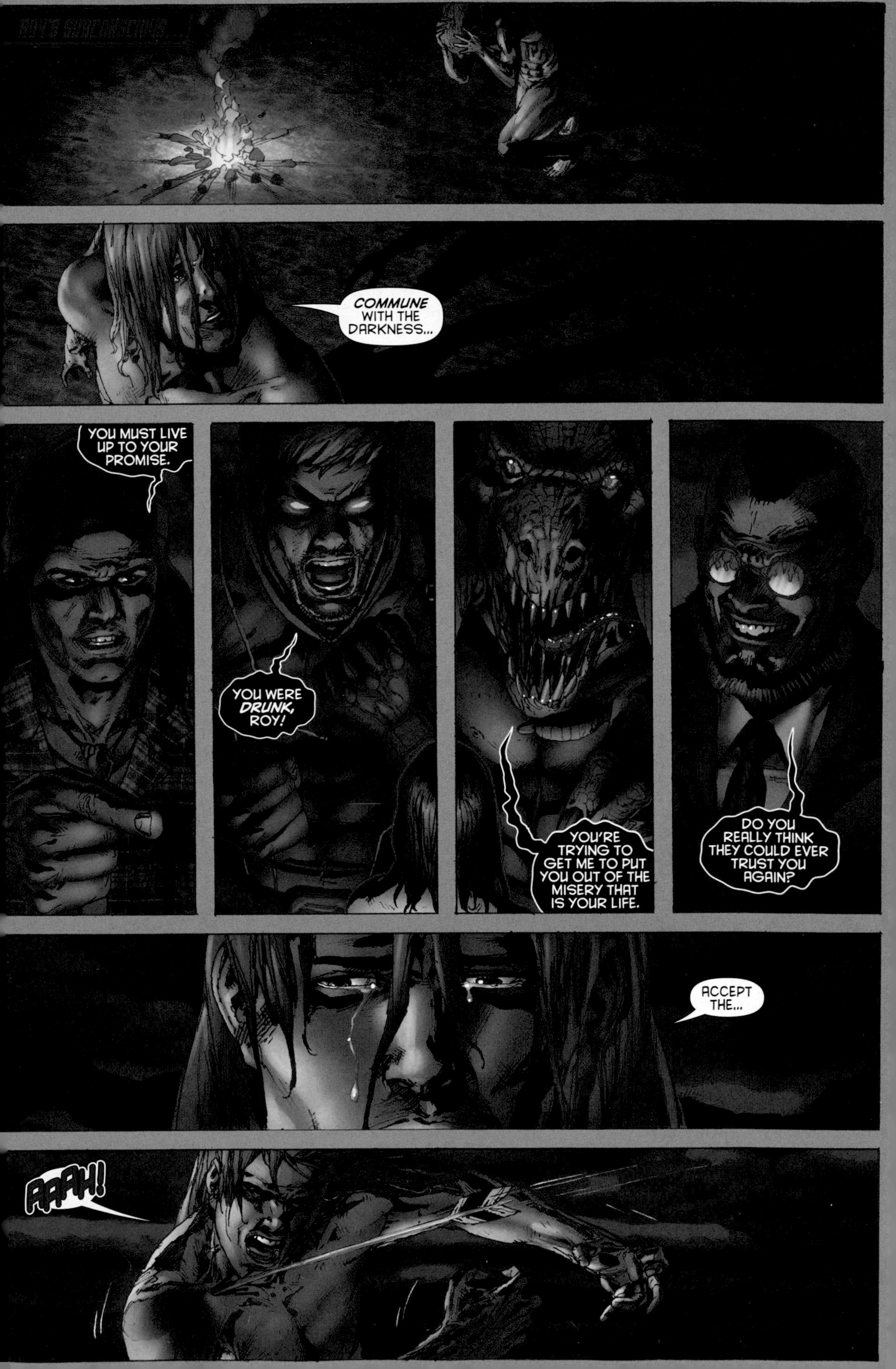
COMMUNE WITH THE DARKNESS...
YOU MUST LIVE UP TO YOUR PROMISE.
YOU WERE DRUNK, ROY!
YOU'RE TRYING TO GET ME TO PUT YOU OUT OF THE MISERY THAT IS YOUR LIFE.
DO YOU REALLY THINK THEY COULD EVER TRUST YOU AGAIN?
ACCEPT THE...
AAAH!

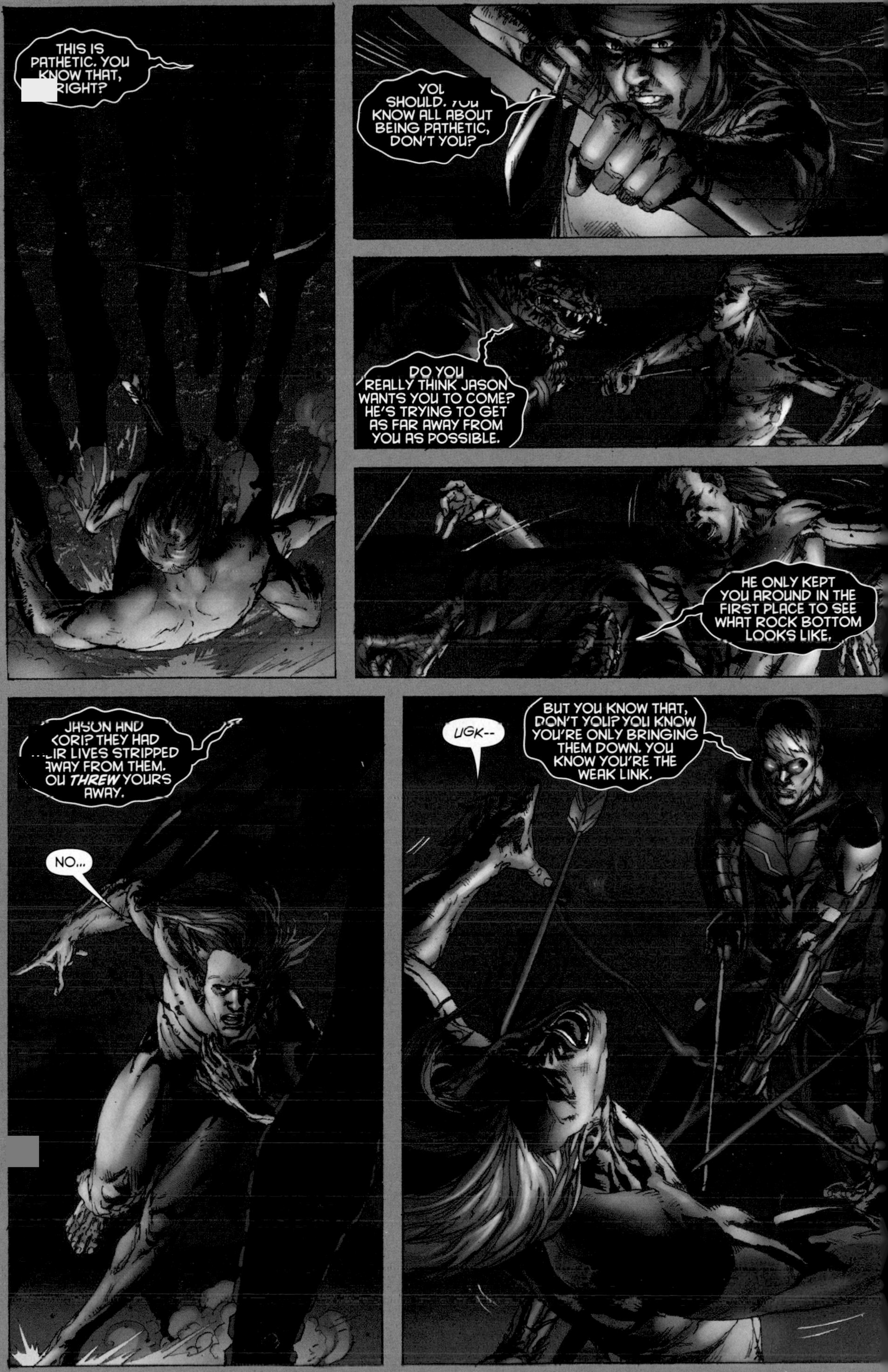
THIS IS PATHETIC. YOU KNOW THAT, RIGHT?
SHOULD. YOU KNOW ALL ABOUT BEING PATHETIC, DON'T YOU?
DO YOU REALLY THINK JASON WANTS YOU TO COME? HE'S TRYING TO GET AS FAR AWAY FROM YOU AS POSSIBLE.
HE ONLY KEPT YOU AROUND IN THE FIRST PLACE TO SEE WHAT ROCK BOTTOM LOOKS LIKE.
JASON AND KORI? THEY HAD IR LIVES STRIPPED AWAY FROM THEM. OU *THREW* YOURS AWAY.
NO...
UGK--
BUT YOU KNOW THAT, DON'T YOU? YOU KNOW YOU'RE ONLY BRINGING THEM DOWN. YOU KNOW YOU'RE THE WEAK LINK.

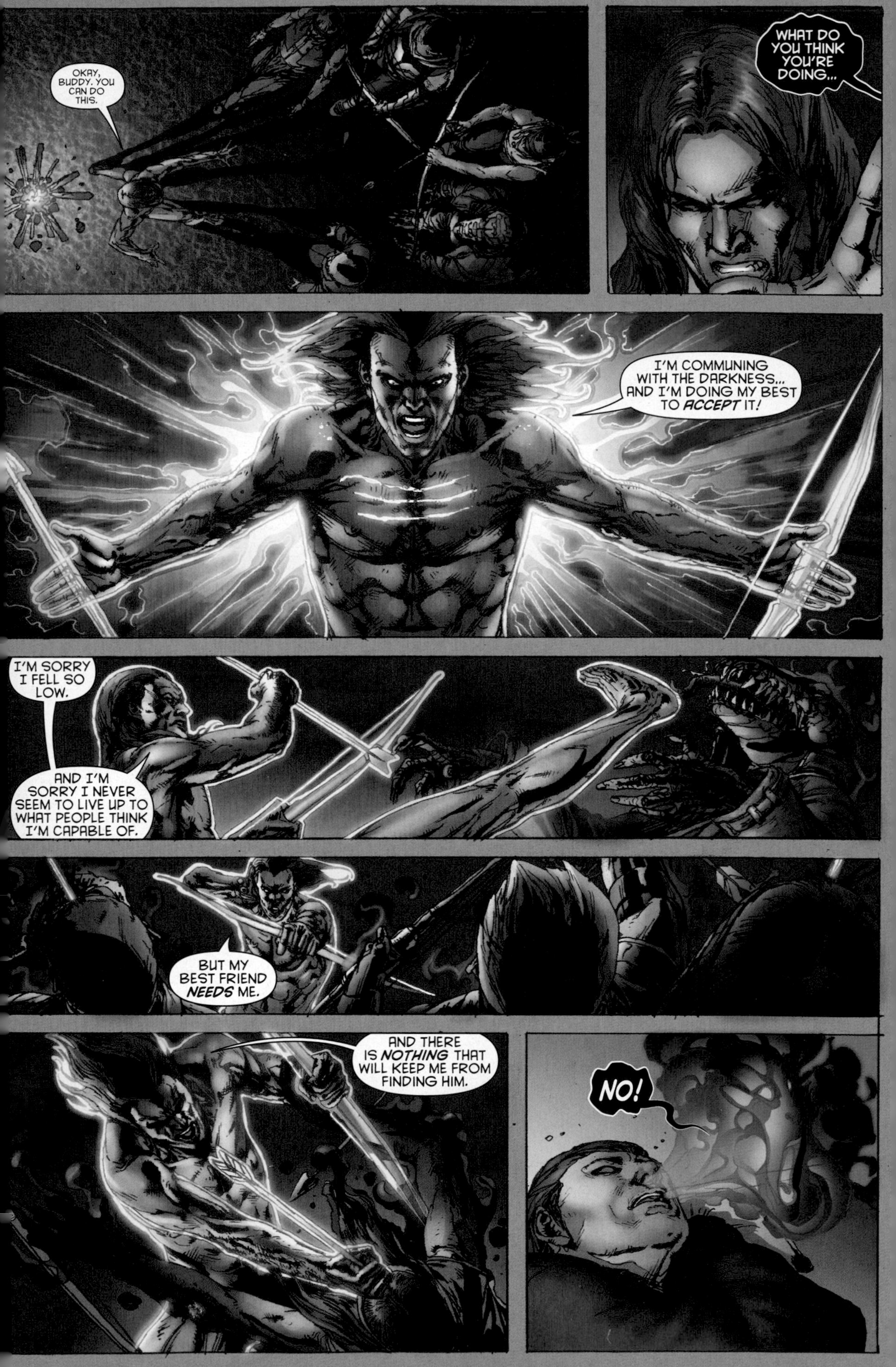
OKAY, BUDDY. YOU CAN DO THIS.
WHAT DO YOU THINK YOU'RE DOING...
I'M COMMUNING WITH THE DARKNESS... AND I'M DOING MY BEST TO *ACCEPT* IT!
I'M SORRY I FELL SO LOW.
AND I'M SORRY I NEVER SEEM TO LIVE UP TO WHAT PEOPLE THINK I'M CAPABLE OF.
BUT MY BEST FRIEND ***NEEDS*** ME.
AND THERE IS ***NOTHING*** THAT WILL KEEP ME FROM FINDING HIM.
NO!

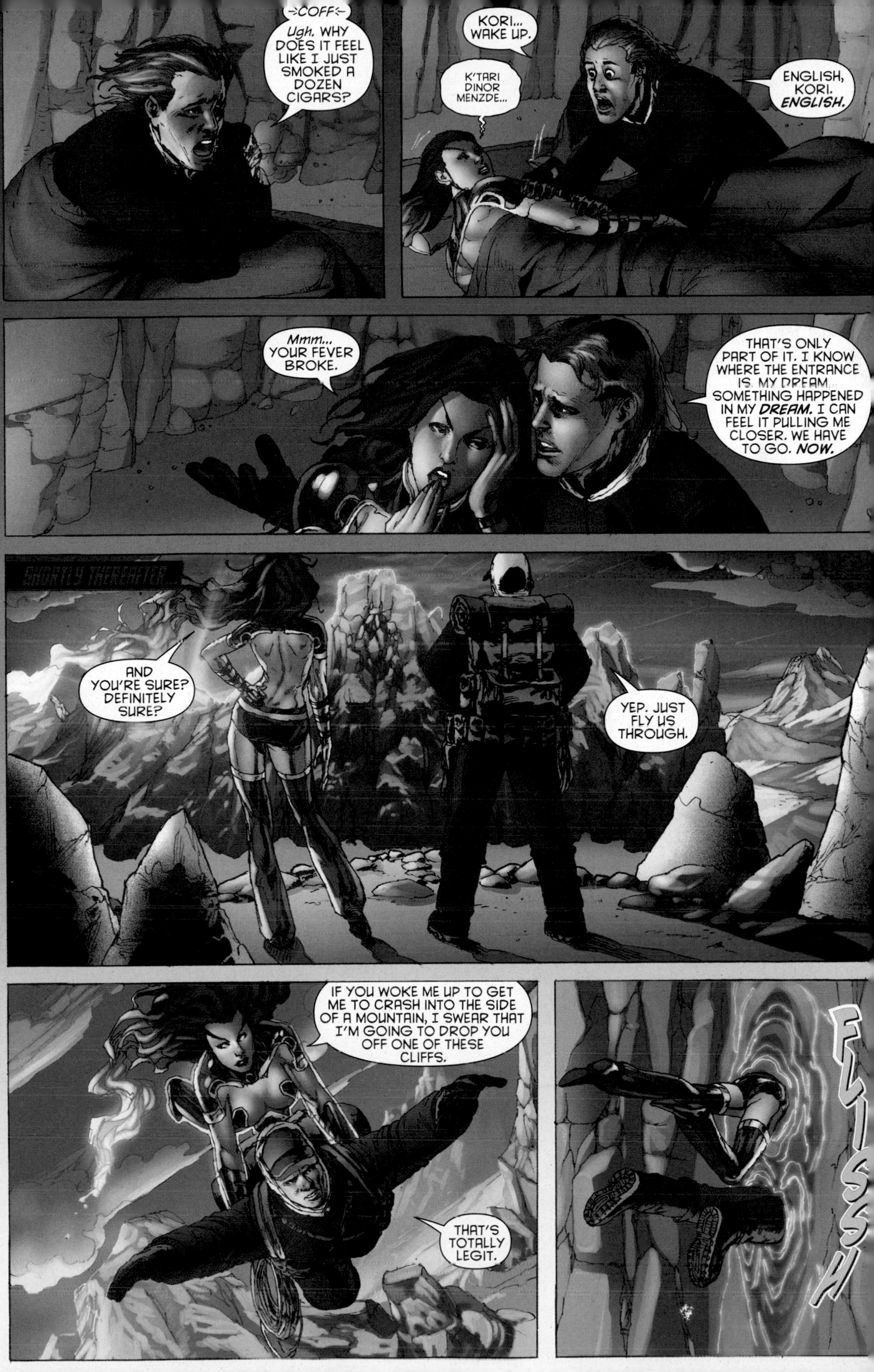

-COFF-
Ugh. WHY DOES IT FEEL LIKE I JUST SMOKED A DOZEN CIGARS?
KORI... WAKE UP.
K'TARI DINOR MENZDE...
ENGLISH, KORI. ENGLISH.
Mmm... YOUR FEVER BROKE.
THAT'S ONLY PART OF IT. I KNOW WHERE THE ENTRANCE IS. MY DREAM... SOMETHING HAPPENED IN MY DREAM. I CAN FEEL IT PULLING ME CLOSER. WE HAVE TO GO. NOW.
SHORTLY THEREAFTER...
AND YOU'RE SURE? DEFINITELY SURE?
YEP. JUST FLY US THROUGH.
IF YOU WOKE ME UP TO GET ME TO CRASH INTO THE SIDE OF A MOUNTAIN, I SWEAR THAT I'M GOING TO DROP YOU OFF ONE OF THESE CLIFFS.
THAT'S TOTALLY LEGIT.
FLISSH

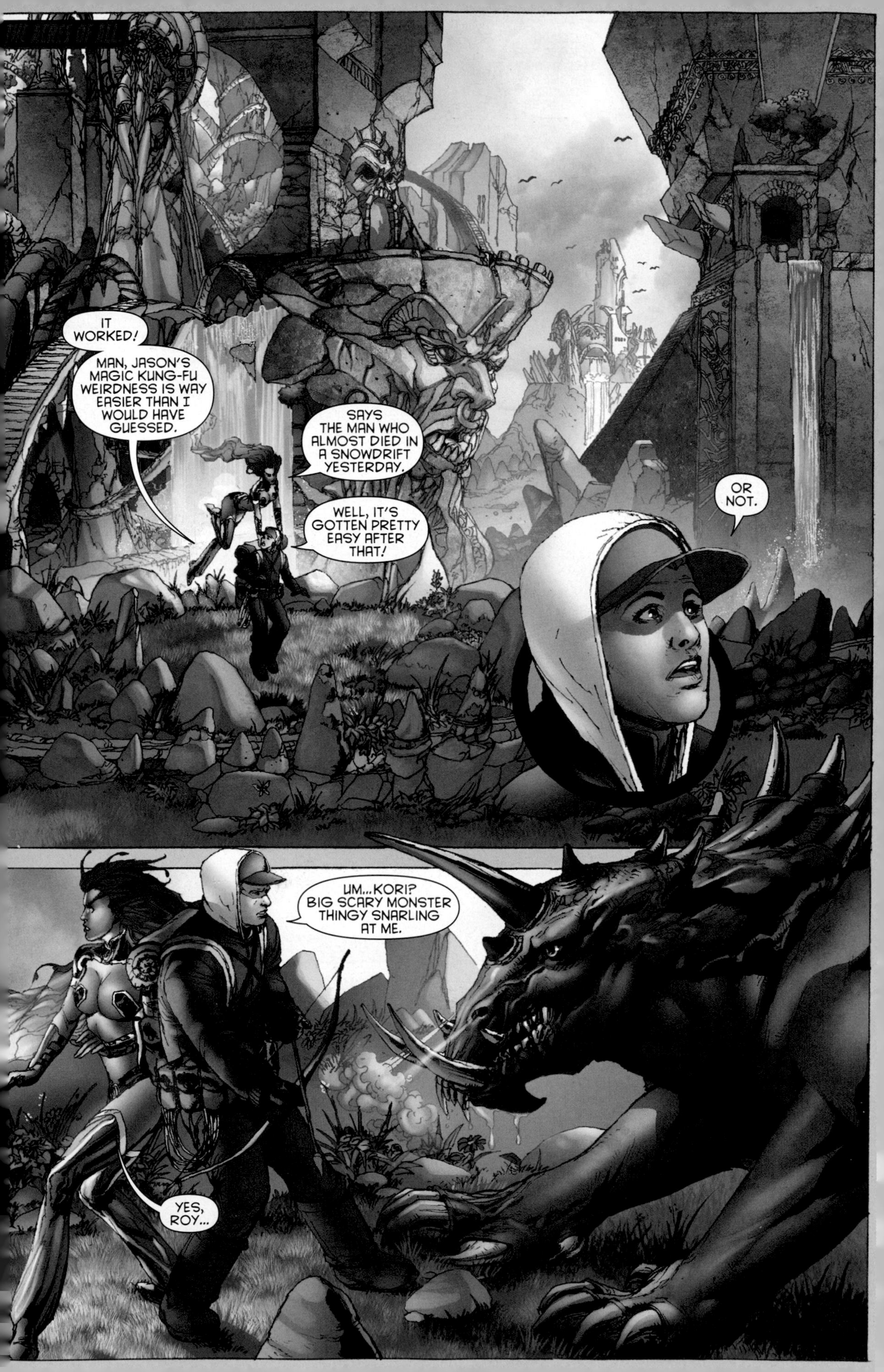
IT WORKED!
MAN, JASON'S MAGIC KUNG-FU WEIRDNESS IS WAY EASIER THAN I WOULD HAVE GUESSED.
SAYS THE MAN WHO ALMOST DIED IN A SNOWDRIFT YESTERDAY.
WELL, IT'S GOTTEN PRETTY EASY AFTER THAT!
OR NOT.
UM...KORI? BIG SCARY MONSTER THINGY SNARLING AT ME.
YES, ROY...

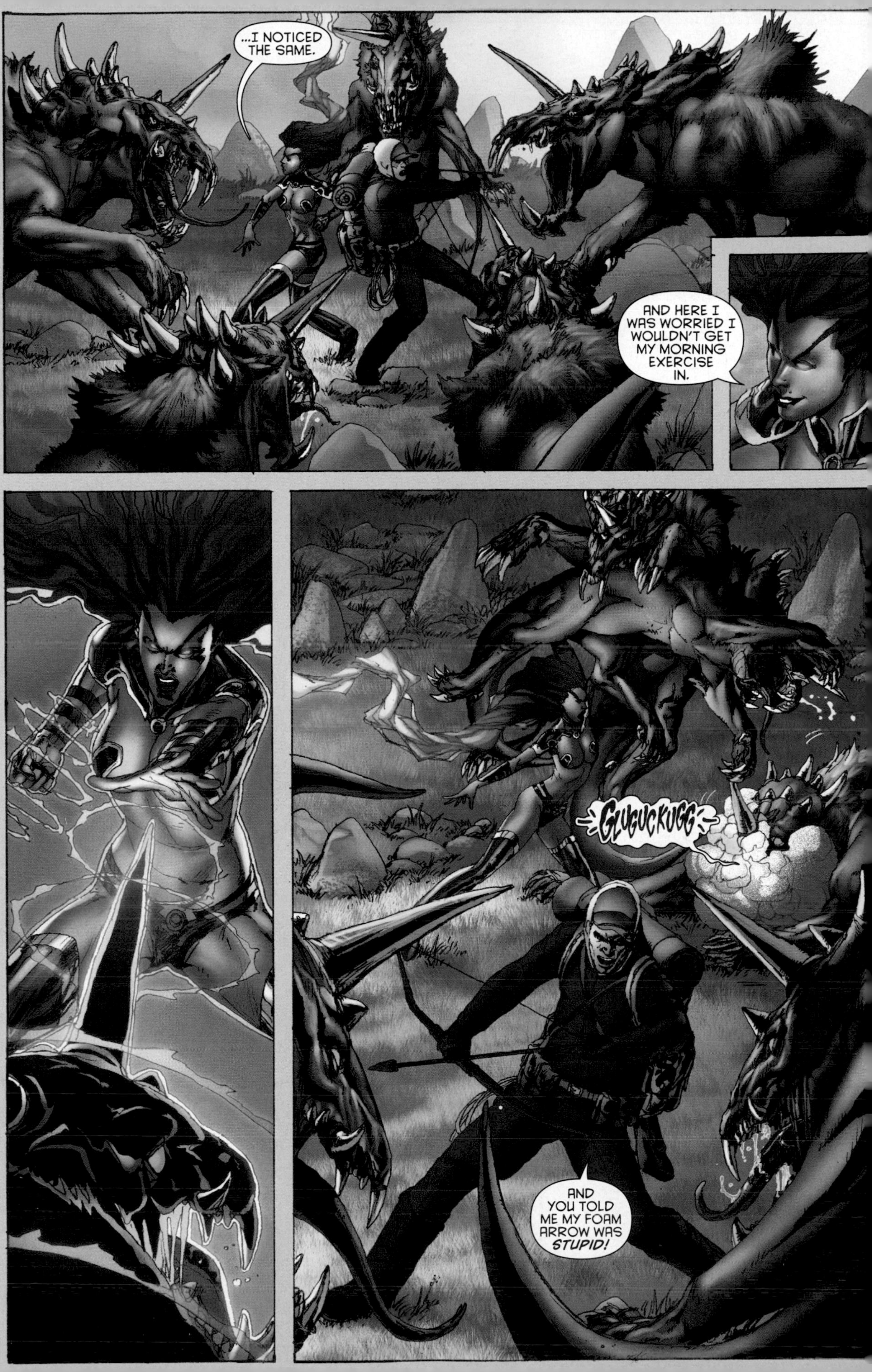
...I NOTICED THE SAME.
AND HERE I WAS WORRIED I WOULDN'T GET MY MORNING EXERCISE IN.
GLUGUCKUGG
AND YOU TOLD ME MY FOAM ARROW WAS *STUPID!*

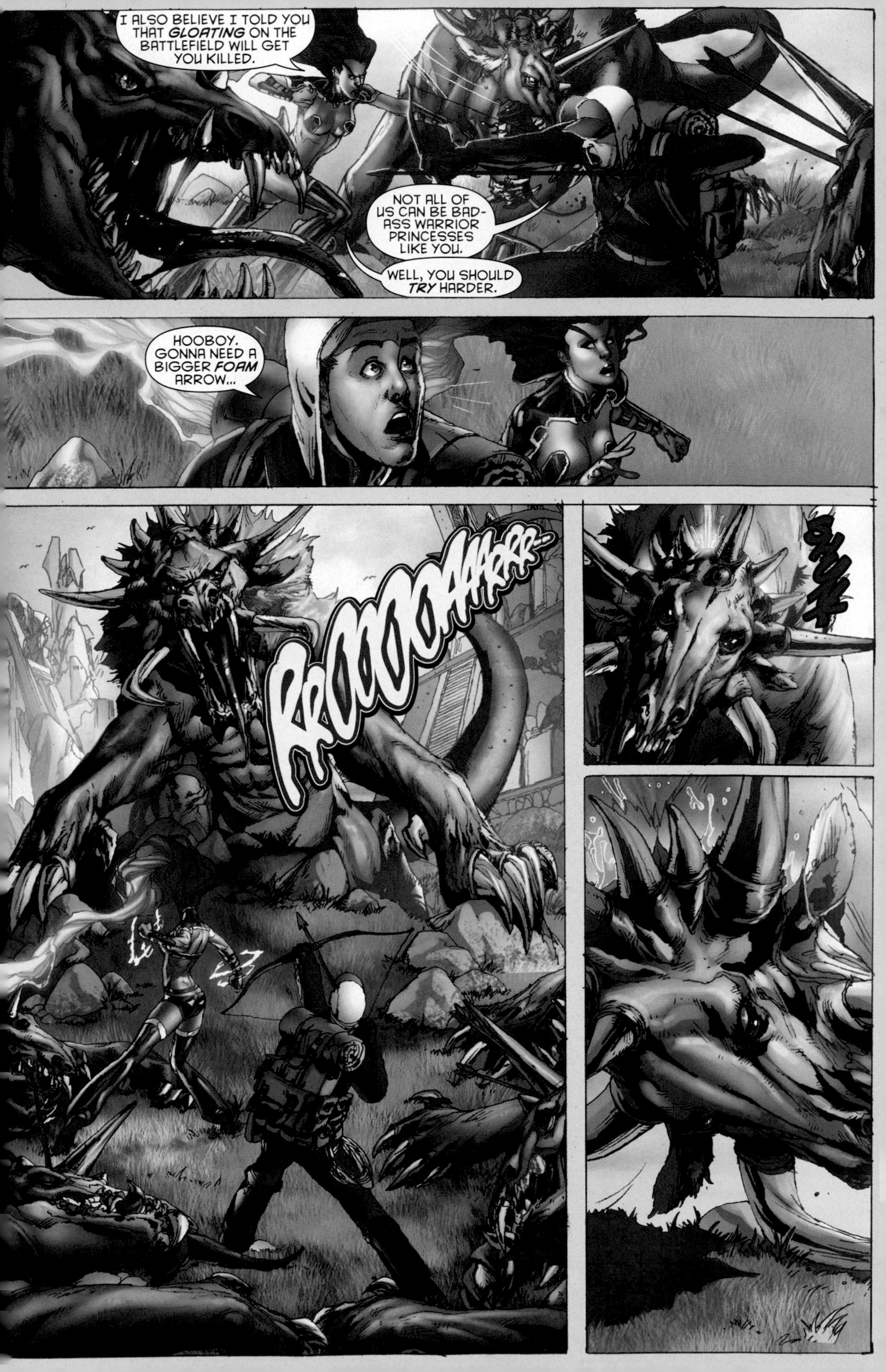
I ALSO BELIEVE I TOLD YOU THAT GLOATING ON THE BATTLEFIELD WILL GET YOU KILLED.
NOT ALL OF US CAN BE BAD-ASS WARRIOR PRINCESSES LIKE YOU.
WELL, YOU SHOULD TRY HARDER.
HOOBOY. GONNA NEED A BIGGER FOAM ARROW...
RROOOOAAARRR--
SHUNK

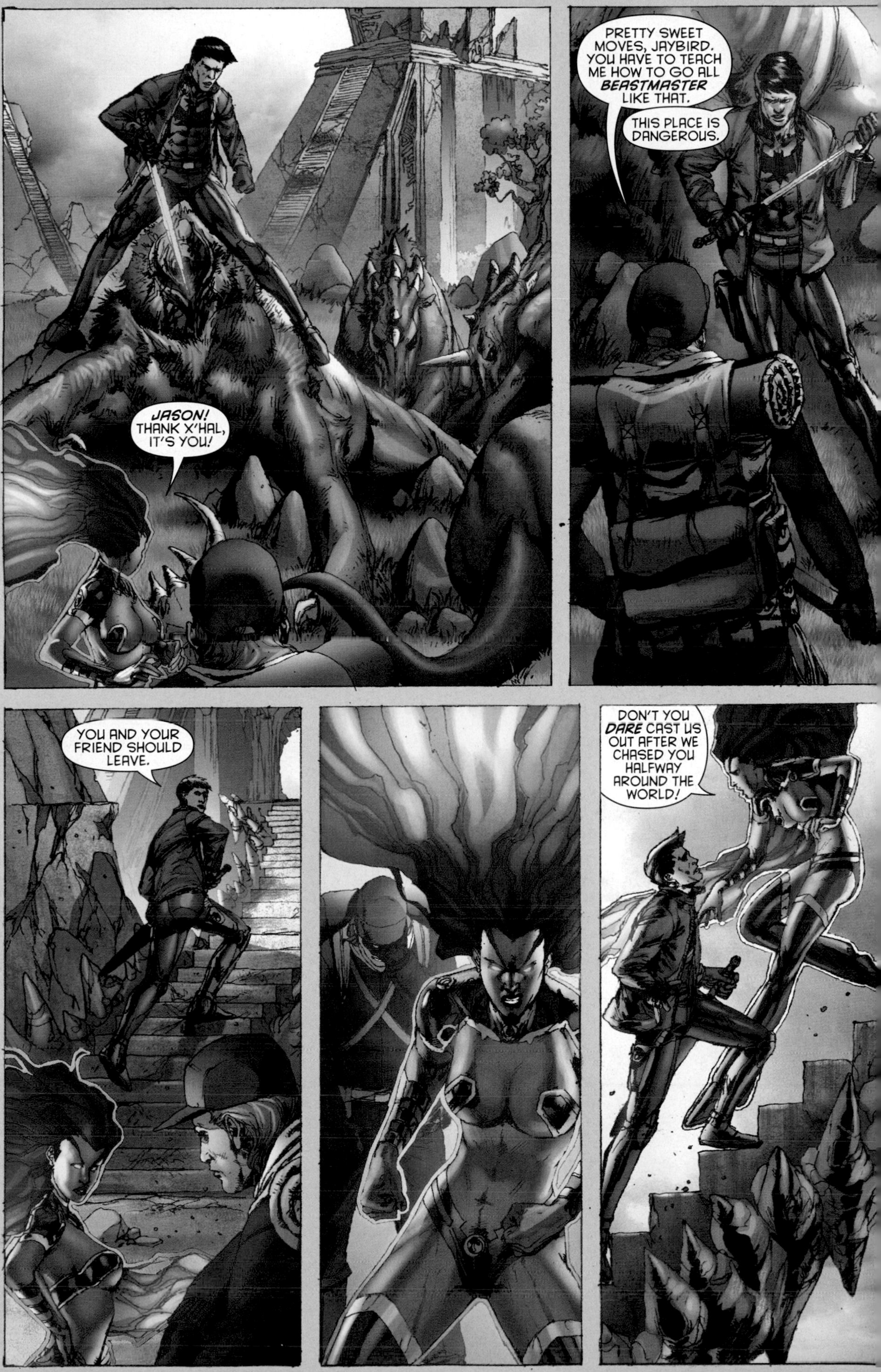
JASON! THANK X'HAL, IT'S YOU!
PRETTY SWEET MOVES, JAYBIRD. YOU HAVE TO TEACH ME HOW TO GO ALL BEASTMASTER LIKE THAT.
THIS PLACE IS DANGEROUS.
YOU AND YOUR FRIEND SHOULD LEAVE.
DON'T YOU DARE CAST US OUT AFTER WE CHASED YOU HALFWAY AROUND THE WORLD!

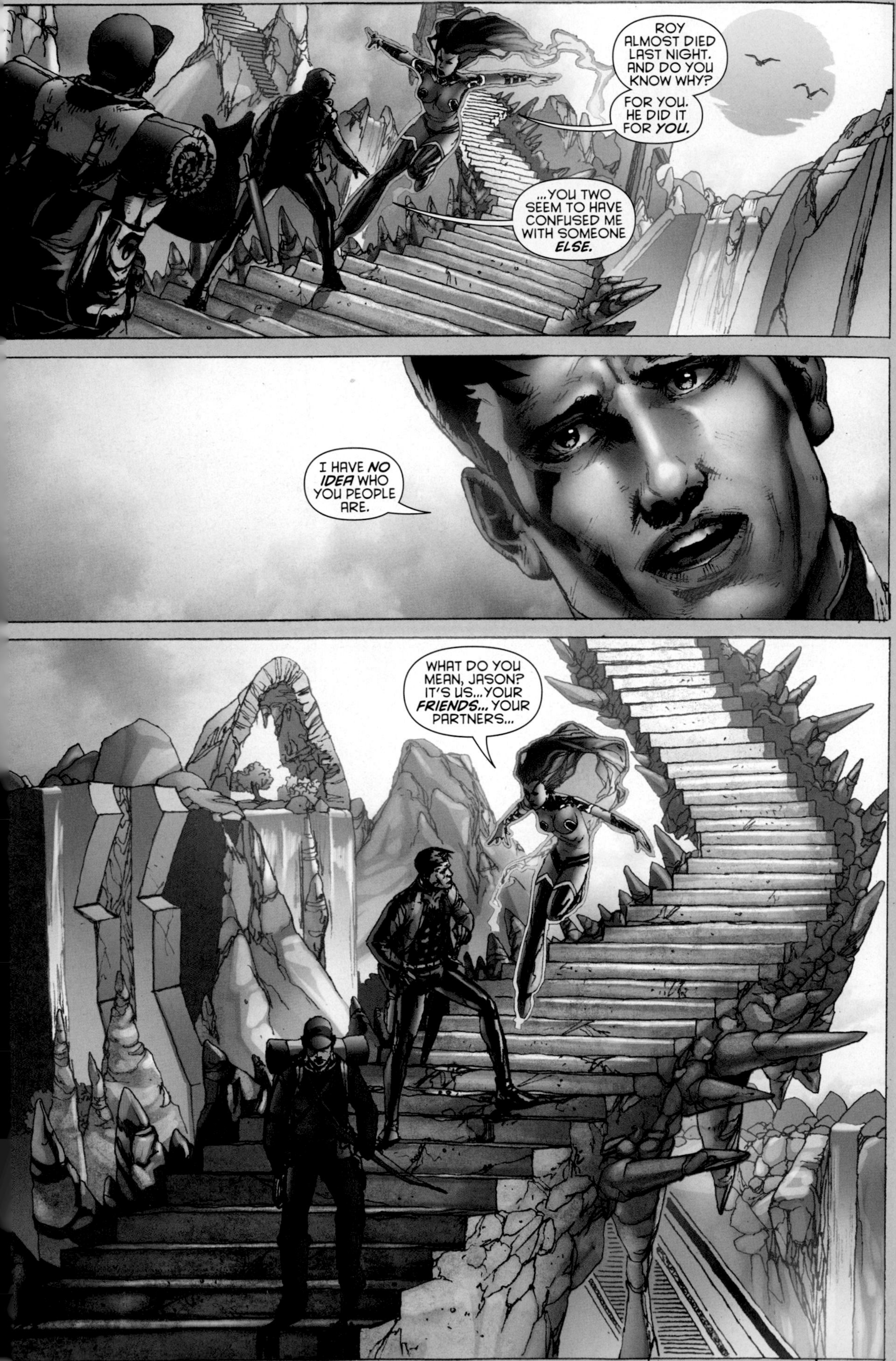
ROY ALMOST DIED LAST NIGHT. AND DO YOU KNOW WHY?
FOR YOU. HE DID IT FOR YOU.
...YOU TWO SEEM TO HAVE CONFUSED ME WITH SOMEONE ELSE.
I HAVE NO IDEA WHO YOU PEOPLE ARE.
WHAT DO YOU MEAN, JASON? IT'S US...YOUR FRIENDS... YOUR PARTNERS...

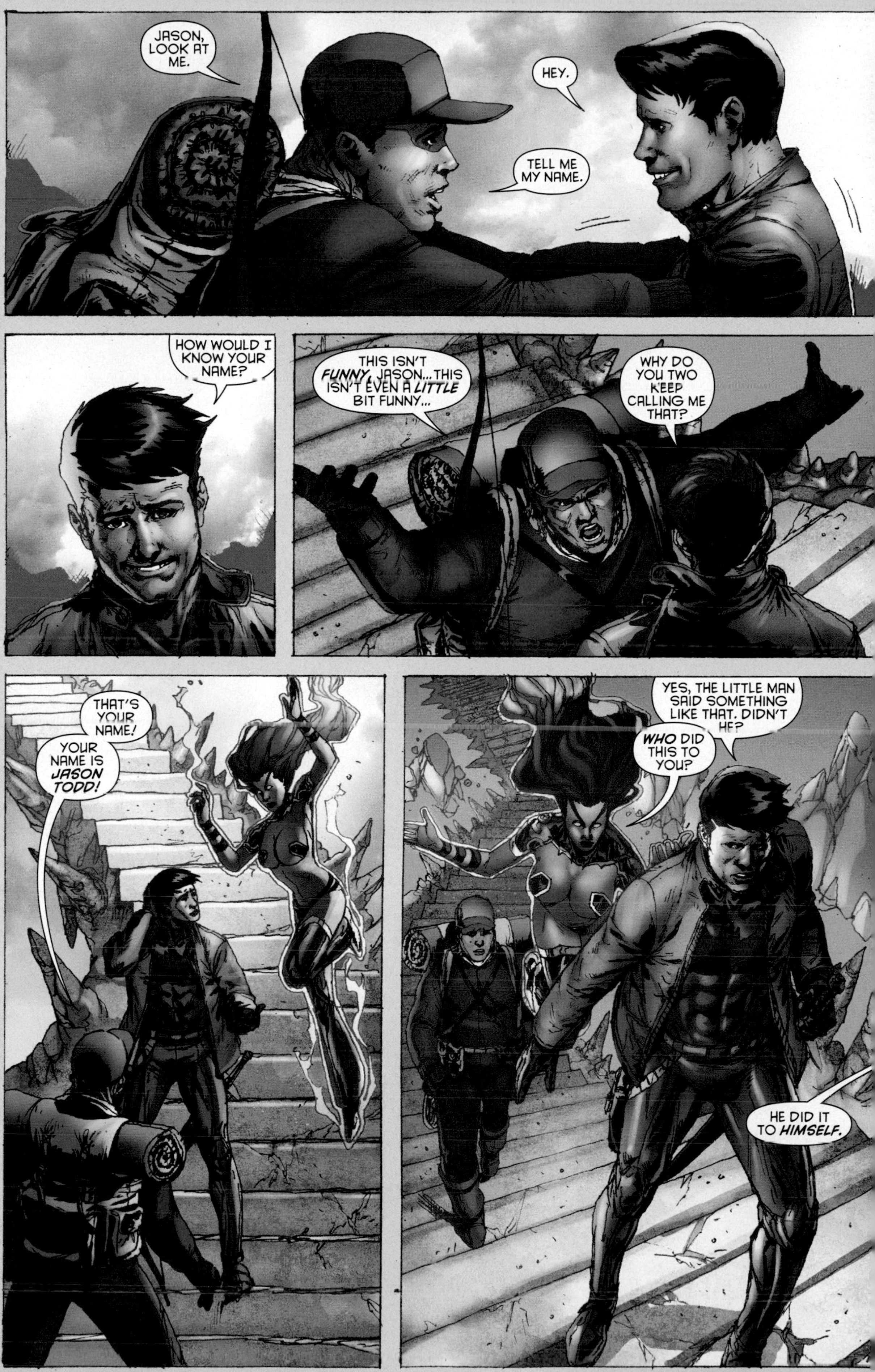

JASON, LOOK AT ME.
HEY.
TELL ME MY NAME.
HOW WOULD I KNOW YOUR NAME?
THIS ISN'T FUNNY, JASON... THIS ISN'T EVEN A LITTLE BIT FUNNY...
WHY DO YOU TWO KEEP CALLING ME THAT?
THAT'S YOUR NAME!
YOUR NAME IS JASON TODD!
YES, THE LITTLE MAN SAID SOMETHING LIKE THAT. DIDN'T HE?
WHO DID THIS TO YOU?
HE DID IT TO HIMSELF.

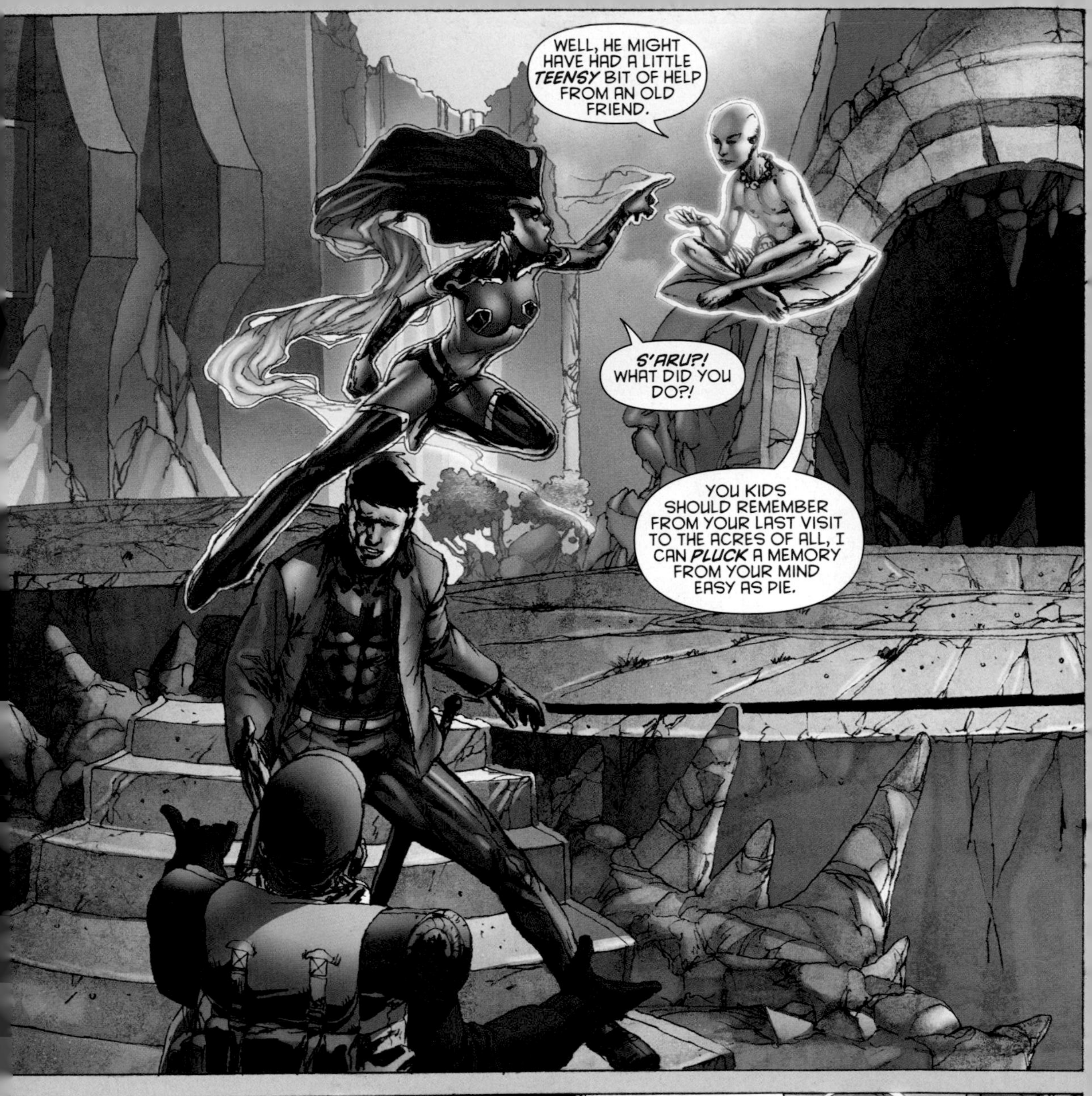
WELL, HE MIGHT HAVE HAD A LITTLE *TEENSY* BIT OF HELP FROM AN OLD FRIEND.
S'ARU?! WHAT DID YOU DO?!
YOU KIDS SHOULD REMEMBER FROM YOUR LAST VISIT TO THE ACRES OF ALL, I CAN *PLUCK* A MEMORY FROM YOUR MIND EASY AS PIE.

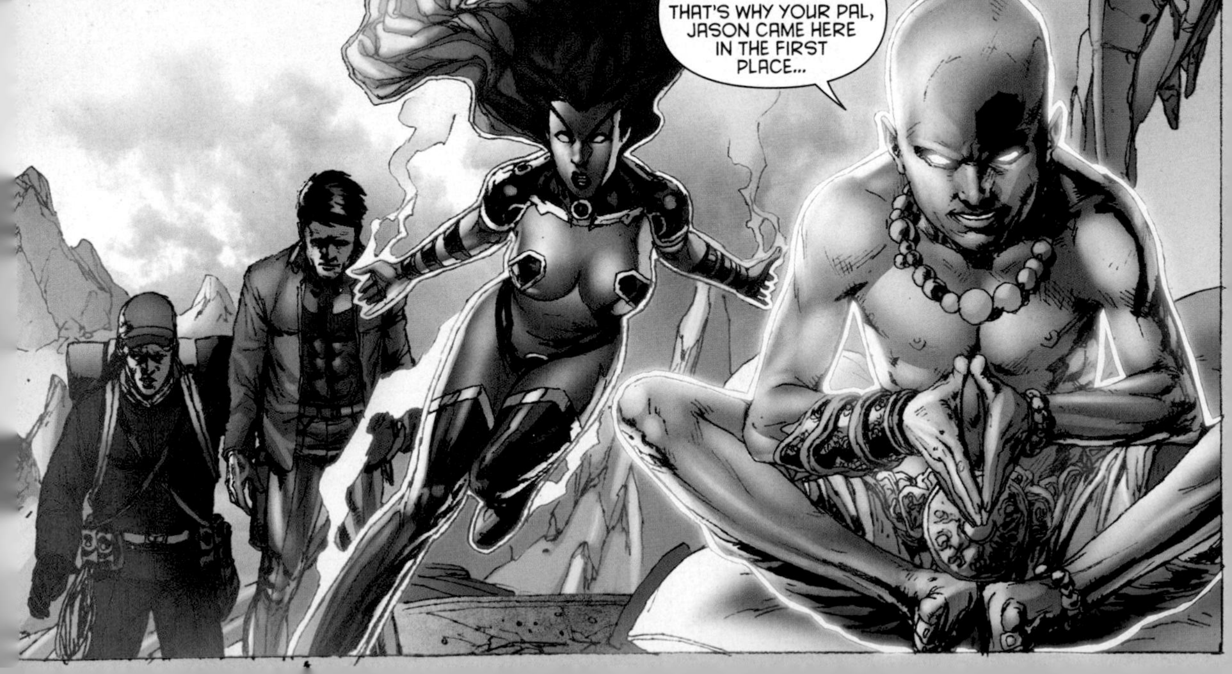
THAT'S WHY YOUR PAL, JASON CAME HERE IN THE FIRST PLACE...

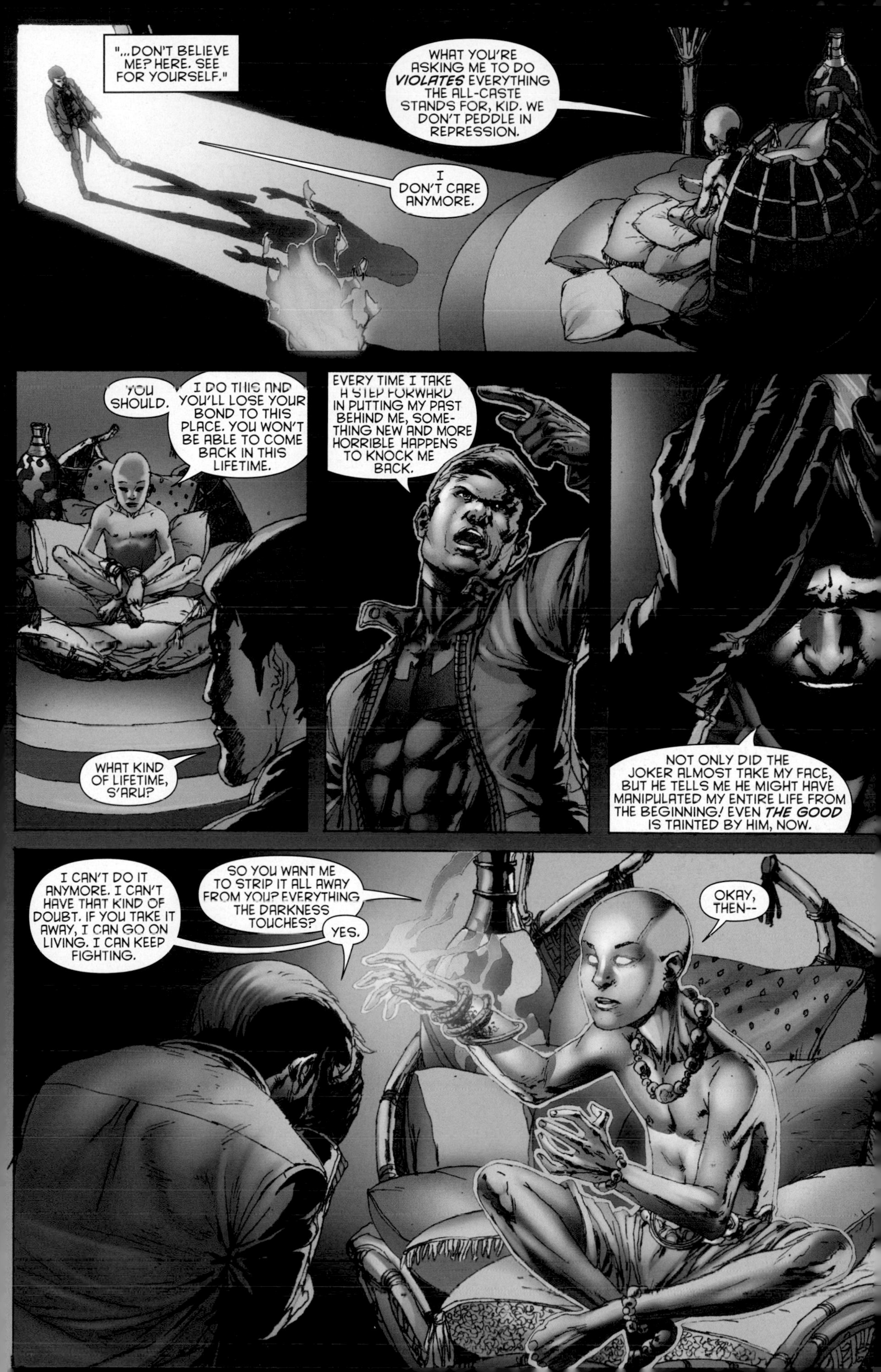
"...DON'T BELIEVE ME? HERE. SEE FOR YOURSELF."
WHAT YOU'RE ASKING ME TO DO VIOLATES EVERYTHING THE ALL-CASTE STANDS FOR, KID. WE DON'T PEDDLE IN REPRESSION.
I DON'T CARE ANYMORE.
YOU SHOULD.
I DO THIS AND YOU'LL LOSE YOUR BOND TO THIS PLACE. YOU WON'T BE ABLE TO COME BACK IN THIS LIFETIME.
WHAT KIND OF LIFETIME, S'ARU?
EVERY TIME I TAKE A STEP FORWARD IN PUTTING MY PAST BEHIND ME, SOMETHING NEW AND MORE HORRIBLE HAPPENS TO KNOCK ME BACK.
NOT ONLY DID THE JOKER ALMOST TAKE MY FACE, BUT HE TELLS ME HE MIGHT HAVE MANIPULATED MY ENTIRE LIFE FROM THE BEGINNING! EVEN THE GOOD IS TAINTED BY HIM, NOW.
I CAN'T DO IT ANYMORE. I CAN'T HAVE THAT KIND OF DOUBT. IF YOU TAKE IT AWAY, I CAN GO ON LIVING. I CAN KEEP FIGHTING.
SO YOU WANT ME TO STRIP IT ALL AWAY FROM YOU? EVERYTHING THE DARKNESS TOUCHES?
YES.
OKAY, THEN--

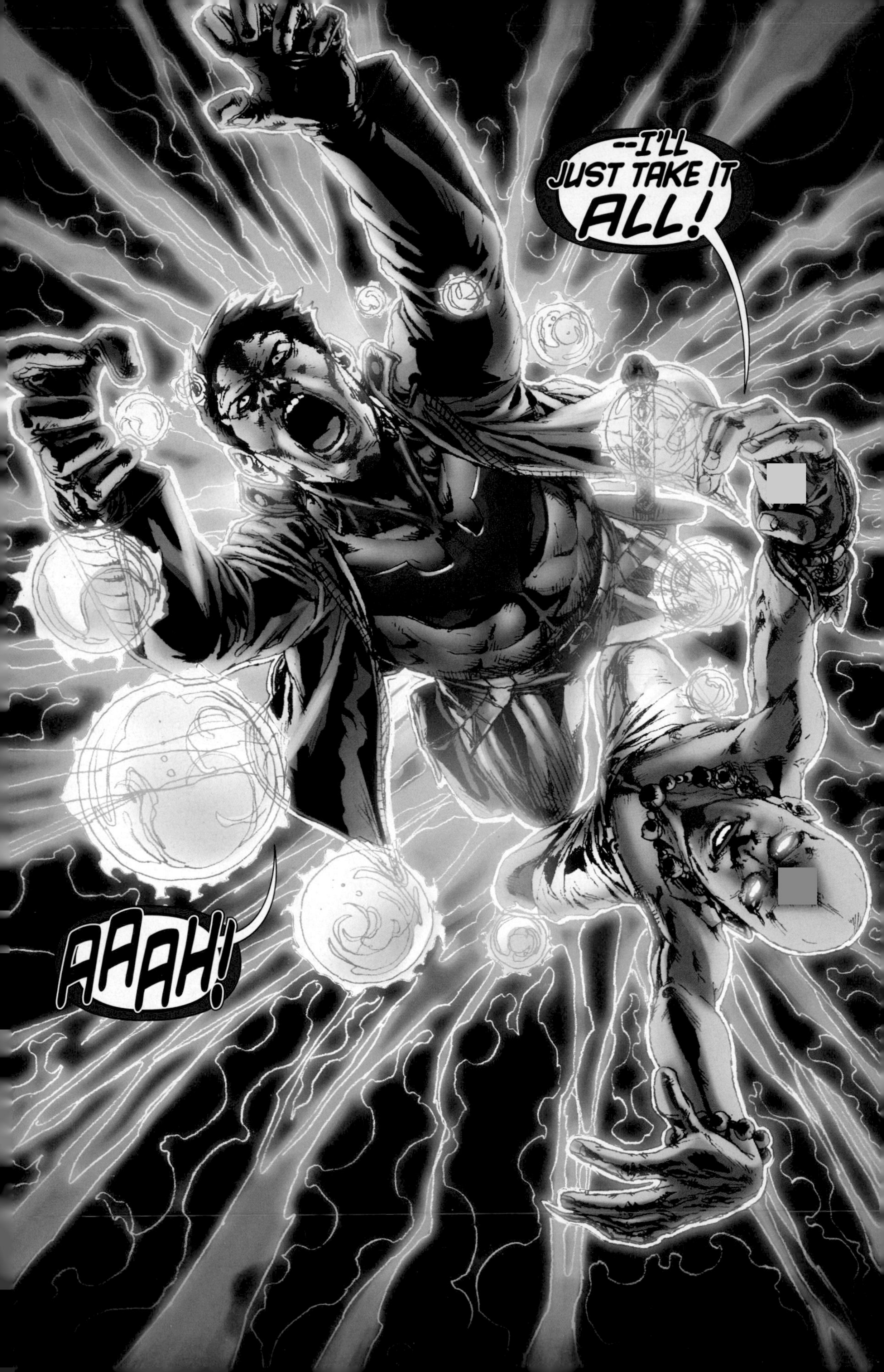
--I'LL JUST TAKE IT ALL!
AAAH!

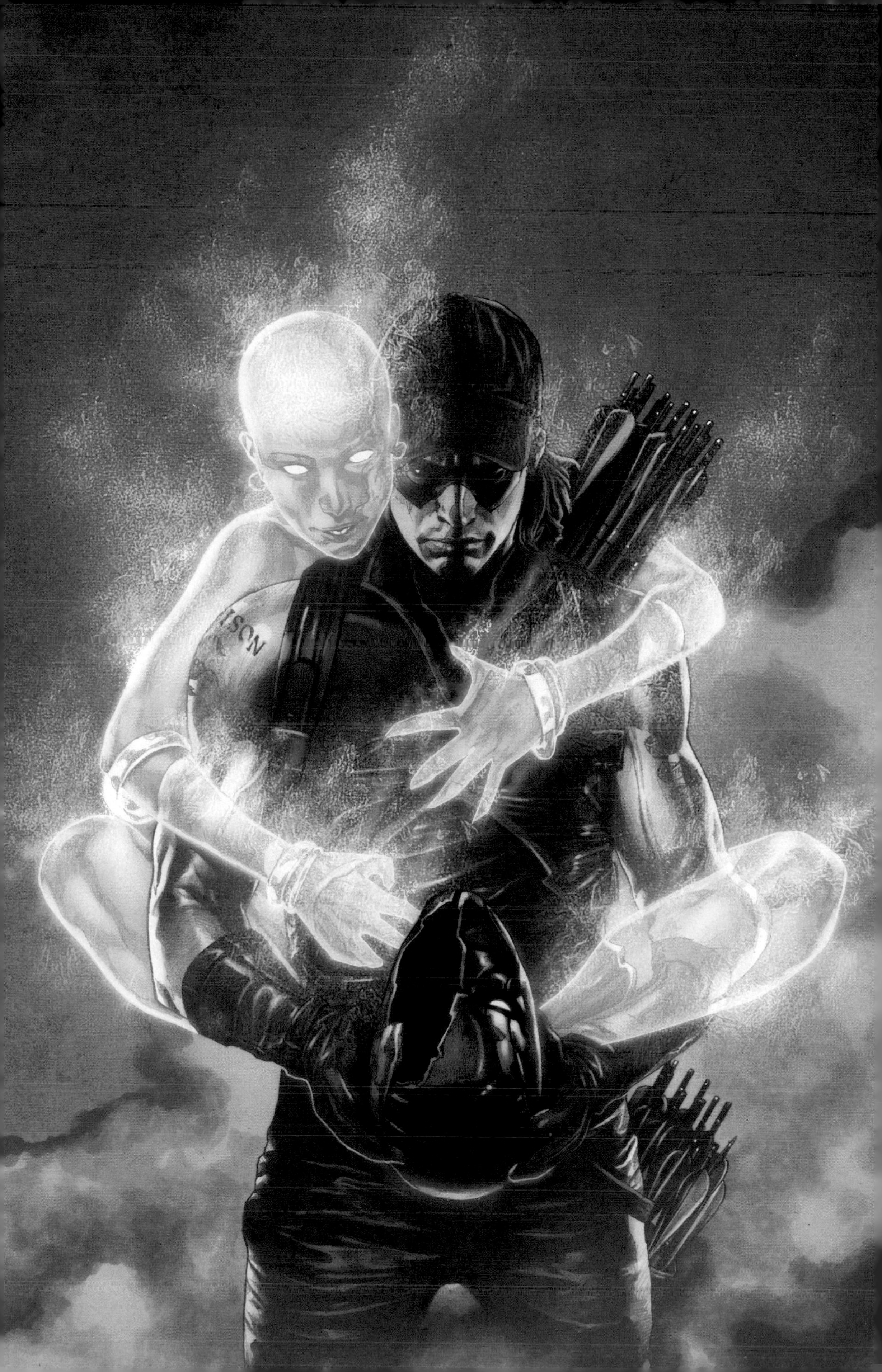

JAMES TYNION IV writer **JULIUS GOPEZ** artist **IAN CHURCHILL** thumbnail artist **NEI RUFFINO** colorist
AL BARRIONUEVO with **JAVIER MENA** cover artists

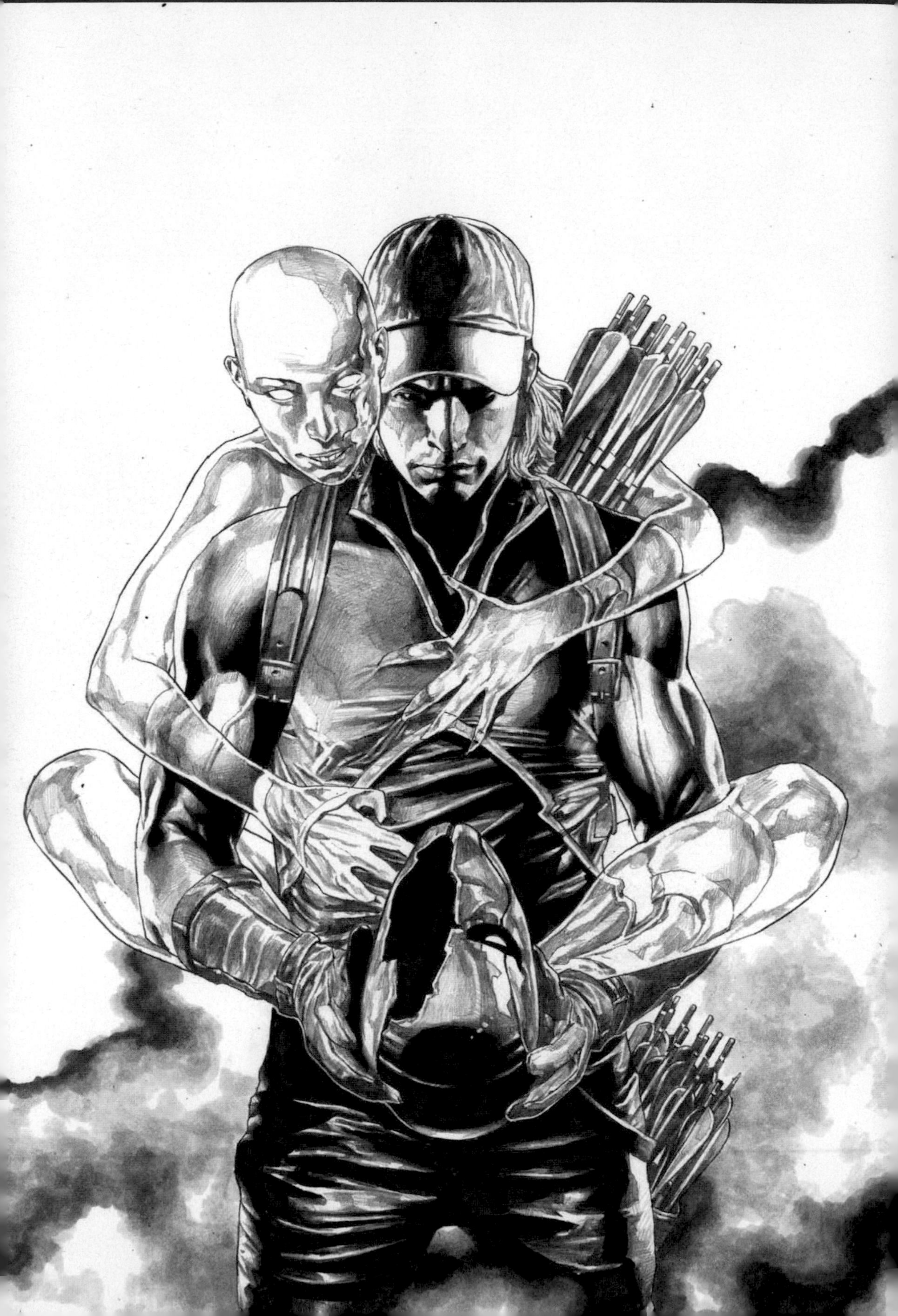

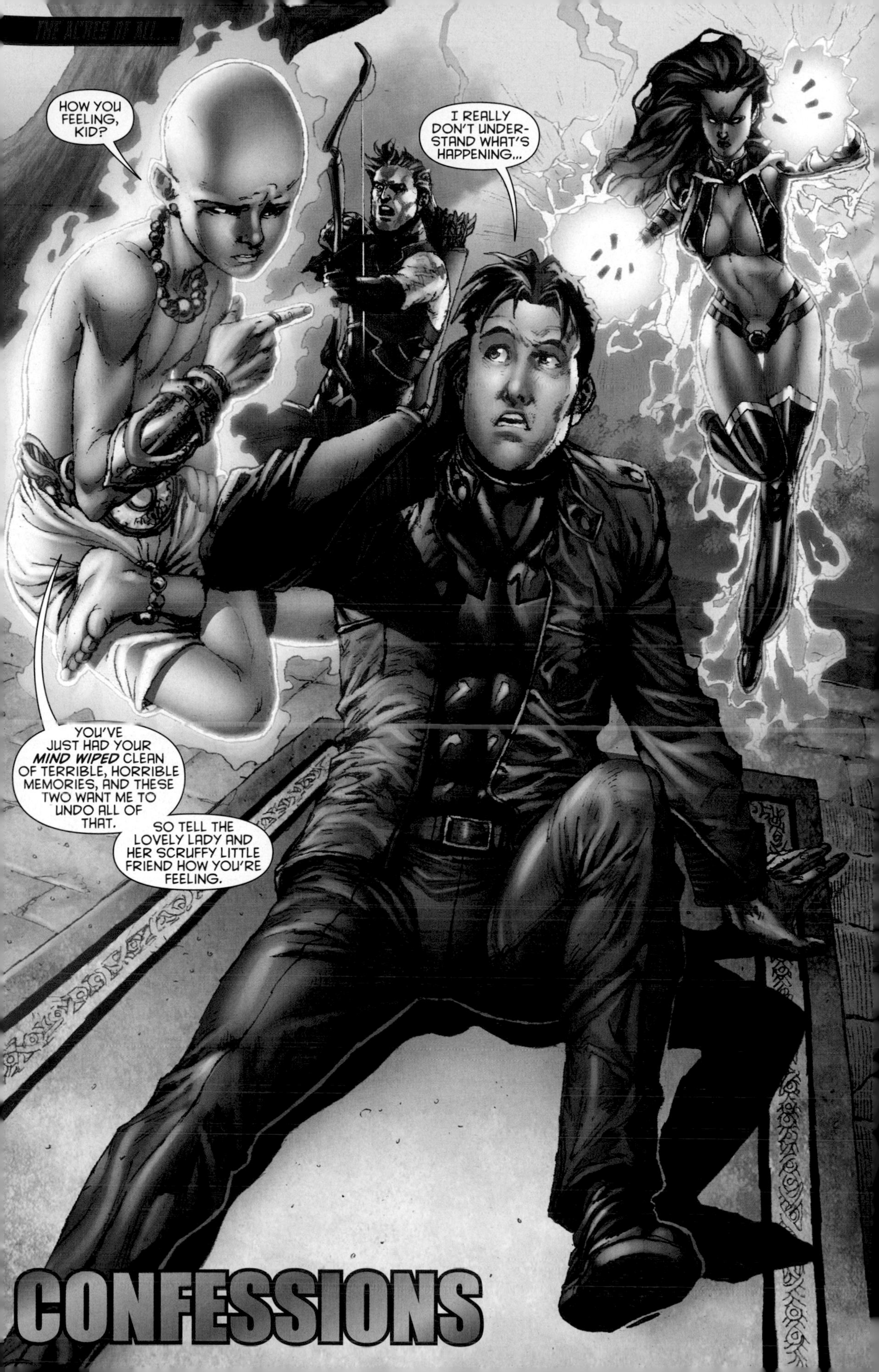
THE ACRES OF ALL . . .
HOW YOU FEELING, KID?
I REALLY DON'T UNDERSTAND WHAT'S HAPPENING...
YOU'VE JUST HAD YOUR MIND WIPED CLEAN OF TERRIBLE, HORRIBLE MEMORIES, AND THESE TWO WANT ME TO UNDO ALL OF THAT.
SO TELL THE LOVELY LADY AND HER SCRUFFY LITTLE FRIEND HOW YOU'RE FEELING.
CONFESSIONS

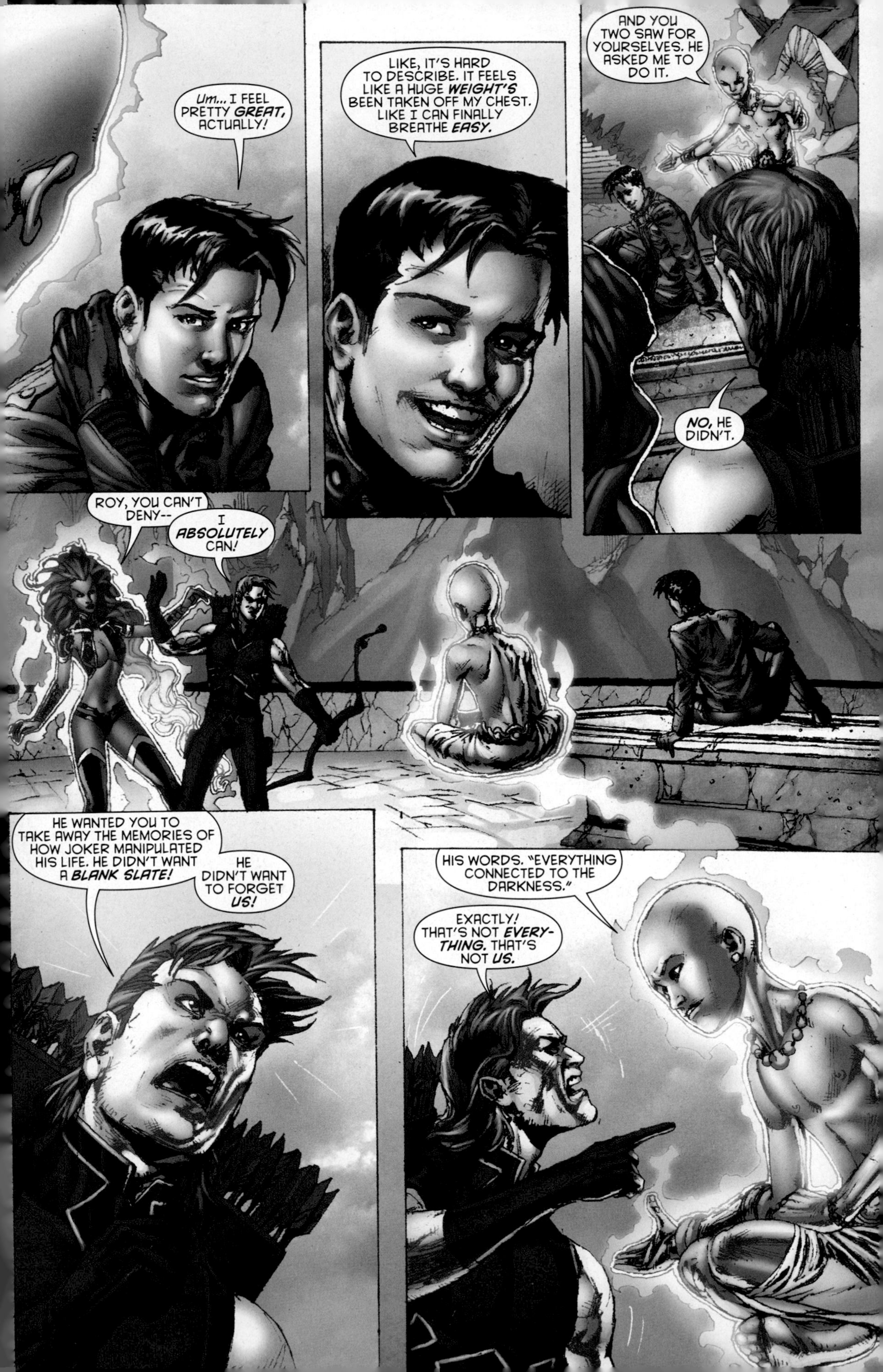
UM... I FEEL PRETTY GREAT, ACTUALLY!
LIKE, IT'S HARD TO DESCRIBE. IT FEELS LIKE A HUGE WEIGHT'S BEEN TAKEN OFF MY CHEST. LIKE I CAN FINALLY BREATHE EASY.
AND YOU TWO SAW FOR YOURSELVES. HE ASKED ME TO DO IT.
NO, HE DIDN'T.
ROY, YOU CAN'T DENY--
I ABSOLUTELY CAN!
HE WANTED YOU TO TAKE AWAY THE MEMORIES OF HOW JOKER MANIPULATED HIS LIFE. HE DIDN'T WANT A BLANK SLATE!
HE DIDN'T WANT TO FORGET US!
HIS WORDS. "EVERYTHING CONNECTED TO THE DARKNESS."
EXACTLY! THAT'S NOT EVERYTHING. THAT'S NOT US.

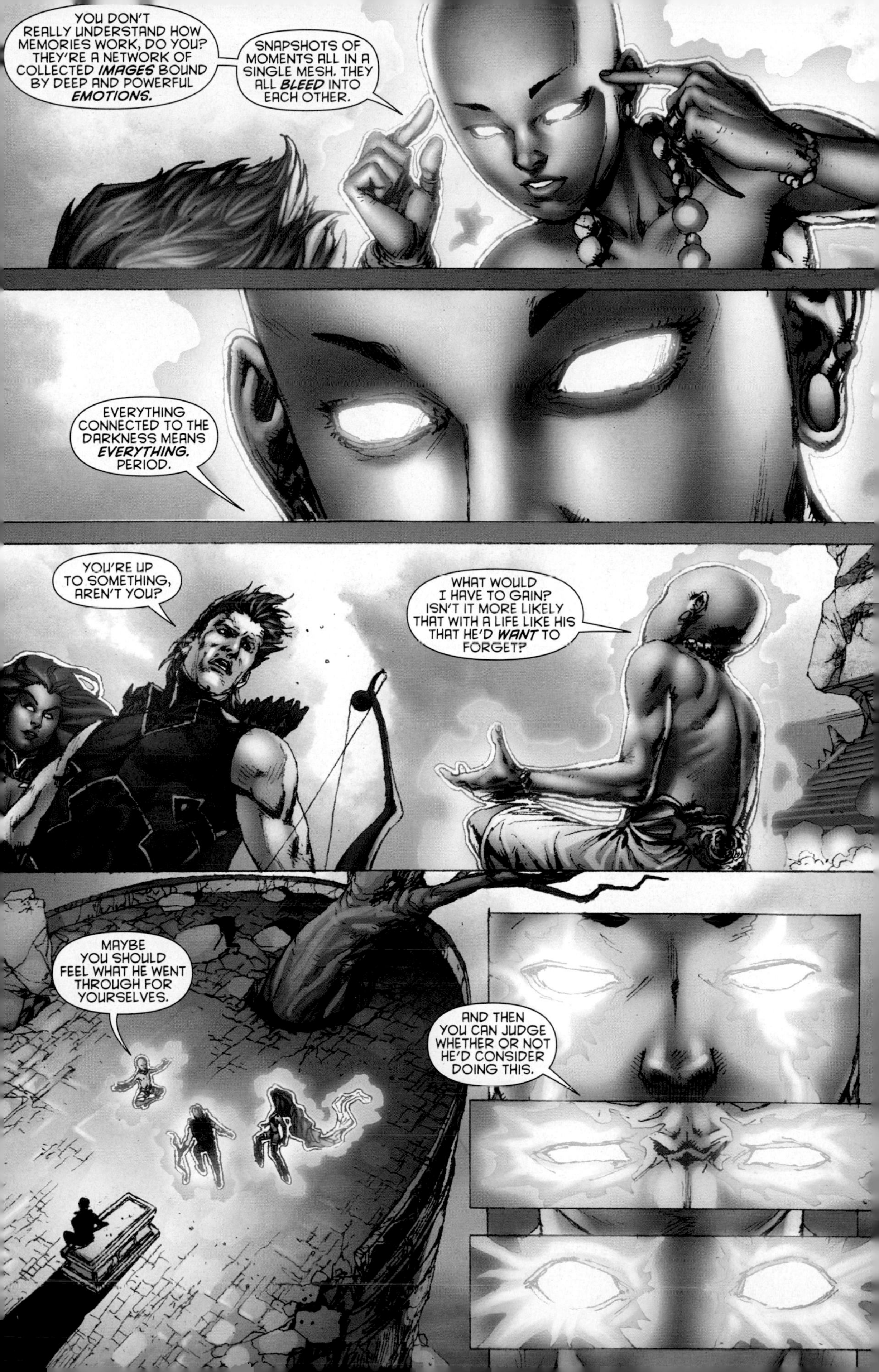
YOU DON'T REALLY UNDERSTAND HOW MEMORIES WORK, DO YOU? THEY'RE A NETWORK OF COLLECTED *IMAGES* BOUND BY DEEP AND POWERFUL *EMOTIONS.*
SNAPSHOTS OF MOMENTS ALL IN A SINGLE MESH. THEY ALL *BLEED* INTO EACH OTHER.
EVERYTHING CONNECTED TO THE DARKNESS MEANS *EVERYTHING.* PERIOD.
YOU'RE UP TO SOMETHING, AREN'T YOU?
WHAT WOULD I HAVE TO GAIN? ISN'T IT MORE LIKELY THAT WITH A LIFE LIKE HIS THAT HE'D *WANT* TO FORGET?
MAYBE YOU SHOULD FEEL WHAT HE WENT THROUGH FOR YOURSELVES.
AND THEN YOU CAN JUDGE WHETHER OR NOT HE'D CONSIDER DOING THIS.

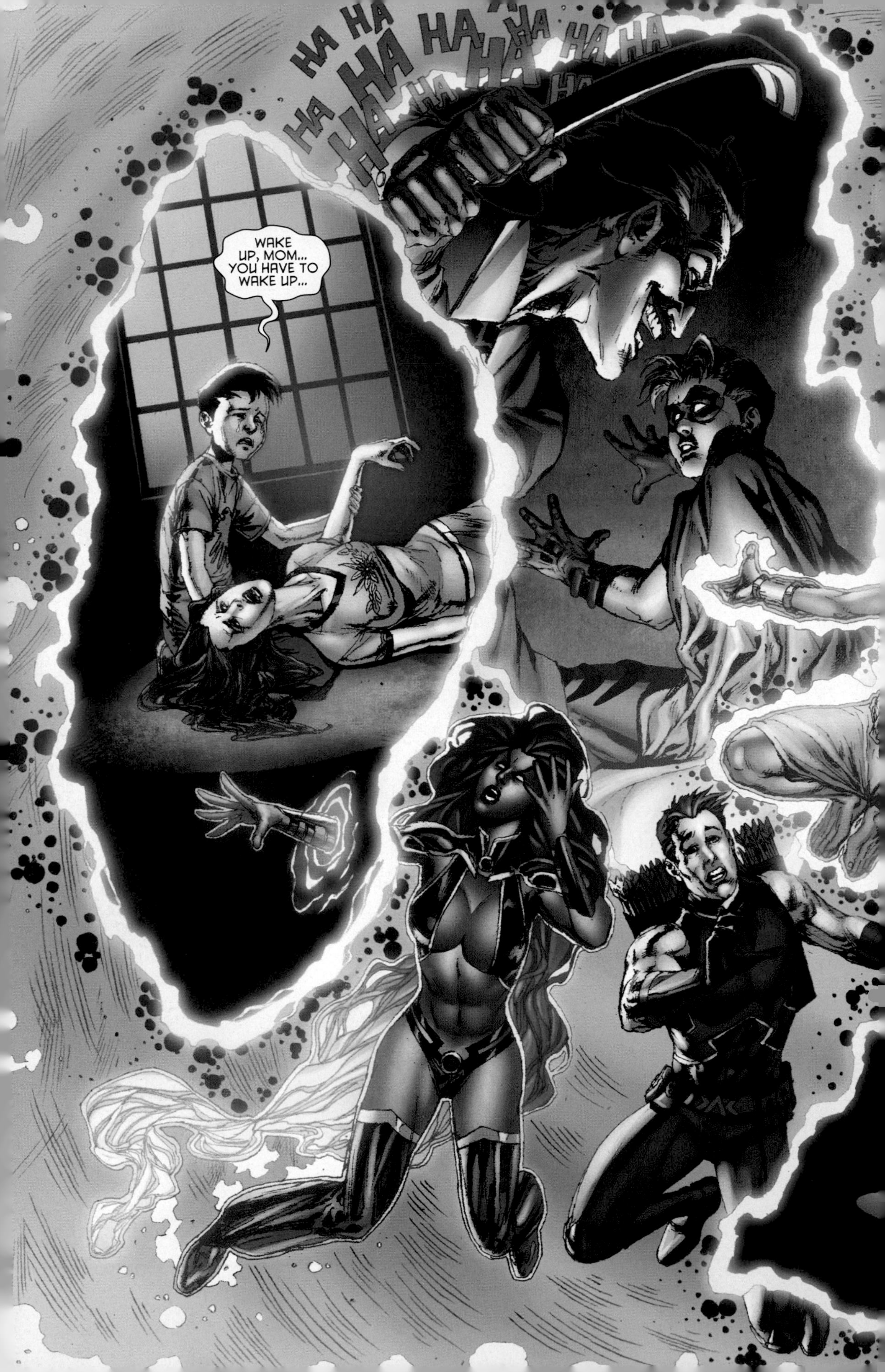
HA HA HA HA HA HA HA HA HA HA HA HA HA
WAKE UP, MOM... YOU HAVE TO WAKE UP...

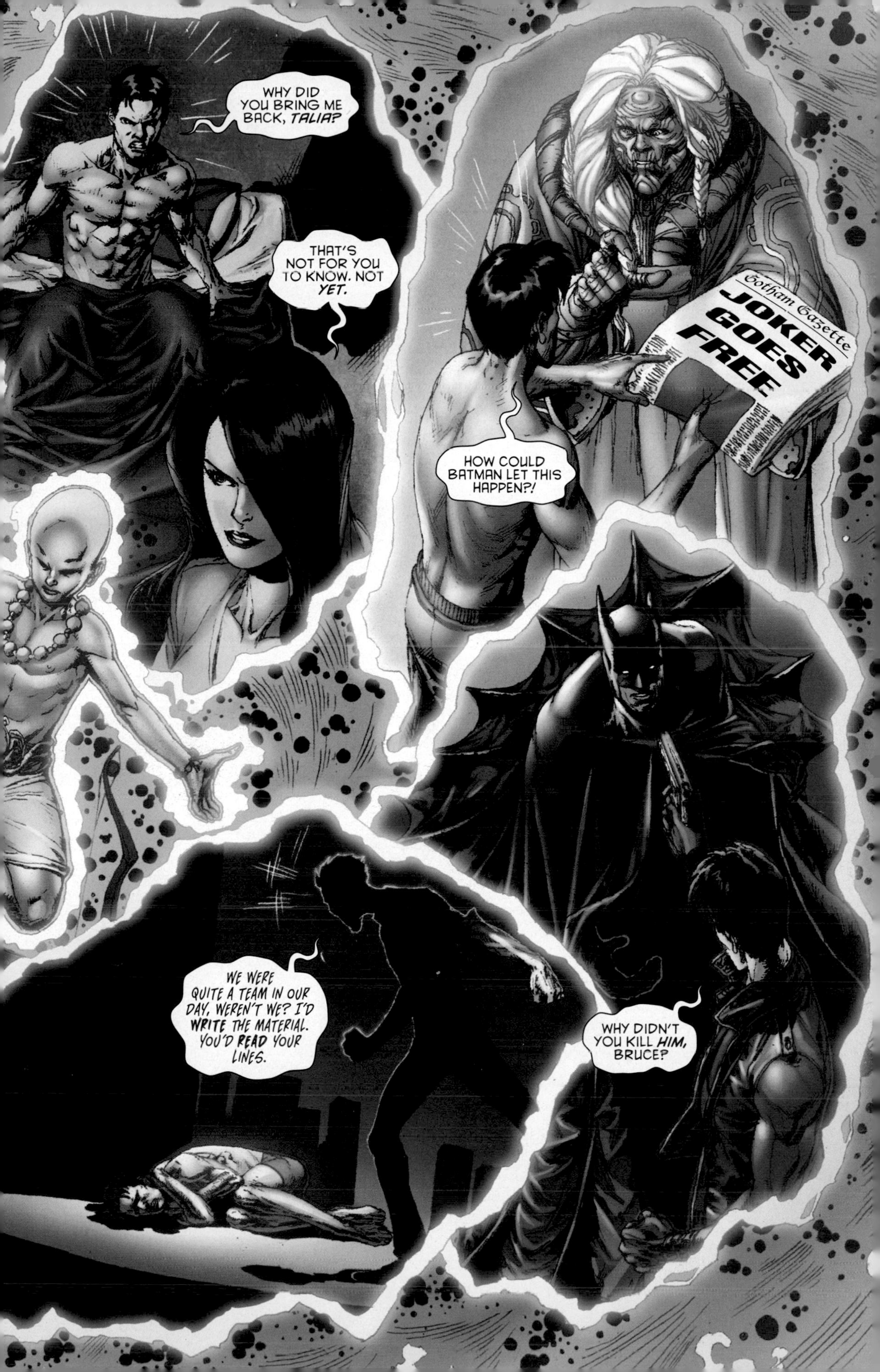
WHY DID YOU BRING ME BACK, TALIA?
THAT'S NOT FOR YOU TO KNOW. NOT YET.
Gotham Gazette
JOKER GOES FREE
HOW COULD BATMAN LET THIS HAPPEN?!
WE WERE QUITE A TEAM IN OUR DAY, WEREN'T WE? I'D WRITE THE MATERIAL. YOU'D READ YOUR LINES.
WHY DIDN'T YOU KILL HIM, BRUCE?

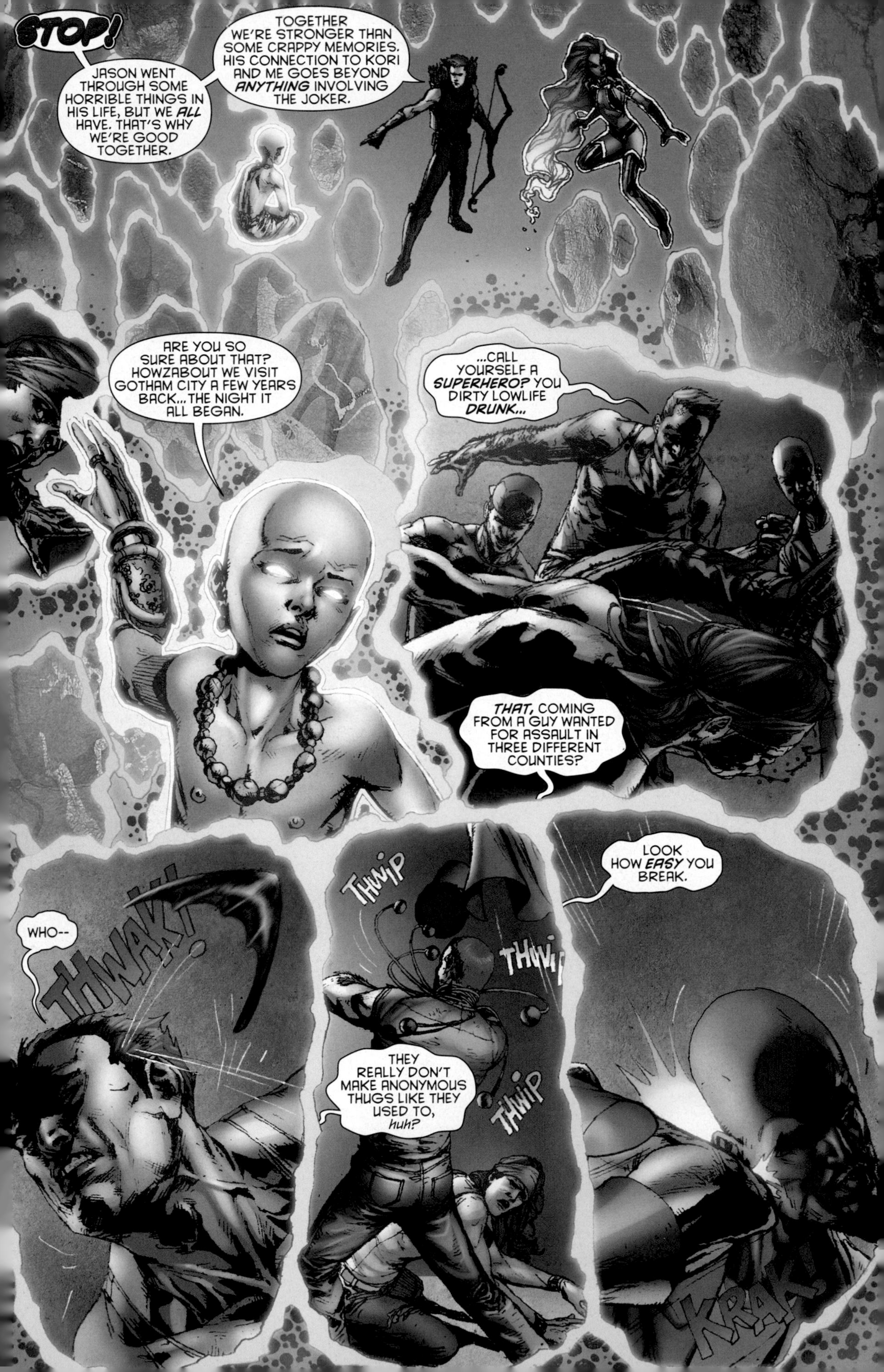
STOP!
JASON WENT THROUGH SOME HORRIBLE THINGS IN HIS LIFE, BUT WE ALL HAVE. THAT'S WHY WE'RE GOOD TOGETHER.
TOGETHER WE'RE STRONGER THAN SOME CRAPPY MEMORIES. HIS CONNECTION TO KORI AND ME GOES BEYOND ANYTHING INVOLVING THE JOKER.
ARE YOU SO SURE ABOUT THAT? HOWZABOUT WE VISIT GOTHAM CITY A FEW YEARS BACK...THE NIGHT IT ALL BEGAN.
...CALL YOURSELF A SUPERHERO? YOU DIRTY LOWLIFE DRUNK...
THAT, COMING FROM A GUY WANTED FOR ASSAULT IN THREE DIFFERENT COUNTIES?
WHO--
THWAK!
THWIP
THWIP
THWIP
THEY REALLY DON'T MAKE ANONYMOUS THUGS LIKE THEY USED TO, huh?
LOOK HOW EASY YOU BREAK.
KRAK

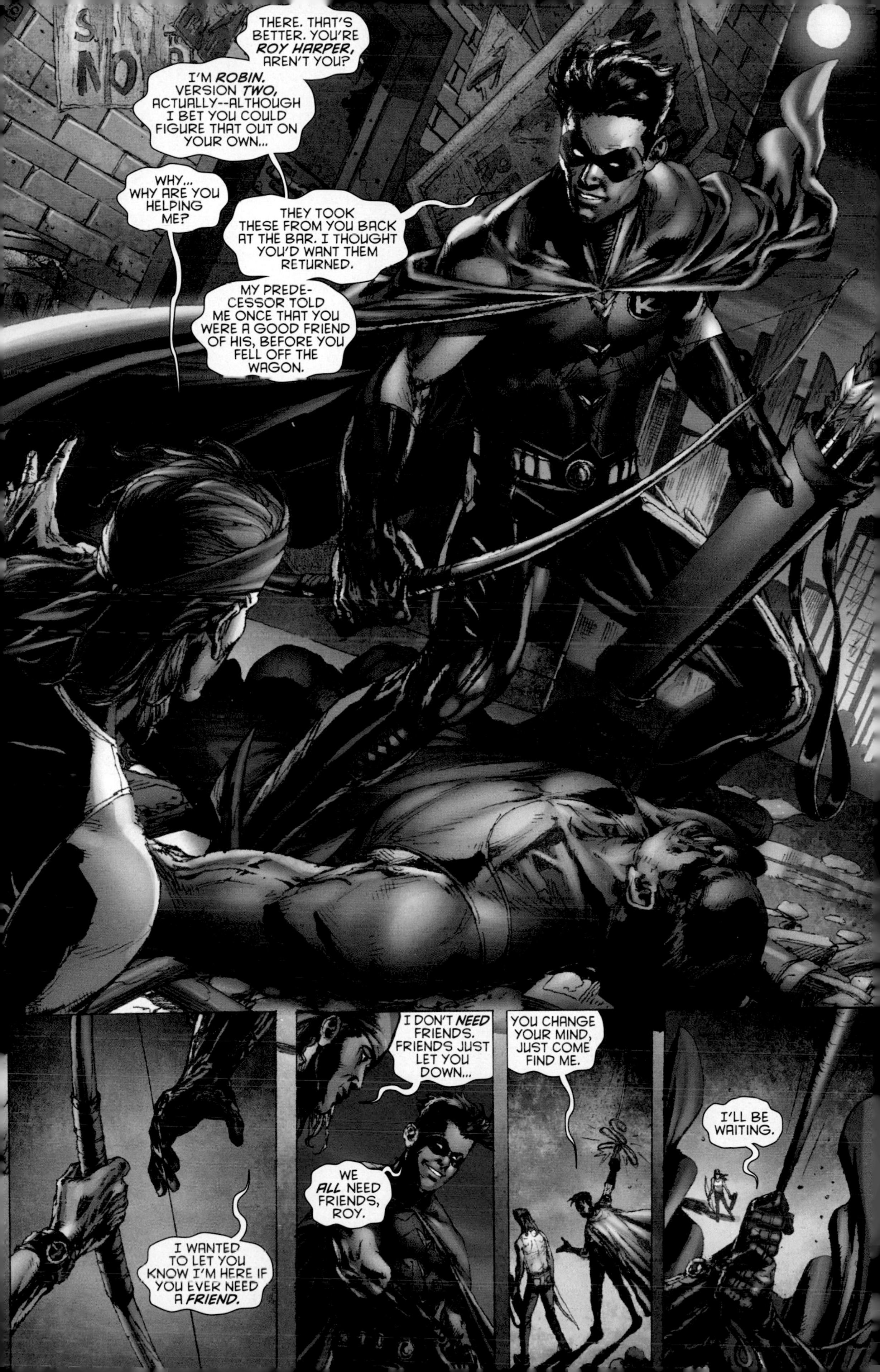

THERE. THAT'S BETTER. YOU'RE *ROY HARPER,* AREN'T YOU?
I'M *ROBIN.* VERSION *TWO,* ACTUALLY--ALTHOUGH I BET YOU COULD FIGURE THAT OUT ON YOUR OWN...
WHY... WHY ARE YOU HELPING ME?
THEY TOOK THESE FROM YOU BACK AT THE BAR. I THOUGHT YOU'D WANT THEM RETURNED.
MY PREDE-CESSOR TOLD ME ONCE THAT YOU WERE A GOOD FRIEND OF HIS, BEFORE YOU FELL OFF THE WAGON.
I WANTED TO LET YOU KNOW I'M HERE IF YOU EVER NEED A *FRIEND.*
I DON'T *NEED* FRIENDS. FRIENDS JUST LET YOU DOWN...
WE *ALL* NEED FRIENDS, ROY.
YOU CHANGE YOUR MIND, JUST COME FIND ME.
I'LL BE WAITING.

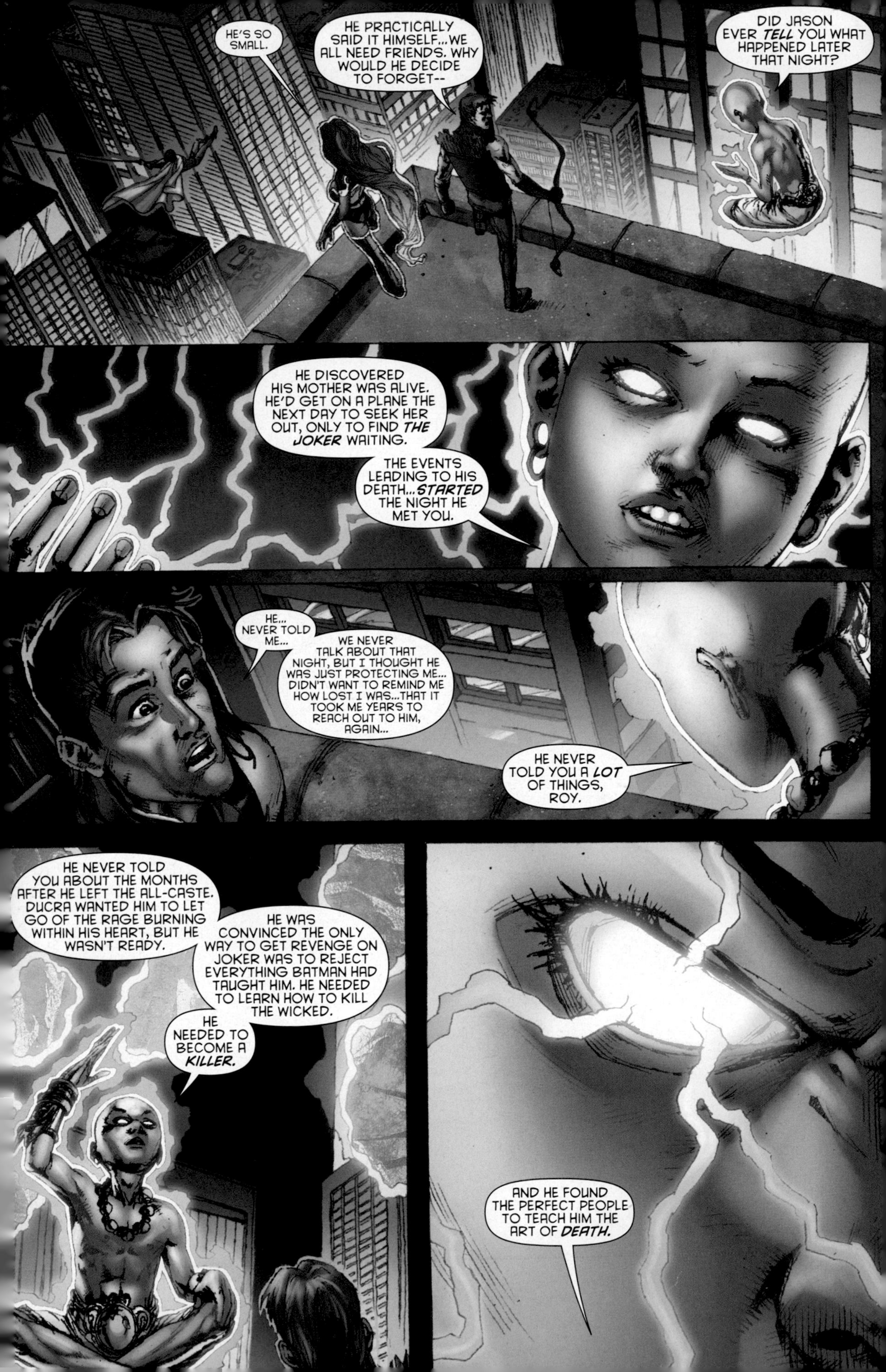
HE'S SO SMALL.
HE PRACTICALLY SAID IT HIMSELF...WE ALL NEED FRIENDS. WHY WOULD HE DECIDE TO FORGET--
DID JASON EVER TELL YOU WHAT HAPPENED LATER THAT NIGHT?
HE DISCOVERED HIS MOTHER WAS ALIVE. HE'D GET ON A PLANE THE NEXT DAY TO SEEK HER OUT, ONLY TO FIND THE JOKER WAITING.
THE EVENTS LEADING TO HIS DEATH...STARTED THE NIGHT HE MET YOU.
HE... NEVER TOLD ME...
WE NEVER TALK ABOUT THAT NIGHT, BUT I THOUGHT HE WAS JUST PROTECTING ME... DIDN'T WANT TO REMIND ME HOW LOST I WAS...THAT IT TOOK ME YEARS TO REACH OUT TO HIM, AGAIN...
HE NEVER TOLD YOU A LOT OF THINGS, ROY.
HE NEVER TOLD YOU ABOUT THE MONTHS AFTER HE LEFT THE ALL-CASTE. DUCRA WANTED HIM TO LET GO OF THE RAGE BURNING WITHIN HIS HEART, BUT HE WASN'T READY.
HE WAS CONVINCED THE ONLY WAY TO GET REVENGE ON JOKER WAS TO REJECT EVERYTHING BATMAN HAD TAUGHT HIM. HE NEEDED TO LEARN HOW TO KILL THE WICKED.
HE NEEDED TO BECOME A KILLER.
AND HE FOUND THE PERFECT PEOPLE TO TEACH HIM THE ART OF DEATH.

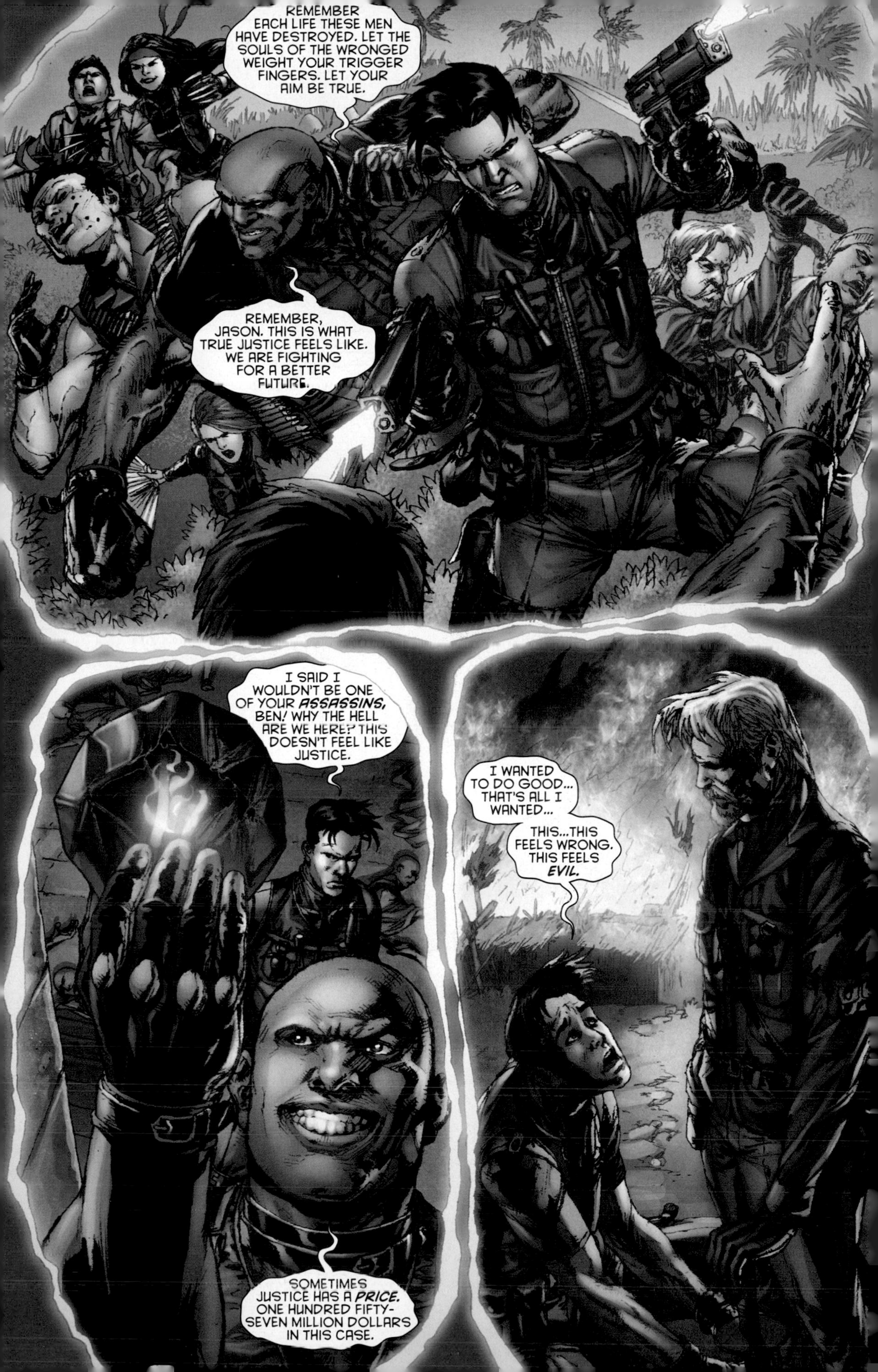
REMEMBER EACH LIFE THESE MEN HAVE DESTROYED. LET THE SOULS OF THE WRONGED WEIGHT YOUR TRIGGER FINGERS. LET YOUR AIM BE TRUE.
REMEMBER, JASON. THIS IS WHAT TRUE JUSTICE FEELS LIKE. WE ARE FIGHTING FOR A BETTER FUTURE.
I SAID I WOULDN'T BE ONE OF YOUR ASSASSINS, BEN! WHY THE HELL ARE WE HERE? THIS DOESN'T FEEL LIKE JUSTICE.
SOMETIMES JUSTICE HAS A PRICE. ONE HUNDRED FIFTY-SEVEN MILLION DOLLARS IN THIS CASE.
I WANTED TO DO GOOD... THAT'S ALL I WANTED...
THIS...THIS FEELS WRONG. THIS FEELS EVIL.

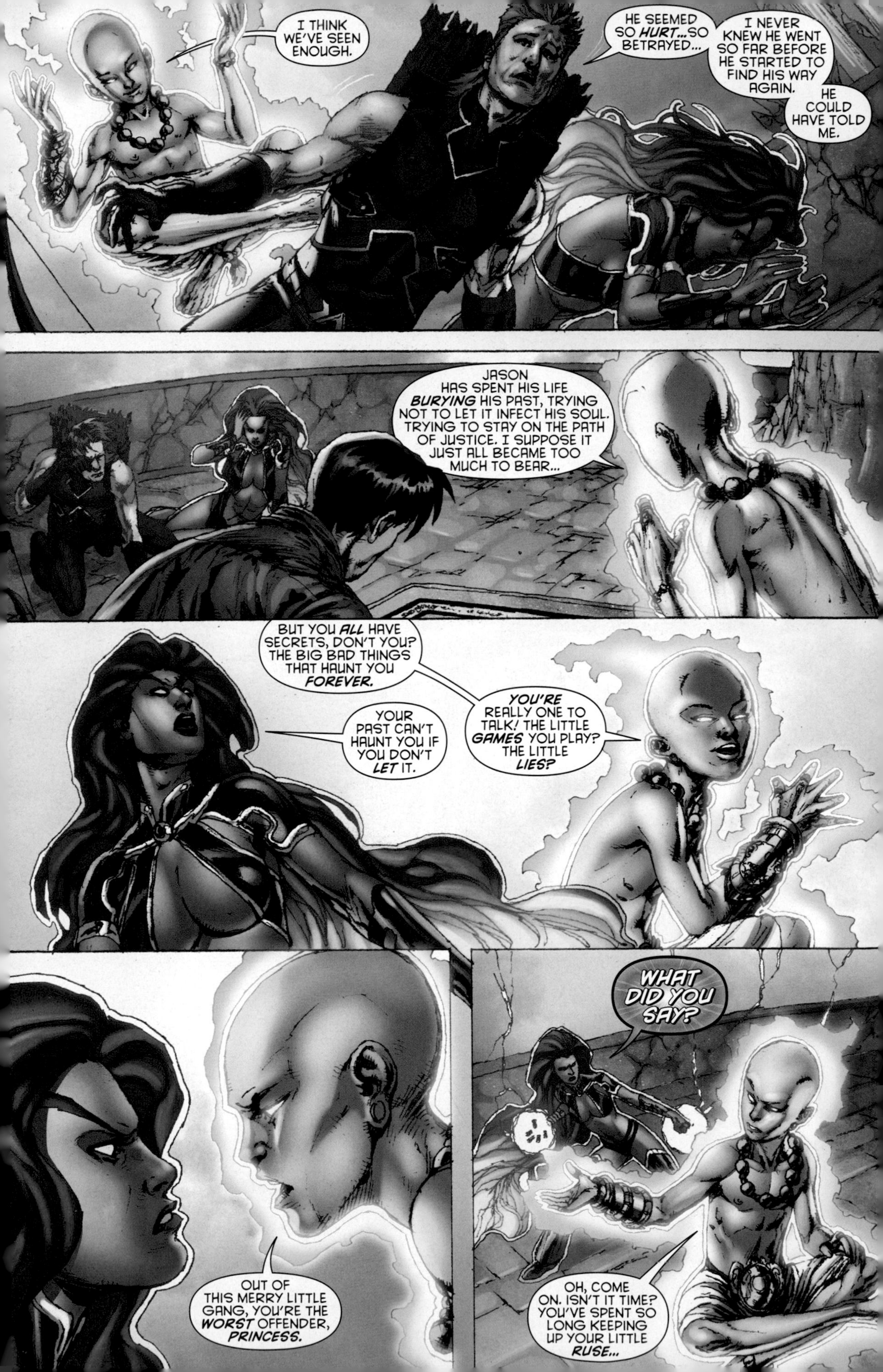
I THINK WE'VE SEEN ENOUGH.
HE SEEMED SO HURT...SO BETRAYED...
I NEVER KNEW HE WENT SO FAR BEFORE HE STARTED TO FIND HIS WAY AGAIN.
HE COULD HAVE TOLD ME.
JASON HAS SPENT HIS LIFE BURYING HIS PAST, TRYING NOT TO LET IT INFECT HIS SOUL. TRYING TO STAY ON THE PATH OF JUSTICE. I SUPPOSE IT JUST ALL BECAME TOO MUCH TO BEAR...
BUT YOU ALL HAVE SECRETS, DON'T YOU? THE BIG BAD THINGS THAT HAUNT YOU FOREVER.
YOUR PAST CAN'T HAUNT YOU IF YOU DON'T LET IT.
YOU'RE REALLY ONE TO TALK! THE LITTLE GAMES YOU PLAY? THE LITTLE LIES?
OUT OF THIS MERRY LITTLE GANG, YOU'RE THE WORST OFFENDER, PRINCESS.
WHAT DID YOU SAY?
OH, COME ON. ISN'T IT TIME? YOU'VE SPENT SO LONG KEEPING UP YOUR LITTLE RUSE...

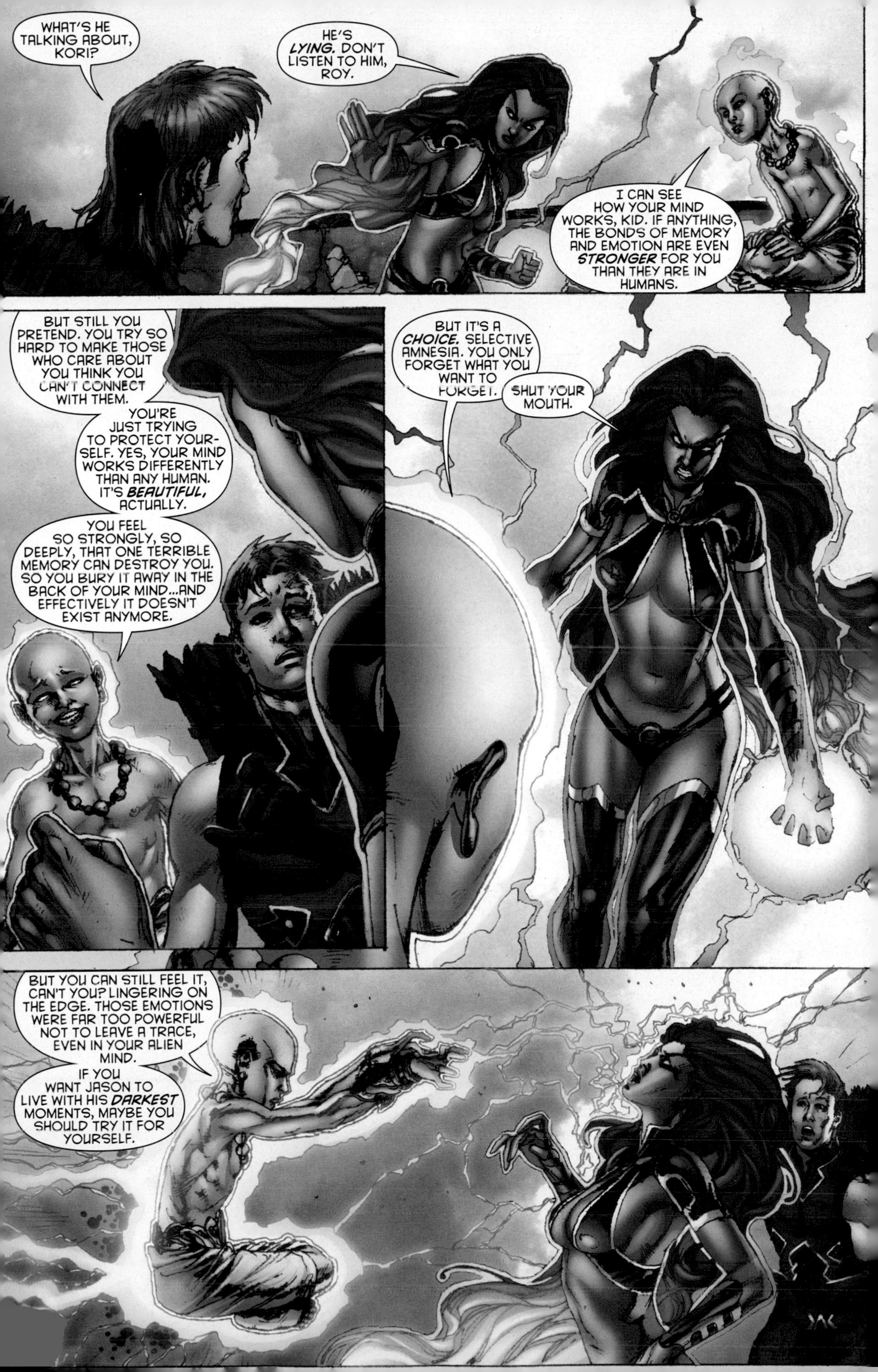

WHAT'S HE TALKING ABOUT, KORI?
HE'S *LYING.* DON'T LISTEN TO HIM, ROY.
I CAN SEE HOW YOUR MIND WORKS, KID. IF ANYTHING, THE BONDS OF MEMORY AND EMOTION ARE EVEN ***STRONGER*** FOR YOU THAN THEY ARE IN HUMANS.
BUT STILL YOU PRETEND. YOU TRY SO HARD TO MAKE THOSE WHO CARE ABOUT YOU THINK YOU CAN'T CONNECT WITH THEM.
YOU'RE JUST TRYING TO PROTECT YOURSELF. YES, YOUR MIND WORKS DIFFERENTLY THAN ANY HUMAN. IT'S ***BEAUTIFUL,*** ACTUALLY.
YOU FEEL SO STRONGLY, SO DEEPLY, THAT ONE TERRIBLE MEMORY CAN DESTROY YOU. SO YOU BURY IT AWAY IN THE BACK OF YOUR MIND...AND EFFECTIVELY IT DOESN'T EXIST ANYMORE.
BUT IT'S A *CHOICE.* SELECTIVE AMNESIA. YOU ONLY FORGET WHAT YOU WANT TO FORGET.
SHUT YOUR MOUTH.
BUT YOU CAN STILL FEEL IT, CAN'T YOU? LINGERING ON THE EDGE. THOSE EMOTIONS WERE FAR TOO POWERFUL NOT TO LEAVE A TRACE, EVEN IN YOUR ALIEN MIND.
IF YOU WANT JASON TO LIVE WITH HIS ***DARKEST*** MOMENTS, MAYBE YOU SHOULD TRY IT FOR YOURSELF.

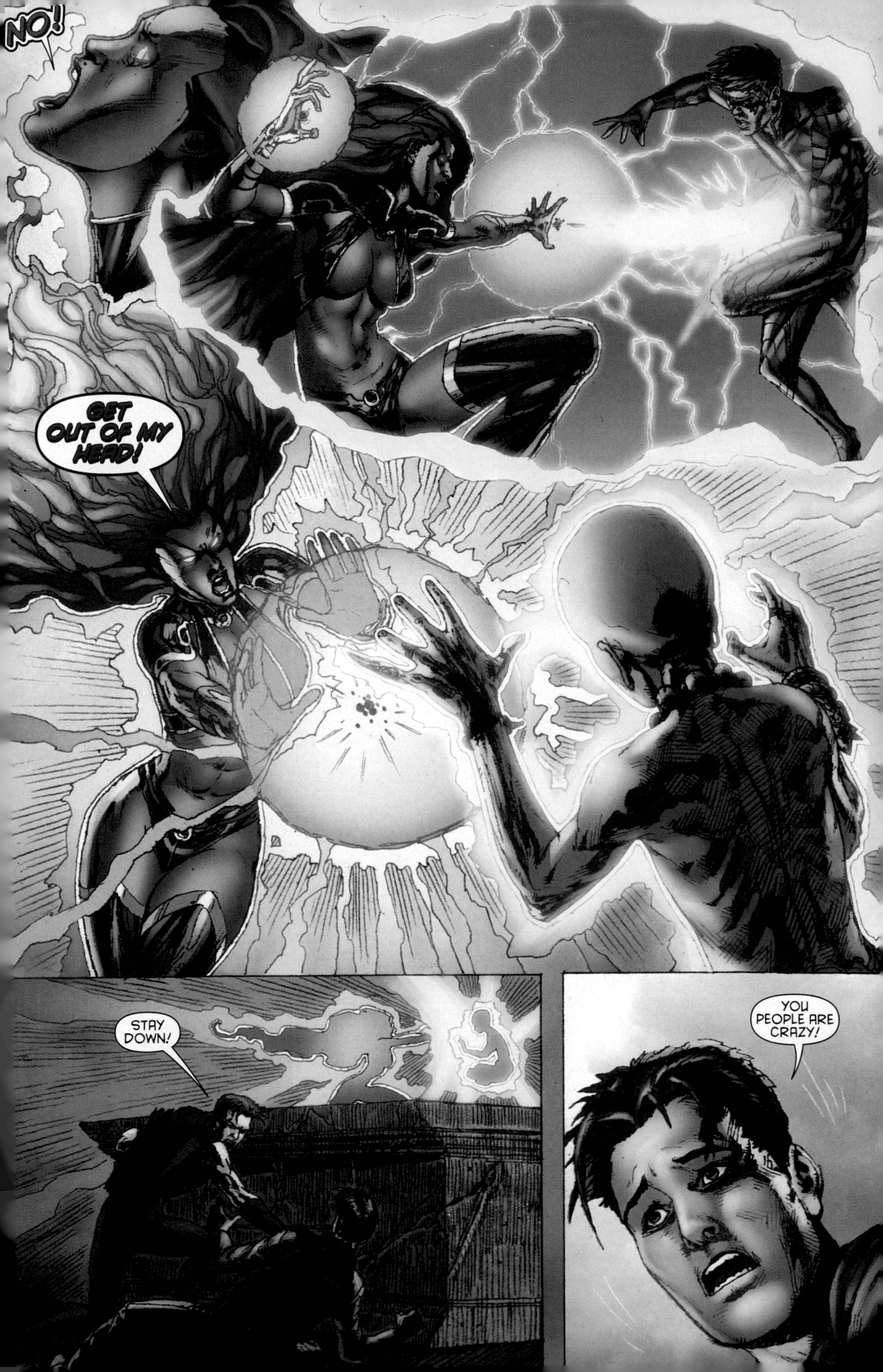
NO!
GET OUT OF MY HEAD!
STAY DOWN!
YOU PEOPLE ARE CRAZY!

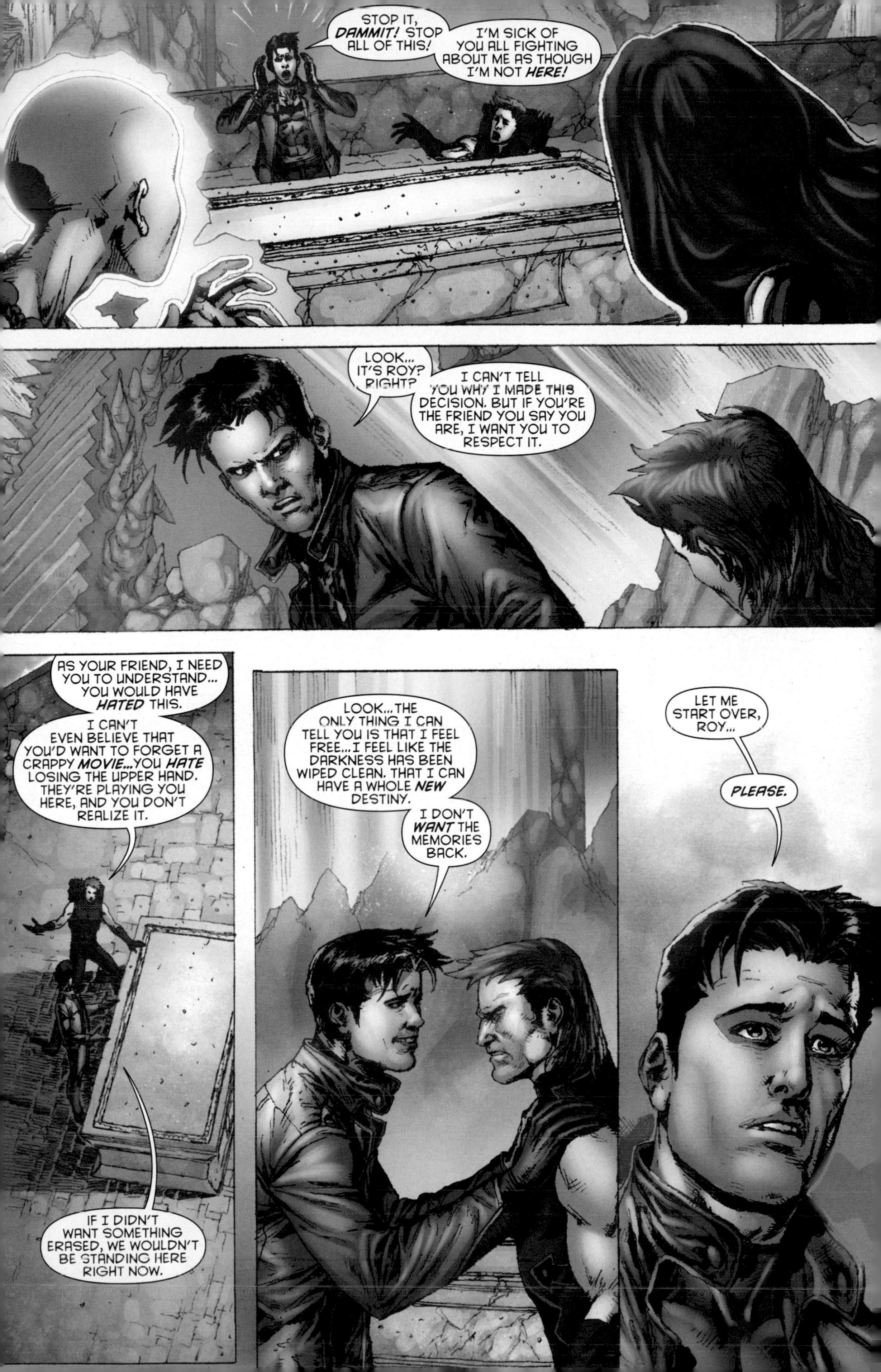
STOP IT, DAMMIT! STOP ALL OF THIS!
I'M SICK OF YOU ALL FIGHTING ABOUT ME AS THOUGH I'M NOT HERE!
LOOK... IT'S ROY? RIGHT?
I CAN'T TELL YOU WHY I MADE THIS DECISION. BUT IF YOU'RE THE FRIEND YOU SAY YOU ARE, I WANT YOU TO RESPECT IT.
AS YOUR FRIEND, I NEED YOU TO UNDERSTAND... YOU WOULD HAVE HATED THIS.
I CAN'T EVEN BELIEVE THAT YOU'D WANT TO FORGET A CRAPPY MOVIE...YOU HATE LOSING THE UPPER HAND. THEY'RE PLAYING YOU HERE, AND YOU DON'T REALIZE IT.
IF I DIDN'T WANT SOMETHING ERASED, WE WOULDN'T BE STANDING HERE RIGHT NOW.
LOOK...THE ONLY THING I CAN TELL YOU IS THAT I FEEL FREE...I FEEL LIKE THE DARKNESS HAS BEEN WIPED CLEAN. THAT I CAN HAVE A WHOLE NEW DESTINY.
I DON'T WANT THE MEMORIES BACK.
LET ME START OVER, ROY...
PLEASE.

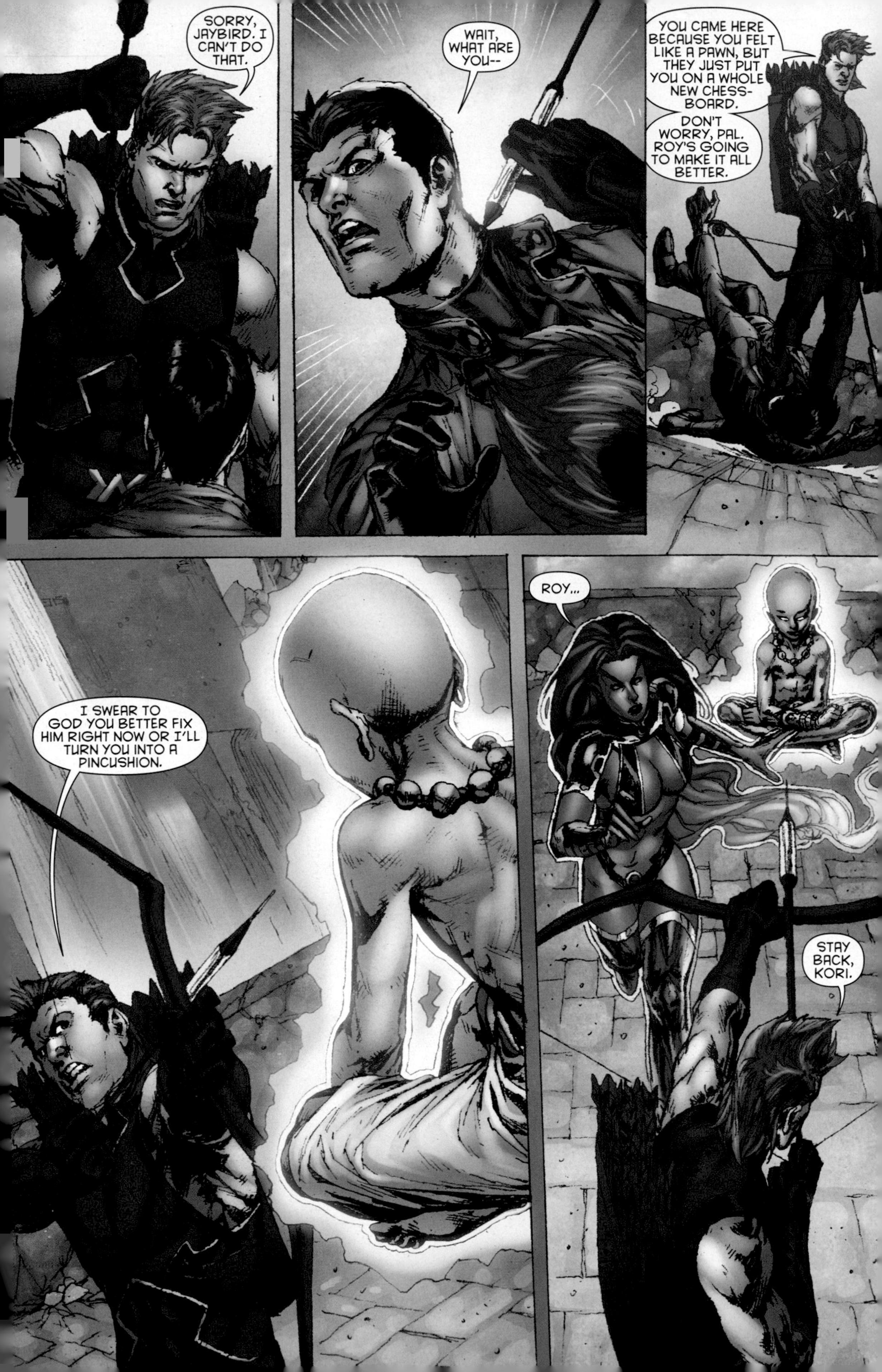
SORRY, JAYBIRD. I CAN'T DO THAT.
WAIT, WHAT ARE YOU--
YOU CAME HERE BECAUSE YOU FELT LIKE A PAWN, BUT THEY JUST PUT YOU ON A WHOLE NEW CHESS-BOARD.
DON'T WORRY, PAL. ROY'S GOING TO MAKE IT ALL BETTER.
I SWEAR TO GOD YOU BETTER FIX HIM RIGHT NOW OR I'LL TURN YOU INTO A PINCUSHION.
ROY...
STAY BACK, KORI.

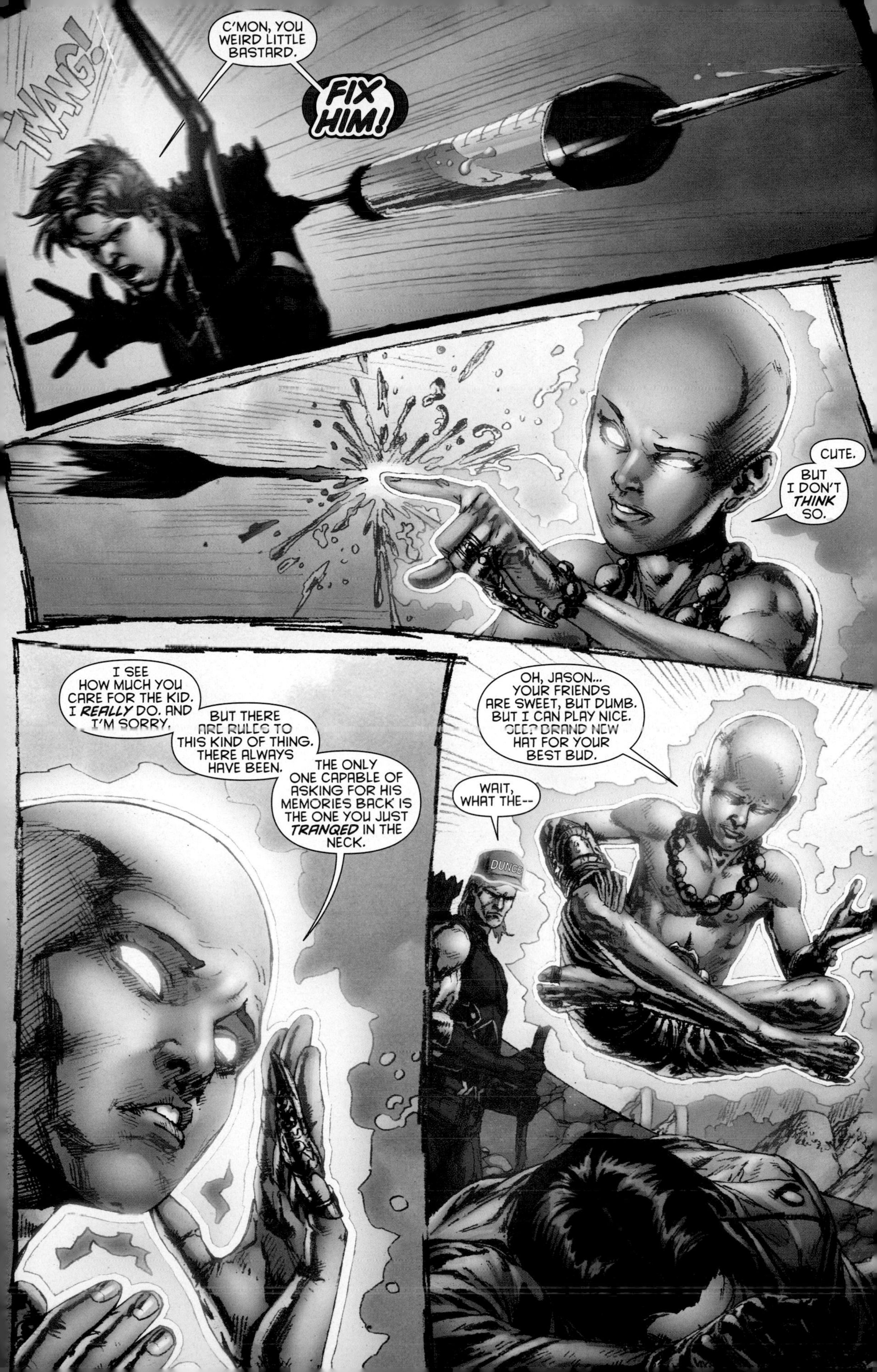
TWANG!
C'MON, YOU WEIRD LITTLE BASTARD.
FIX HIM!
CUTE.
BUT I DON'T THINK SO.
I SEE HOW MUCH YOU CARE FOR THE KID. I REALLY DO. AND I'M SORRY.
BUT THERE ARE RULES TO THIS KIND OF THING. THERE ALWAYS HAVE BEEN.
THE ONLY ONE CAPABLE OF ASKING FOR HIS MEMORIES BACK IS THE ONE YOU JUST TRANQED IN THE NECK.
OH, JASON... YOUR FRIENDS ARE SWEET, BUT DUMB. BUT I CAN PLAY NICE. SEE? BRAND NEW HAT FOR YOUR BEST BUD.
WAIT, WHAT THE--
DUNCE

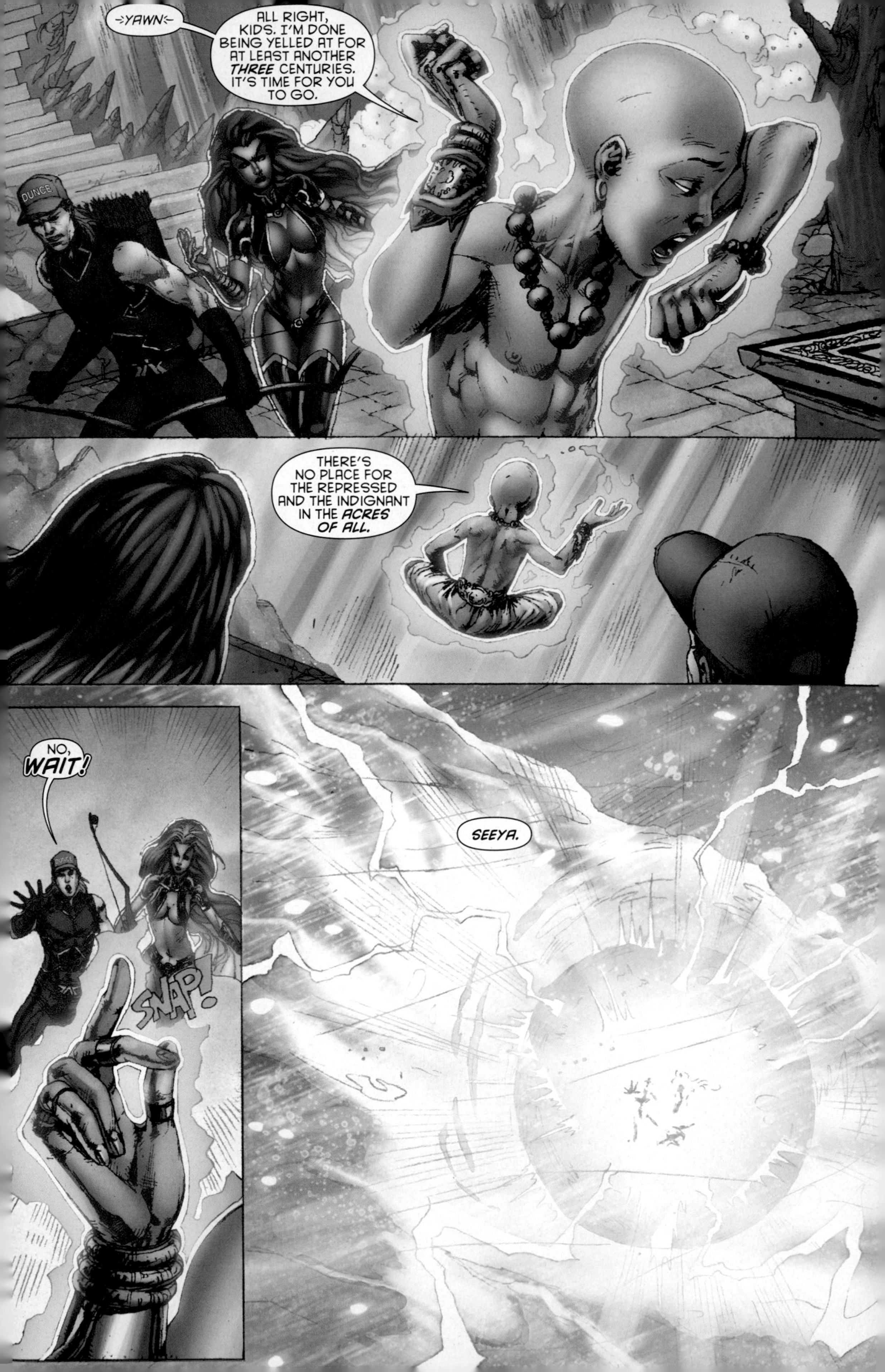

~YAWN~
ALL RIGHT, KIDS. I'M DONE BEING YELLED AT FOR AT LEAST ANOTHER THREE CENTURIES. IT'S TIME FOR YOU TO GO.
DUNCE
THERE'S NO PLACE FOR THE REPRESSED AND THE INDIGNANT IN THE ACRES OF ALL.
NO, WAIT!
DUNCE
SNAP!
SEEYA.

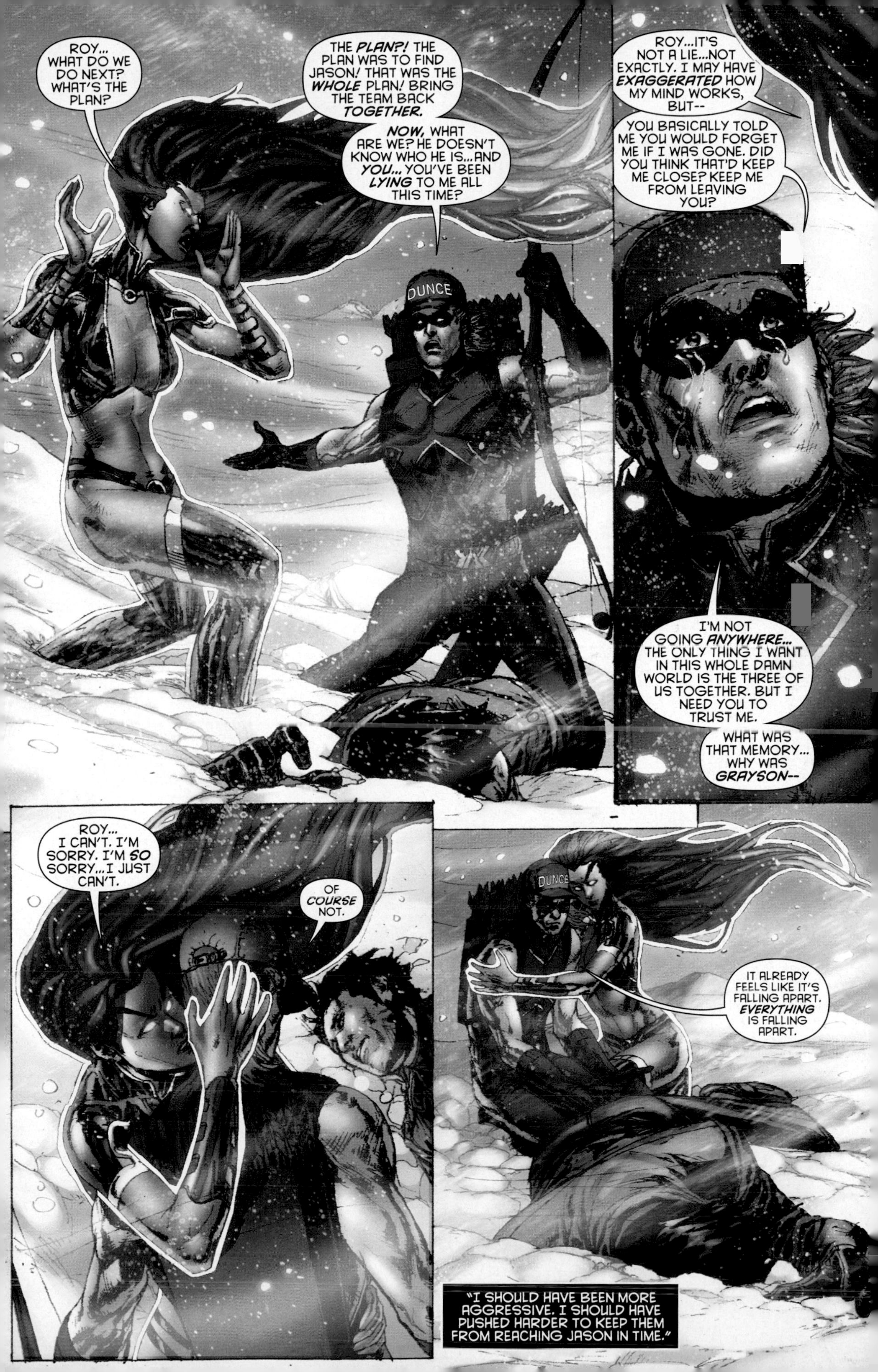
ROY... WHAT DO WE DO NEXT? WHAT'S THE PLAN?
THE PLAN?! THE PLAN WAS TO FIND JASON! THAT WAS THE WHOLE PLAN! BRING THE TEAM BACK TOGETHER.
NOW, WHAT ARE WE? HE DOESN'T KNOW WHO HE IS...AND YOU... YOU'VE BEEN LYING TO ME ALL THIS TIME?
DUNCE
ROY...IT'S NOT A LIE...NOT EXACTLY. I MAY HAVE EXAGGERATED HOW MY MIND WORKS, BUT--
YOU BASICALLY TOLD ME YOU WOULD FORGET ME IF I WAS GONE. DID YOU THINK THAT'D KEEP ME CLOSE? KEEP ME FROM LEAVING YOU?
I'M NOT GOING ANYWHERE... THE ONLY THING I WANT IN THIS WHOLE DAMN WORLD IS THE THREE OF US TOGETHER. BUT I NEED YOU TO TRUST ME.
WHAT WAS THAT MEMORY... WHY WAS GRAYSON--
ROY... I CAN'T. I'M SORRY. I'M SO SORRY...I JUST CAN'T.
OF COURSE NOT.
DUNCE
IT ALREADY FEELS LIKE IT'S FALLING APART. EVERYTHING IS FALLING APART.
"I SHOULD HAVE BEEN MORE AGGRESSIVE. I SHOULD HAVE PUSHED HARDER TO KEEP THEM FROM REACHING JASON IN TIME."

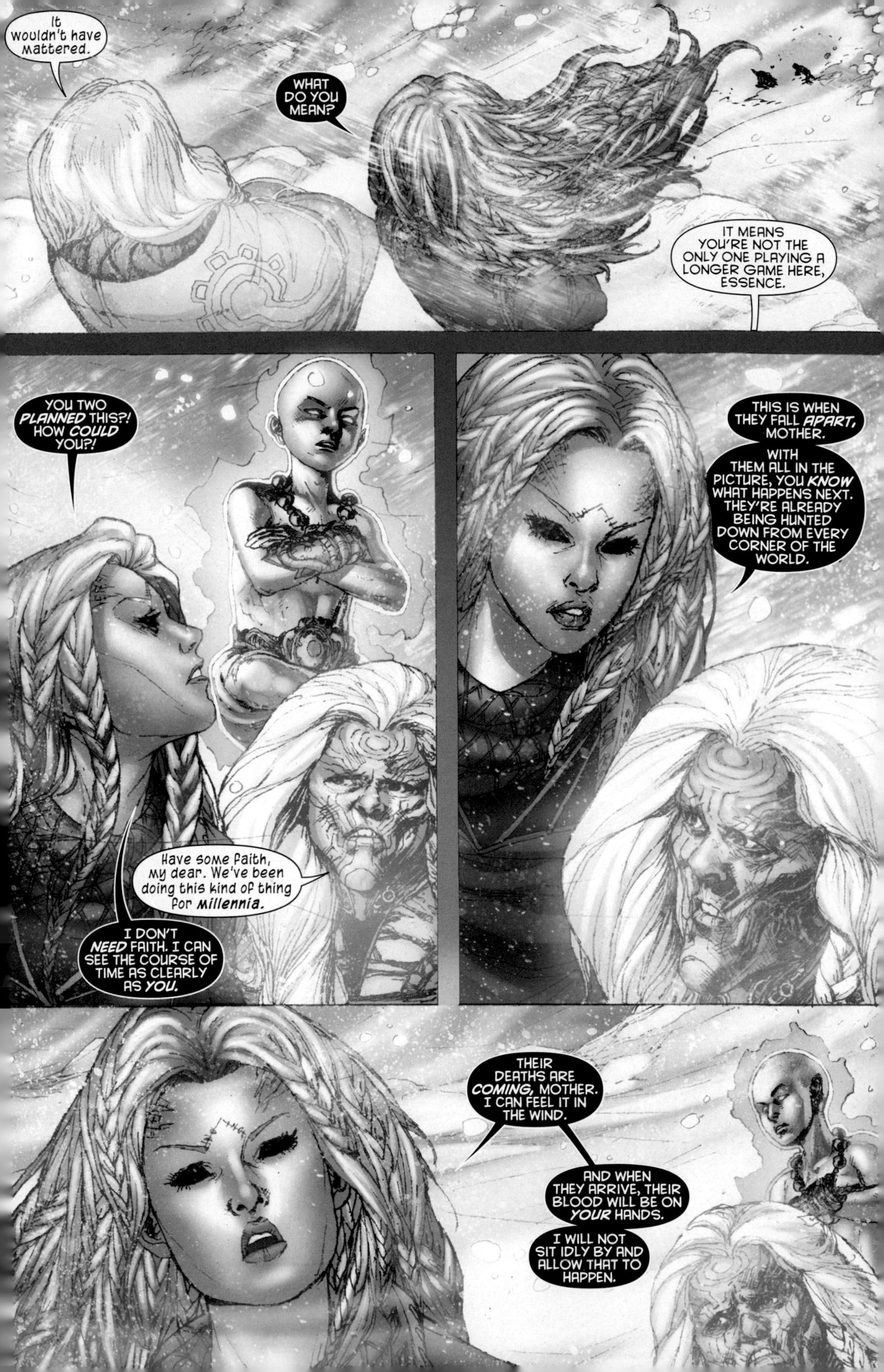
It wouldn't have Mattered.
WHAT DO YOU MEAN?
IT MEANS YOU'RE NOT THE ONLY ONE PLAYING A LONGER GAME HERE, ESSENCE.
YOU TWO *PLANNED* THIS?! HOW *COULD* YOU?!
Have some faith, my dear. We've been doing this kind of thing for *Millennia.*
I DON'T *NEED* FAITH. I CAN SEE THE COURSE OF TIME AS CLEARLY AS *YOU.*
THIS IS WHEN THEY FALL *APART,* MOTHER.
WITH THEM ALL IN THE PICTURE, YOU *KNOW* WHAT HAPPENS NEXT. THEY'RE ALREADY BEING HUNTED DOWN FROM EVERY CORNER OF THE WORLD.
THEIR DEATHS ARE *COMING,* MOTHER. I CAN FEEL IT IN THE WIND.
AND WHEN THEY ARRIVE, THEIR BLOOD WILL BE ON *YOUR* HANDS.
I WILL NOT SIT IDLY BY AND ALLOW THAT TO HAPPEN.

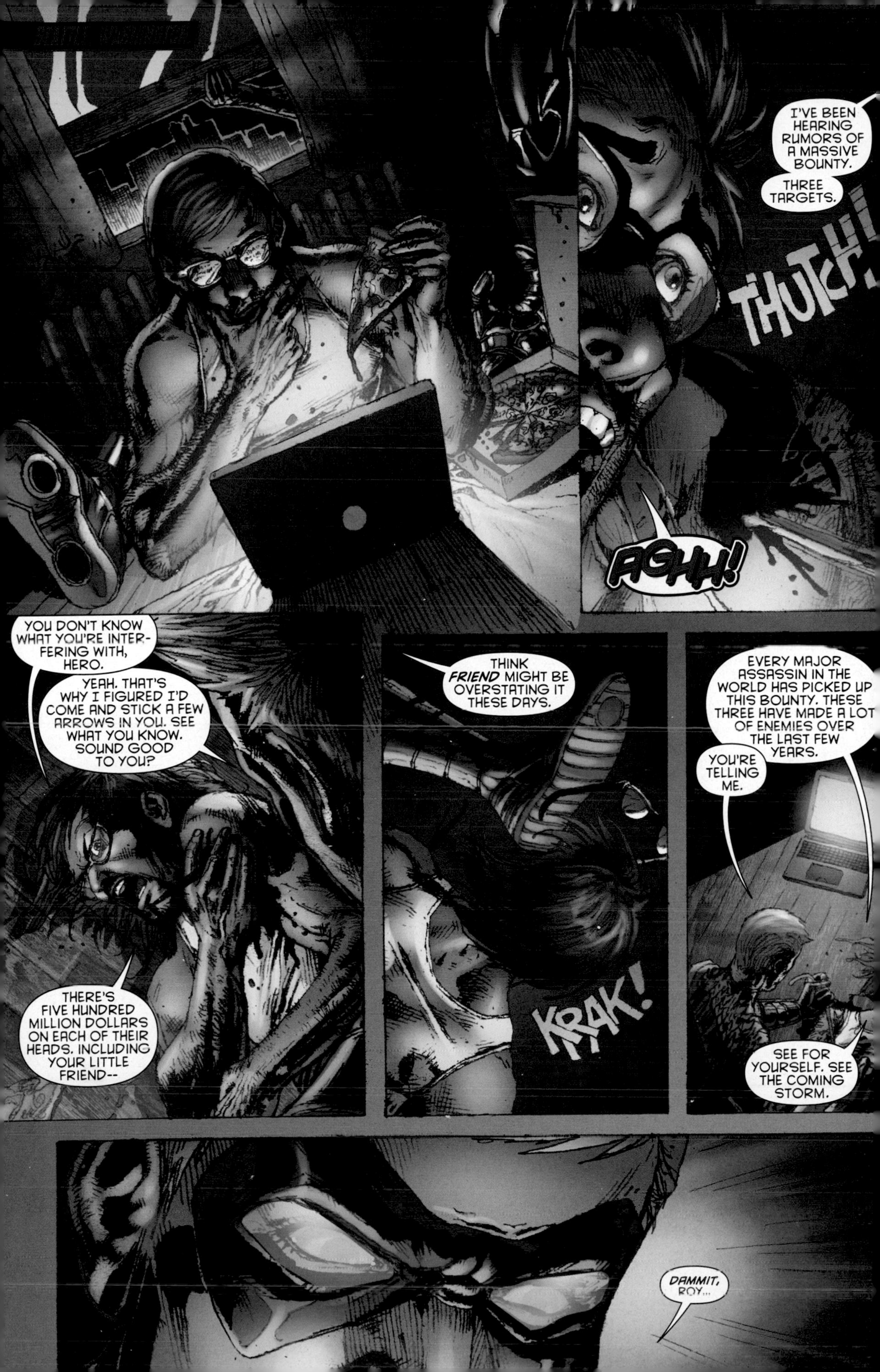
I'VE BEEN HEARING RUMORS OF A MASSIVE BOUNTY.
THREE TARGETS.
THUCK!
AGHH!
YOU DON'T KNOW WHAT YOU'RE INTERFERING WITH, HERO.
YEAH. THAT'S WHY I FIGURED I'D COME AND STICK A FEW ARROWS IN YOU. SEE WHAT YOU KNOW. SOUND GOOD TO YOU?
THERE'S FIVE HUNDRED MILLION DOLLARS ON EACH OF THEIR HEADS. INCLUDING YOUR LITTLE FRIEND--
THINK FRIEND MIGHT BE OVERSTATING IT THESE DAYS.
KRAK!
EVERY MAJOR ASSASSIN IN THE WORLD HAS PICKED UP THIS BOUNTY. THESE THREE HAVE MADE A LOT OF ENEMIES OVER THE LAST FEW YEARS.
YOU'RE TELLING ME.
SEE FOR YOURSELF. SEE THE COMING STORM.
DAMMIT, ROY...

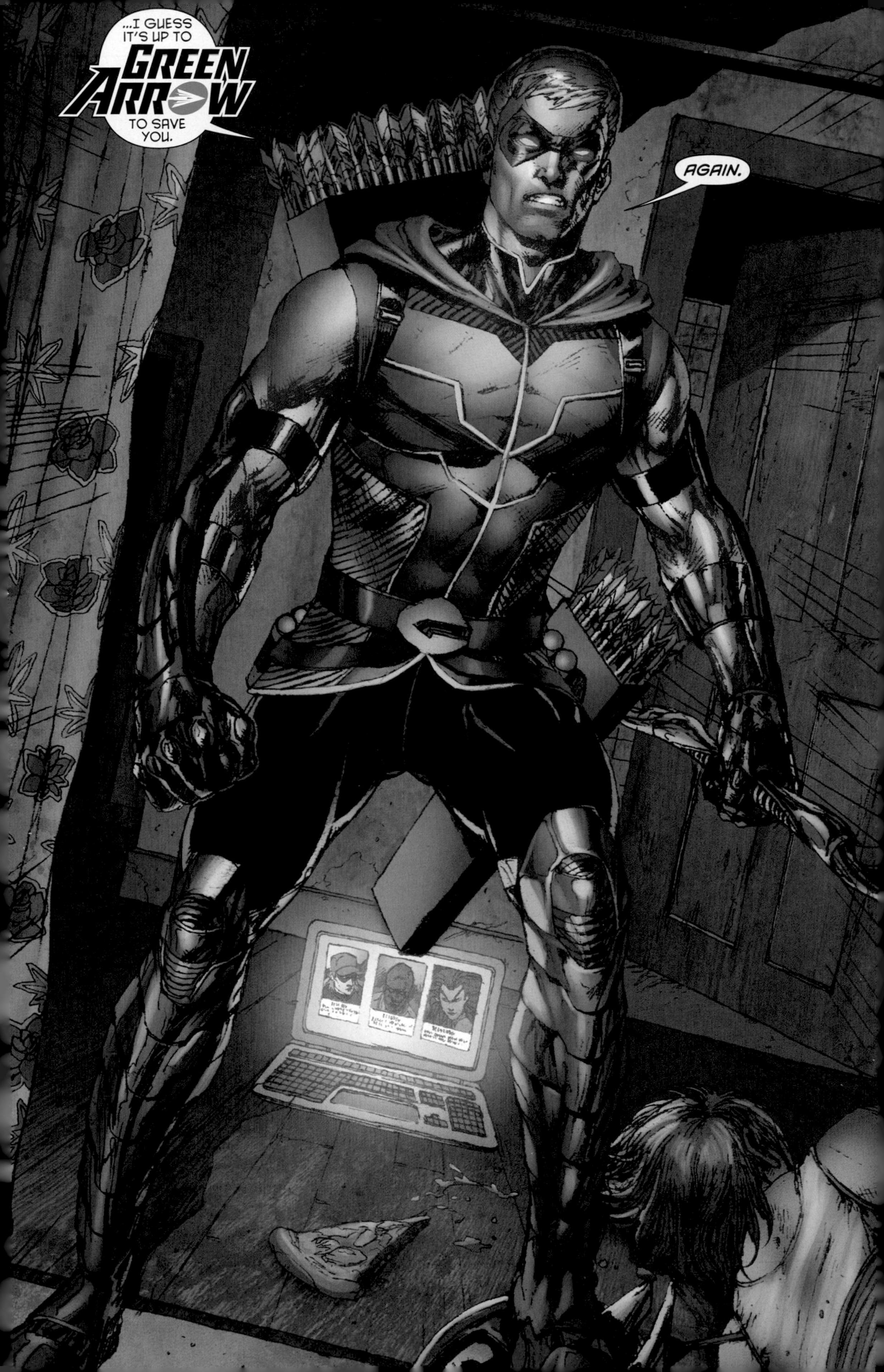
...I GUESS IT'S UP TO GREEN ARROW TO SAVE YOU.
AGAIN.

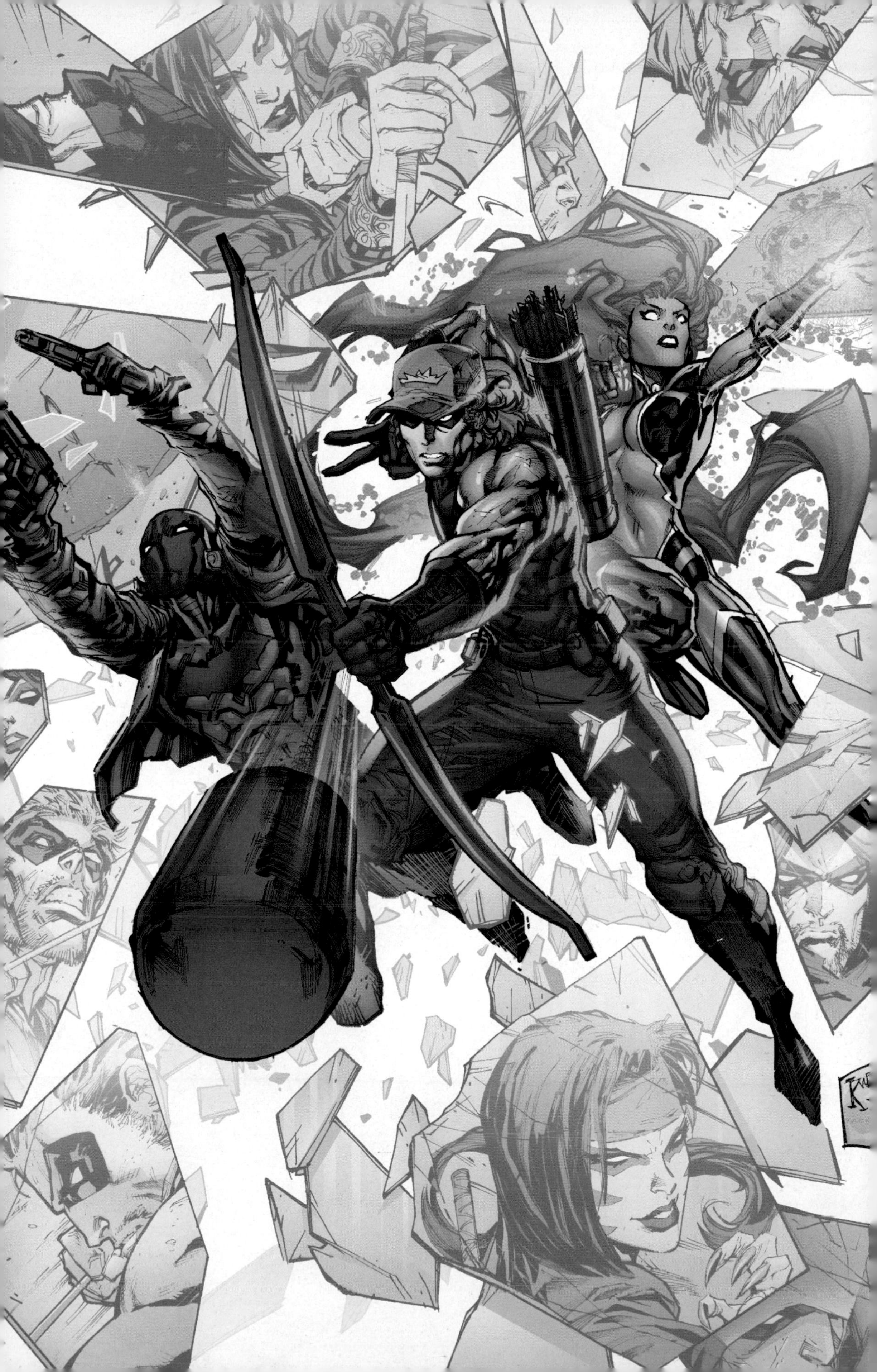

JAMES TYNION IV writer AL BARRIONUEVO artist JAVIER MENA & BIT colorists KEN LASHLEY with MATT YACKEY cover artists

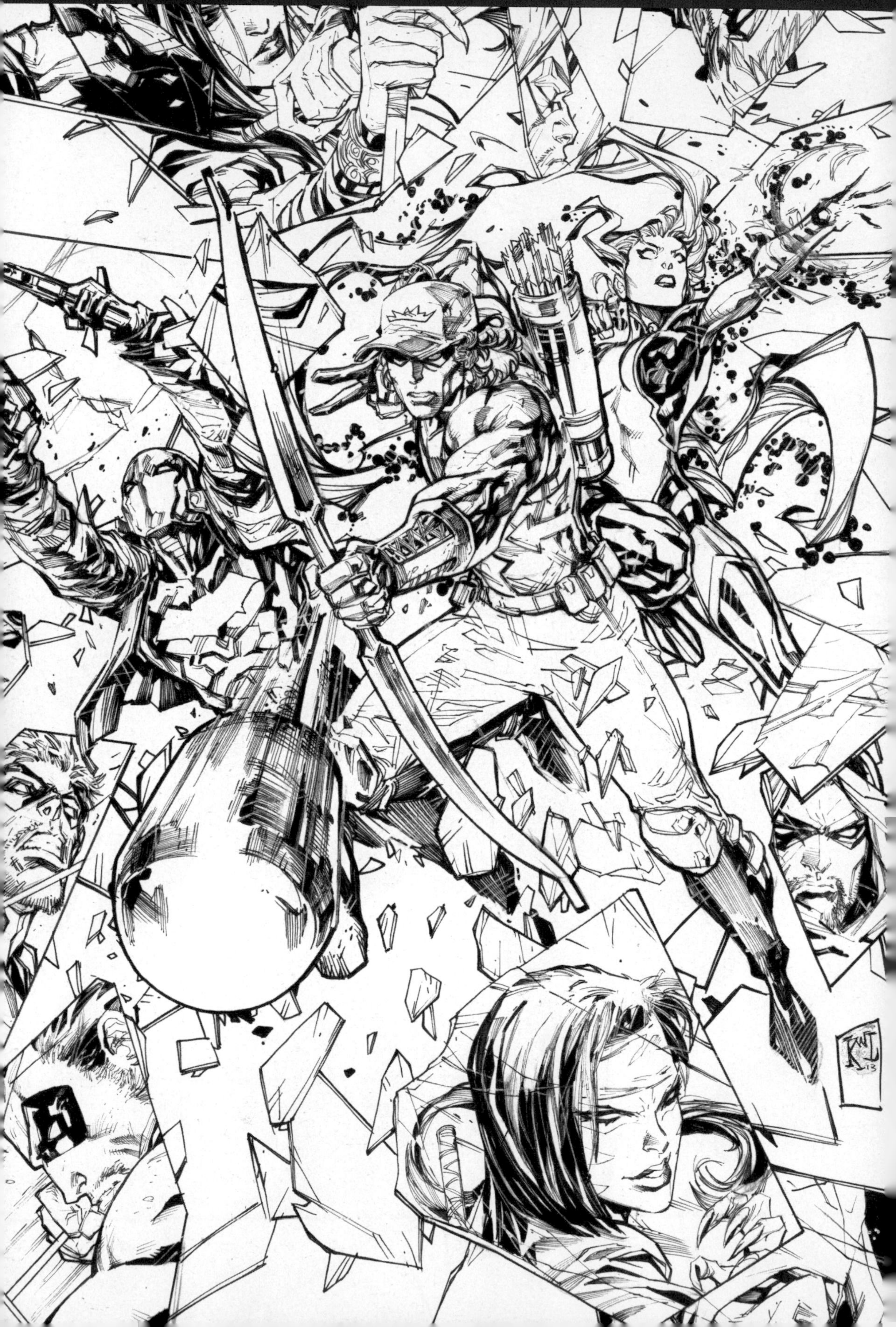

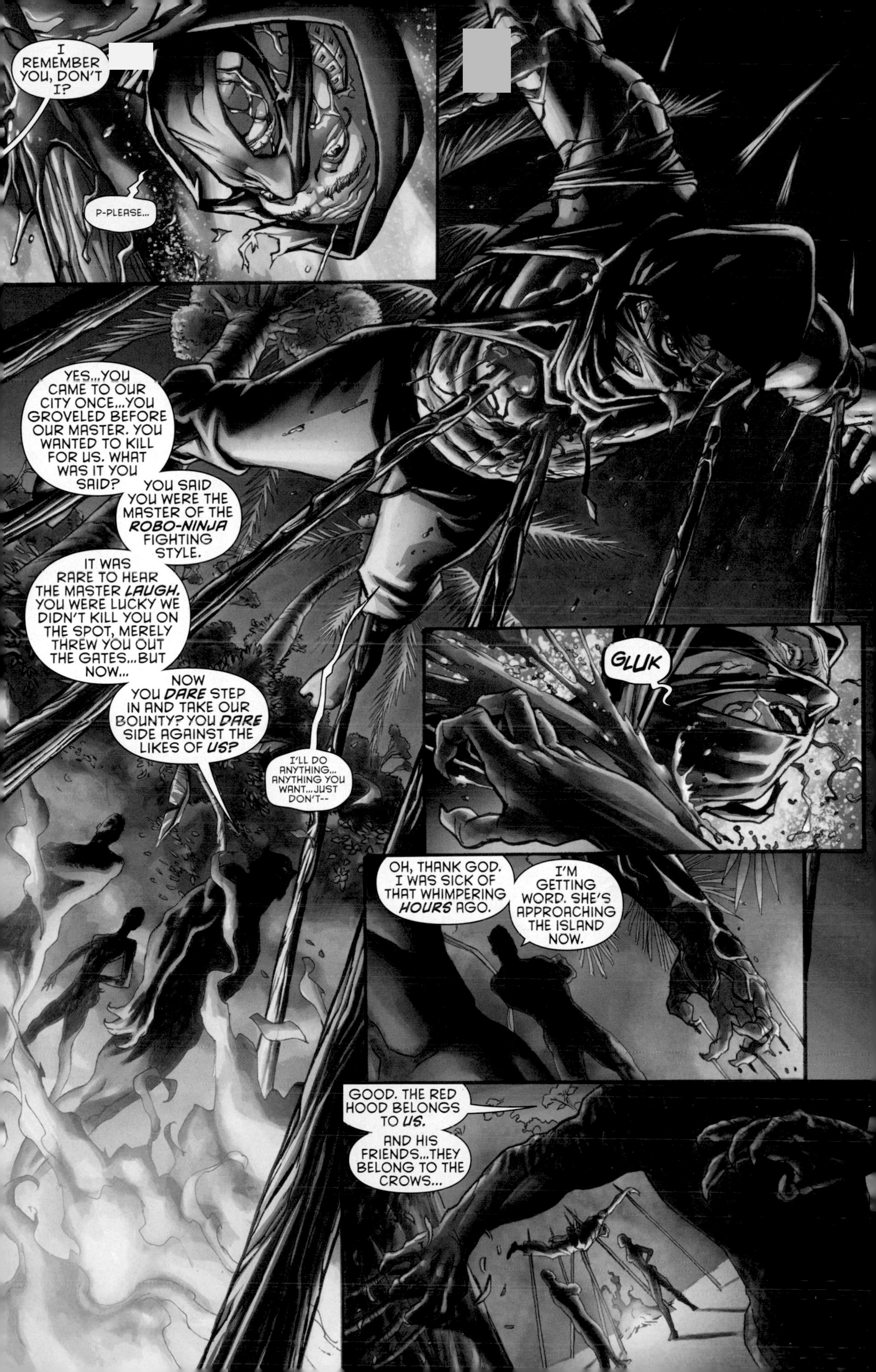
I REMEMBER YOU, DON'T I?
P-PLEASE...
YES...YOU CAME TO OUR CITY ONCE...YOU GROVELED BEFORE OUR MASTER. YOU WANTED TO KILL FOR US. WHAT WAS IT YOU SAID?
YOU SAID YOU WERE THE MASTER OF THE ROBO-NINJA FIGHTING STYLE.
IT WAS RARE TO HEAR THE MASTER LAUGH. YOU WERE LUCKY WE DIDN'T KILL YOU ON THE SPOT, MERELY THREW YOU OUT THE GATES...BUT NOW...
NOW YOU DARE STEP IN AND TAKE OUR BOUNTY? YOU DARE SIDE AGAINST THE LIKES OF US?
I'LL DO ANYTHING... ANYTHING YOU WANT...JUST DON'T--
GLUK
OH, THANK GOD. I WAS SICK OF THAT WHIMPERING HOURS AGO.
I'M GETTING WORD. SHE'S APPROACHING THE ISLAND NOW.
GOOD. THE RED HOOD BELONGS TO US.
AND HIS FRIENDS...THEY BELONG TO THE CROWS...

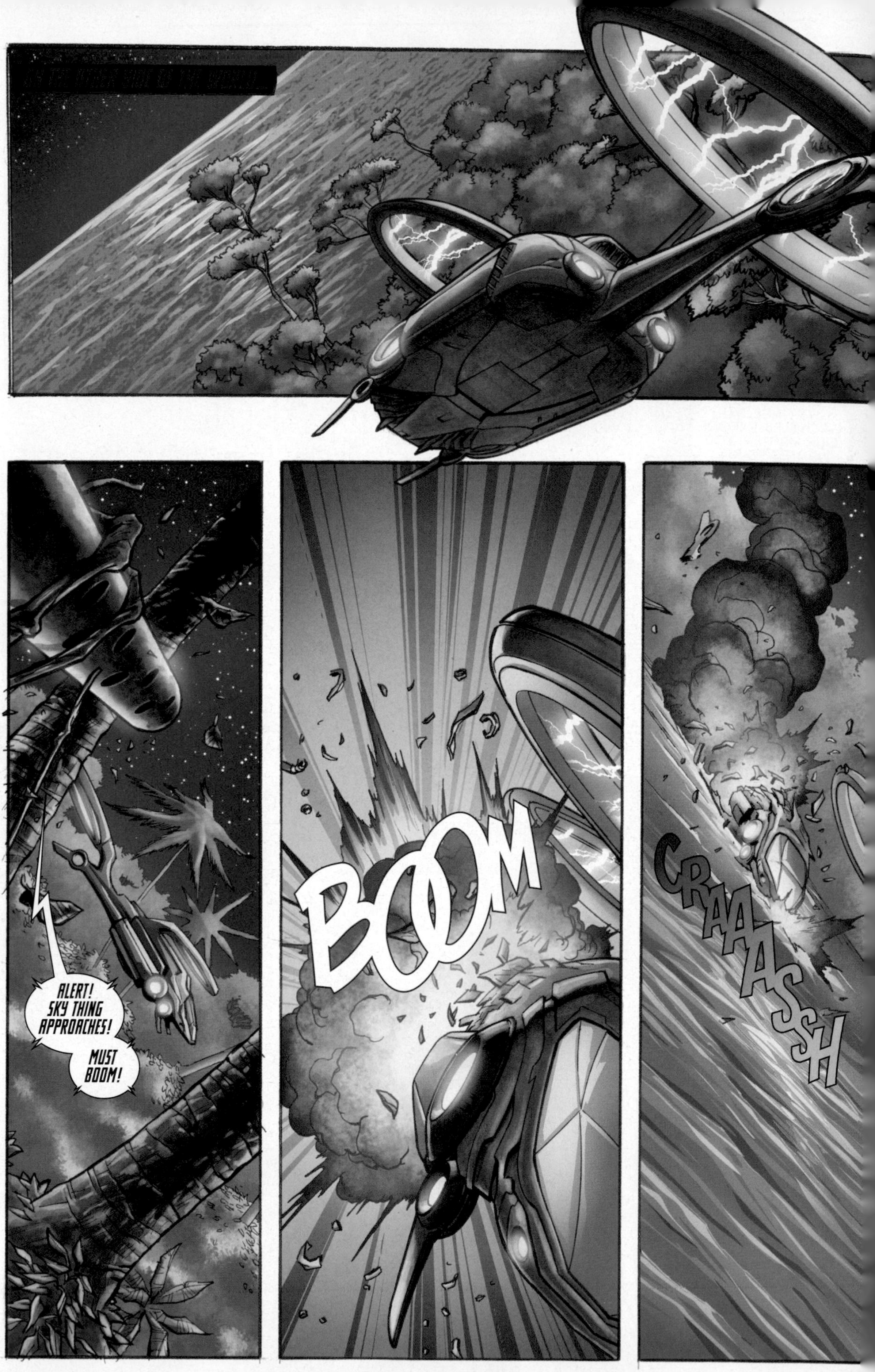

ALERT! SKY THING APPROACHES!
MUST BOOM!
BOOM
CRAAASSH

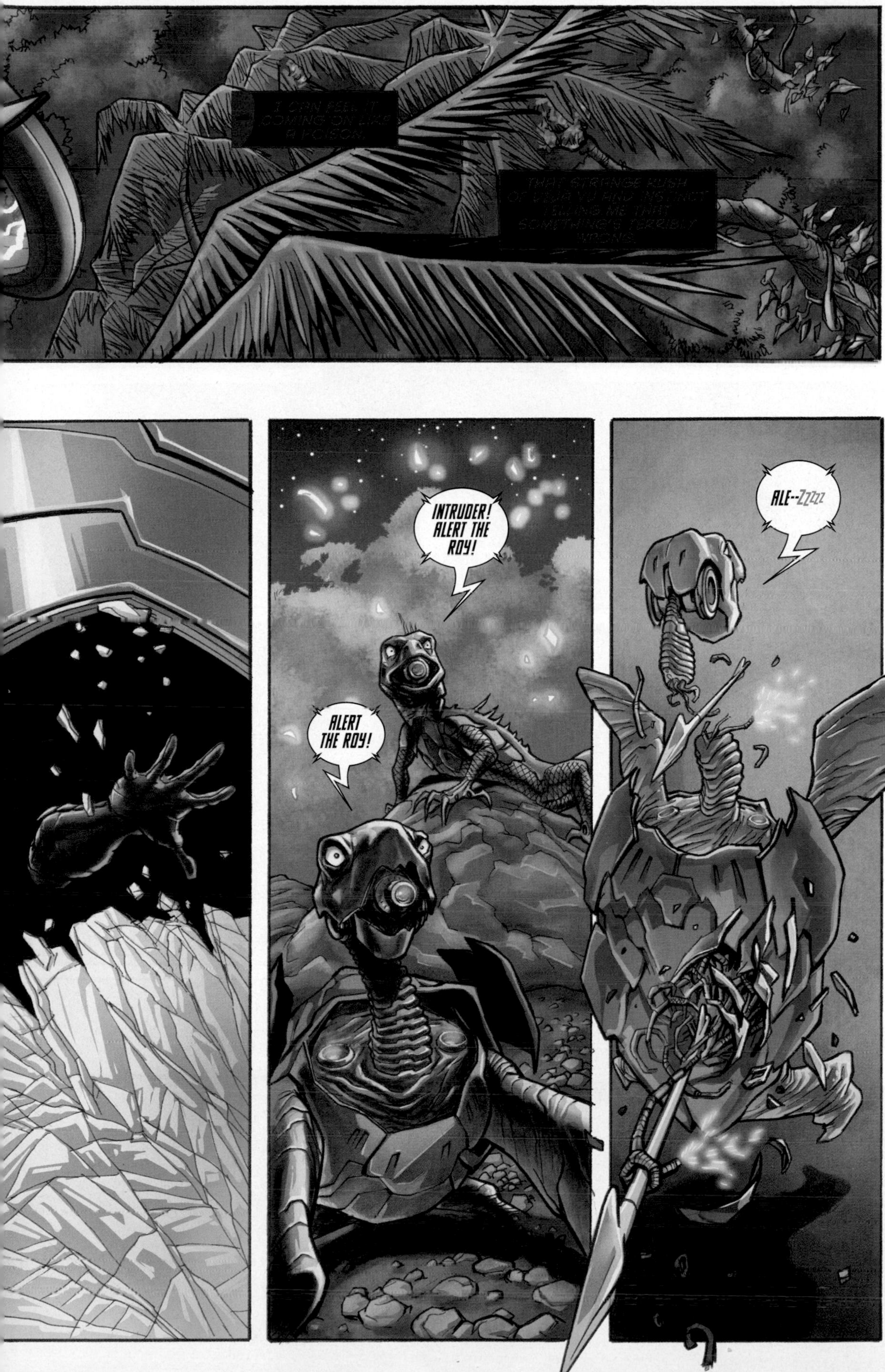
I CAN FEEL IT COMING ON LIKE A POISON.
THAT STRANGE RUSH OF DEJA VU AND INSTINCT TELLING ME THAT SOMETHING'S TERRIBLY WRONG.
INTRUDER! ALERT THE ROY!
ALERT THE ROY!
ALE--Zzzzz

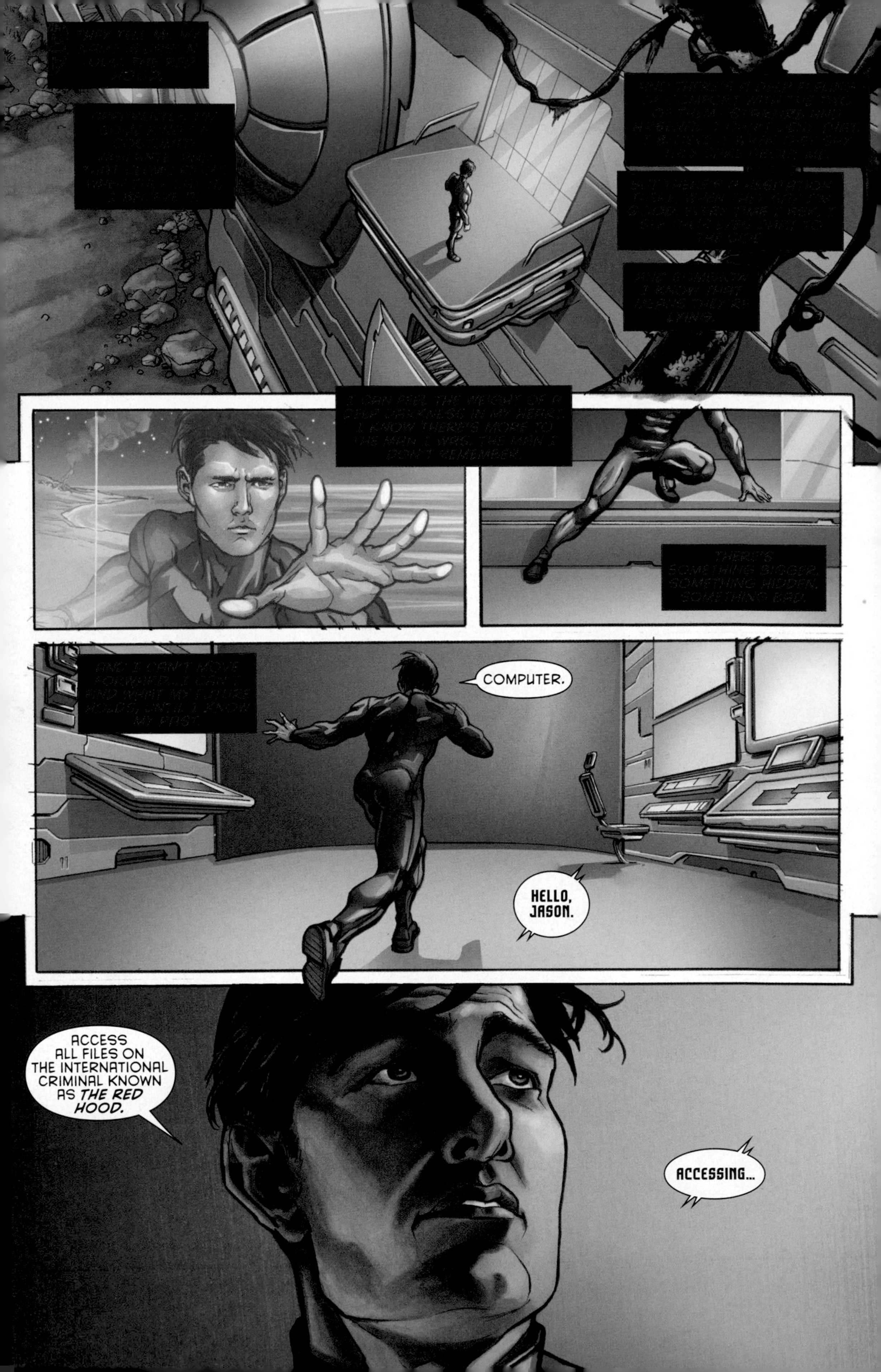
[redacted]
[redacted]
[redacted]
[redacted]
[redacted]
[redacted]
[redacted]
[redacted]
COMPUTER.
HELLO, JASON.
ACCESS ALL FILES ON THE INTERNATIONAL CRIMINAL KNOWN AS *THE RED HOOD.*
ACCESSING...

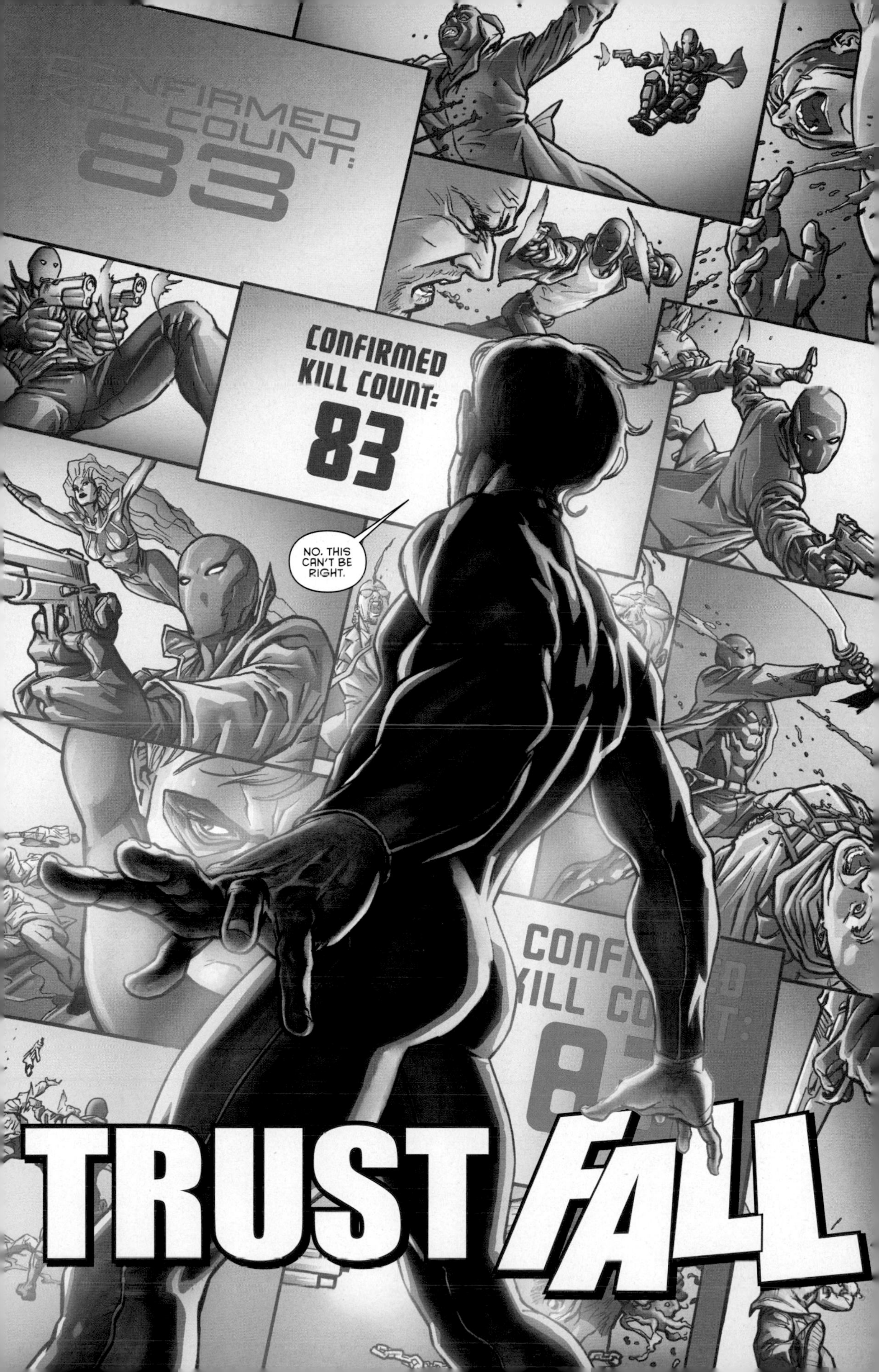
CONFIRMED KILL COUNT: 83
CONFIRMED KILL COUNT: 83
NO. THIS CAN'T BE RIGHT.
TRUST FALL

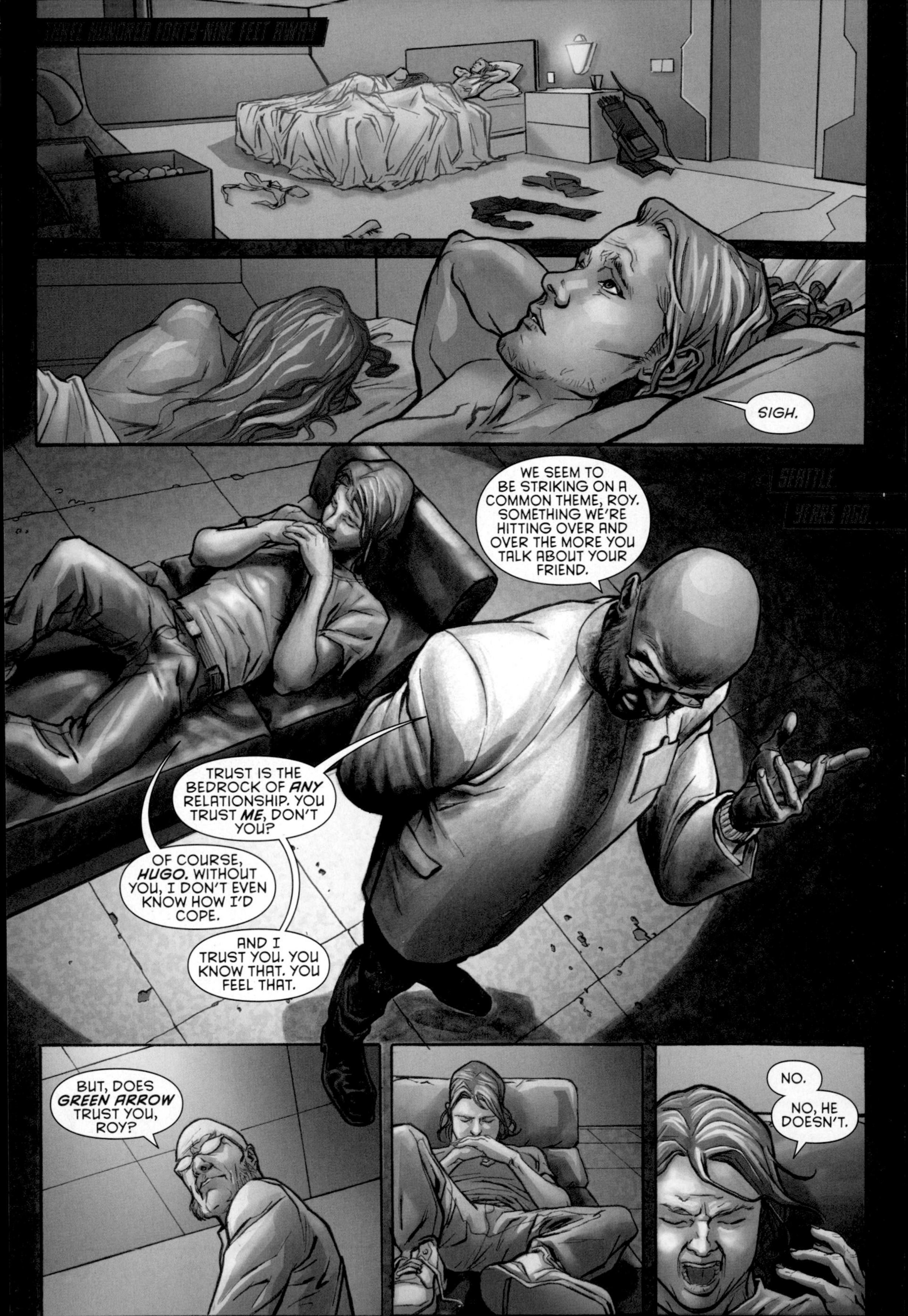
THREE HUNDRED FORTY-NINE FEET AWAY
SIGH.
SEATTLE.
YEARS AGO...
WE SEEM TO BE STRIKING ON A COMMON THEME, ROY. SOMETHING WE'RE HITTING OVER AND OVER THE MORE YOU TALK ABOUT YOUR FRIEND.
TRUST IS THE BEDROCK OF *ANY* RELATIONSHIP. YOU TRUST *ME*, DON'T YOU?
OF COURSE, **HUGO.** WITHOUT YOU, I DON'T EVEN KNOW HOW I'D COPE.
AND I TRUST YOU. YOU KNOW THAT. YOU FEEL THAT.
BUT, DOES ***GREEN ARROW*** TRUST YOU, ROY?
NO.
NO, HE DOESN'T.

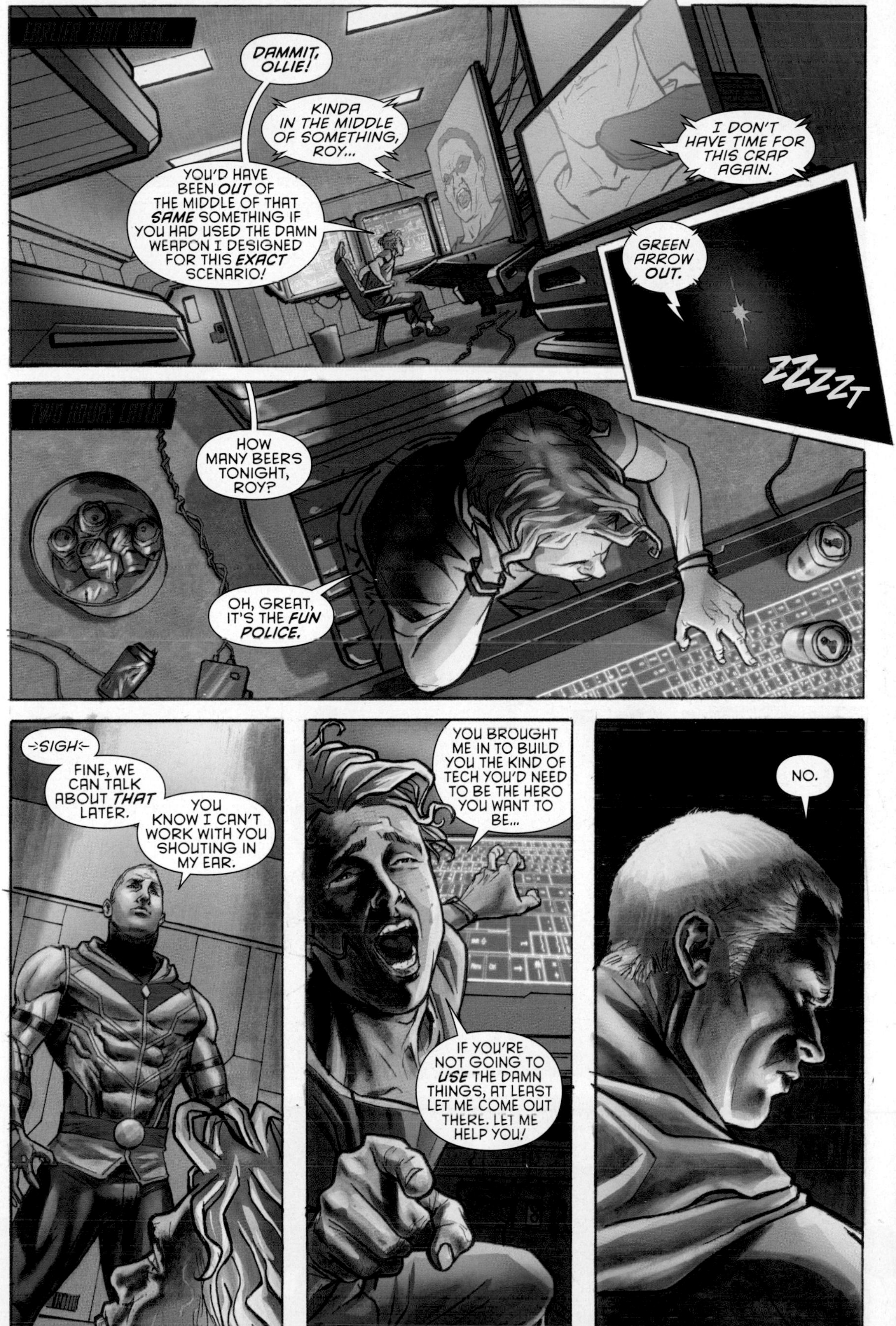
EARLIER THAT WEEK...
DAMMIT, OLLIE!
KINDA IN THE MIDDLE OF SOMETHING, ROY...
YOU'D HAVE BEEN OUT OF THE MIDDLE OF THAT SAME SOMETHING IF YOU HAD USED THE DAMN WEAPON I DESIGNED FOR THIS EXACT SCENARIO!
I DON'T HAVE TIME FOR THIS CRAP AGAIN.
GREEN ARROW OUT.
ZZZZT
TWO HOURS LATER.
HOW MANY BEERS TONIGHT, ROY?
OH, GREAT, IT'S THE FUN POLICE.
-SIGH-
FINE, WE CAN TALK ABOUT THAT LATER.
YOU KNOW I CAN'T WORK WITH YOU SHOUTING IN MY EAR.
YOU BROUGHT ME IN TO BUILD YOU THE KIND OF TECH YOU'D NEED TO BE THE HERO YOU WANT TO BE...
IF YOU'RE NOT GOING TO USE THE DAMN THINGS, AT LEAST LET ME COME OUT THERE. LET ME HELP YOU!
NO.

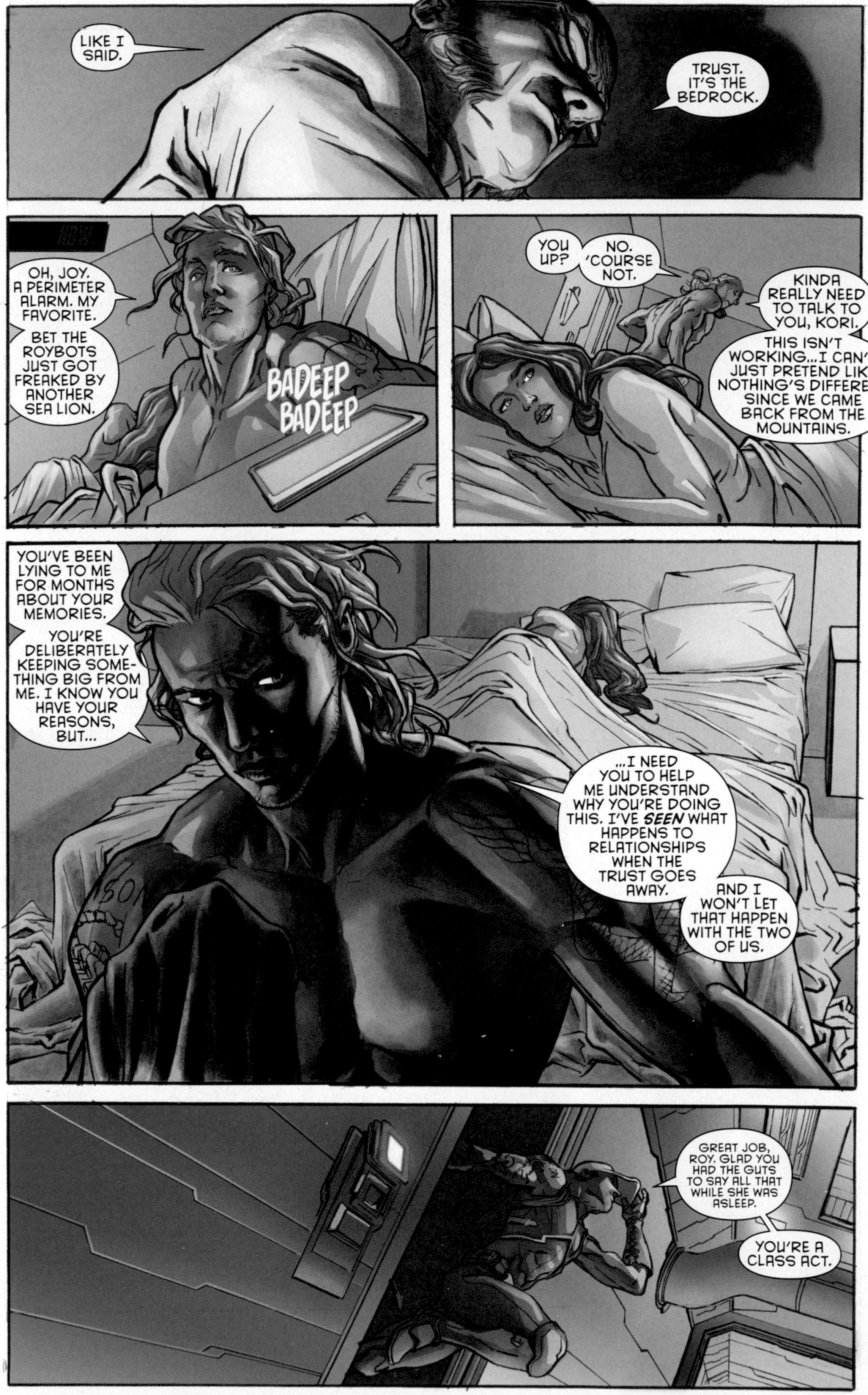
LIKE I SAID.
TRUST. IT'S THE BEDROCK.
NOW.
OH, JOY. A PERIMETER ALARM. MY FAVORITE.
BET THE ROYBOTS JUST GOT FREAKED BY ANOTHER SEA LION.
BADEEP BADEEP
YOU UP?
NO. 'COURSE NOT.
KINDA REALLY NEED TO TALK TO YOU, KORI.
THIS ISN'T WORKING...I CAN'T JUST PRETEND LIKE NOTHING'S DIFFERENT SINCE WE CAME BACK FROM THE MOUNTAINS.
YOU'VE BEEN LYING TO ME FOR MONTHS ABOUT YOUR MEMORIES.
YOU'RE DELIBERATELY KEEPING SOME-THING BIG FROM ME. I KNOW YOU HAVE YOUR REASONS, BUT...
...I NEED YOU TO HELP ME UNDERSTAND WHY YOU'RE DOING THIS. I'VE *SEEN* WHAT HAPPENS TO RELATIONSHIPS WHEN THE TRUST GOES AWAY.
AND I WON'T LET THAT HAPPEN WITH THE TWO OF US.
GREAT JOB, ROY. GLAD YOU HAD THE GUTS TO SAY ALL THAT WHILE SHE WAS ASLEEP.
YOU'RE A CLASS ACT.

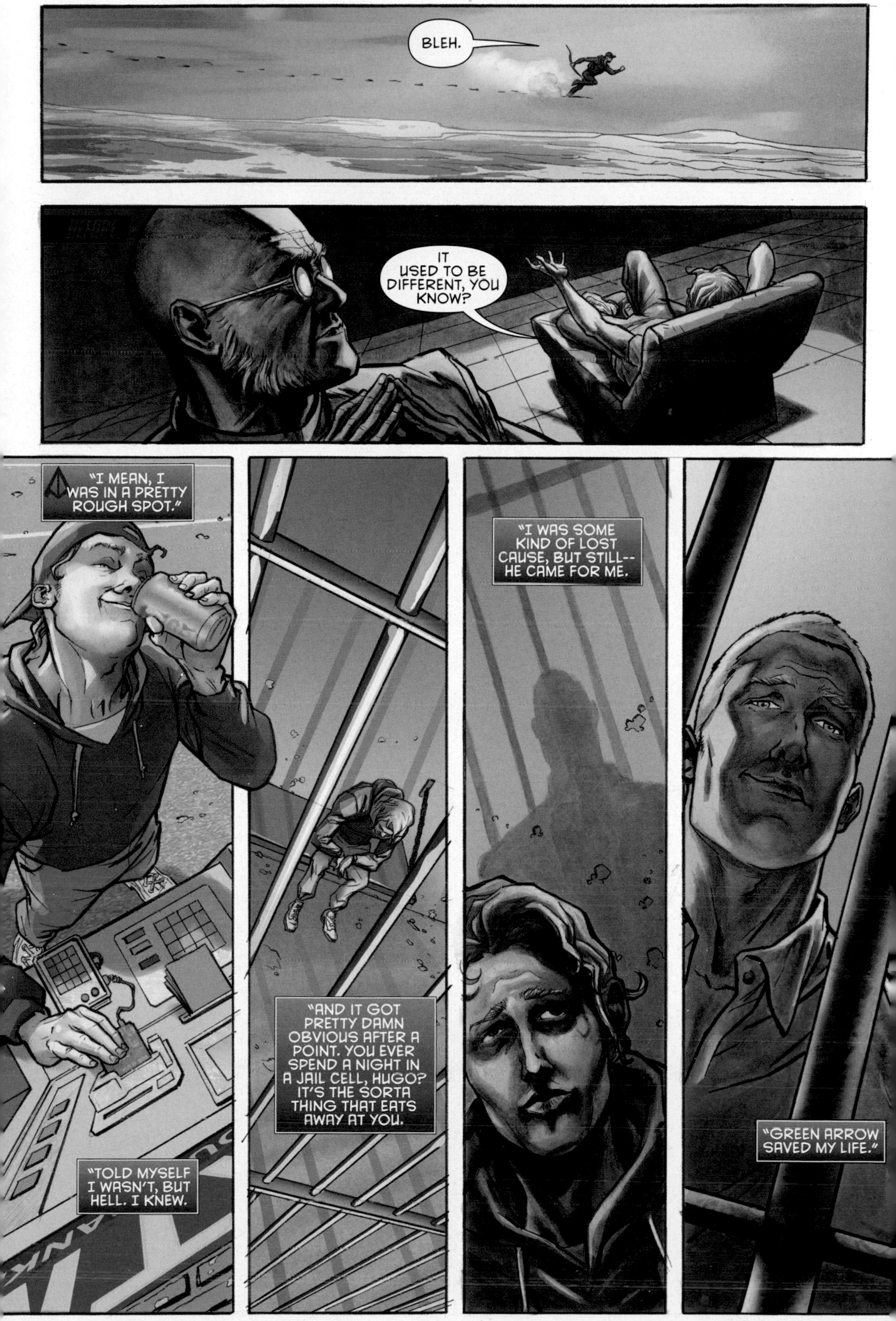
BLEH.
IT USED TO BE DIFFERENT, YOU KNOW?
"I MEAN, I WAS IN A PRETTY ROUGH SPOT."
"TOLD MYSELF I WASN'T, BUT HELL. I KNEW.
"AND IT GOT PRETTY DAMN OBVIOUS AFTER A POINT. YOU EVER SPEND A NIGHT IN A JAIL CELL, HUGO? IT'S THE SORTA THING THAT EATS AWAY AT YOU.
"I WAS SOME KIND OF LOST CAUSE, BUT STILL-- HE CAME FOR ME.
"GREEN ARROW SAVED MY LIFE."

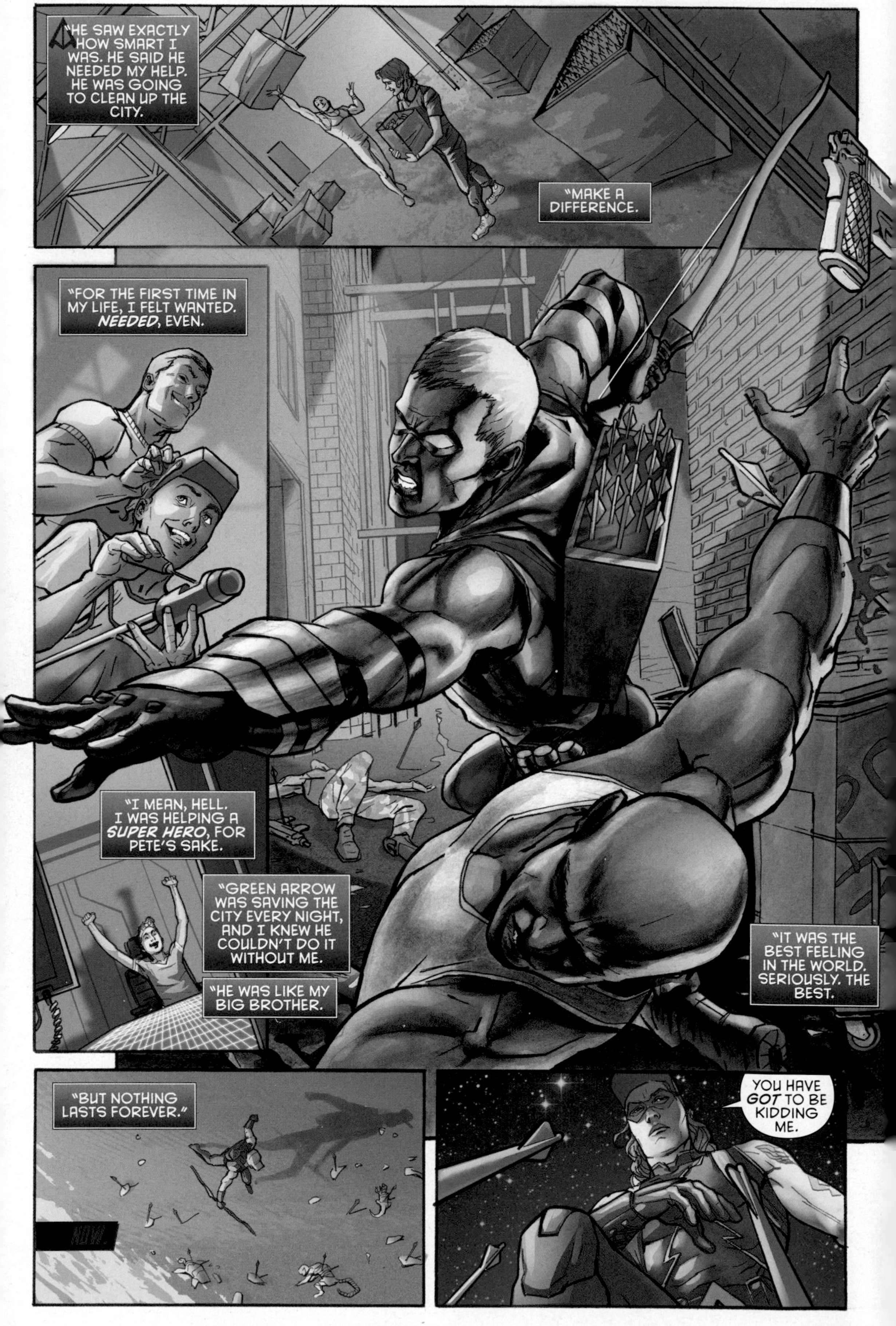
"HE SAW EXACTLY HOW SMART I WAS. HE SAID HE NEEDED MY HELP. HE WAS GOING TO CLEAN UP THE CITY.
"MAKE A DIFFERENCE.
"FOR THE FIRST TIME IN MY LIFE, I FELT WANTED. NEEDED, EVEN.
"I MEAN, HELL. I WAS HELPING A SUPER HERO, FOR PETE'S SAKE.
"GREEN ARROW WAS SAVING THE CITY EVERY NIGHT, AND I KNEW HE COULDN'T DO IT WITHOUT ME.
"HE WAS LIKE MY BIG BROTHER.
"IT WAS THE BEST FEELING IN THE WORLD. SERIOUSLY. THE BEST.
"BUT NOTHING LASTS FOREVER."
NOW.
YOU HAVE GOT TO BE KIDDING ME.

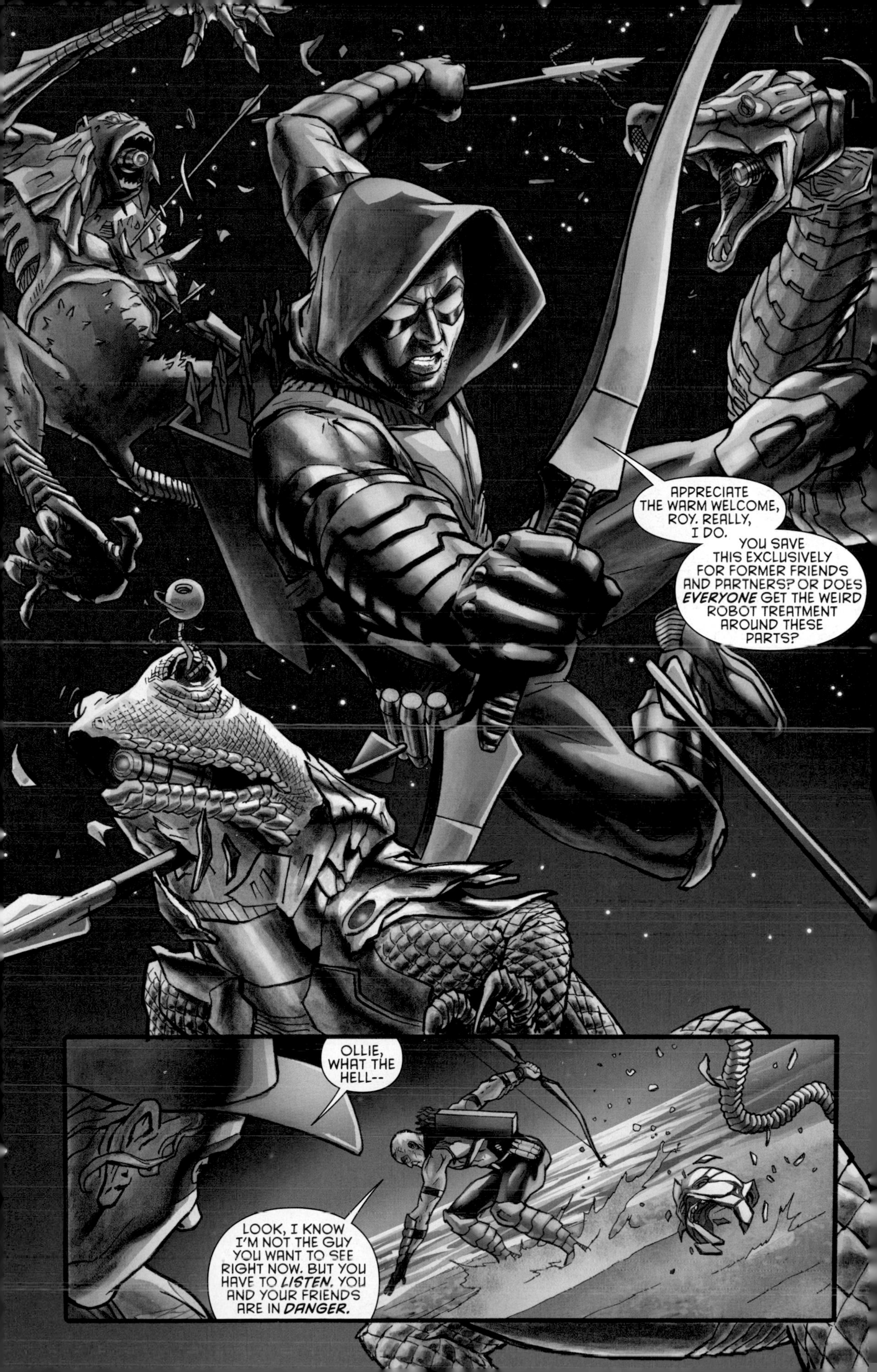
APPRECIATE THE WARM WELCOME, ROY. REALLY, I DO.
YOU SAVE THIS EXCLUSIVELY FOR FORMER FRIENDS AND PARTNERS? OR DOES *EVERYONE* GET THE WEIRD ROBOT TREATMENT AROUND THESE PARTS?
OLLIE, WHAT THE HELL--
LOOK, I KNOW I'M NOT THE GUY YOU WANT TO SEE RIGHT NOW. BUT YOU HAVE TO *LISTEN*. YOU AND YOUR FRIENDS ARE IN *DANGER*.

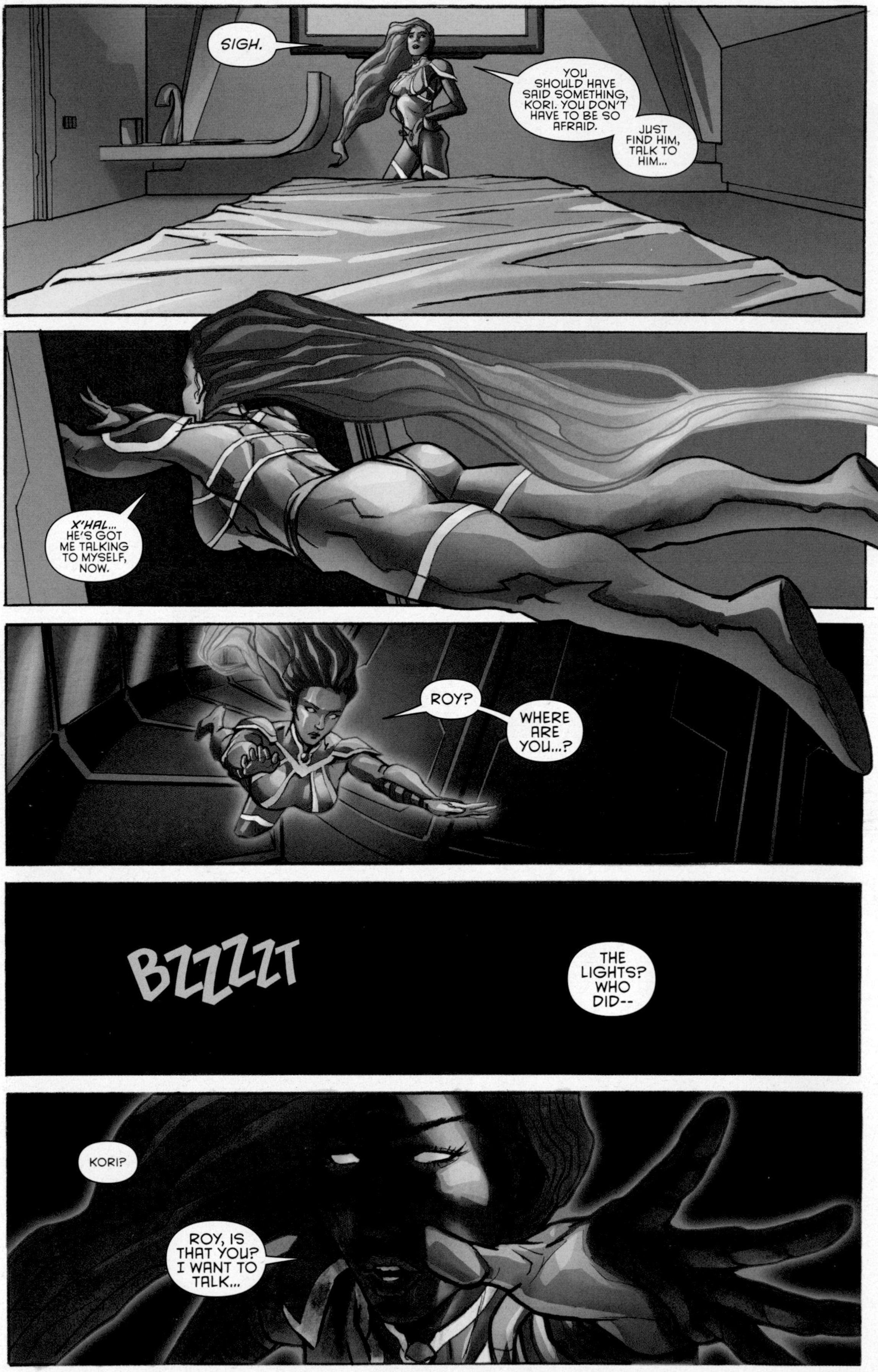
SIGH.
YOU SHOULD HAVE SAID SOMETHING, KORI. YOU DON'T HAVE TO BE SO AFRAID.
JUST FIND HIM, TALK TO HIM...
X'HAL... HE'S GOT ME TALKING TO MYSELF, NOW.
ROY?
WHERE ARE YOU...?
BZZZZZT
THE LIGHTS? WHO DID--
KORI?
ROY, IS THAT YOU? I WANT TO TALK...

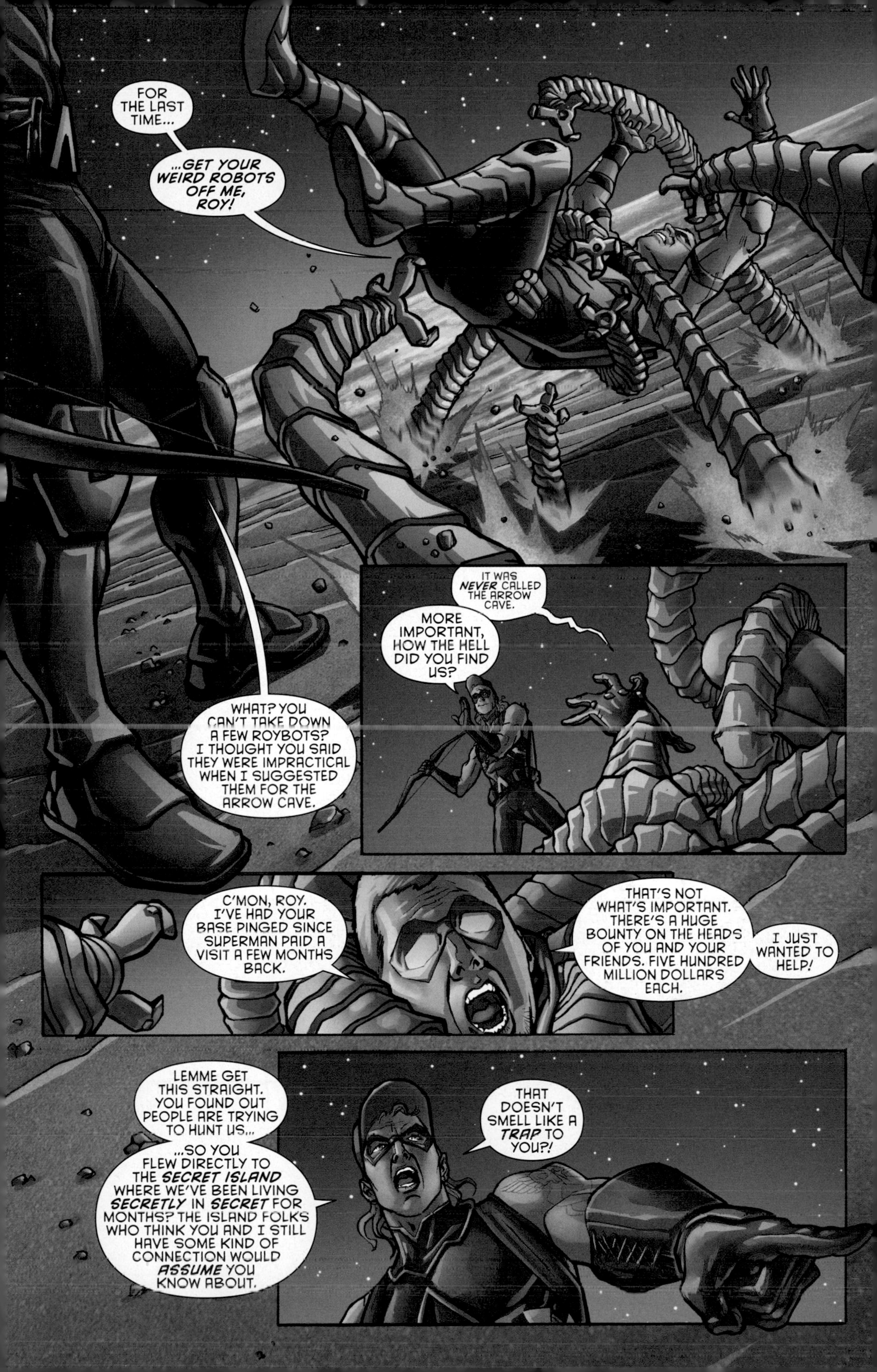
FOR THE LAST TIME...
...GET YOUR WEIRD ROBOTS OFF ME, ROY!
WHAT? YOU CAN'T TAKE DOWN A FEW ROYBOTS? I THOUGHT YOU SAID THEY WERE IMPRACTICAL WHEN I SUGGESTED THEM FOR THE ARROW CAVE.
IT WAS NEVER CALLED THE ARROW CAVE.
MORE IMPORTANT, HOW THE HELL DID YOU FIND US?
C'MON, ROY. I'VE HAD YOUR BASE PINGED SINCE SUPERMAN PAID A VISIT A FEW MONTHS BACK.
THAT'S NOT WHAT'S IMPORTANT. THERE'S A HUGE BOUNTY ON THE HEADS OF YOU AND YOUR FRIENDS. FIVE HUNDRED MILLION DOLLARS EACH.
I JUST WANTED TO HELP!
LEMME GET THIS STRAIGHT. YOU FOUND OUT PEOPLE ARE TRYING TO HUNT US...
...SO YOU FLEW DIRECTLY TO THE SECRET ISLAND WHERE WE'VE BEEN LIVING SECRETLY IN SECRET FOR MONTHS? THE ISLAND FOLKS WHO THINK YOU AND I STILL HAVE SOME KIND OF CONNECTION WOULD ASSUME YOU KNOW ABOUT.
THAT DOESN'T SMELL LIKE A TRAP TO YOU?!

IT'S HARD, ROY. THOSE MEMORIES...IT WAS LIKE A POISON RIPPING ME APART FROM THE INSIDE. I HAD NO CHOICE BUT TO BURY THEM AWAY.

I KNOW THAT IT SCARES YOU... I GUESS I *WAS* TRYING TO KEEP YOU AT ARM'S LENGTH. I DIDN'T WANT TO GET CLOSE ENOUGH...I DIDN'T WANT TO GET THAT HURT AGAIN.

YOU HAVE EVERY RIGHT TO BE MAD AT ME...

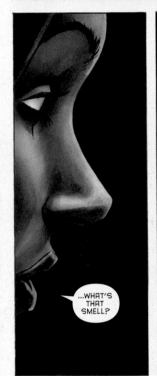

...WHAT'S THAT SMELL?

IT'S TOO DARK TO SEE...

ROY, IF YOU'RE GOING TO BE BUILDING YOUR SILLY ROBOTS ALL DAY, YOU REALLY HAVE TO SHOWER.

SERIOUSLY... WHAT *IS* THAT?

IT'S GASOLINE.

BOOOM!!

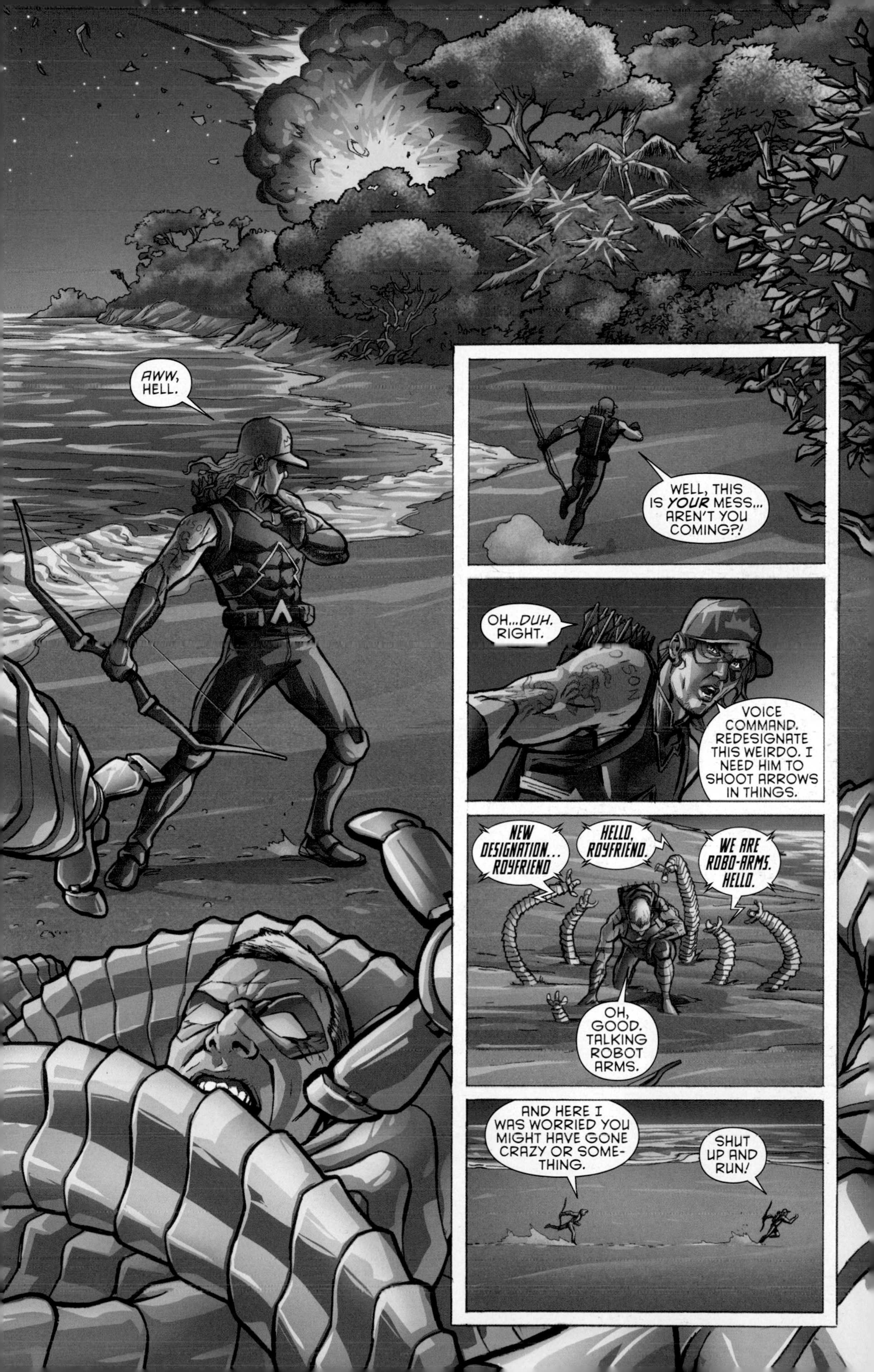

AWW, HELL.
WELL, THIS IS YOUR MESS... AREN'T YOU COMING?!
OH...DUH. RIGHT.
VOICE COMMAND. REDESIGNATE THIS WEIRDO. I NEED HIM TO SHOOT ARROWS IN THINGS.
NEW DESIGNATION... ROYFRIEND
HELLO, ROYFRIEND.
WE ARE ROBO-ARMS. HELLO.
OH, GOOD. TALKING ROBOT ARMS.
AND HERE I WAS WORRIED YOU MIGHT HAVE GONE CRAZY OR SOME-THING.
SHUT UP AND RUN!

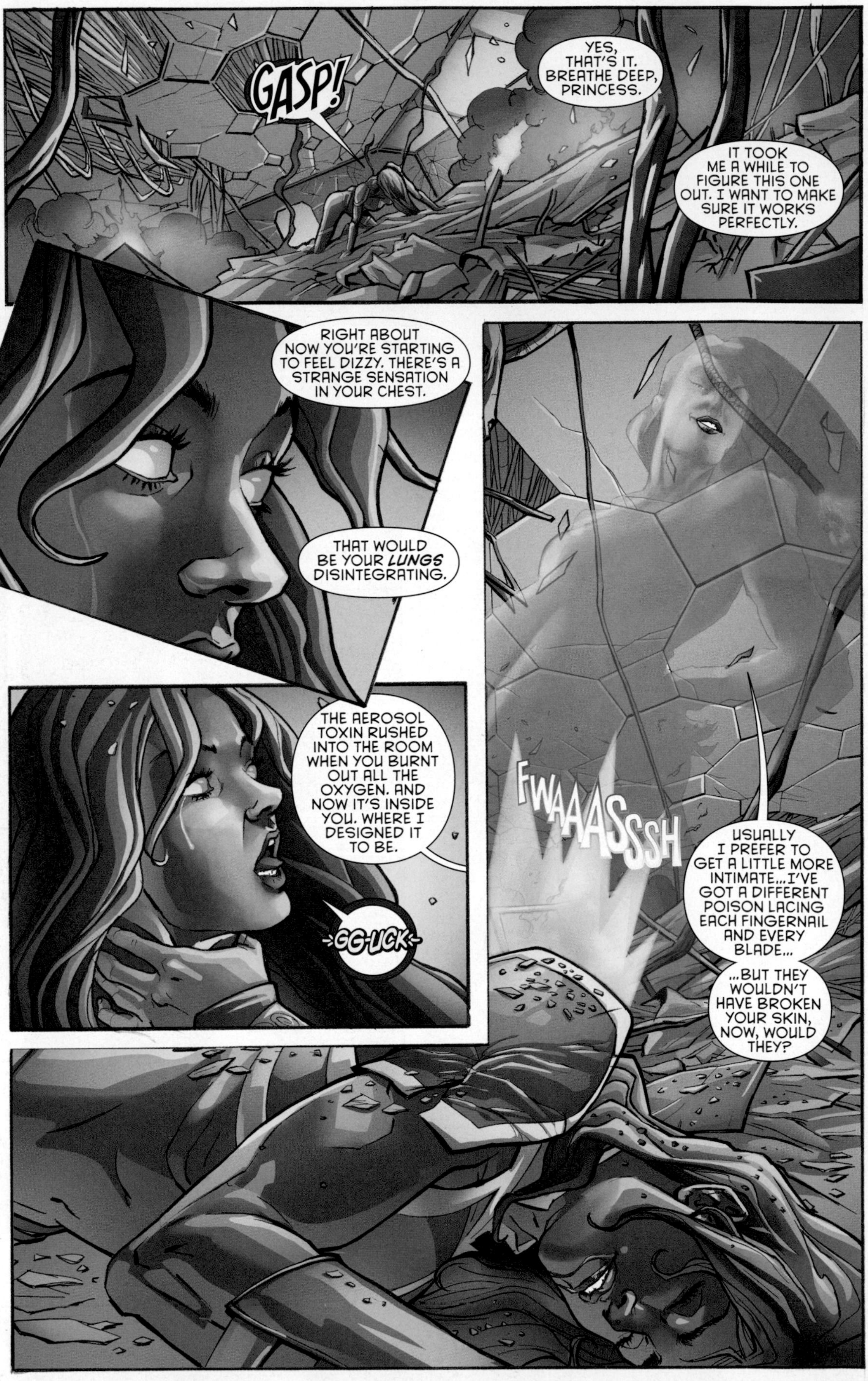
GASP!
YES, THAT'S IT. BREATHE DEEP, PRINCESS.
IT TOOK ME A WHILE TO FIGURE THIS ONE OUT. I WANT TO MAKE SURE IT WORKS PERFECTLY.
RIGHT ABOUT NOW YOU'RE STARTING TO FEEL DIZZY. THERE'S A STRANGE SENSATION IN YOUR CHEST.
THAT WOULD BE YOUR *LUNGS* DISINTEGRATING.
THE AEROSOL TOXIN RUSHED INTO THE ROOM WHEN YOU BURNT OUT ALL THE OXYGEN. AND NOW IT'S INSIDE YOU. WHERE I DESIGNED IT TO BE.
GG-UCK
FWAAASSSH
USUALLY I PREFER TO GET A LITTLE MORE INTIMATE... I'VE GOT A DIFFERENT POISON LACING EACH FINGERNAIL AND EVERY BLADE...
...BUT THEY WOULDN'T HAVE BROKEN YOUR SKIN, NOW, WOULD THEY?

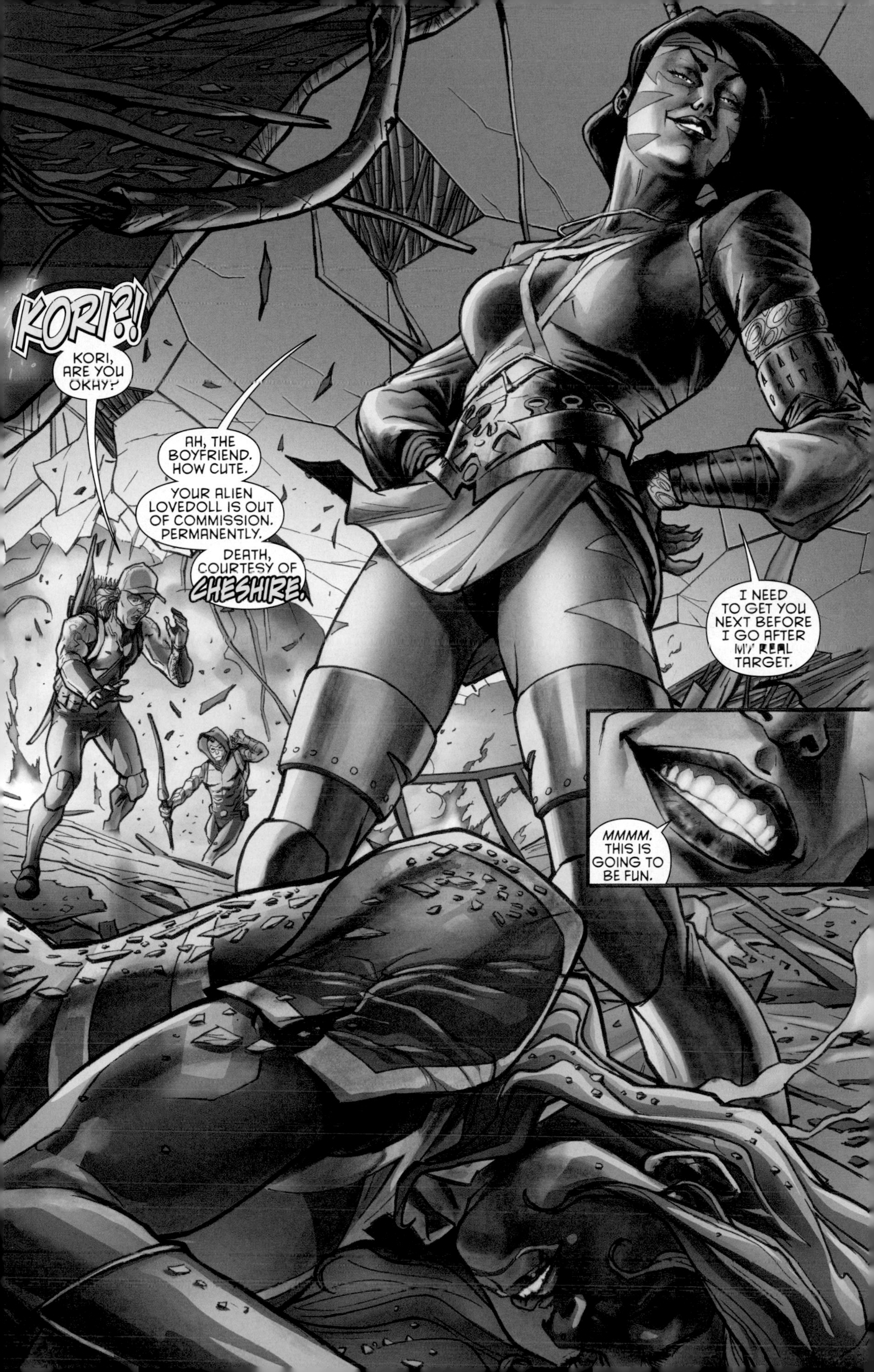
KORI?!
KORI, ARE YOU OKAY?
AH, THE BOYFRIEND. HOW CUTE.
YOUR ALIEN LOVEDOLL IS OUT OF COMMISSION. PERMANENTLY.
DEATH, COURTESY OF CHESHIRE.
I NEED TO GET YOU NEXT BEFORE I GO AFTER MY REAL TARGET.
MMMM. THIS IS GOING TO BE FUN.

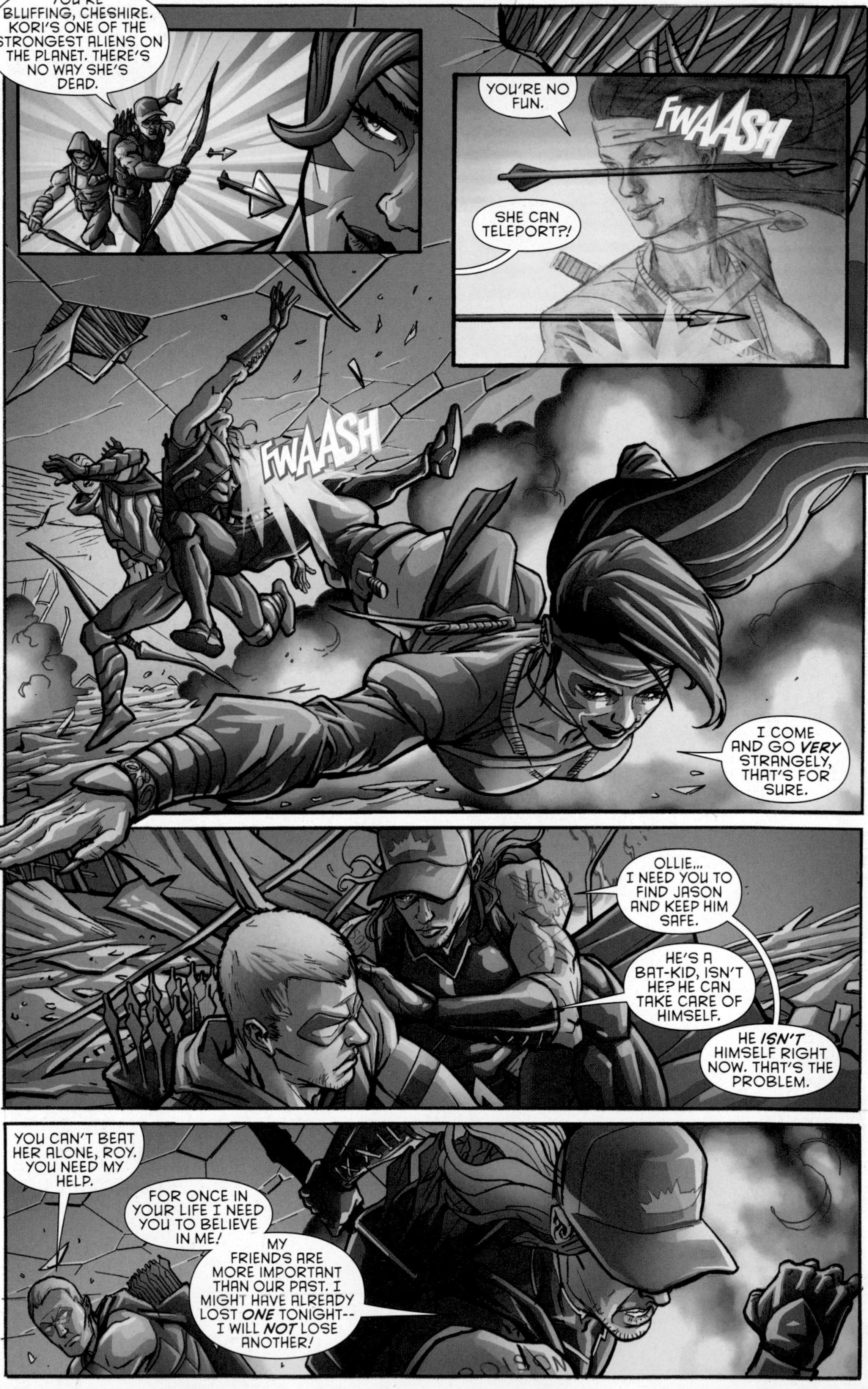
YOU'RE BLUFFING, CHESHIRE. KORI'S ONE OF THE STRONGEST ALIENS ON THE PLANET. THERE'S NO WAY SHE'S DEAD.
YOU'RE NO FUN.
FWAASH
SHE CAN TELEPORT?!
FWAASH
I COME AND GO VERY STRANGELY, THAT'S FOR SURE.
OLLIE... I NEED YOU TO FIND JASON AND KEEP HIM SAFE.
HE'S A BAT-KID, ISN'T HE? HE CAN TAKE CARE OF HIMSELF.
HE ISN'T HIMSELF RIGHT NOW. THAT'S THE PROBLEM.
YOU CAN'T BEAT HER ALONE, ROY. YOU NEED MY HELP.
FOR ONCE IN YOUR LIFE I NEED YOU TO BELIEVE IN ME!
MY FRIENDS ARE MORE IMPORTANT THAN OUR PAST. I MIGHT HAVE ALREADY LOST ONE TONIGHT-- I WILL NOT LOSE ANOTHER!

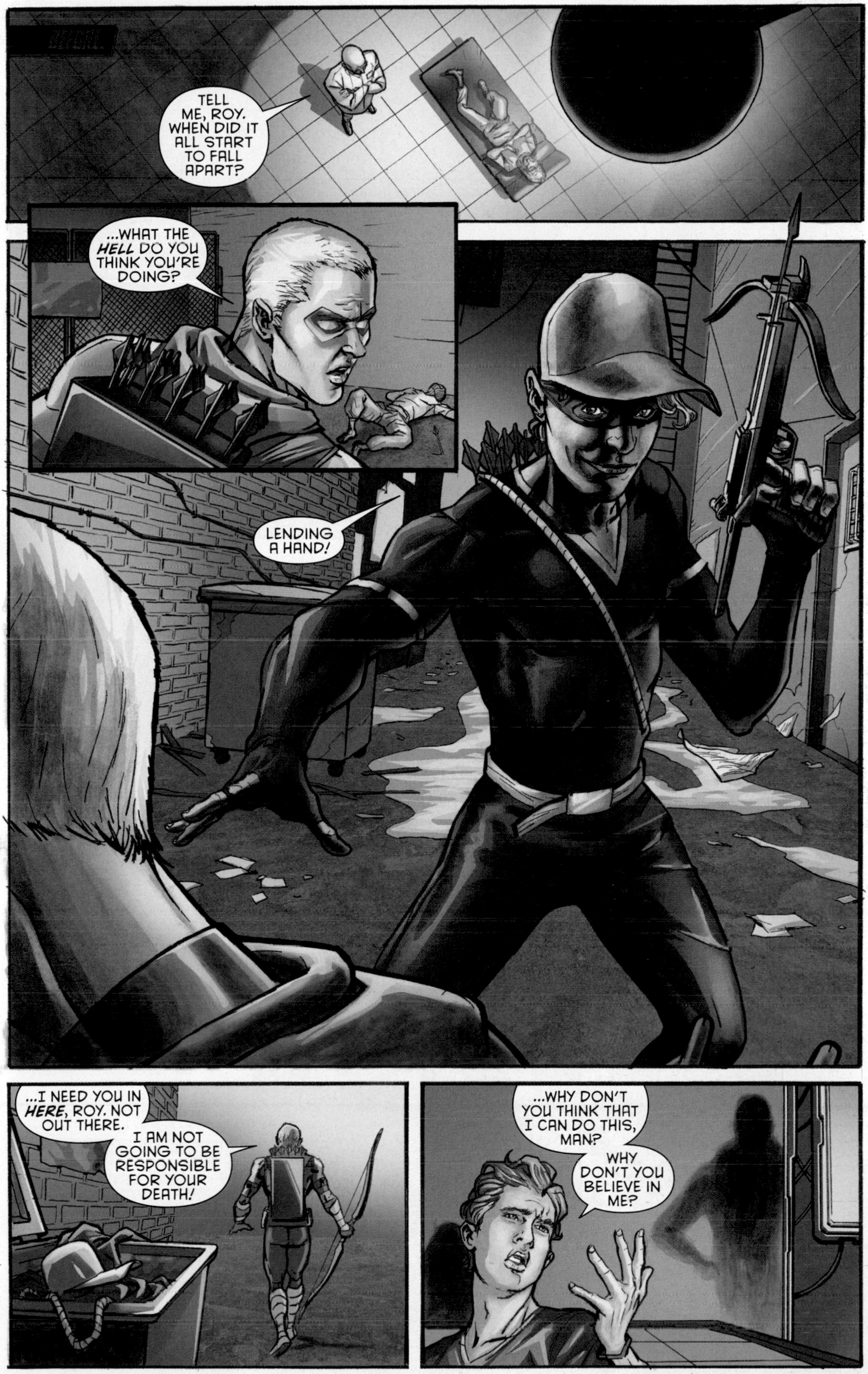
TELL ME, ROY. WHEN DID IT ALL START TO FALL APART?
...WHAT THE *HELL* DO YOU THINK YOU'RE DOING?
LENDING A HAND!
...I NEED YOU IN *HERE*, ROY. NOT OUT THERE.
I AM NOT GOING TO BE RESPONSIBLE FOR YOUR DEATH!
...WHY DON'T YOU THINK THAT I CAN DO THIS, MAN?
WHY DON'T YOU BELIEVE IN ME?

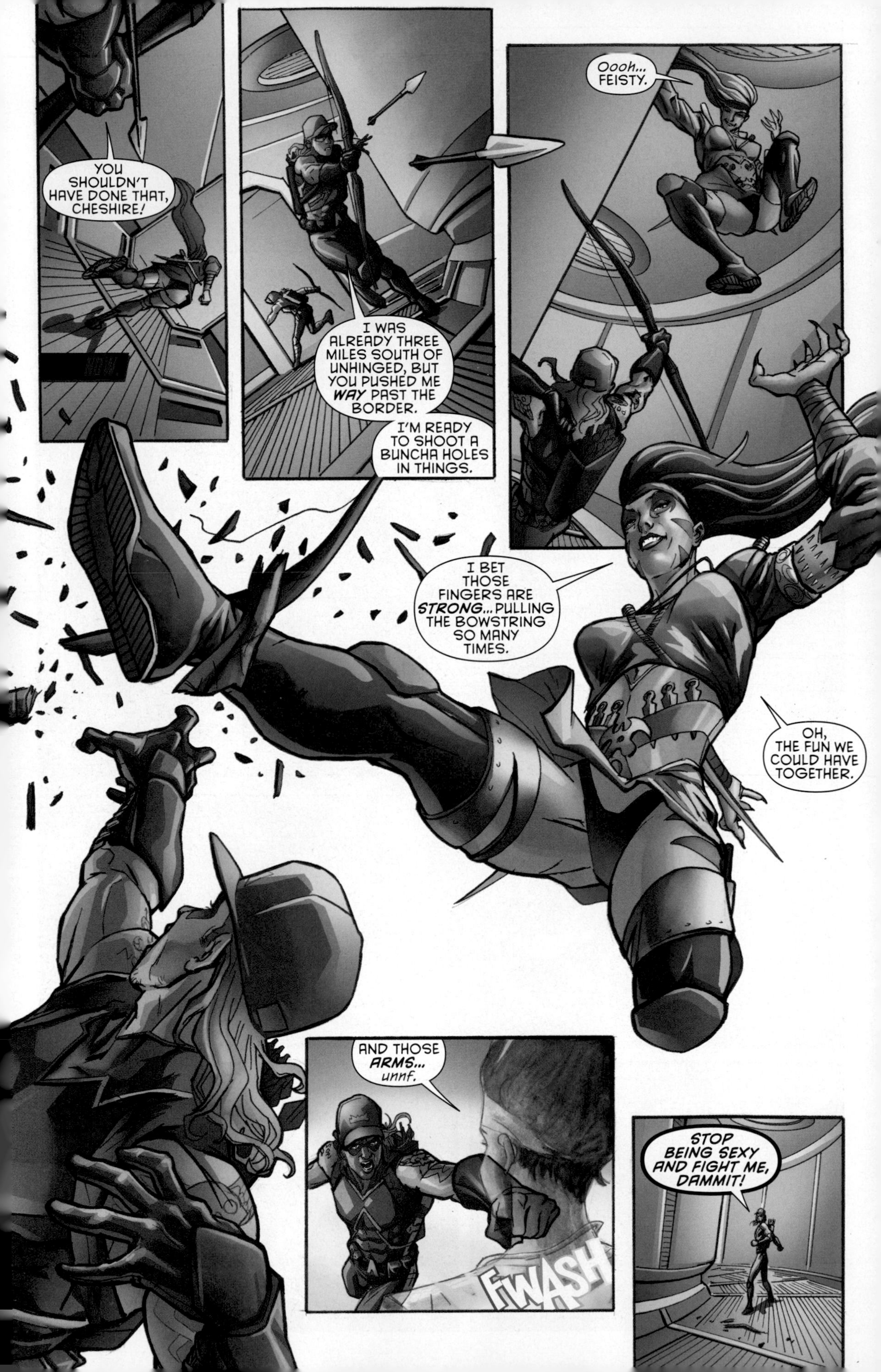
YOU SHOULDN'T HAVE DONE THAT, CHESHIRE!
I WAS ALREADY THREE MILES SOUTH OF UNHINGED, BUT YOU PUSHED ME WAY PAST THE BORDER.
I'M READY TO SHOOT A BUNCHA HOLES IN THINGS.
Oooh... FEISTY.
I BET THOSE FINGERS ARE STRONG... PULLING THE BOWSTRING SO MANY TIMES.
OH, THE FUN WE COULD HAVE TOGETHER.
AND THOSE ARMS... unnf.
FWASH
STOP BEING SEXY AND FIGHT ME, DAMMIT!

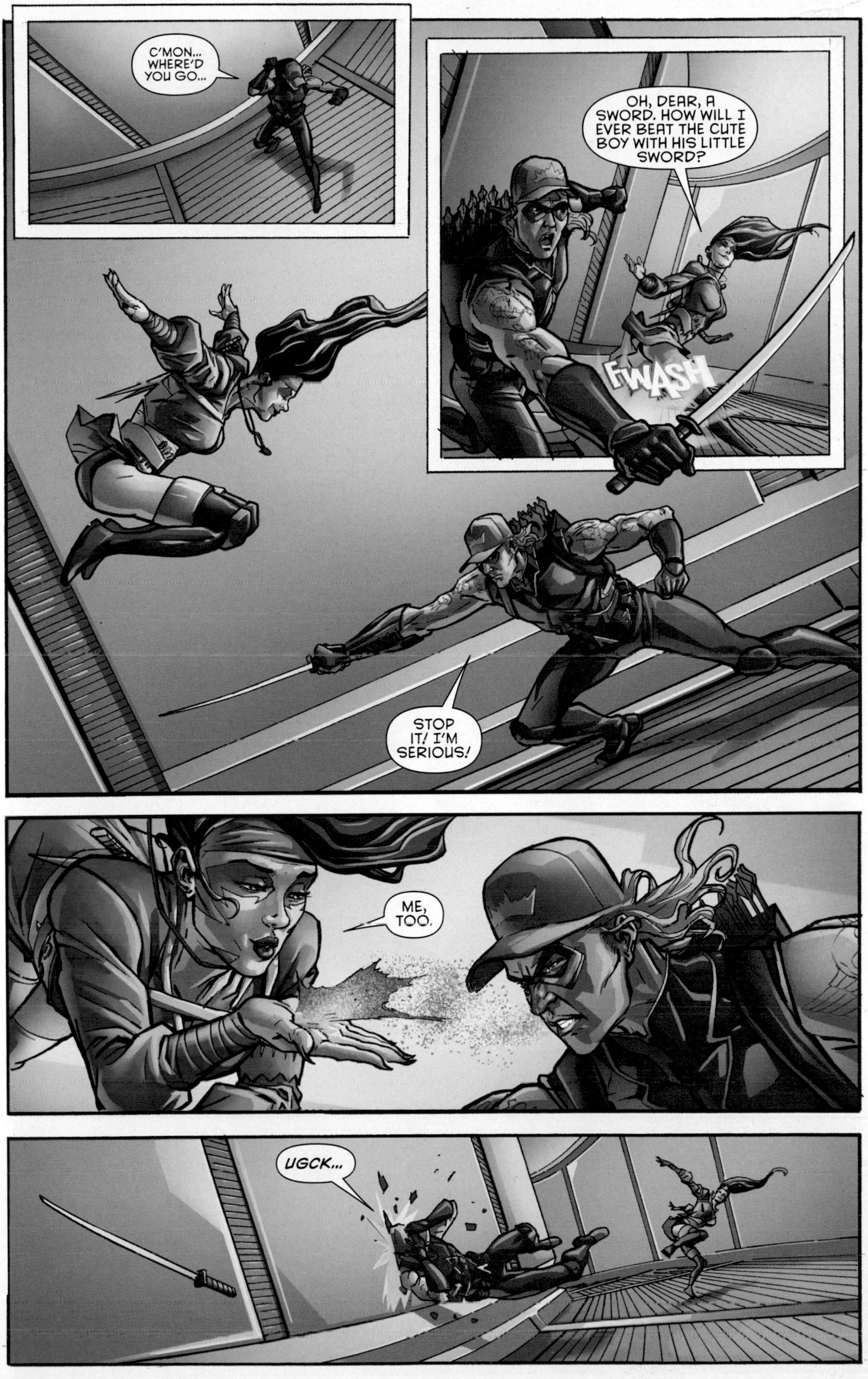
C'MON... WHERE'D YOU GO...
OH, DEAR, A SWORD. HOW WILL I EVER BEAT THE CUTE BOY WITH HIS LITTLE SWORD?
FWASH
STOP IT! I'M SERIOUS!
ME, TOO.
UGCK...

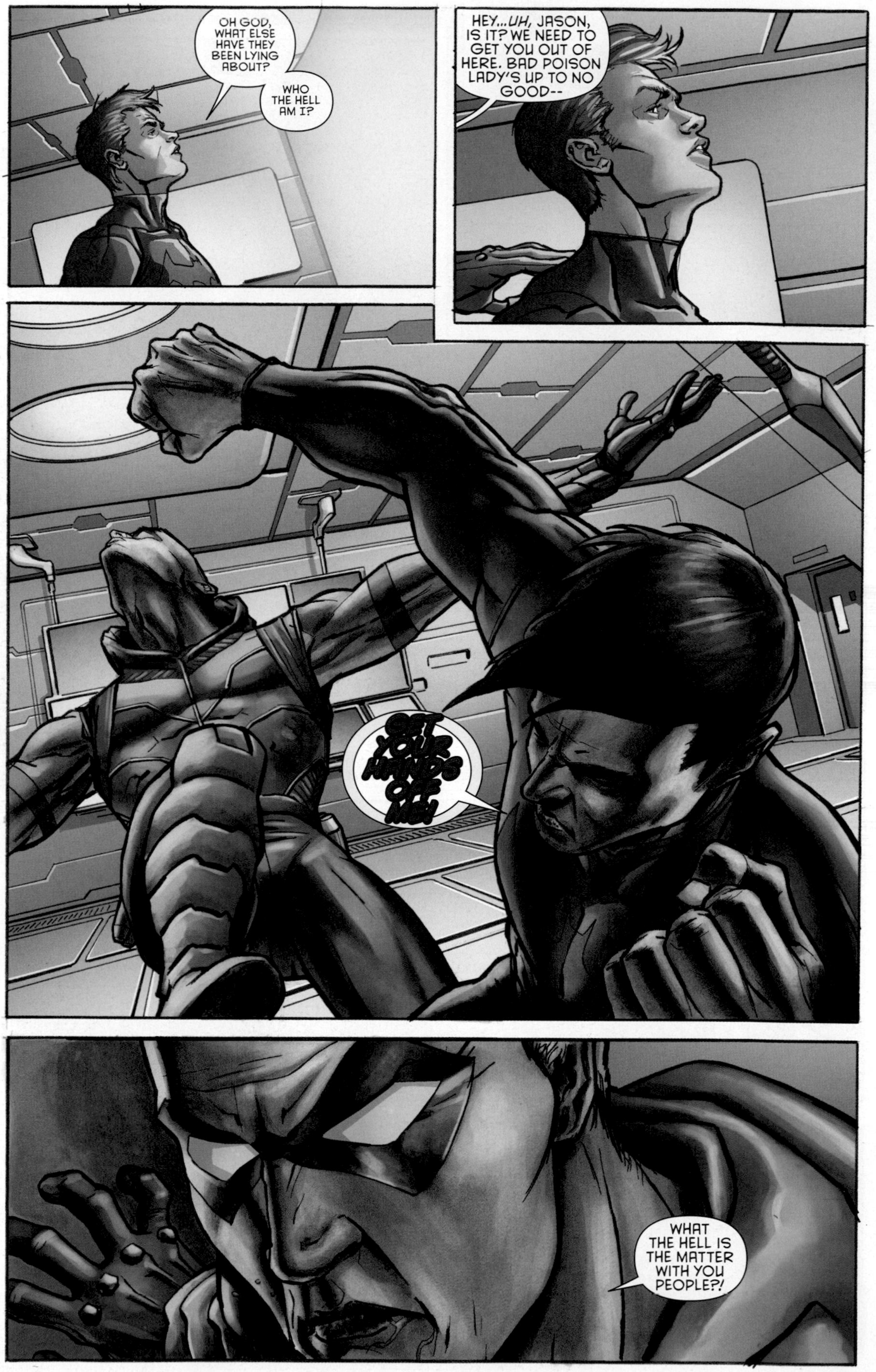
OH GOD, WHAT ELSE HAVE THEY BEEN LYING ABOUT?
WHO THE HELL AM I?
HEY...UH, JASON, IS IT? WE NEED TO GET YOU OUT OF HERE. BAD POISON LADY'S UP TO NO GOOD--
GET YOUR HANDS OFF ME!
WHAT THE HELL IS THE MATTER WITH YOU PEOPLE?!

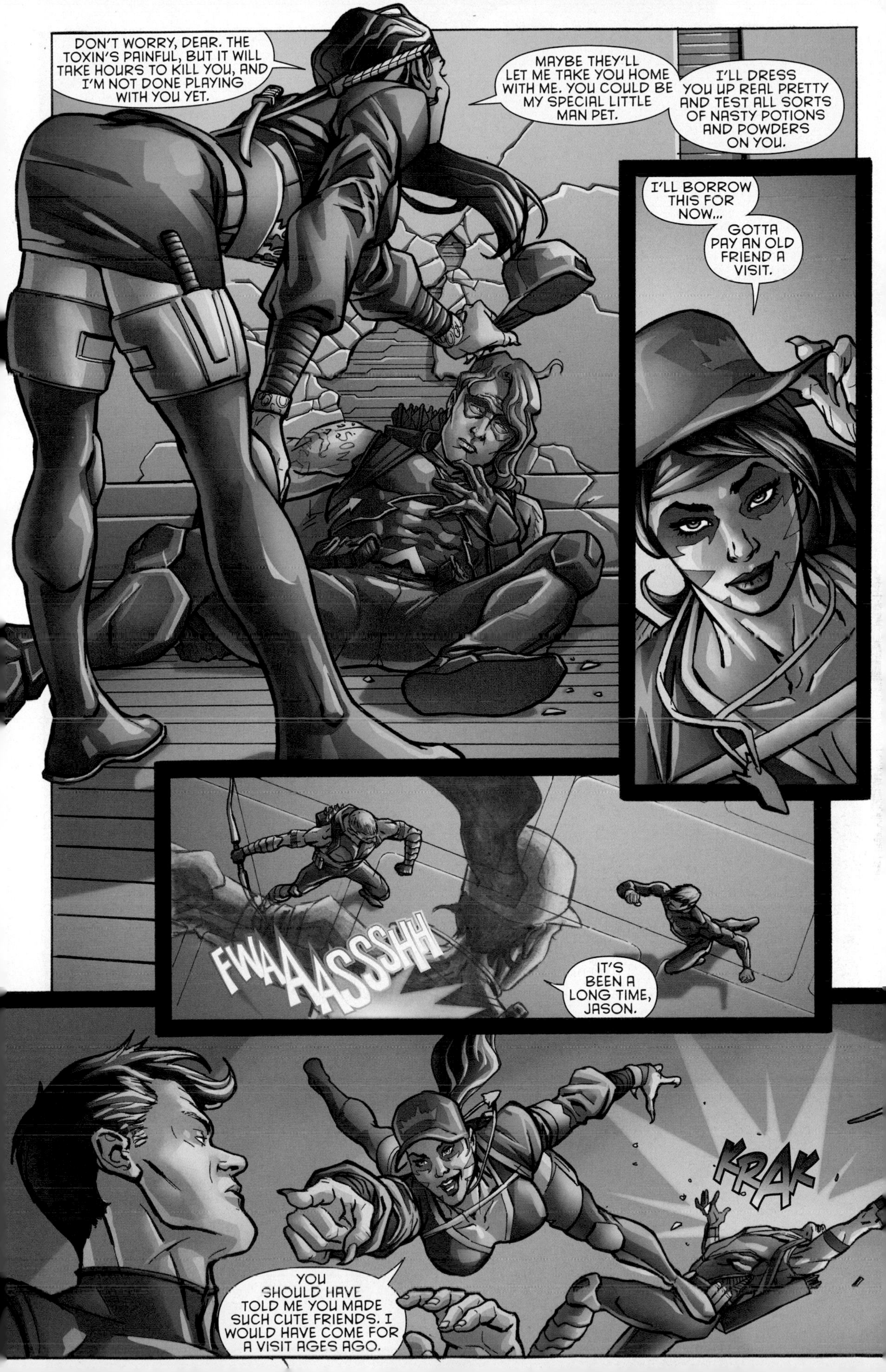

DON'T WORRY, DEAR. THE TOXIN'S PAINFUL, BUT IT WILL TAKE HOURS TO KILL YOU, AND I'M NOT DONE PLAYING WITH YOU YET.
MAYBE THEY'LL LET ME TAKE YOU HOME WITH ME. YOU COULD BE MY SPECIAL LITTLE MAN PET.
I'LL DRESS YOU UP REAL PRETTY AND TEST ALL SORTS OF NASTY POTIONS AND POWDERS ON YOU.
I'LL BORROW THIS FOR NOW...
GOTTA PAY AN OLD FRIEND A VISIT.
FWAAAASSSHH
IT'S BEEN A LONG TIME, JASON.
KRAK
YOU SHOULD HAVE TOLD ME YOU MADE SUCH CUTE FRIENDS. I WOULD HAVE COME FOR A VISIT AGES AGO.

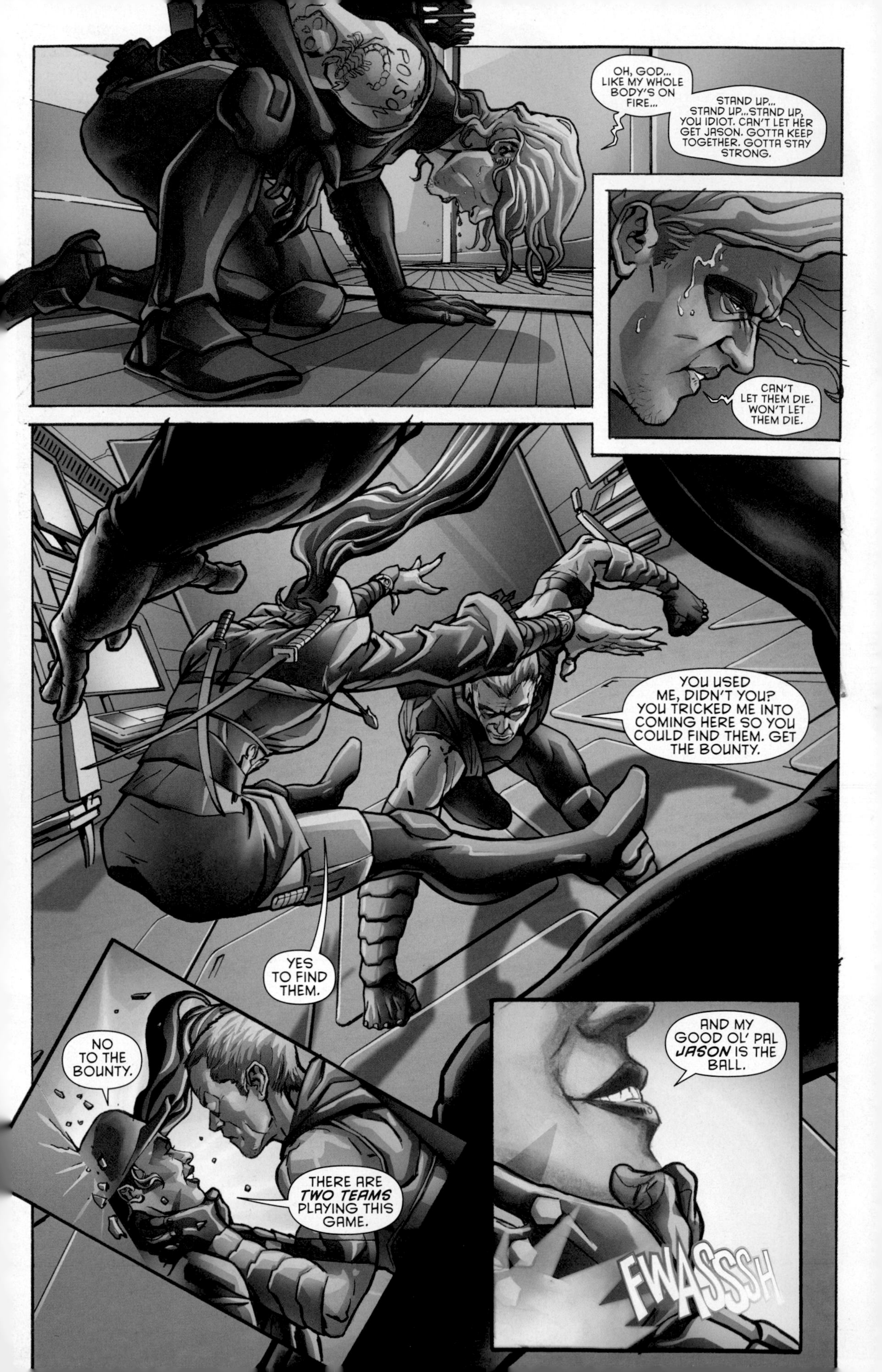

OH, GOD... LIKE MY WHOLE BODY'S ON FIRE...
STAND UP... STAND UP...STAND UP, YOU IDIOT. CAN'T LET HER GET JASON. GOTTA KEEP TOGETHER. GOTTA STAY STRONG.
POISON
CAN'T LET THEM DIE. WON'T LET THEM DIE.
YOU USED ME, DIDN'T YOU? YOU TRICKED ME INTO COMING HERE SO YOU COULD FIND THEM. GET THE BOUNTY.
YES TO FIND THEM.
NO TO THE BOUNTY.
THERE ARE TWO TEAMS PLAYING THIS GAME.
AND MY GOOD OL' PAL JASON IS THE BALL.
FWASSSH

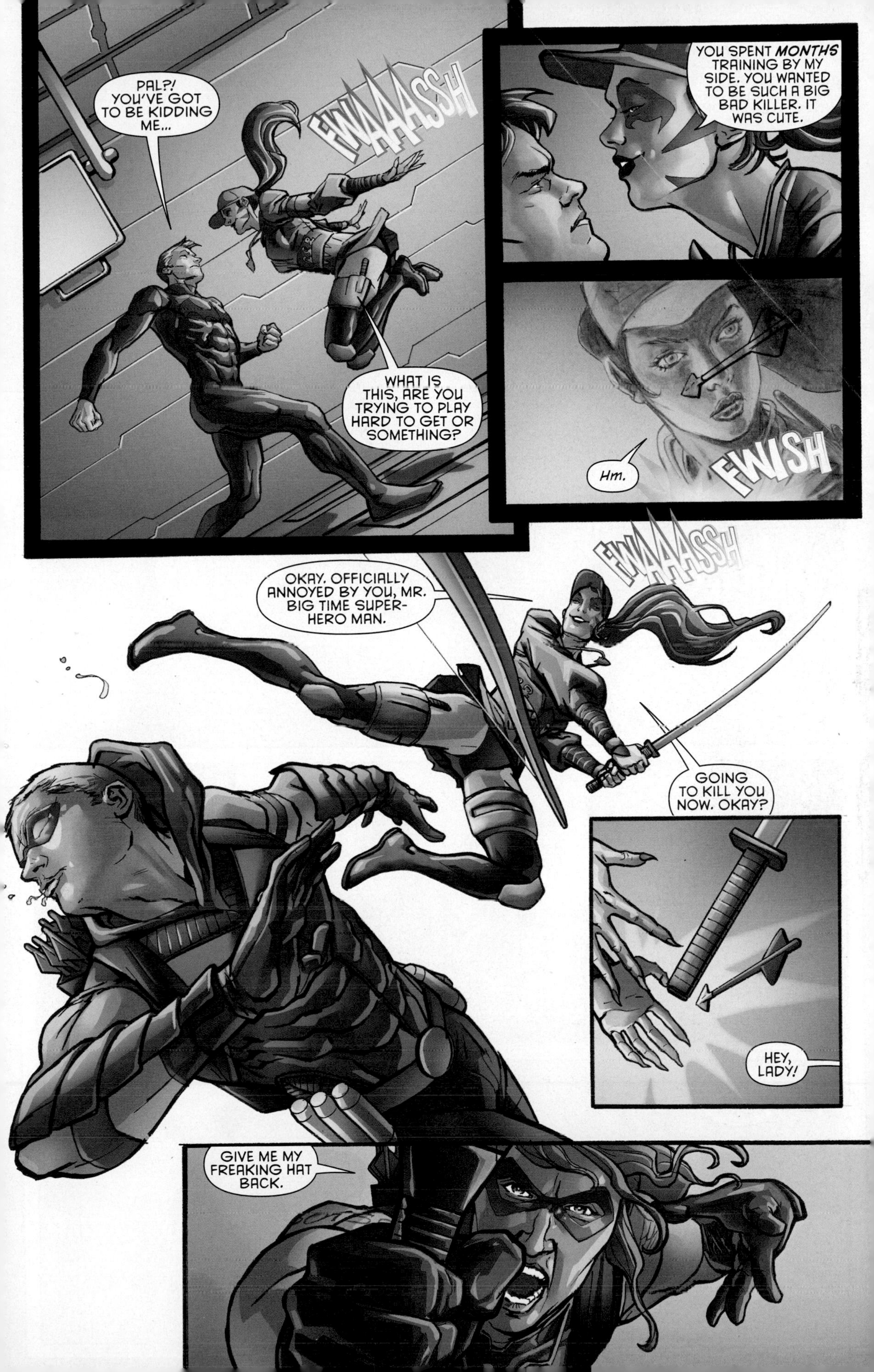

PAL?! YOU'VE GOT TO BE KIDDING ME...
FWAAASSH
WHAT IS THIS, ARE YOU TRYING TO PLAY HARD TO GET OR SOMETHING?
YOU SPENT MONTHS TRAINING BY MY SIDE. YOU WANTED TO BE SUCH A BIG BAD KILLER. IT WAS CUTE.
Hm.
FWISH
FWAAASSH
OKAY. OFFICIALLY ANNOYED BY YOU, MR. BIG TIME SUPER-HERO MAN.
GOING TO KILL YOU NOW. OKAY?
HEY, LADY!
GIVE ME MY FREAKING HAT BACK.

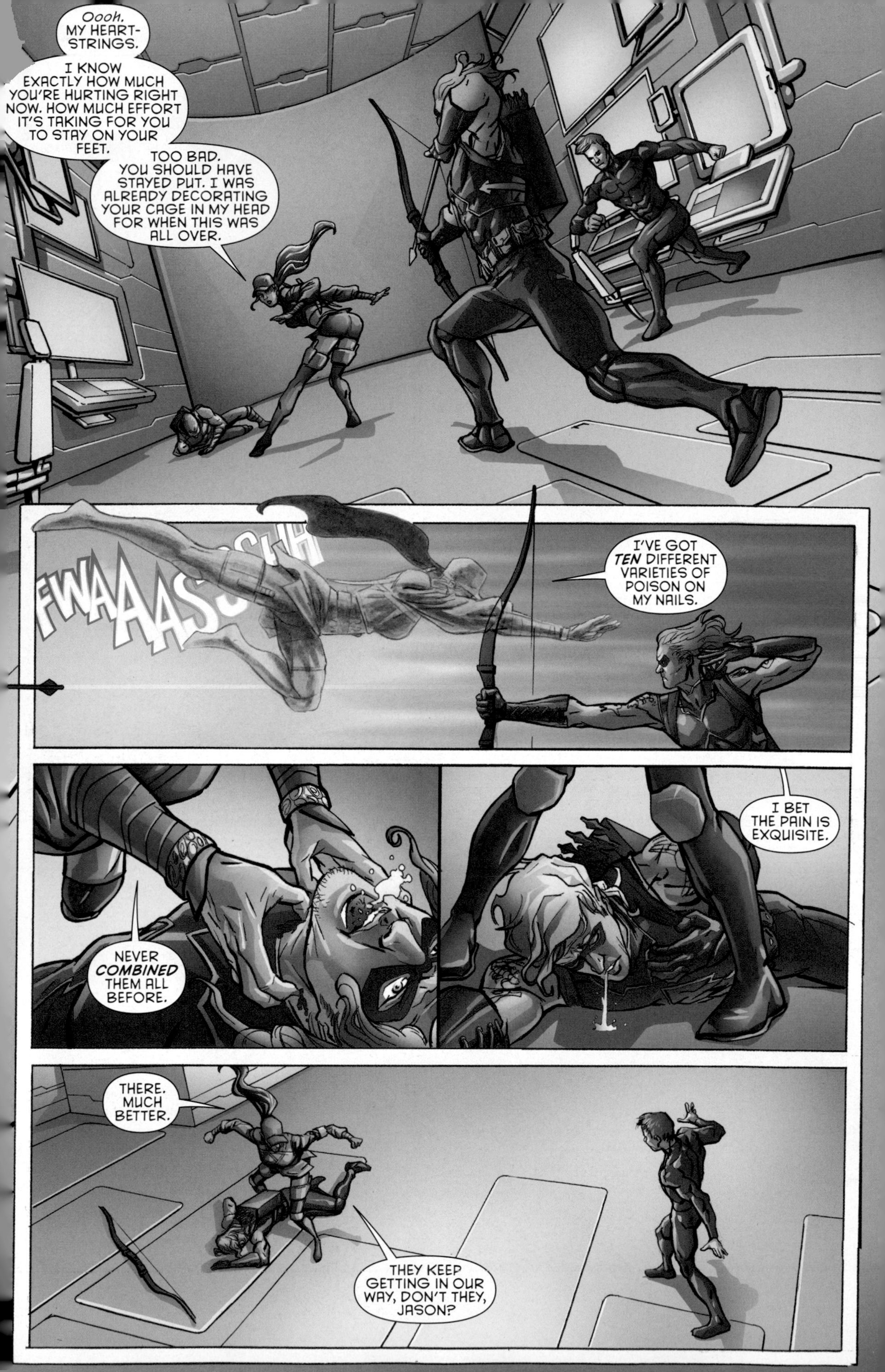
Oooh. MY HEART-STRINGS.
I KNOW EXACTLY HOW MUCH YOU'RE HURTING RIGHT NOW. HOW MUCH EFFORT IT'S TAKING FOR YOU TO STAY ON YOUR FEET.
TOO BAD. YOU SHOULD HAVE STAYED PUT. I WAS ALREADY DECORATING YOUR CAGE IN MY HEAD FOR WHEN THIS WAS ALL OVER.
FWAAASSHH
I'VE GOT TEN DIFFERENT VARIETIES OF POISON ON MY NAILS.
NEVER COMBINED THEM ALL BEFORE.
I BET THE PAIN IS EXQUISITE.
THERE. MUCH BETTER.
THEY KEEP GETTING IN OUR WAY, DON'T THEY, JASON?

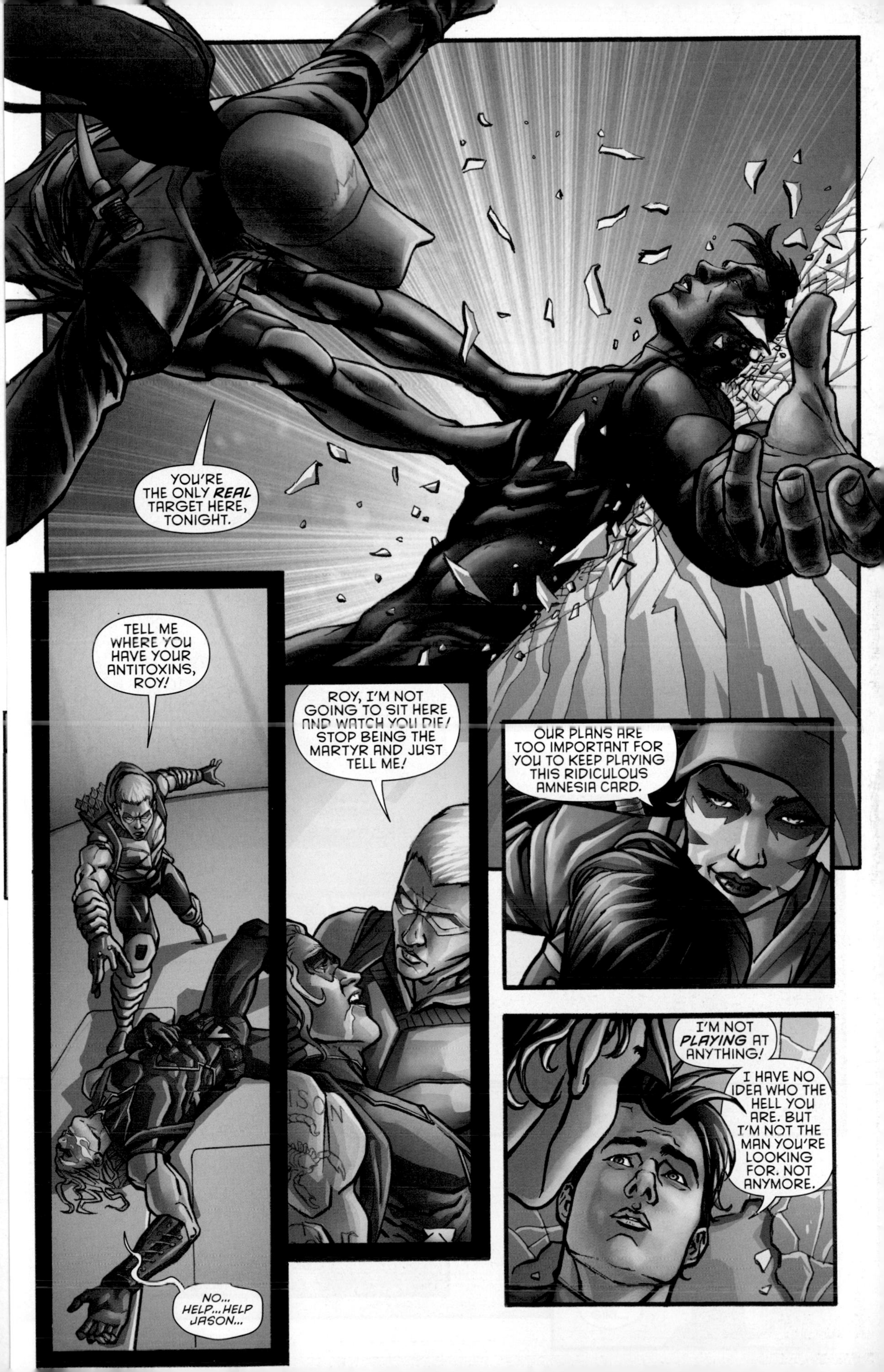
YOU'RE THE ONLY REAL TARGET HERE, TONIGHT.
TELL ME WHERE YOU HAVE YOUR ANTITOXINS, ROY!
NO... HELP...HELP JASON...
ROY, I'M NOT GOING TO SIT HERE AND WATCH YOU DIE! STOP BEING THE MARTYR AND JUST TELL ME!
OUR PLANS ARE TOO IMPORTANT FOR YOU TO KEEP PLAYING THIS RIDICULOUS AMNESIA CARD.
I'M NOT PLAYING AT ANYTHING!
I HAVE NO IDEA WHO THE HELL YOU ARE. BUT I'M NOT THE MAN YOU'RE LOOKING FOR. NOT ANYMORE.

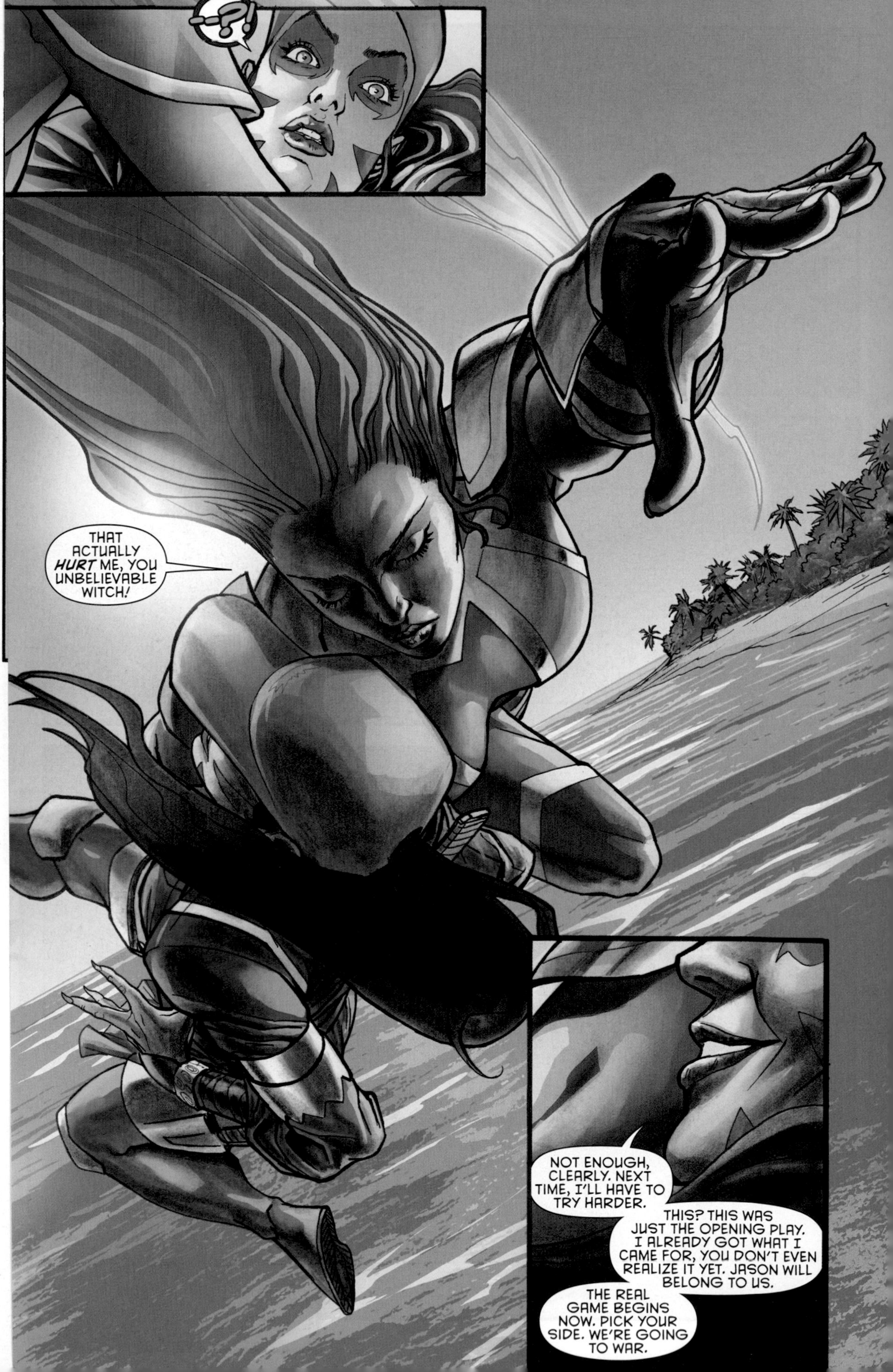

?!
THAT ACTUALLY HURT ME, YOU UNBELIEVABLE WITCH!
NOT ENOUGH, CLEARLY. NEXT TIME, I'LL HAVE TO TRY HARDER.
THIS? THIS WAS JUST THE OPENING PLAY. I ALREADY GOT WHAT I CAME FOR, YOU DON'T EVEN REALIZE IT YET. JASON WILL BELONG TO US.
THE REAL GAME BEGINS NOW. PICK YOUR SIDE. WE'RE GOING TO WAR.

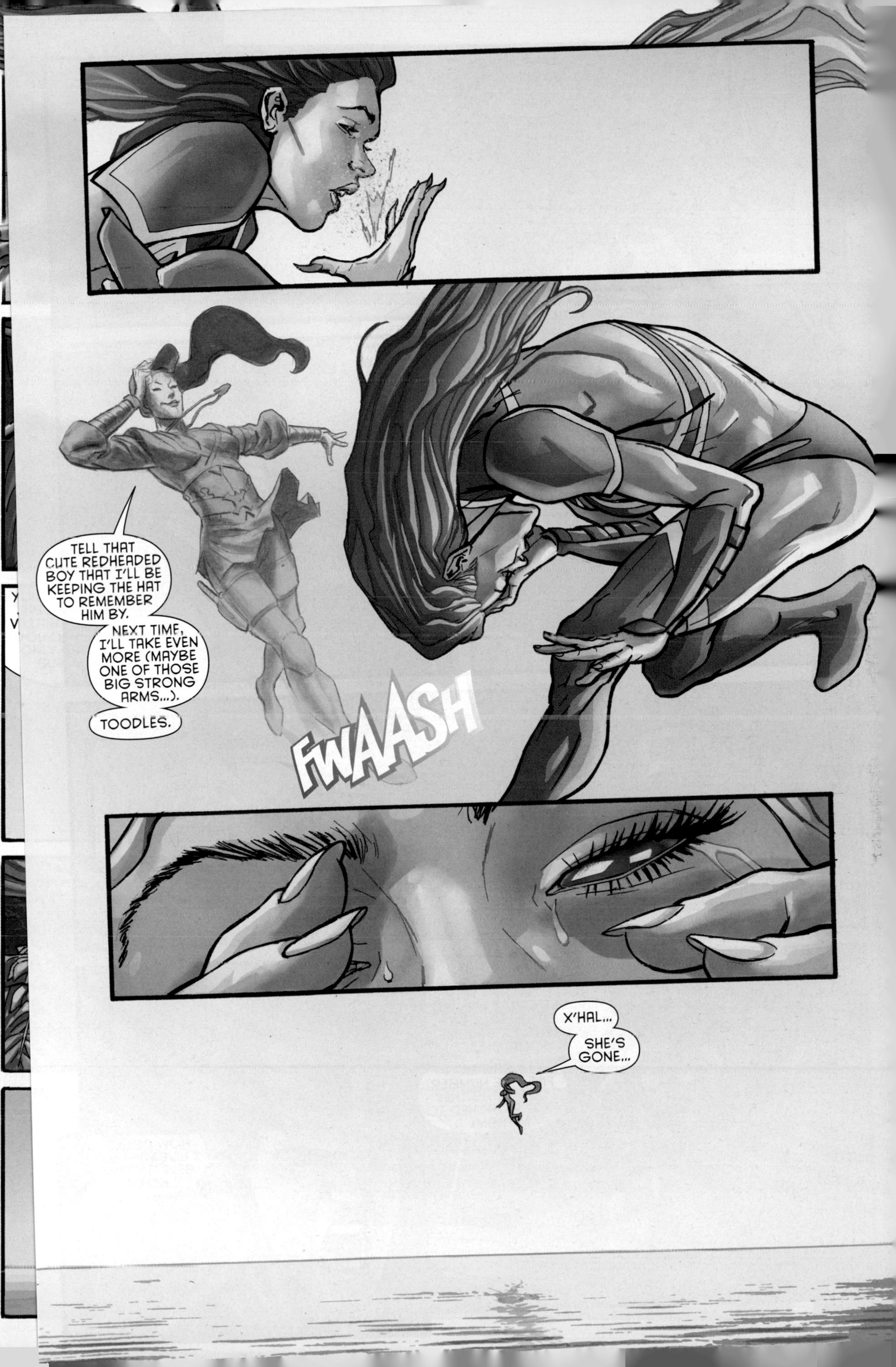
TELL THAT CUTE REDHEADED BOY THAT I'LL BE KEEPING THE HAT TO REMEMBER HIM BY.
NEXT TIME, I'LL TAKE EVEN MORE (MAYBE ONE OF THOSE BIG STRONG ARMS...).
TOODLES.
FWAASH
X'HAL...
SHE'S GONE...

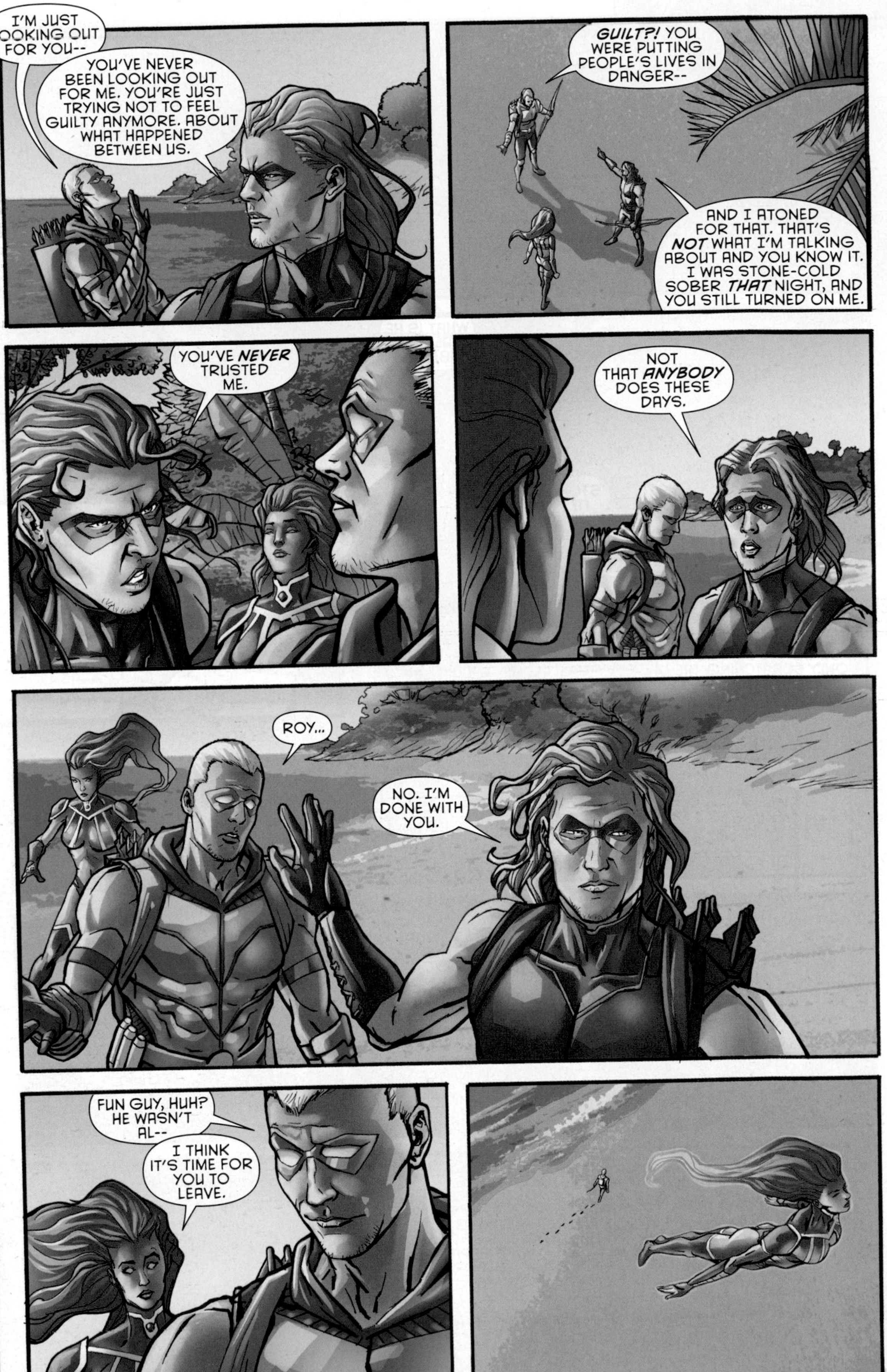
I'M JUST LOOKING OUT FOR YOU--
YOU'VE NEVER BEEN LOOKING OUT FOR ME. YOU'RE JUST TRYING NOT TO FEEL GUILTY ANYMORE. ABOUT WHAT HAPPENED BETWEEN US.
GUILT?! YOU WERE PUTTING PEOPLE'S LIVES IN DANGER--
AND I ATONED FOR THAT. THAT'S NOT WHAT I'M TALKING ABOUT AND YOU KNOW IT. I WAS STONE-COLD SOBER THAT NIGHT, AND YOU STILL TURNED ON ME.
YOU'VE NEVER TRUSTED ME.
NOT THAT ANYBODY DOES THESE DAYS.
ROY...
NO. I'M DONE WITH YOU.
FUN GUY, HUH? HE WASN'T AL--
I THINK IT'S TIME FOR YOU TO LEAVE.

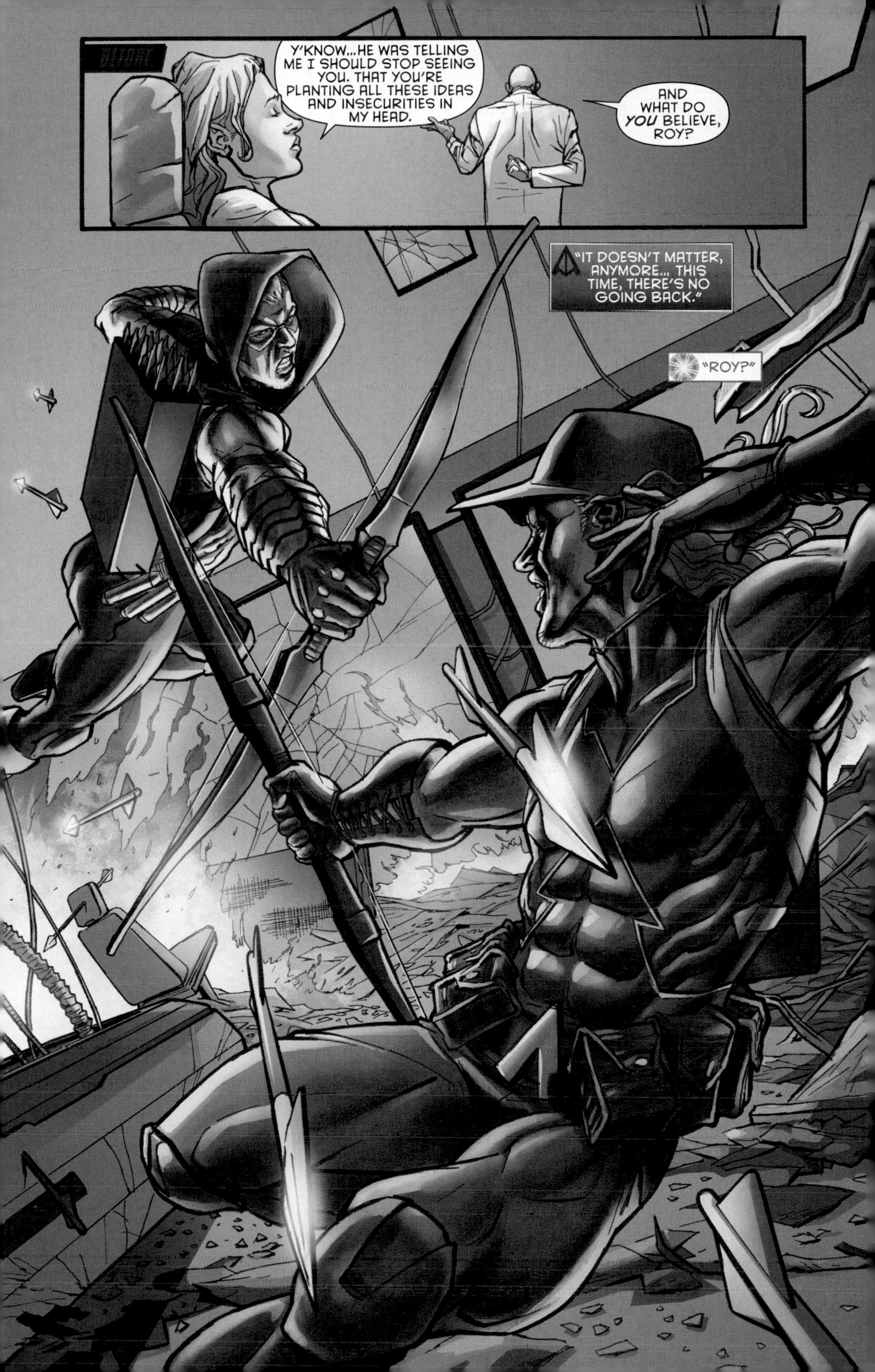
Y'KNOW...HE WAS TELLING ME I SHOULD STOP SEEING YOU. THAT YOU'RE PLANTING ALL THESE IDEAS AND INSECURITIES IN MY HEAD.
AND WHAT DO YOU BELIEVE, ROY?
"IT DOESN'T MATTER, ANYMORE... THIS TIME, THERE'S NO GOING BACK."
"ROY?"

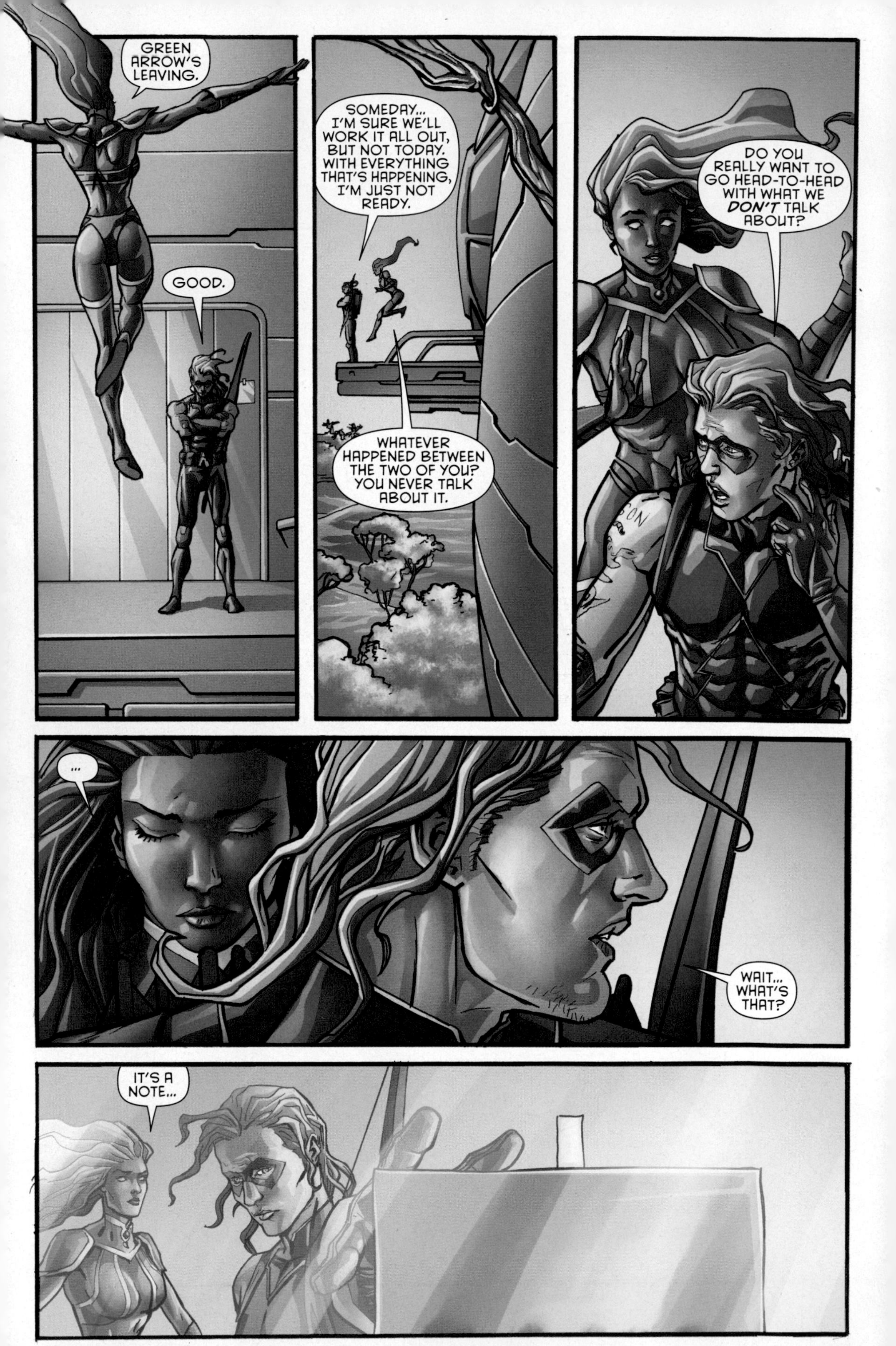
GREEN ARROW'S LEAVING.
GOOD.
SOMEDAY... I'M SURE WE'LL WORK IT ALL OUT, BUT NOT TODAY. WITH EVERYTHING THAT'S HAPPENING, I'M JUST NOT READY.
WHATEVER HAPPENED BETWEEN THE TWO OF YOU? YOU NEVER TALK ABOUT IT.
DO YOU REALLY WANT TO GO HEAD-TO-HEAD WITH WHAT WE DON'T TALK ABOUT?
...
WAIT... WHAT'S THAT?
IT'S A NOTE...

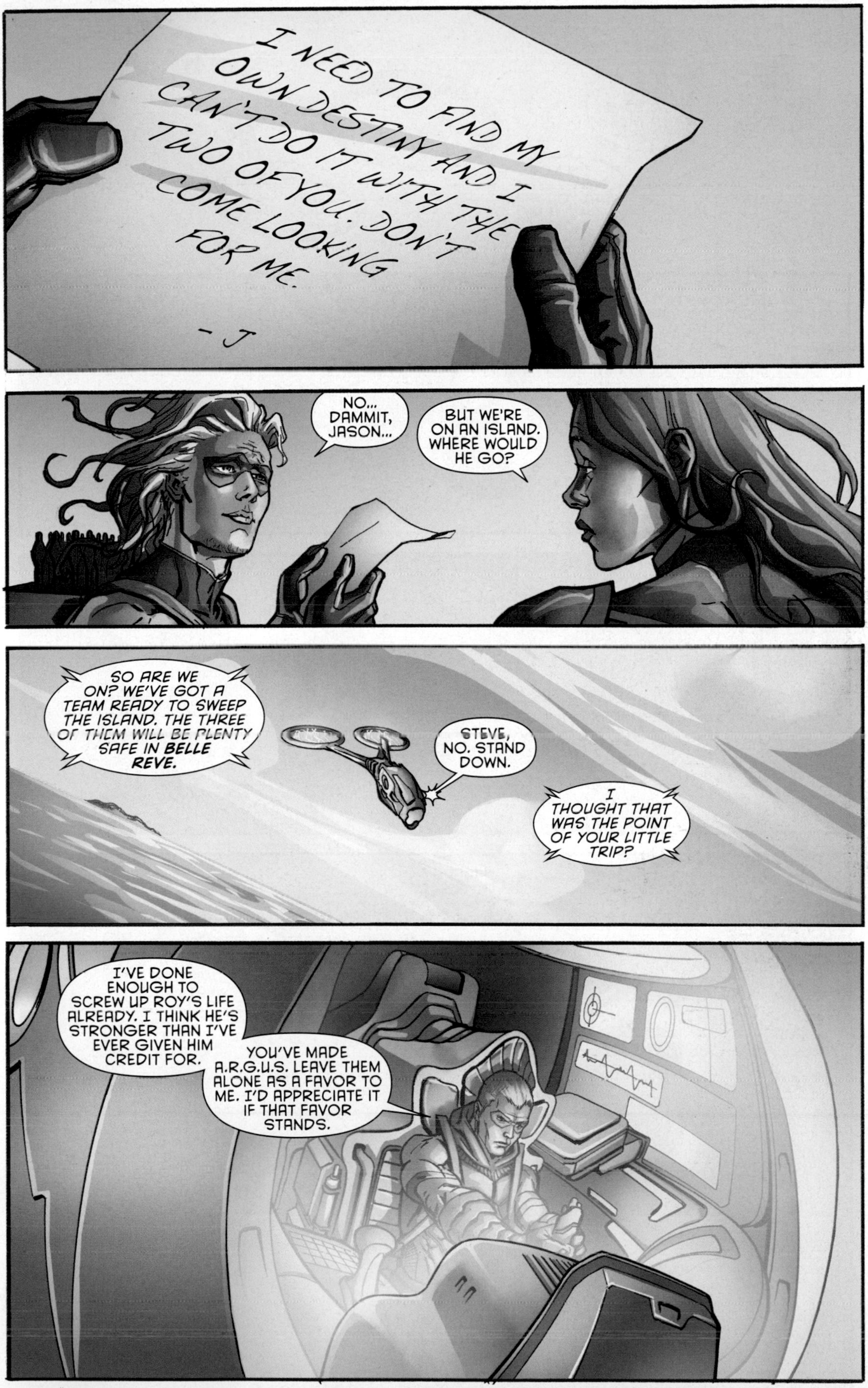
I NEED TO FIND MY OWN DESTINY AND I CAN'T DO IT WITH THE TWO OF YOU. DON'T COME LOOKING FOR ME.
- J
NO... DAMMIT, JASON...
BUT WE'RE ON AN ISLAND. WHERE WOULD HE GO?
SO ARE WE ON? WE'VE GOT A TEAM READY TO SWEEP THE ISLAND. THE THREE OF THEM WILL BE PLENTY SAFE IN BELLE REVE.
STEVE, NO. STAND DOWN.
I THOUGHT THAT WAS THE POINT OF YOUR LITTLE TRIP?
I'VE DONE ENOUGH TO SCREW UP ROY'S LIFE ALREADY. I THINK HE'S STRONGER THAN I'VE EVER GIVEN HIM CREDIT FOR.
YOU'VE MADE A.R.G.U.S. LEAVE THEM ALONE AS A FAVOR TO ME. I'D APPRECIATE IT IF THAT FAVOR STANDS.

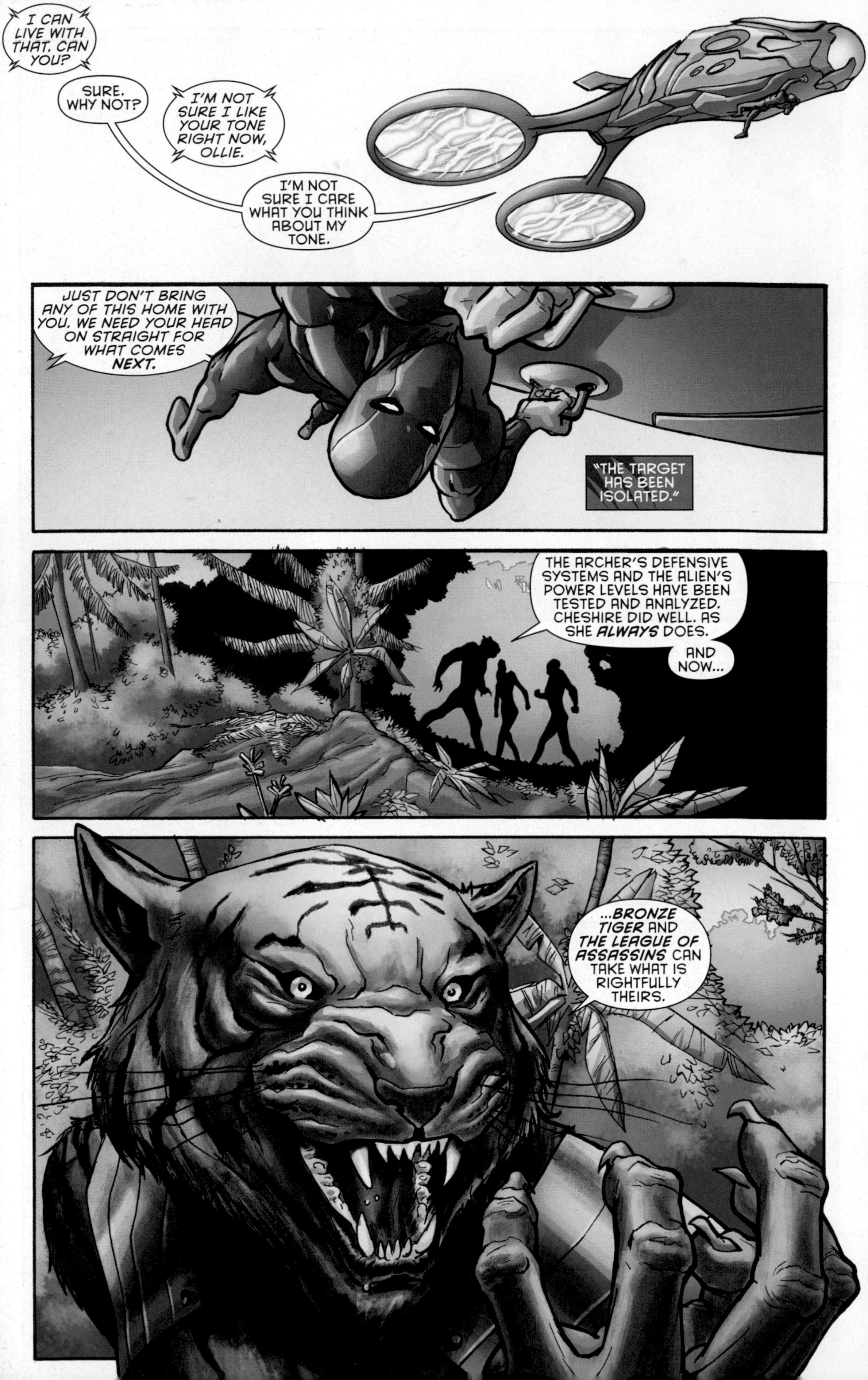
I CAN LIVE WITH THAT. CAN YOU?
SURE. WHY NOT?
I'M NOT SURE I LIKE YOUR TONE RIGHT NOW, OLLIE.
I'M NOT SURE I CARE WHAT YOU THINK ABOUT MY TONE.
JUST DON'T BRING ANY OF THIS HOME WITH YOU. WE NEED YOUR HEAD ON STRAIGHT FOR WHAT COMES NEXT.
"THE TARGET HAS BEEN ISOLATED."
THE ARCHER'S DEFENSIVE SYSTEMS AND THE ALIEN'S POWER LEVELS HAVE BEEN TESTED AND ANALYZED. CHESHIRE DID WELL. AS SHE ALWAYS DOES.
AND NOW...
...BRONZE TIGER AND THE LEAGUE OF ASSASSINS CAN TAKE WHAT IS RIGHTFULLY THEIRS.

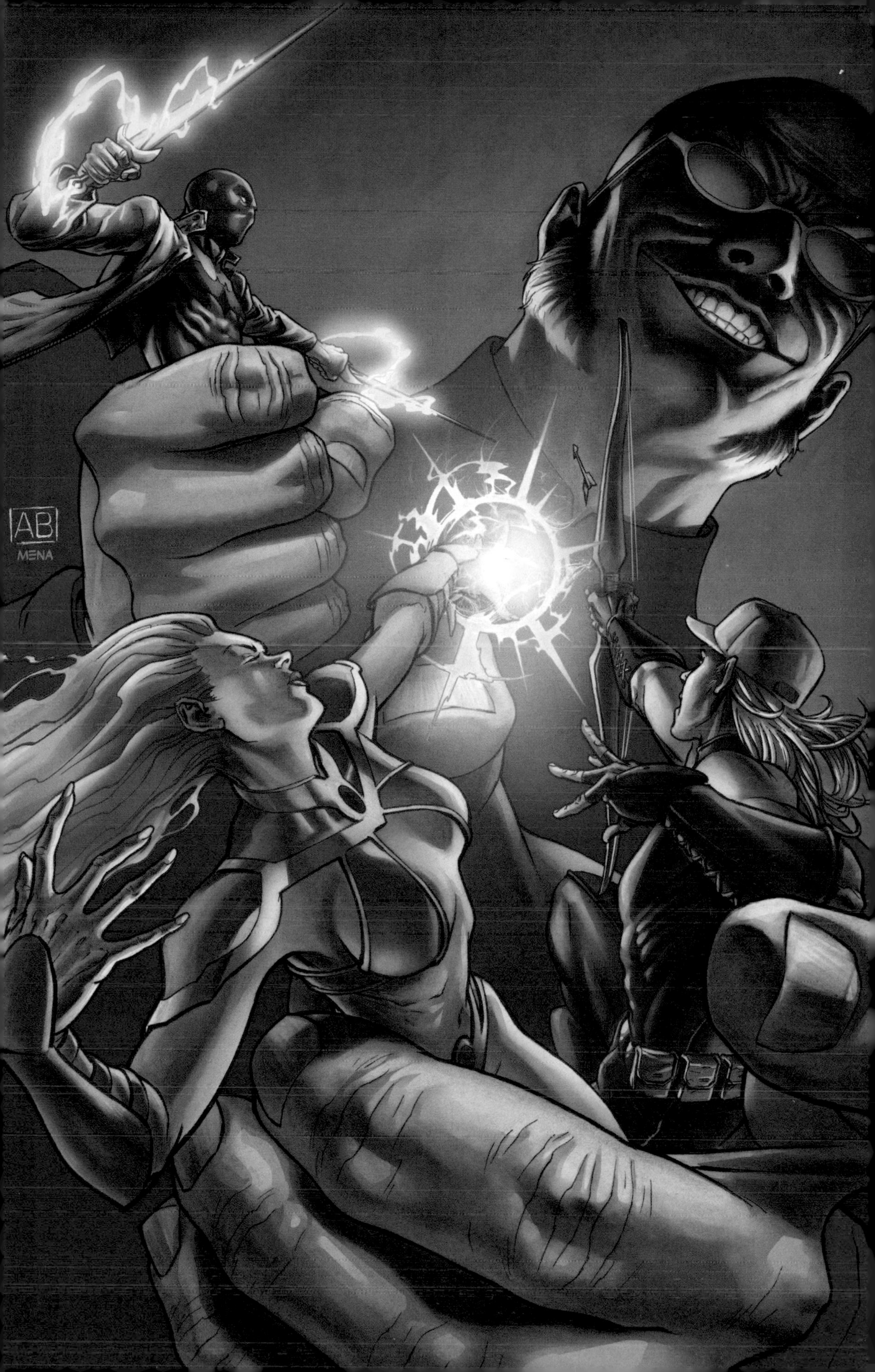
AB
MENA

JAMES TYNION IV writer JULIUS GOPEZ artist KEN LASHLEY thumbnail artist NEI RUFFINO colorist
AL BARRIONUEVO with JAVIER MENA cover artists

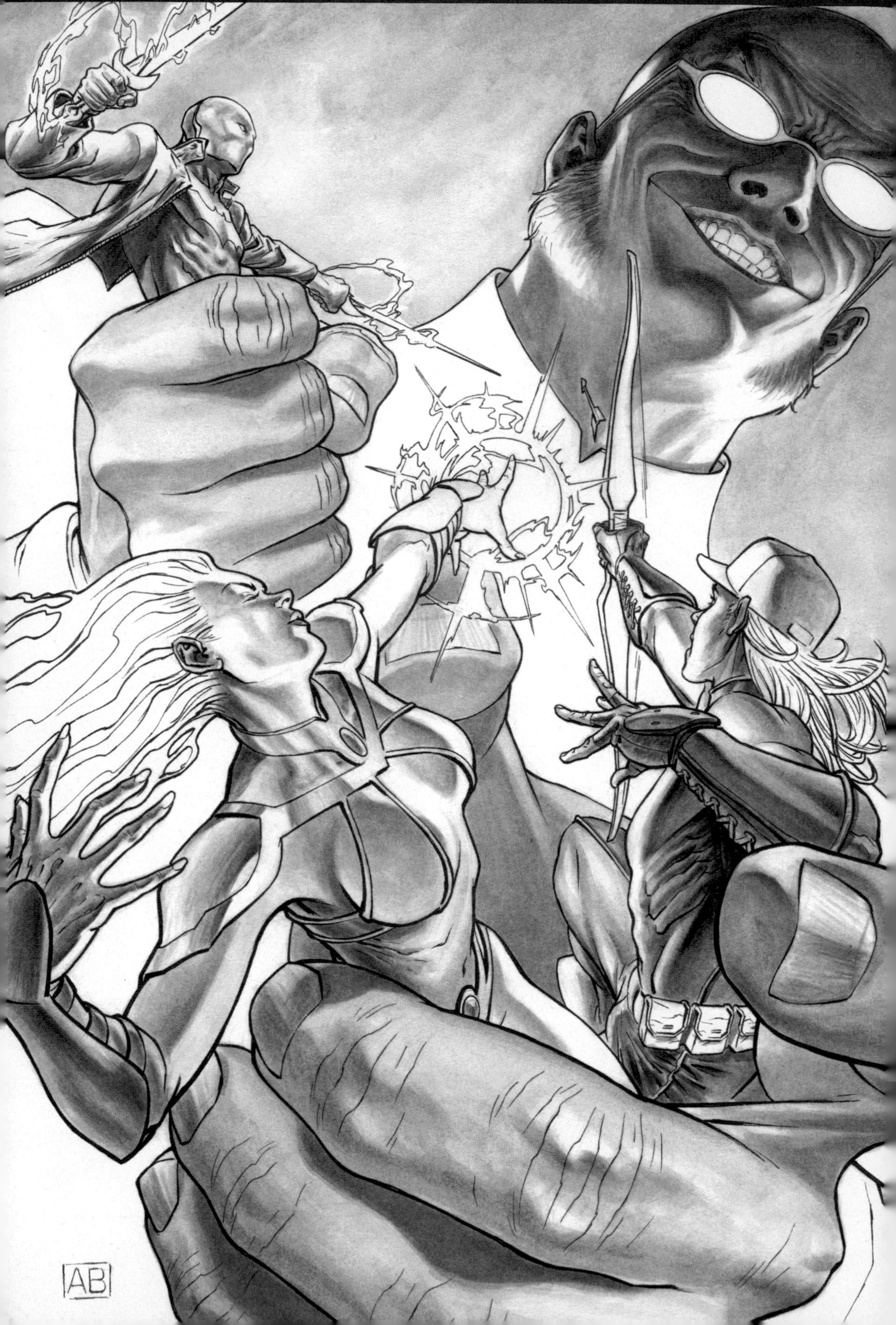

AB

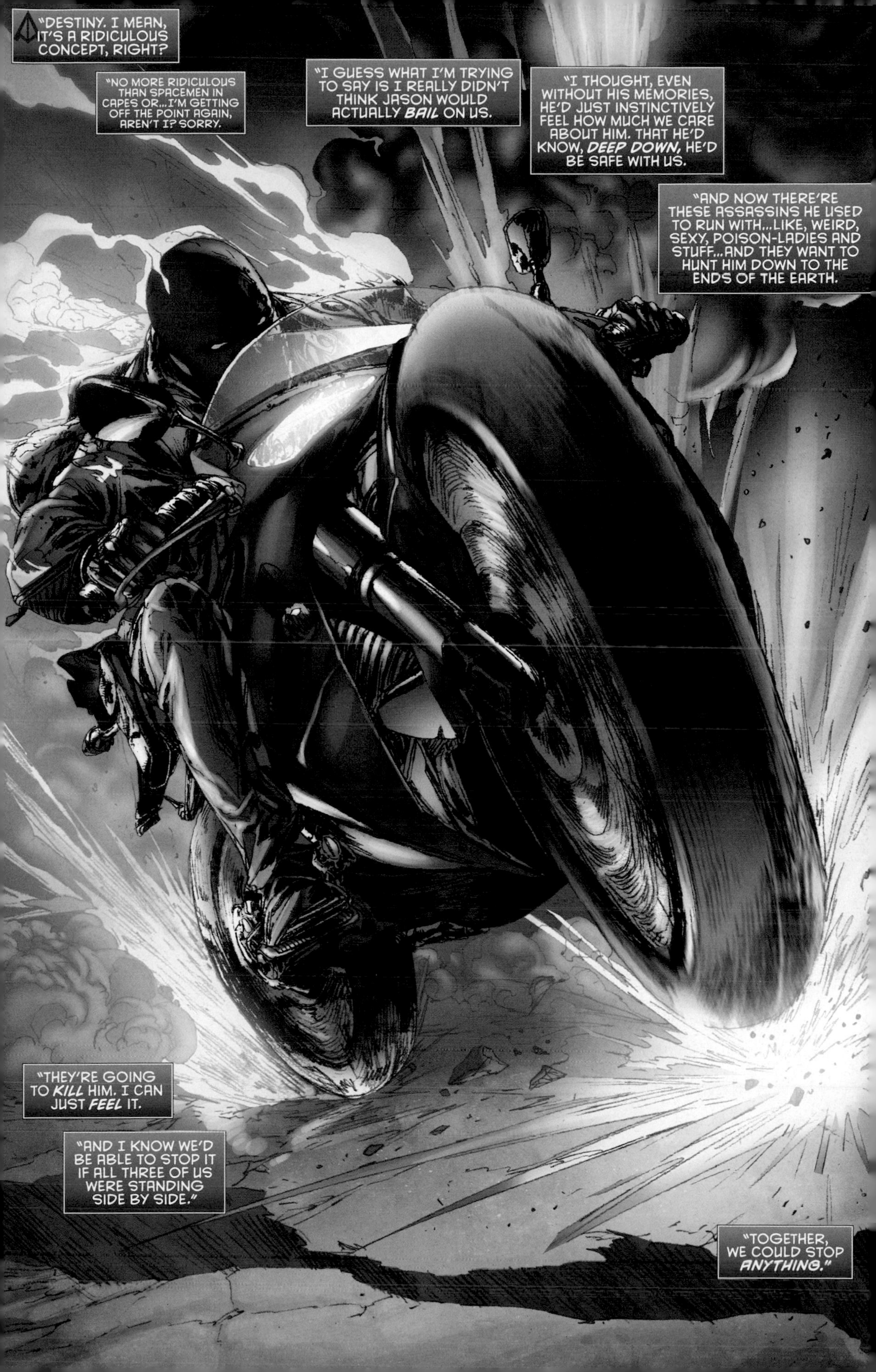
"DESTINY. I MEAN, IT'S A RIDICULOUS CONCEPT, RIGHT?
"NO MORE RIDICULOUS THAN SPACEMEN IN CAPES OR...I'M GETTING OFF THE POINT AGAIN, AREN'T I? SORRY.
"I GUESS WHAT I'M TRYING TO SAY IS I REALLY DIDN'T THINK JASON WOULD ACTUALLY BAIL ON US.
"I THOUGHT, EVEN WITHOUT HIS MEMORIES, HE'D JUST INSTINCTIVELY FEEL HOW MUCH WE CARE ABOUT HIM. THAT HE'D KNOW, DEEP DOWN, HE'D BE SAFE WITH US.
"AND NOW THERE'RE THESE ASSASSINS HE USED TO RUN WITH...LIKE, WEIRD, SEXY, POISON-LADIES AND STUFF...AND THEY WANT TO HUNT HIM DOWN TO THE ENDS OF THE EARTH.
"THEY'RE GOING TO KILL HIM. I CAN JUST FEEL IT.
"AND I KNOW WE'D BE ABLE TO STOP IT IF ALL THREE OF US WERE STANDING SIDE BY SIDE."
"TOGETHER, WE COULD STOP ANYTHING."

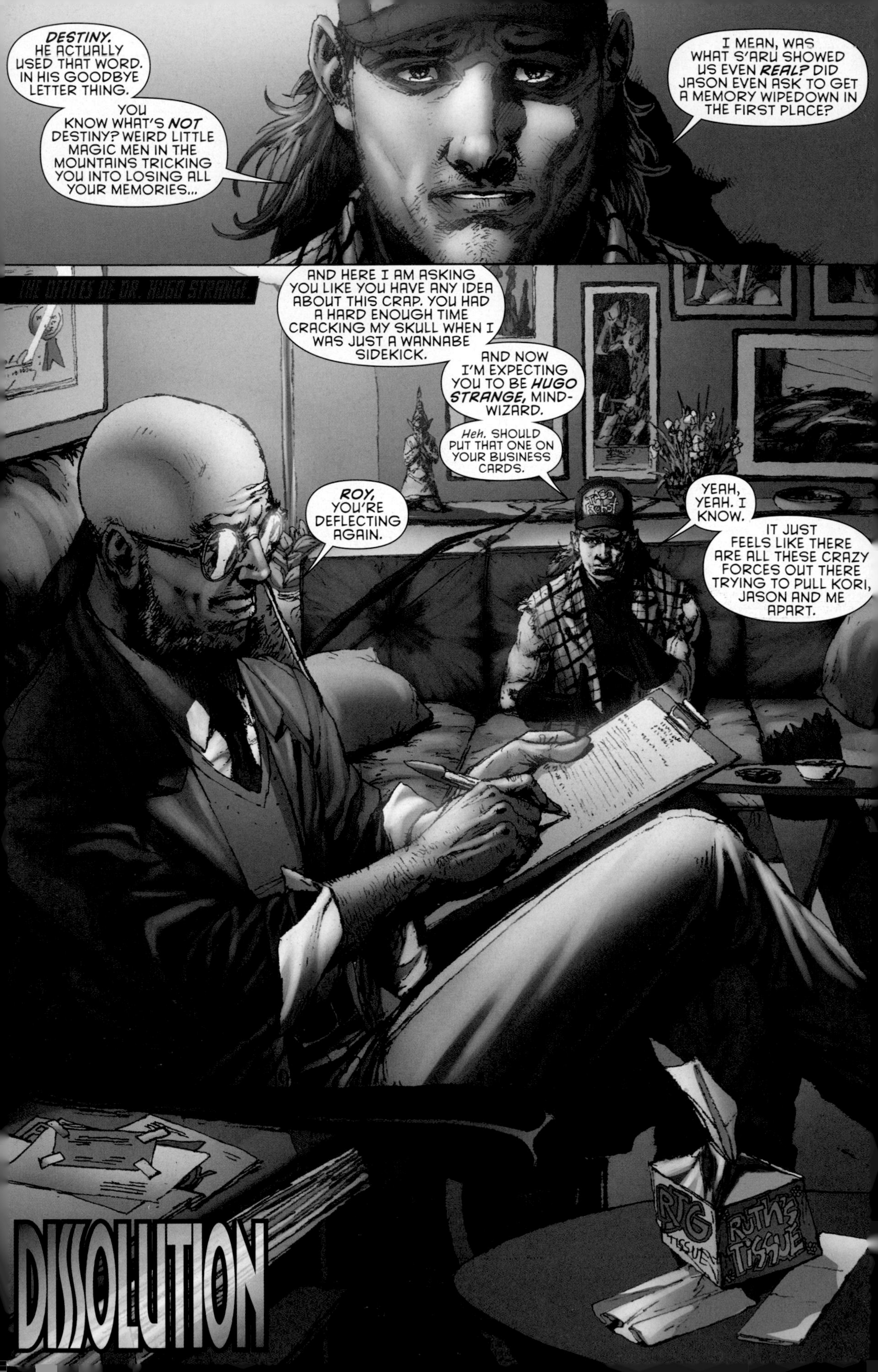

DESTINY. HE ACTUALLY USED THAT WORD. IN HIS GOODBYE LETTER THING.
YOU KNOW WHAT'S NOT DESTINY? WEIRD LITTLE MAGIC MEN IN THE MOUNTAINS TRICKING YOU INTO LOSING ALL YOUR MEMORIES...
I MEAN, WAS WHAT S'ARU SHOWED US EVEN REAL? DID JASON EVEN ASK TO GET A MEMORY WIPEDOWN IN THE FIRST PLACE?
THE OFFICES OF DR. HUGO STRANGE.
AND HERE I AM ASKING YOU LIKE YOU HAVE ANY IDEA ABOUT THIS CRAP. YOU HAD A HARD ENOUGH TIME CRACKING MY SKULL WHEN I WAS JUST A WANNABE SIDEKICK.
AND NOW I'M EXPECTING YOU TO BE HUGO STRANGE, MIND-WIZARD.
Heh. SHOULD PUT THAT ONE ON YOUR BUSINESS CARDS.
ROY, YOU'RE DEFLECTING AGAIN.
YEAH, YEAH. I KNOW.
IT JUST FEELS LIKE THERE ARE ALL THESE CRAZY FORCES OUT THERE TRYING TO PULL KORI, JASON AND ME APART.
RTG TISSUE
RUTH'S TISSUE
DISSOLUTION

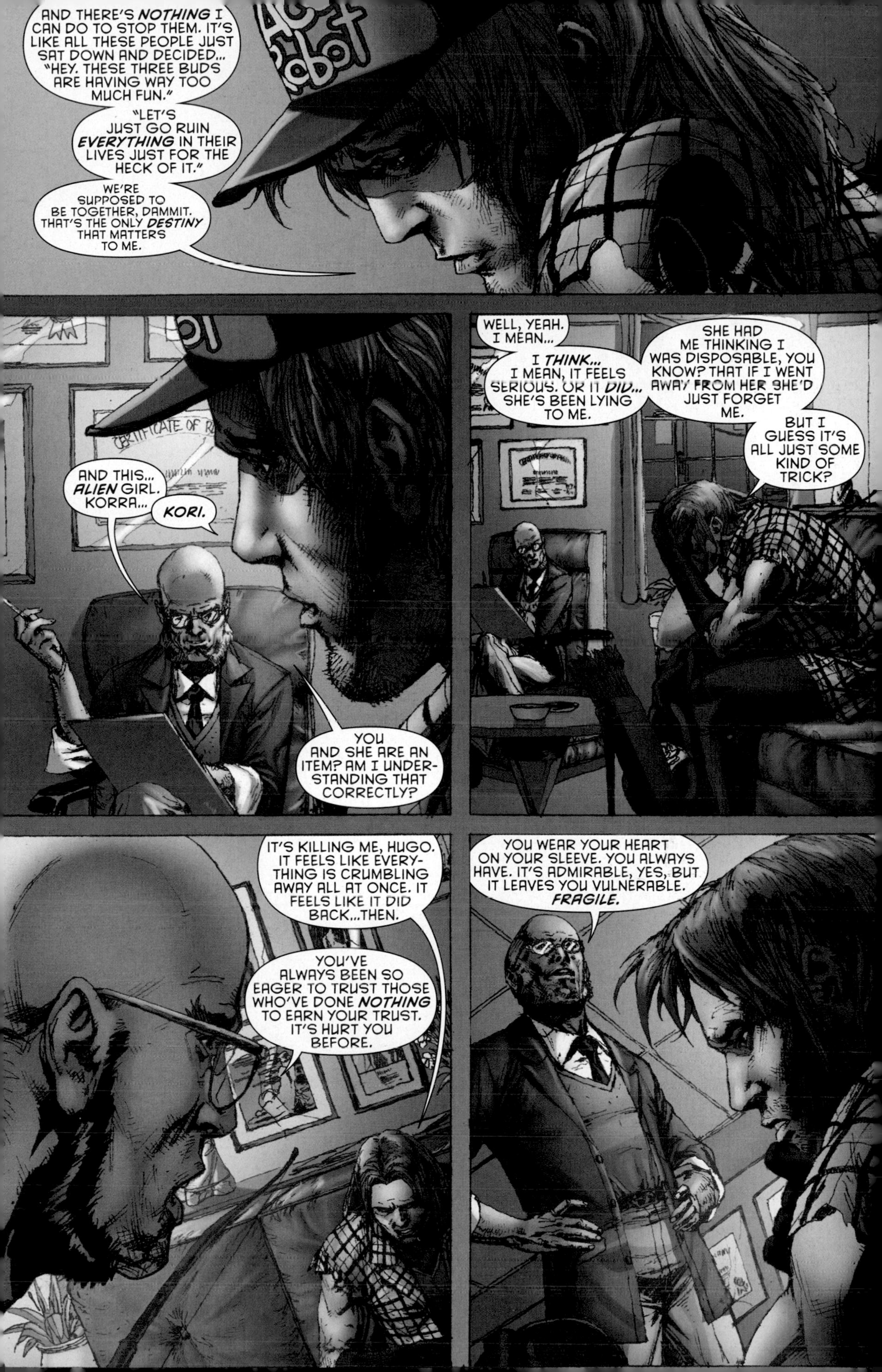

AND THERE'S NOTHING I CAN DO TO STOP THEM. IT'S LIKE ALL THESE PEOPLE JUST SAT DOWN AND DECIDED... "HEY. THESE THREE BUDS ARE HAVING WAY TOO MUCH FUN."
"LET'S JUST GO RUIN EVERYTHING IN THEIR LIVES JUST FOR THE HECK OF IT."
WE'RE SUPPOSED TO BE TOGETHER, DAMMIT. THAT'S THE ONLY DESTINY THAT MATTERS TO ME.
AND THIS... ALIEN GIRL. KORRA...
KORI.
YOU AND SHE ARE AN ITEM? AM I UNDERSTANDING THAT CORRECTLY?
WELL, YEAH. I MEAN...
I THINK... I MEAN, IT FEELS SERIOUS. OR IT DID... SHE'S BEEN LYING TO ME.
SHE HAD ME THINKING I WAS DISPOSABLE, YOU KNOW? THAT IF I WENT AWAY FROM HER SHE'D JUST FORGET ME.
BUT I GUESS IT'S ALL JUST SOME KIND OF TRICK?
IT'S KILLING ME, HUGO. IT FEELS LIKE EVERYTHING IS CRUMBLING AWAY ALL AT ONCE. IT FEELS LIKE IT DID BACK...THEN.
YOU'VE ALWAYS BEEN SO EAGER TO TRUST THOSE WHO'VE DONE NOTHING TO EARN YOUR TRUST. IT'S HURT YOU BEFORE.
YOU WEAR YOUR HEART ON YOUR SLEEVE. YOU ALWAYS HAVE. IT'S ADMIRABLE, YES, BUT IT LEAVES YOU VULNERABLE. FRAGILE.

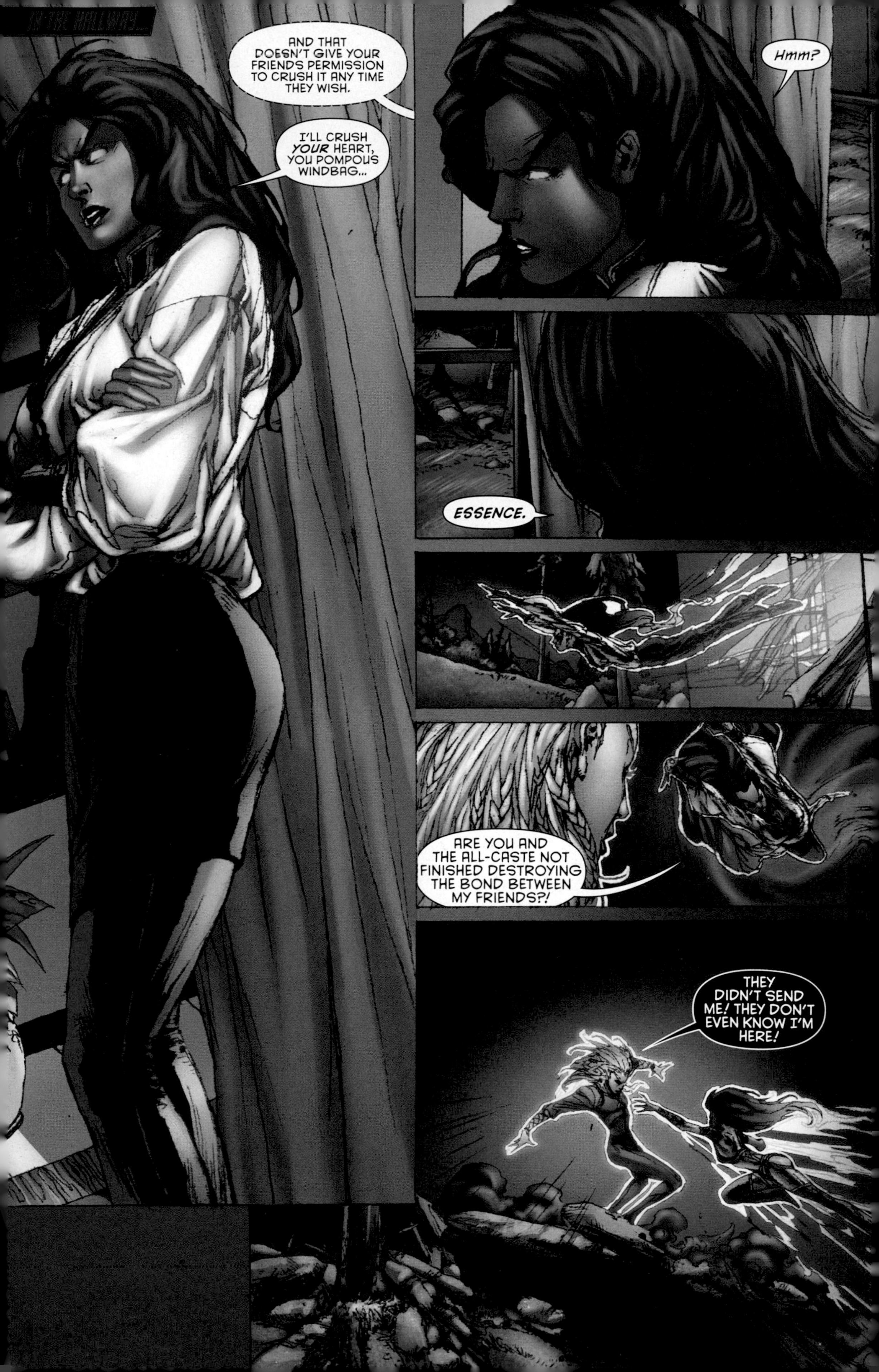
IN THE HALLWAY...
AND THAT DOESN'T GIVE YOUR FRIENDS PERMISSION TO CRUSH IT ANY TIME THEY WISH.
I'LL CRUSH *YOUR* HEART, YOU POMPOUS WINDBAG...
Hmm?
ESSENCE.
ARE YOU AND THE ALL-CASTE NOT FINISHED DESTROYING THE BOND BETWEEN MY FRIENDS?!
THEY DIDN'T SEND ME! THEY DON'T EVEN KNOW I'M HERE!

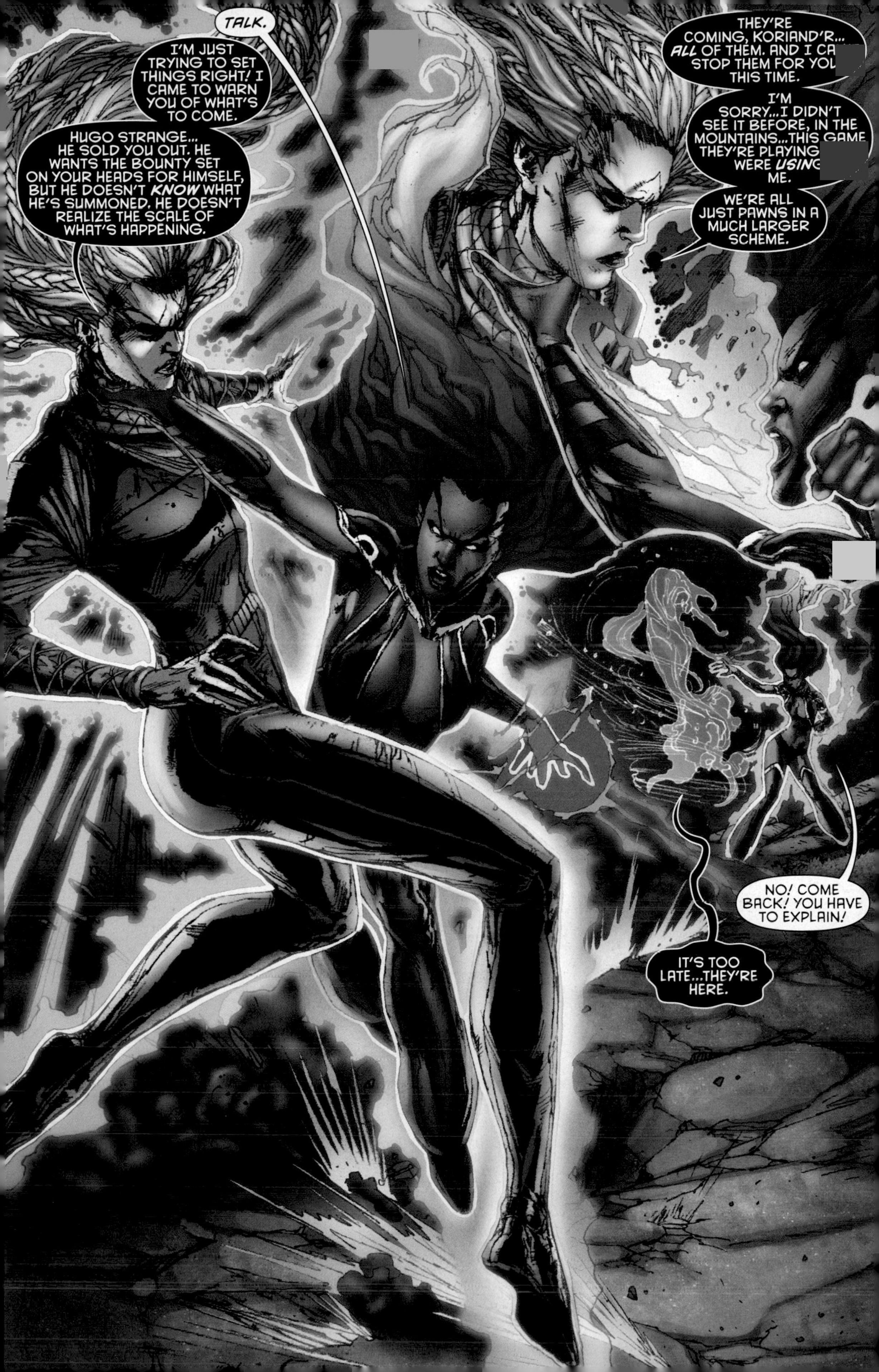
TALK.
I'M JUST TRYING TO SET THINGS RIGHT! I CAME TO WARN YOU OF WHAT'S TO COME.
HUGO STRANGE... HE SOLD YOU OUT. HE WANTS THE BOUNTY SET ON YOUR HEADS FOR HIMSELF, BUT HE DOESN'T KNOW WHAT HE'S SUMMONED. HE DOESN'T REALIZE THE SCALE OF WHAT'S HAPPENING.
THEY'RE COMING, KORIAND'R... ALL OF THEM. AND I CA STOP THEM FOR YOU THIS TIME.
I'M SORRY...I DIDN'T SEE IT BEFORE, IN THE MOUNTAINS...THIS GAME THEY'RE PLAYING WERE USIN ME.
WE'RE ALL JUST PAWNS IN A MUCH LARGER SCHEME.
NO! COME BACK! YOU HAVE TO EXPLAIN!
IT'S TOO LATE...THEY'RE HERE.

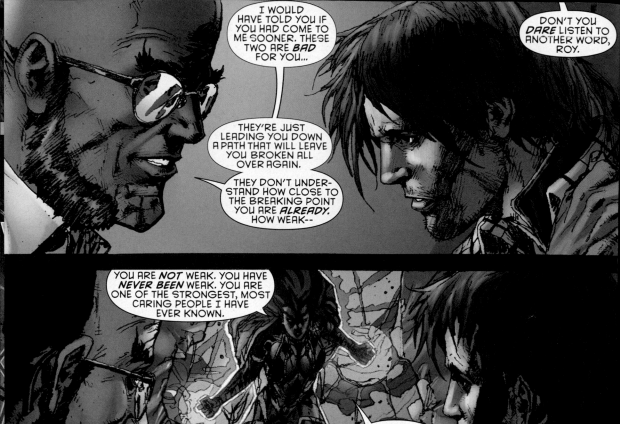

I WOULD HAVE TOLD YOU IF YOU HAD COME TO ME SOONER. THESE TWO ARE *BAD* FOR YOU...

DON'T YOU *DARE* LISTEN TO ANOTHER WORD, ROY.

THEY'RE JUST LEADING YOU DOWN A PATH THAT WILL LEAVE YOU BROKEN ALL OVER AGAIN.

THEY DON'T UNDERSTAND HOW CLOSE TO THE BREAKING POINT YOU ARE *ALREADY.* HOW WEAK--

YOU ARE *NOT* WEAK. YOU HAVE *NEVER BEEN* WEAK. YOU ARE ONE OF THE STRONGEST, MOST CARING PEOPLE I HAVE EVER KNOWN.

THIS MAN IS LYING. HE'S TRYING TO TWIST YOUR MIND AGAINST YOU.

THIS IS KINDA SUPPOSED TO BE A *PRIVATE* SESSION, KORI...I'VE KNOWN HUGO FOR YEARS. HE'S JUST TRYING TO HELP.

TELL HER IT'S NOT TRUE, HUGO. YOU CAN'T HAVE SOLD US OUT TO THEM...NOT *THEM.*

IT'S NOT TRUE. I DON'T KNOW WHAT SHE'S TALKING ABOUT!

AMUSING, HOW YOU MORTALS BICKER AND TURN ON ONE ANOTHER.

HE SOLD US *OUT,* ROY. HE SOLD US OUT TO SOMEONE POWERFUL ENOUGH TO SCARE ESSENCE AWAY.

ROY, WE HAVE TO GET OUT OF HERE...

ESSENCE?! SHE WAS *HERE?* BUT THAT WOULD MEAN--

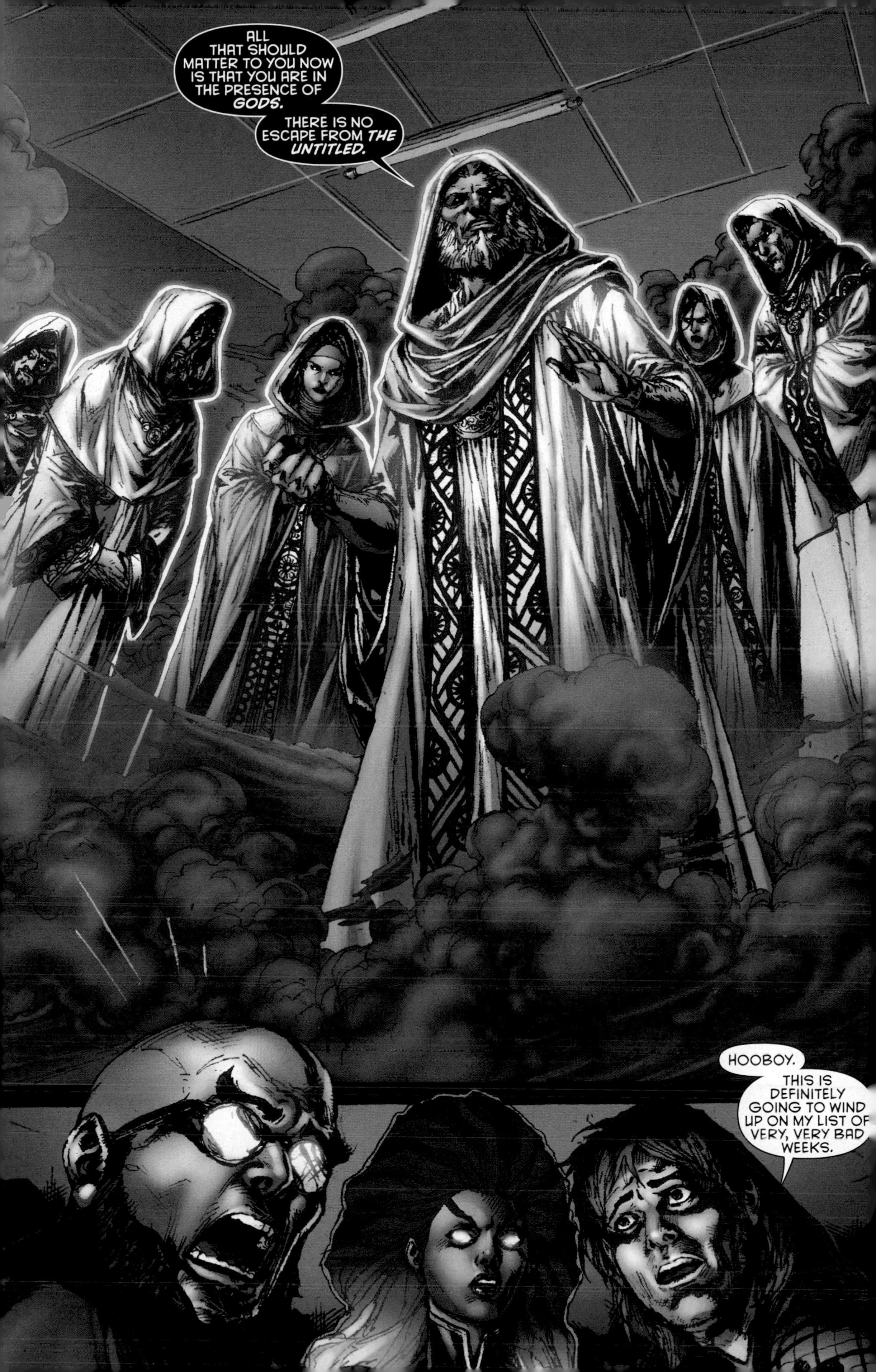
ALL THAT SHOULD MATTER TO YOU NOW IS THAT YOU ARE IN THE PRESENCE OF *GODS.*
THERE IS NO ESCAPE FROM *THE UNTITLED.*
HOOBOY.
THIS IS DEFINITELY GOING TO WIND UP ON MY LIST OF VERY, VERY BAD WEEKS.

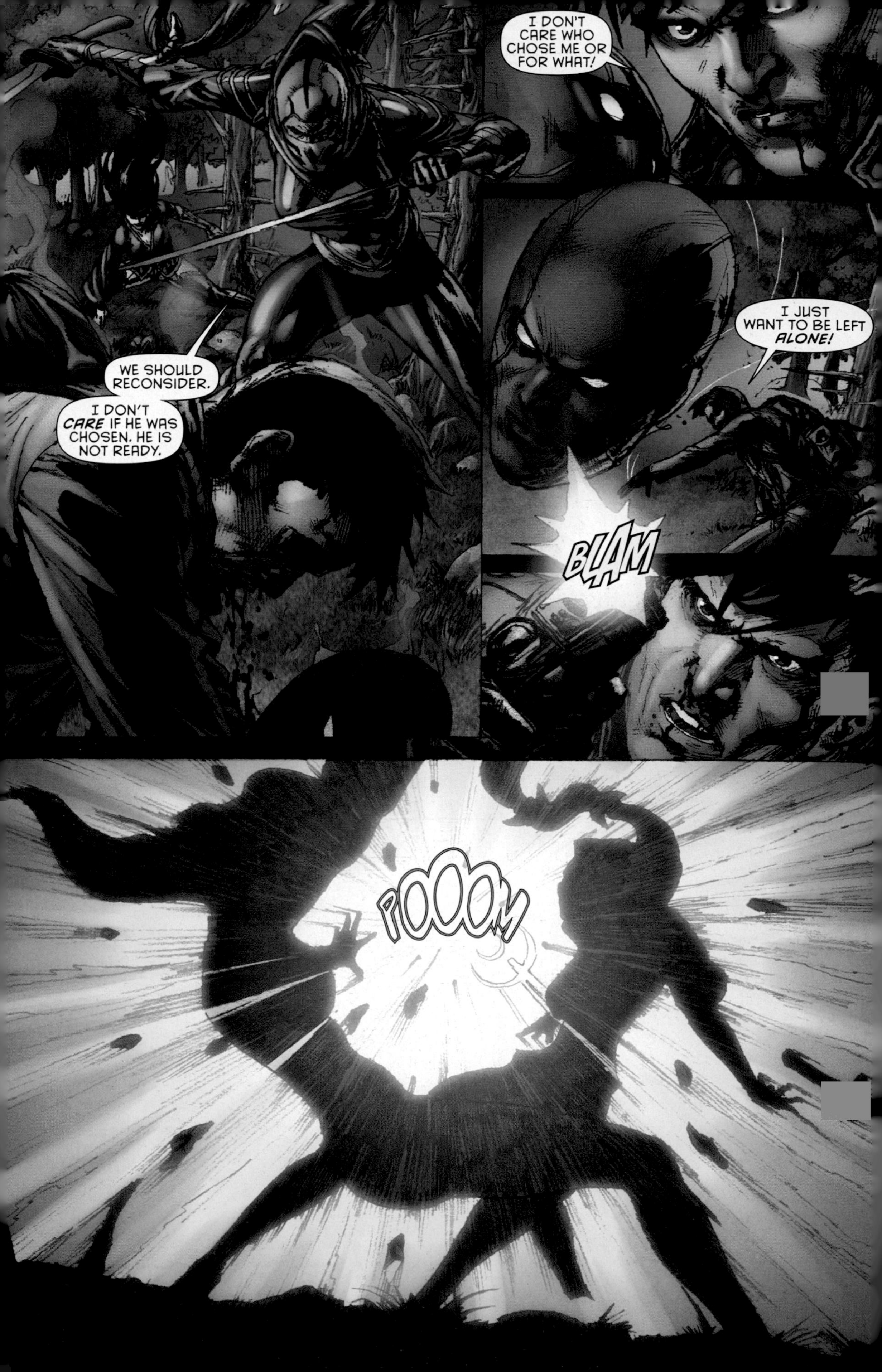

I DON'T CARE WHO CHOSE ME OR FOR WHAT!
WE SHOULD RECONSIDER.
I DON'T CARE IF HE WAS CHOSEN. HE IS NOT READY.
I JUST WANT TO BE LEFT ALONE!
BLAM
POOOM

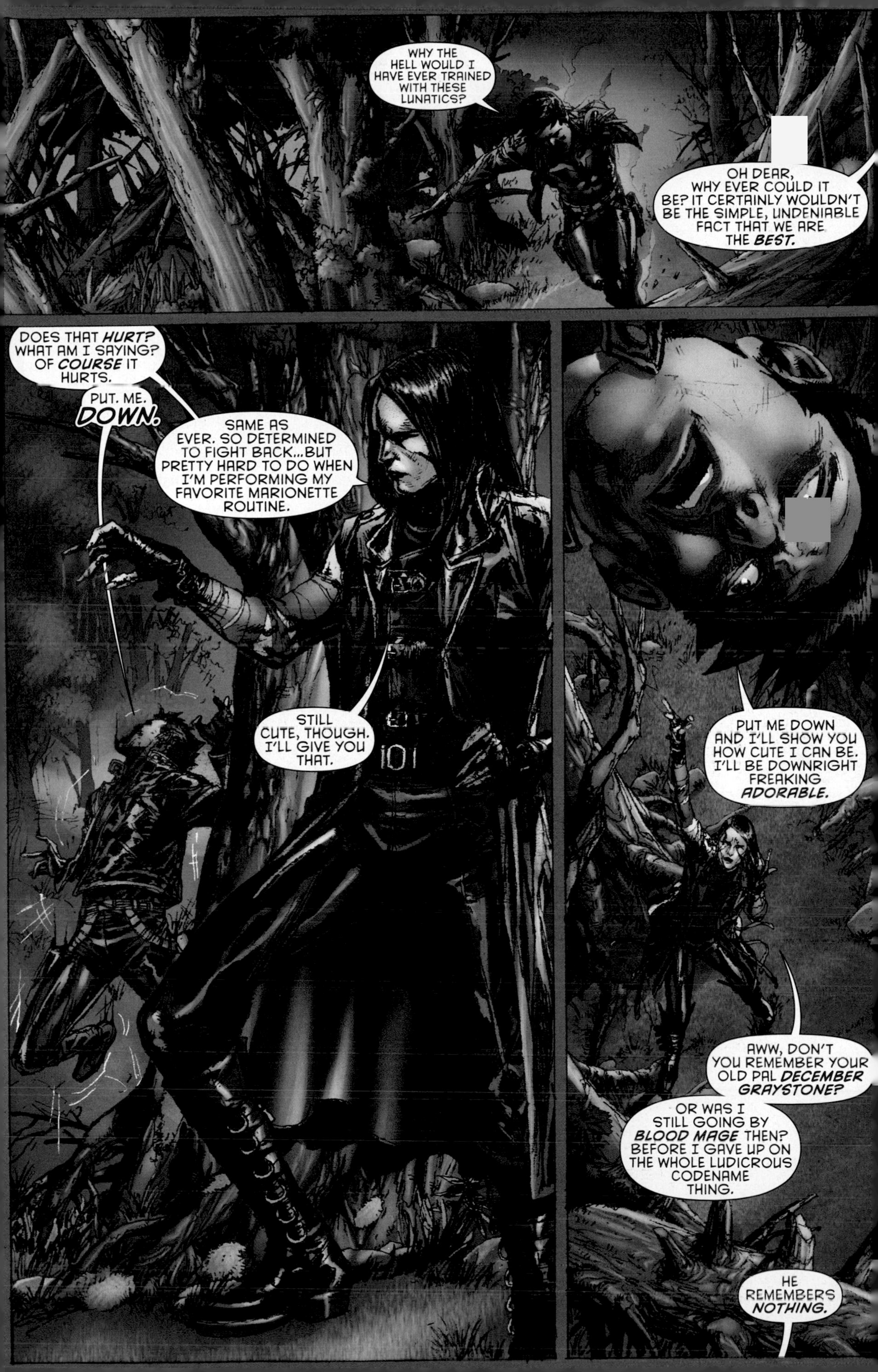
WHY THE HELL WOULD I HAVE EVER TRAINED WITH THESE LUNATICS?
OH DEAR, WHY EVER COULD IT BE? IT CERTAINLY WOULDN'T BE THE SIMPLE, UNDENIABLE FACT THAT WE ARE THE BEST.
DOES THAT HURT? WHAT AM I SAYING? OF COURSE IT HURTS.
PUT. ME. DOWN.
SAME AS EVER. SO DETERMINED TO FIGHT BACK...BUT PRETTY HARD TO DO WHEN I'M PERFORMING MY FAVORITE MARIONETTE ROUTINE.
STILL CUTE, THOUGH. I'LL GIVE YOU THAT.
PUT ME DOWN AND I'LL SHOW YOU HOW CUTE I CAN BE. I'LL BE DOWNRIGHT FREAKING ADORABLE.
AWW, DON'T YOU REMEMBER YOUR OLD PAL DECEMBER GRAYSTONE?
OR WAS I STILL GOING BY BLOOD MAGE THEN? BEFORE I GAVE UP ON THE WHOLE LUDICROUS CODENAME THING.
HE REMEMBERS NOTHING.

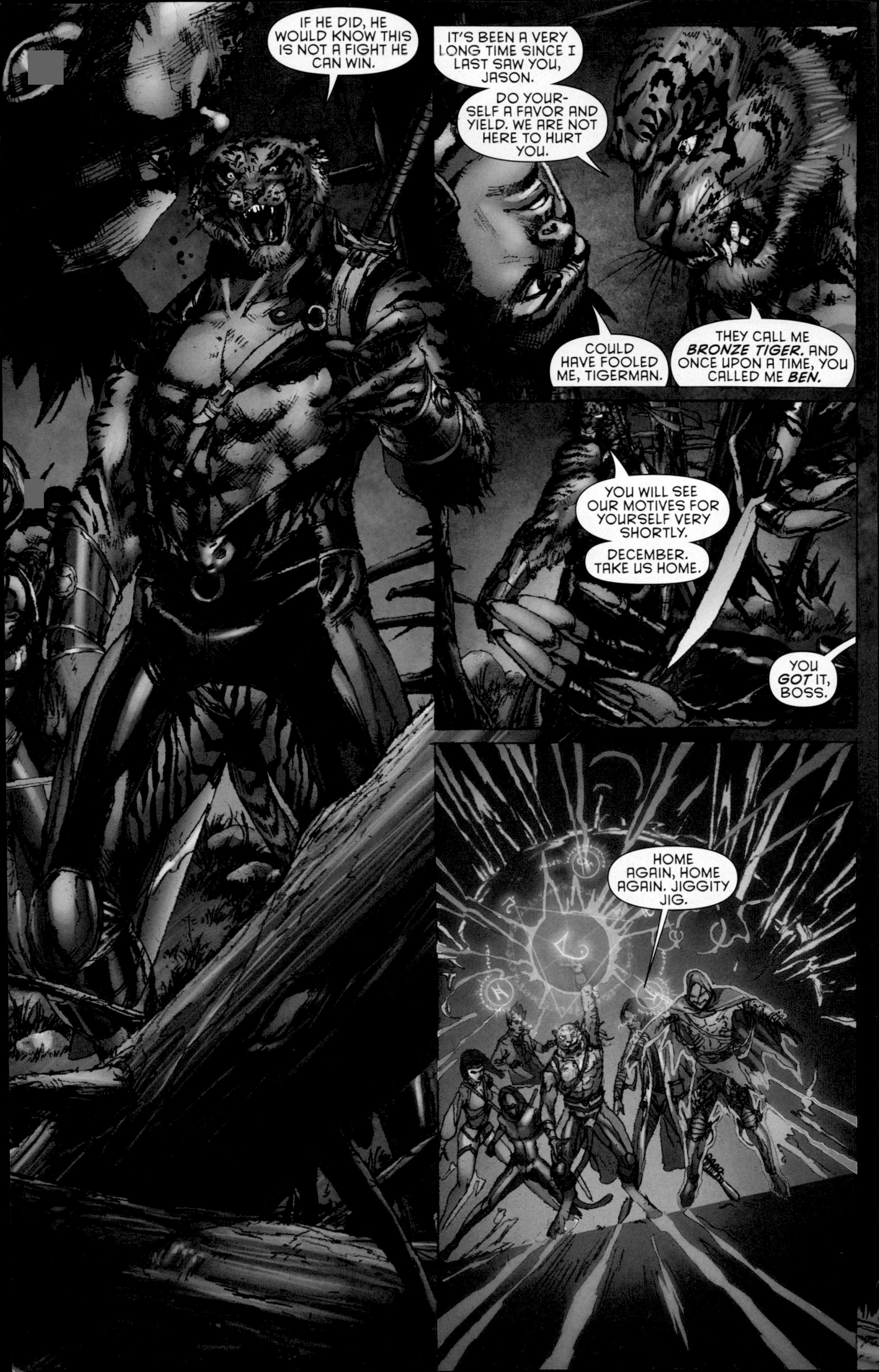
IF HE DID, HE WOULD KNOW THIS IS NOT A FIGHT HE CAN WIN.
IT'S BEEN A VERY LONG TIME SINCE I LAST SAW YOU, JASON.
DO YOUR-SELF A FAVOR AND YIELD. WE ARE NOT HERE TO HURT YOU.
COULD HAVE FOOLED ME, TIGERMAN.
THEY CALL ME ***BRONZE TIGER.*** AND ONCE UPON A TIME, YOU CALLED ME ***BEN.***
YOU WILL SEE OUR MOTIVES FOR YOURSELF VERY SHORTLY.
DECEMBER. TAKE US HOME.
YOU ***GOT*** IT, BOSS.
HOME AGAIN, HOME AGAIN. JIGGITY JIG.

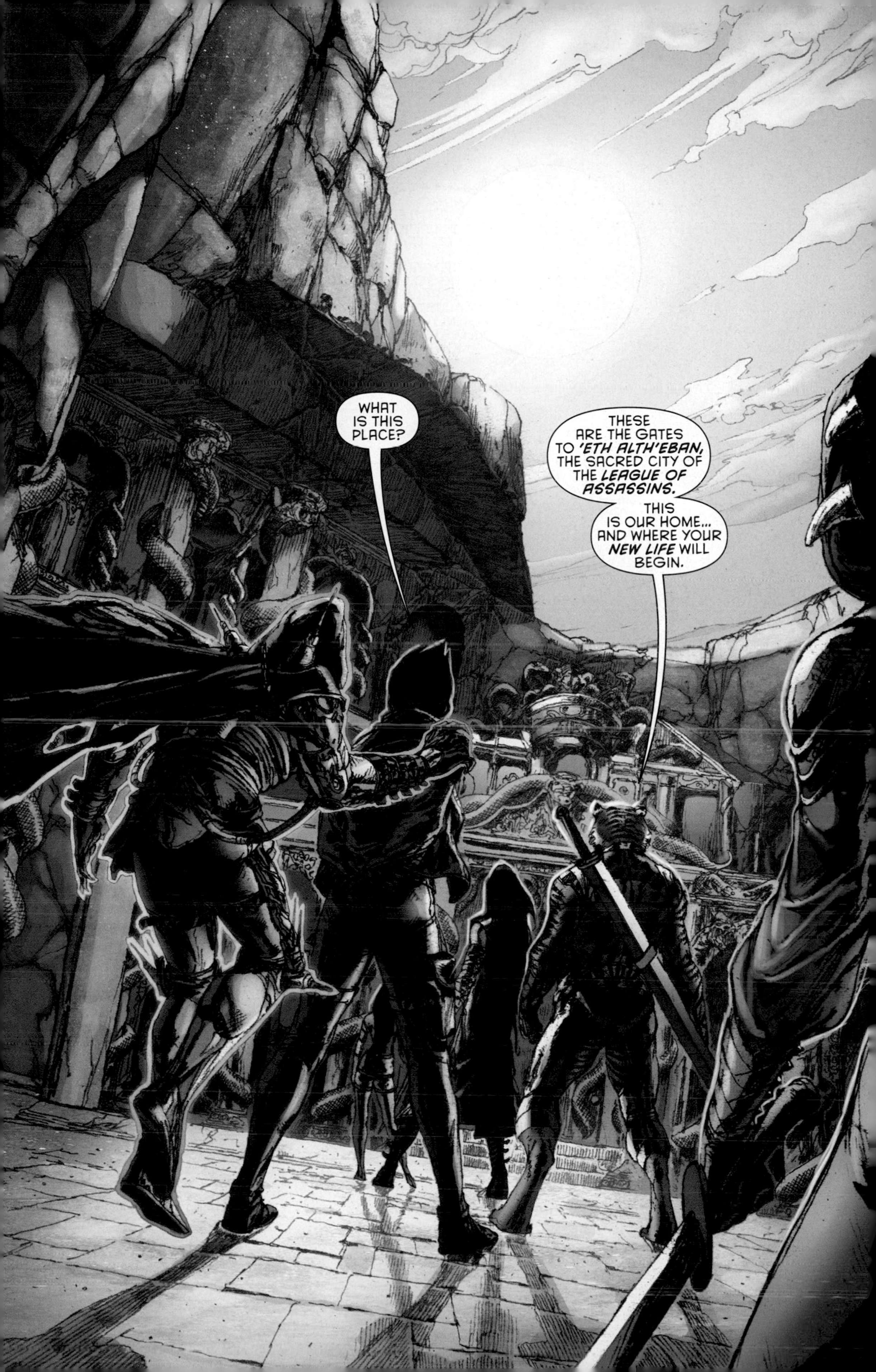
WHAT IS THIS PLACE?
THESE ARE THE GATES TO *'ETH ALTH'EBAN,* THE SACRED CITY OF THE *LEAGUE OF ASSASSINS.*
THIS IS OUR HOME... AND WHERE YOUR *NEW LIFE* WILL BEGIN.

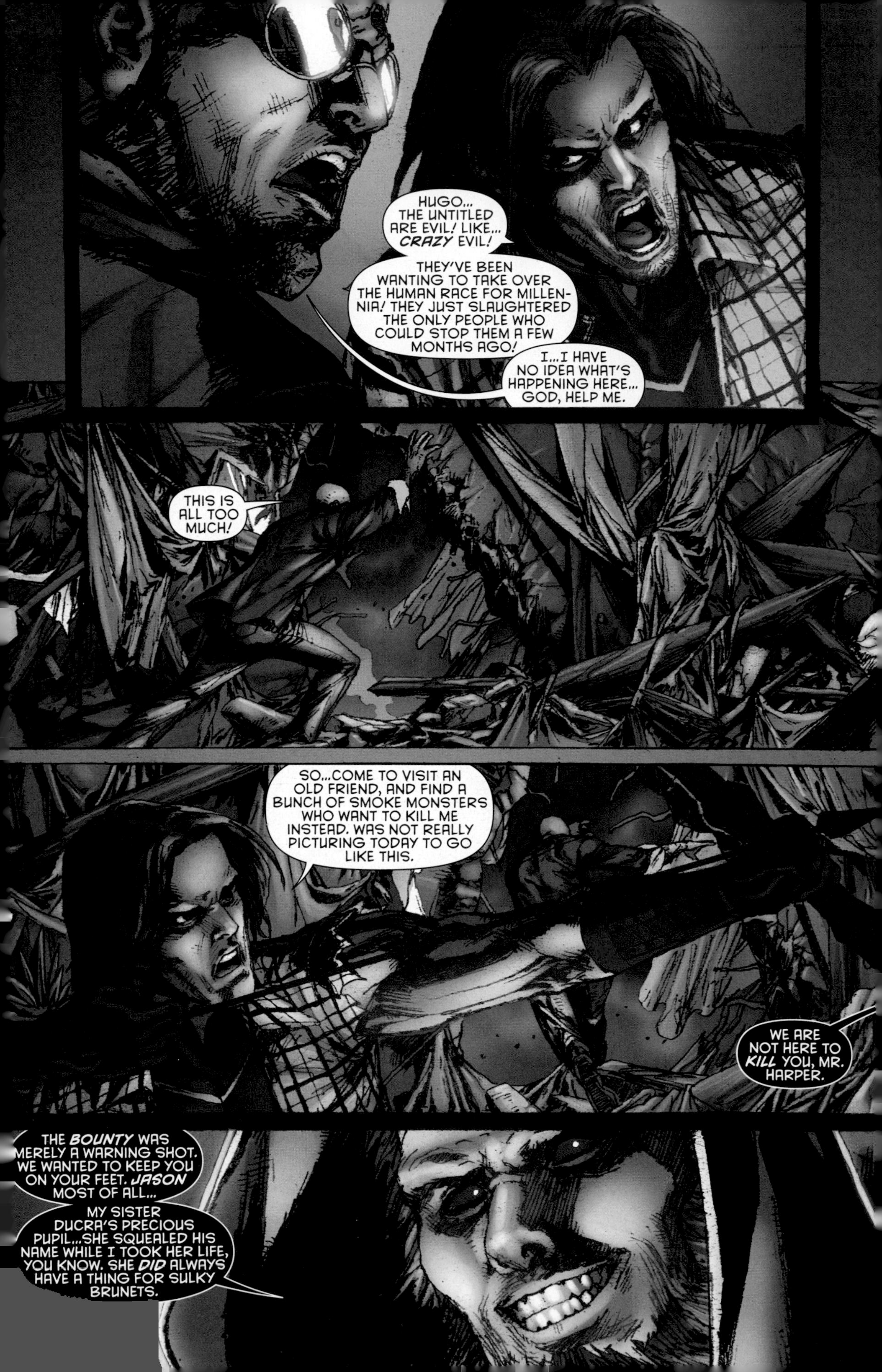
HUGO... THE UNTITLED ARE EVIL! LIKE... CRAZY EVIL!
THEY'VE BEEN WANTING TO TAKE OVER THE HUMAN RACE FOR MILLEN-NIA! THEY JUST SLAUGHTERED THE ONLY PEOPLE WHO COULD STOP THEM A FEW MONTHS AGO!
I...I HAVE NO IDEA WHAT'S HAPPENING HERE... GOD, HELP ME.
THIS IS ALL TOO MUCH!
SO...COME TO VISIT AN OLD FRIEND, AND FIND A BUNCH OF SMOKE MONSTERS WHO WANT TO KILL ME INSTEAD. WAS NOT REALLY PICTURING TODAY TO GO LIKE THIS.
WE ARE NOT HERE TO KILL YOU, MR. HARPER.
THE BOUNTY WAS MERELY A WARNING SHOT. WE WANTED TO KEEP YOU ON YOUR FEET. JASON MOST OF ALL...
MY SISTER DUCRA'S PRECIOUS PUPIL...SHE SQUEALED HIS NAME WHILE I TOOK HER LIFE, YOU KNOW. SHE DID ALWAYS HAVE A THING FOR SULKY BRUNETS.

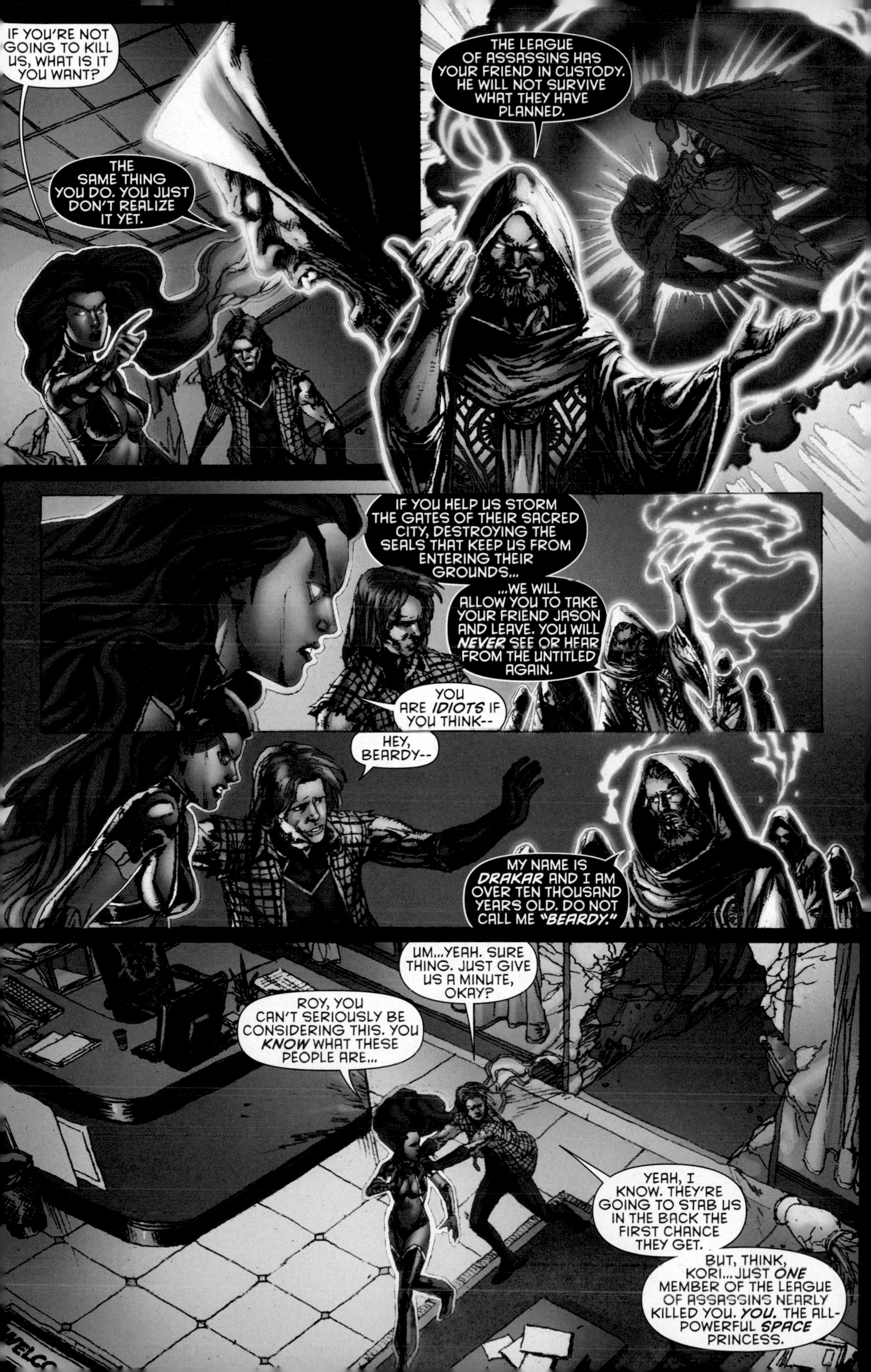
IF YOU'RE NOT GOING TO KILL US, WHAT IS IT YOU WANT?
THE SAME THING YOU DO. YOU JUST DON'T REALIZE IT YET.
THE LEAGUE OF ASSASSINS HAS YOUR FRIEND IN CUSTODY. HE WILL NOT SURVIVE WHAT THEY HAVE PLANNED.
IF YOU HELP US STORM THE GATES OF THEIR SACRED CITY, DESTROYING THE SEALS THAT KEEP US FROM ENTERING THEIR GROUNDS...
...WE WILL ALLOW YOU TO TAKE YOUR FRIEND JASON AND LEAVE. YOU WILL NEVER SEE OR HEAR FROM THE UNTITLED AGAIN.
YOU ARE IDIOTS IF YOU THINK--
HEY, BEARDY--
MY NAME IS DRAKAR AND I AM OVER TEN THOUSAND YEARS OLD. DO NOT CALL ME "BEARDY."
UM...YEAH. SURE THING. JUST GIVE US A MINUTE, OKAY?
ROY, YOU CAN'T SERIOUSLY BE CONSIDERING THIS. YOU KNOW WHAT THESE PEOPLE ARE...
YEAH, I KNOW. THEY'RE GOING TO STAB US IN THE BACK THE FIRST CHANCE THEY GET.
BUT, THINK, KORI...JUST ONE MEMBER OF THE LEAGUE OF ASSASSINS NEARLY KILLED YOU. YOU. THE ALL-POWERFUL SPACE PRINCESS.

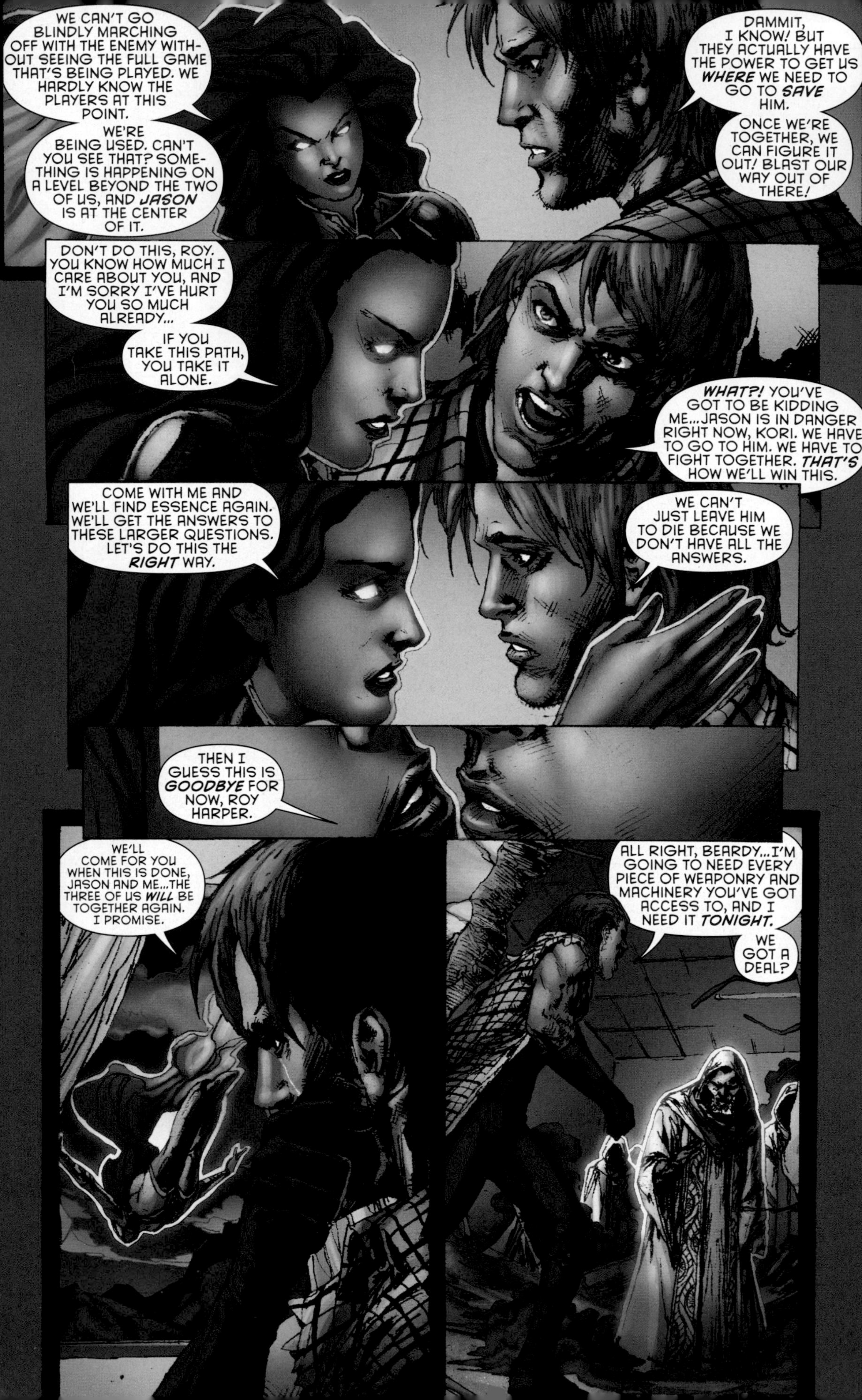
WE CAN'T GO BLINDLY MARCHING OFF WITH THE ENEMY WITH-OUT SEEING THE FULL GAME THAT'S BEING PLAYED. WE HARDLY KNOW THE PLAYERS AT THIS POINT.
WE'RE BEING USED. CAN'T YOU SEE THAT? SOME-THING IS HAPPENING ON A LEVEL BEYOND THE TWO OF US, AND JASON IS AT THE CENTER OF IT.
DAMMIT, I KNOW! BUT THEY ACTUALLY HAVE THE POWER TO GET US WHERE WE NEED TO GO TO SAVE HIM.
ONCE WE'RE TOGETHER, WE CAN FIGURE IT OUT! BLAST OUR WAY OUT OF THERE!
DON'T DO THIS, ROY. YOU KNOW HOW MUCH I CARE ABOUT YOU, AND I'M SORRY I'VE HURT YOU SO MUCH ALREADY...
IF YOU TAKE THIS PATH, YOU TAKE IT ALONE.
WHAT?! YOU'VE GOT TO BE KIDDING ME...JASON IS IN DANGER RIGHT NOW, KORI. WE HAVE TO GO TO HIM. WE HAVE TO FIGHT TOGETHER. THAT'S HOW WE'LL WIN THIS.
COME WITH ME AND WE'LL FIND ESSENCE AGAIN. WE'LL GET THE ANSWERS TO THESE LARGER QUESTIONS. LET'S DO THIS THE RIGHT WAY.
WE CAN'T JUST LEAVE HIM TO DIE BECAUSE WE DON'T HAVE ALL THE ANSWERS.
THEN I GUESS THIS IS GOODBYE FOR NOW, ROY HARPER.
WE'LL COME FOR YOU WHEN THIS IS DONE, JASON AND ME...THE THREE OF US WILL BE TOGETHER AGAIN. I PROMISE.
ALL RIGHT, BEARDY...I'M GOING TO NEED EVERY PIECE OF WEAPONRY AND MACHINERY YOU'VE GOT ACCESS TO, AND I NEED IT TONIGHT.
WE GOT A DEAL?

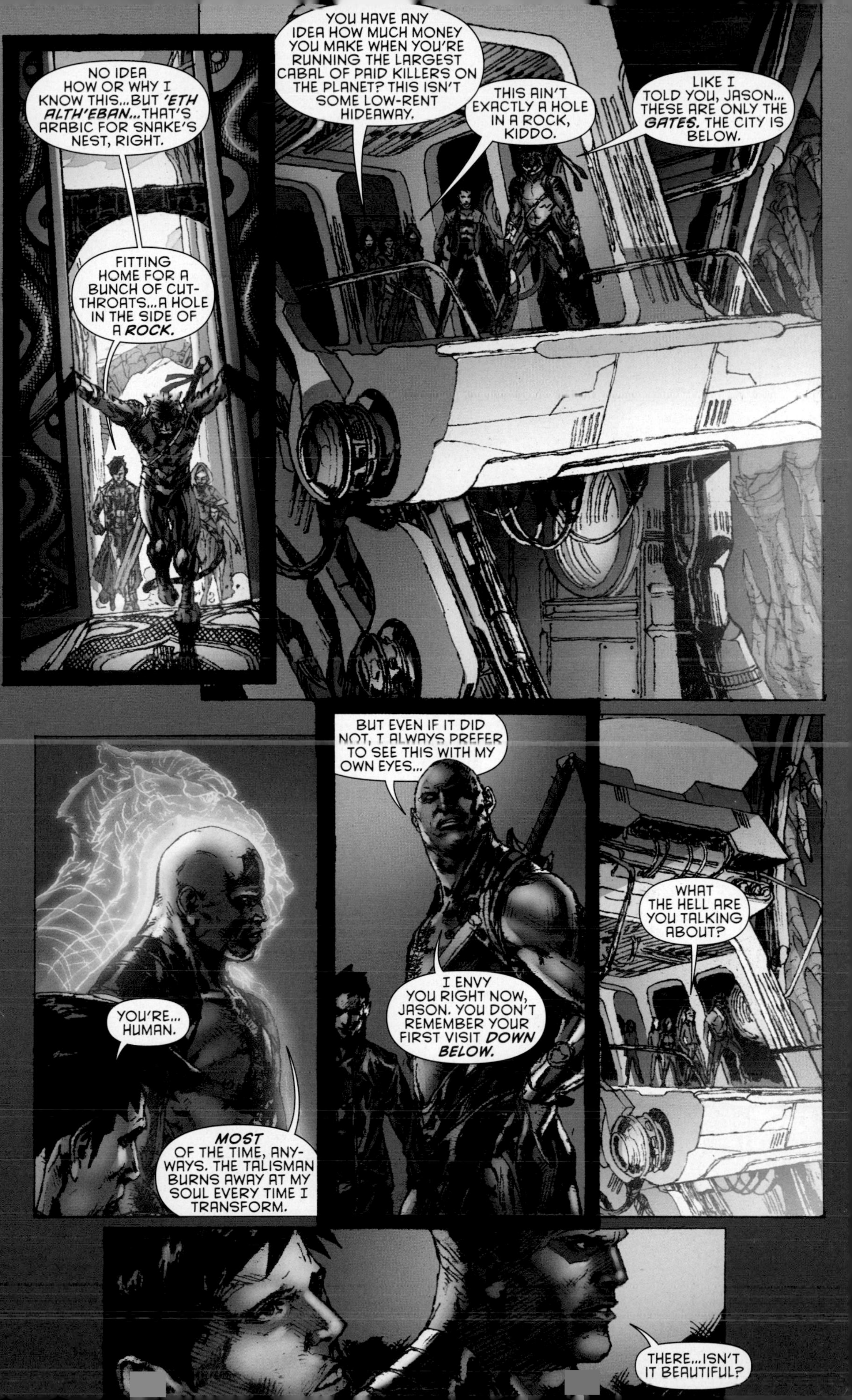
NO IDEA HOW OR WHY I KNOW THIS...BUT 'ETH ALTH'EBAN...THAT'S ARABIC FOR SNAKE'S NEST, RIGHT.
FITTING HOME FOR A BUNCH OF CUT-THROATS...A HOLE IN THE SIDE OF A ROCK.
YOU HAVE ANY IDEA HOW MUCH MONEY YOU MAKE WHEN YOU'RE RUNNING THE LARGEST CABAL OF PAID KILLERS ON THE PLANET? THIS ISN'T SOME LOW-RENT HIDEAWAY.
THIS AIN'T EXACTLY A HOLE IN A ROCK, KIDDO.
LIKE I TOLD YOU, JASON... THESE ARE ONLY THE GATES. THE CITY IS BELOW.
YOU'RE... HUMAN.
MOST OF THE TIME, ANY-WAYS. THE TALISMAN BURNS AWAY AT MY SOUL EVERY TIME I TRANSFORM.
BUT EVEN IF IT DID NOT, I ALWAYS PREFER TO SEE THIS WITH MY OWN EYES...
I ENVY YOU RIGHT NOW, JASON. YOU DON'T REMEMBER YOUR FIRST VISIT DOWN BELOW.
WHAT THE HELL ARE YOU TALKING ABOUT?
THERE...ISN'T IT BEAUTIFUL?

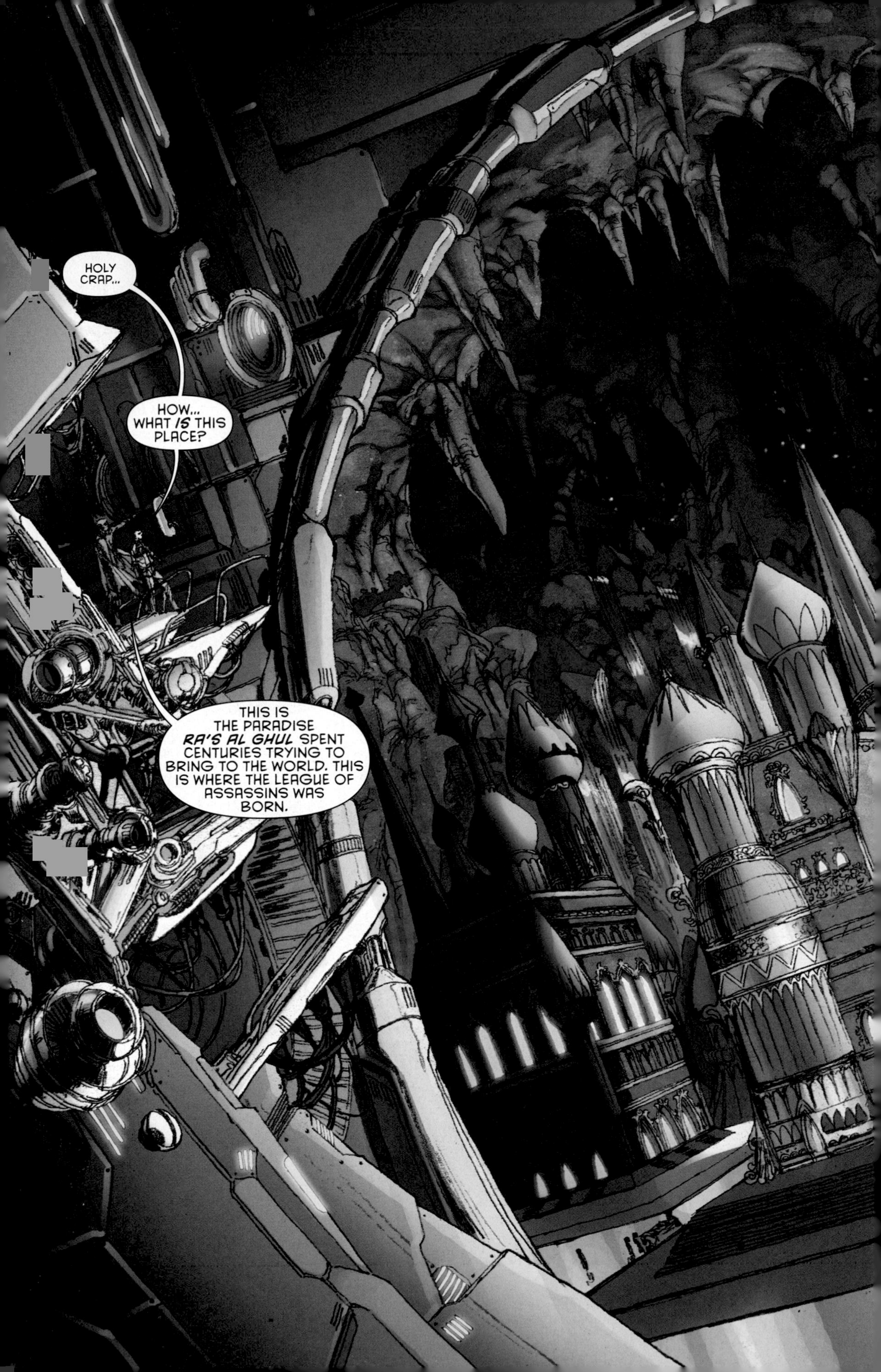
HOLY CRAP...
HOW... WHAT *IS* THIS PLACE?
THIS IS THE PARADISE ***RA'S AL GHUL*** SPENT CENTURIES TRYING TO BRING TO THE WORLD. THIS IS WHERE THE LEAGUE OF ASSASSINS WAS BORN.

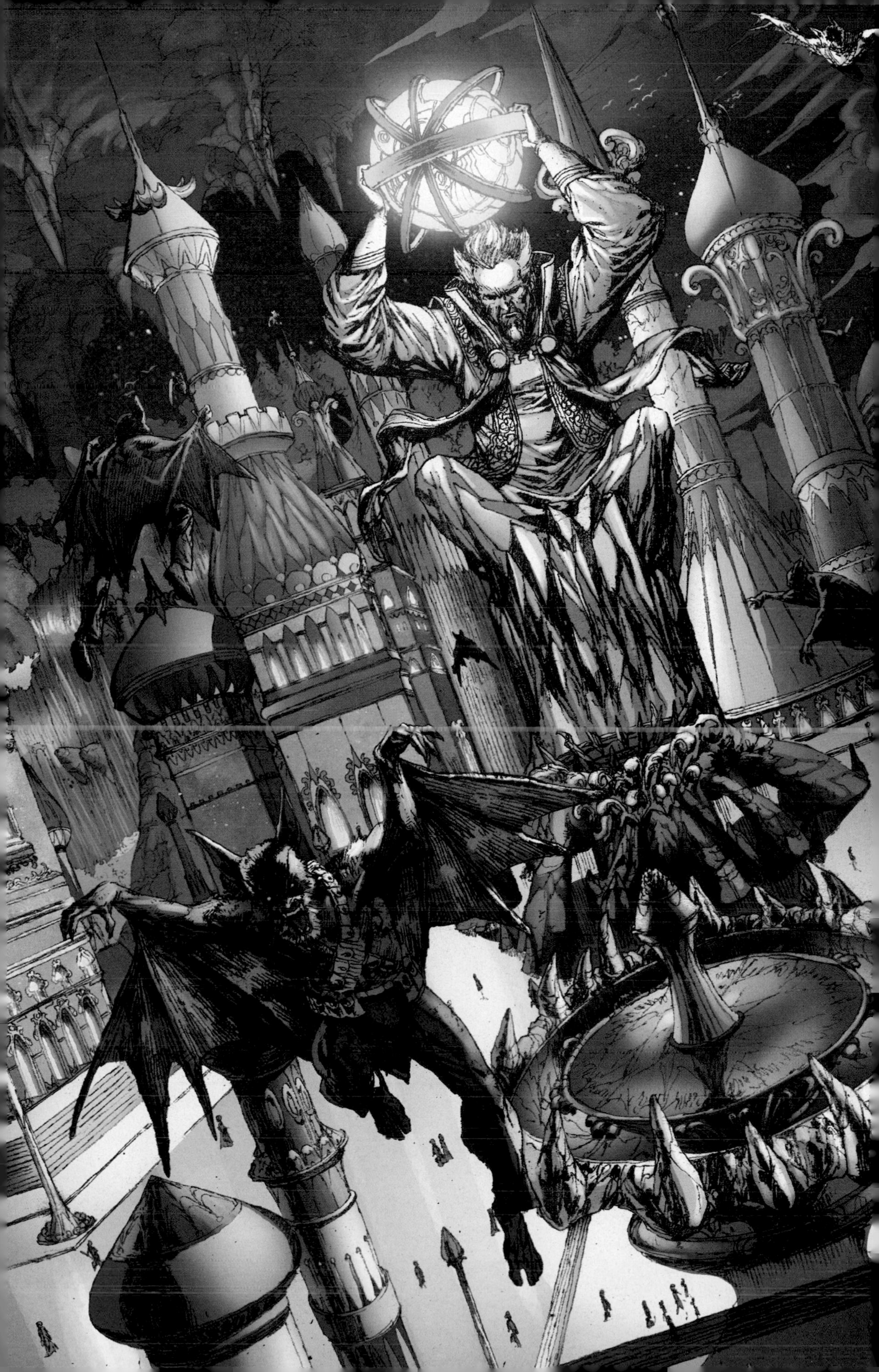

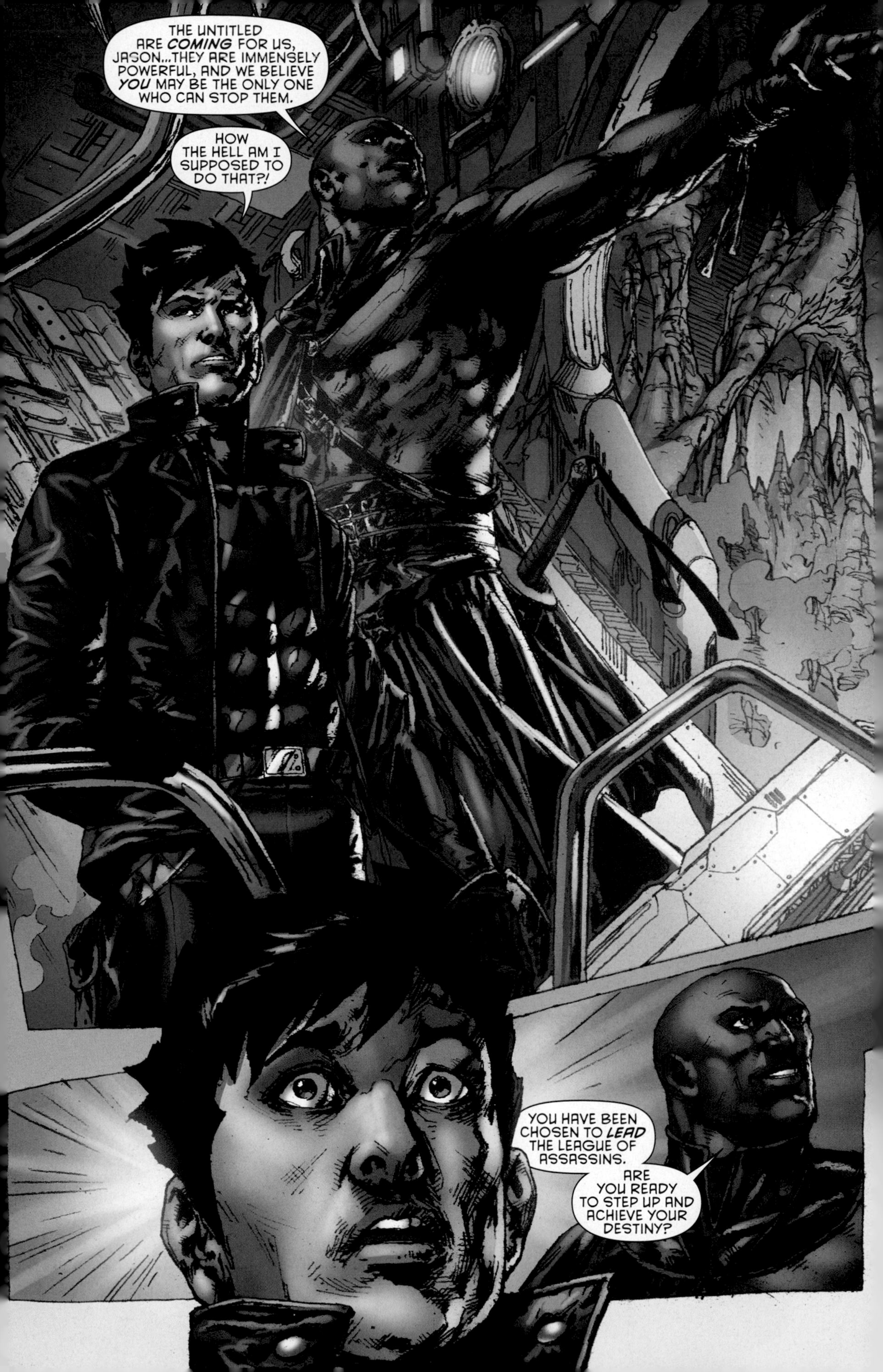
THE UNTITLED ARE COMING FOR US, JASON...THEY ARE IMMENSELY POWERFUL, AND WE BELIEVE YOU MAY BE THE ONLY ONE WHO CAN STOP THEM.
HOW THE HELL AM I SUPPOSED TO DO THAT?!
YOU HAVE BEEN CHOSEN TO LEAD THE LEAGUE OF ASSASSINS.
ARE YOU READY TO STEP UP AND ACHIEVE YOUR DESTINY?

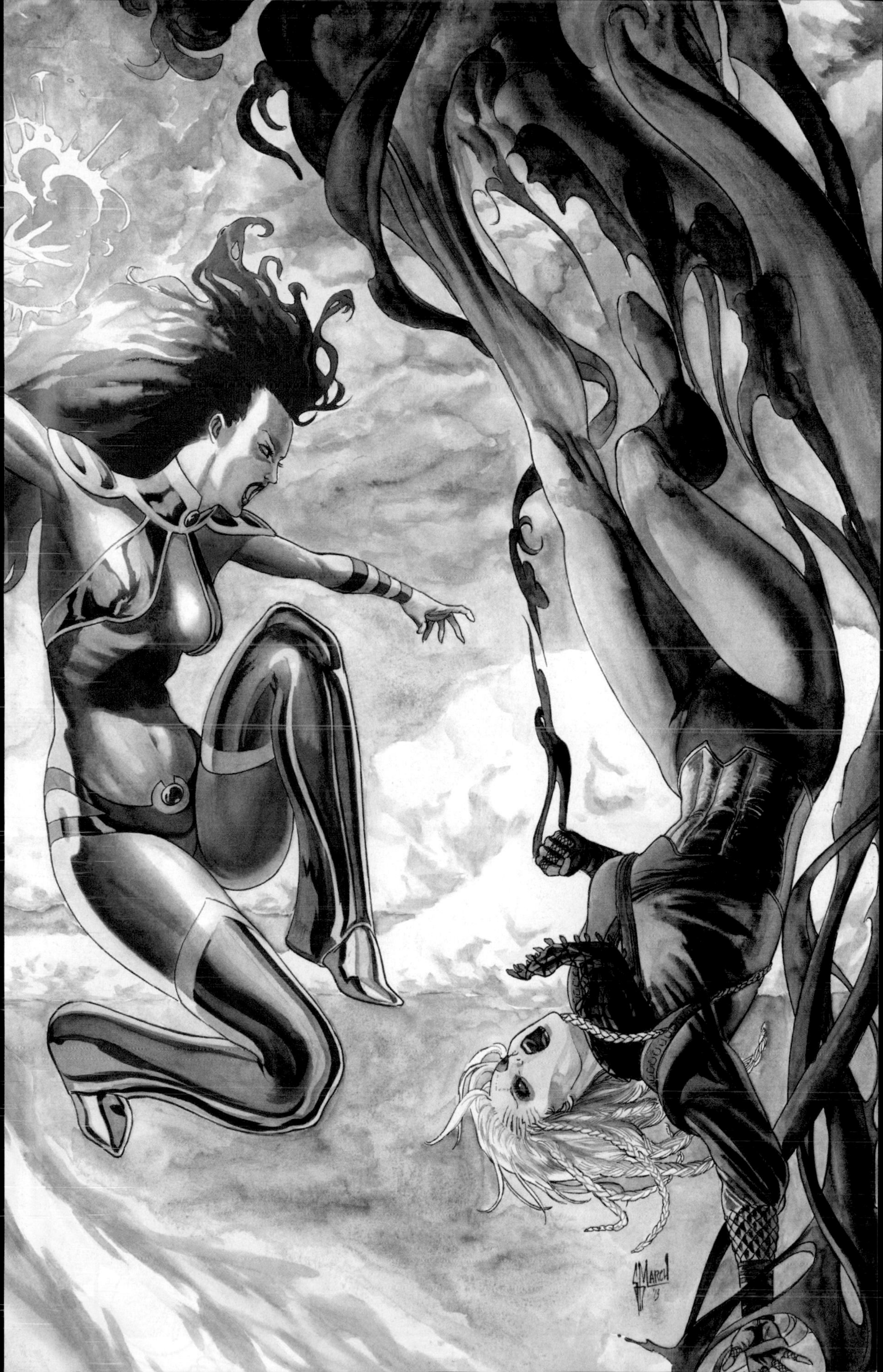

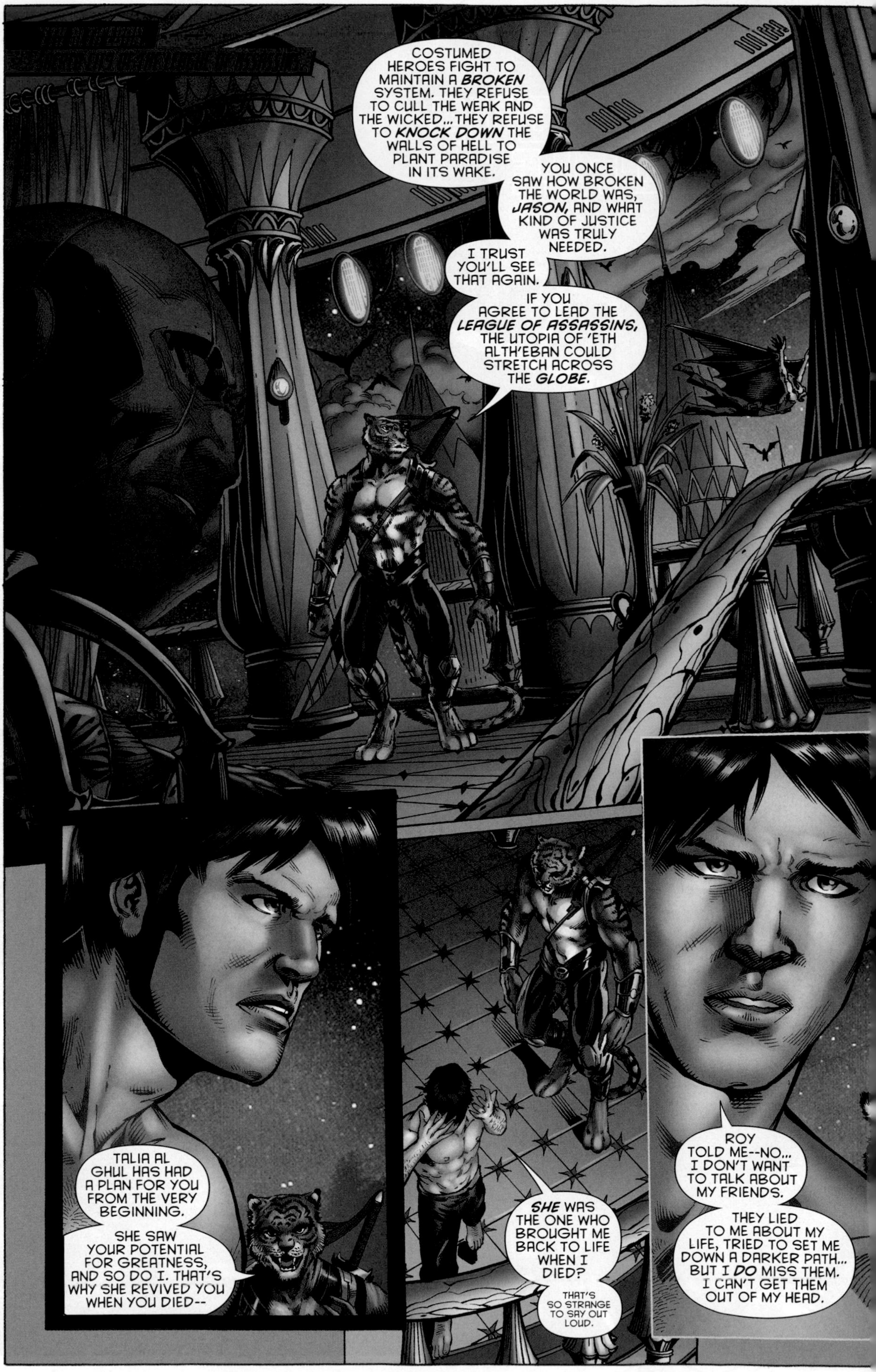
COSTUMED HEROES FIGHT TO MAINTAIN A BROKEN SYSTEM. THEY REFUSE TO CULL THE WEAK AND THE WICKED... THEY REFUSE TO KNOCK DOWN THE WALLS OF HELL TO PLANT PARADISE IN ITS WAKE.
YOU ONCE SAW HOW BROKEN THE WORLD WAS, JASON, AND WHAT KIND OF JUSTICE WAS TRULY NEEDED.
I TRUST YOU'LL SEE THAT AGAIN.
IF YOU AGREE TO LEAD THE LEAGUE OF ASSASSINS, THE UTOPIA OF 'ETH ALTH'EBAN COULD STRETCH ACROSS THE GLOBE.
TALIA AL GHUL HAS HAD A PLAN FOR YOU FROM THE VERY BEGINNING.
SHE SAW YOUR POTENTIAL FOR GREATNESS, AND SO DO I. THAT'S WHY SHE REVIVED YOU WHEN YOU DIED--
SHE WAS THE ONE WHO BROUGHT ME BACK TO LIFE WHEN I DIED?
THAT'S SO STRANGE TO SAY OUT LOUD.
ROY TOLD ME--NO... I DON'T WANT TO TALK ABOUT MY FRIENDS.
THEY LIED TO ME ABOUT MY LIFE, TRIED TO SET ME DOWN A DARKER PATH... BUT I DO MISS THEM. I CAN'T GET THEM OUT OF MY HEAD.

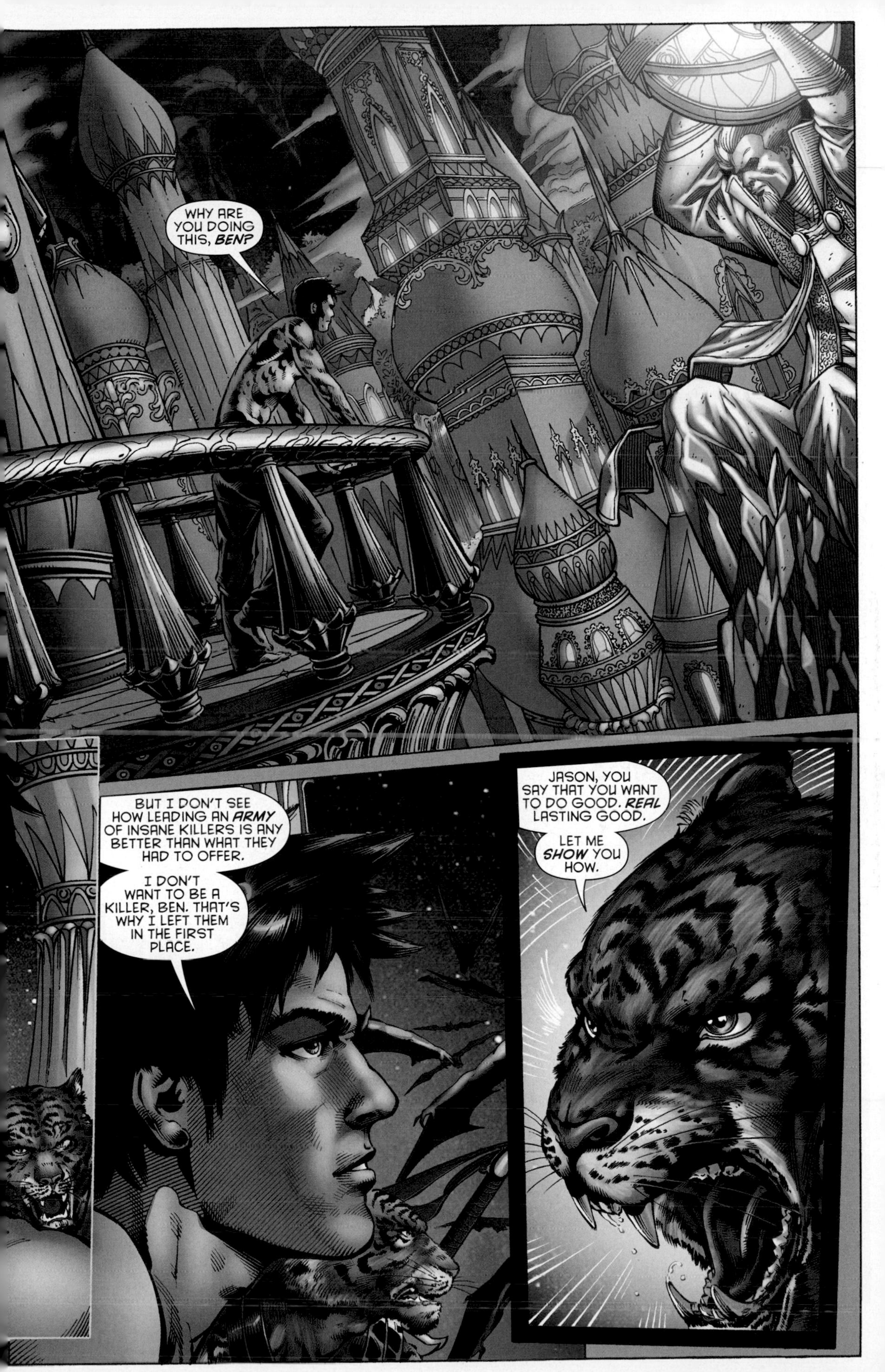
WHY ARE YOU DOING THIS, BEN?
BUT I DON'T SEE HOW LEADING AN ARMY OF INSANE KILLERS IS ANY BETTER THAN WHAT THEY HAD TO OFFER.
I DON'T WANT TO BE A KILLER, BEN. THAT'S WHY I LEFT THEM IN THE FIRST PLACE.
JASON, YOU SAY THAT YOU WANT TO DO GOOD. REAL LASTING GOOD.
LET ME SHOW YOU HOW.

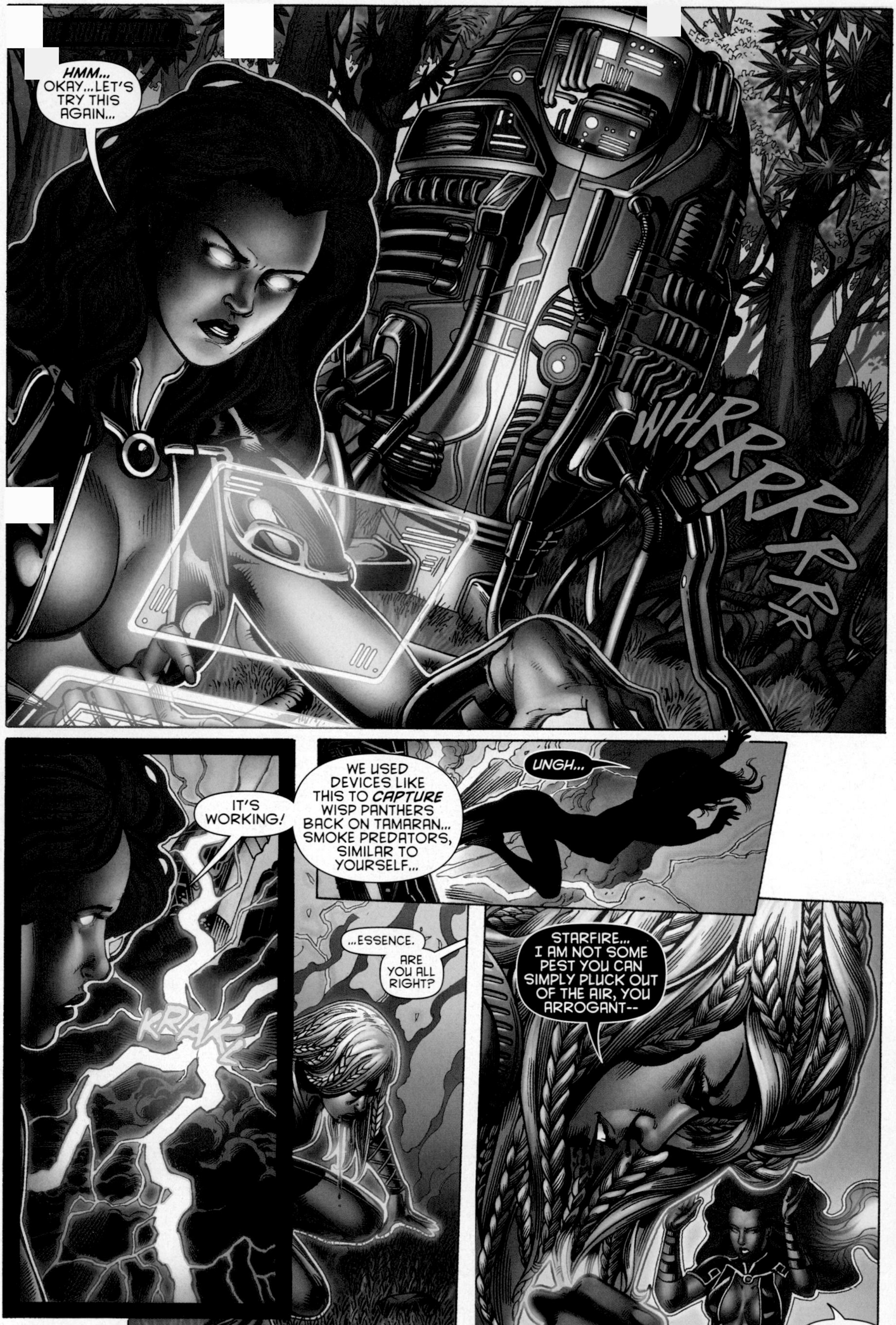
HMM... OKAY...LET'S TRY THIS AGAIN...
WHRRRRRRR
IT'S WORKING!
WE USED DEVICES LIKE THIS TO CAPTURE WISP PANTHERS BACK ON TAMARAN... SMOKE PREDATORS, SIMILAR TO YOURSELF...
UNGH...
KRAK
...ESSENCE.
ARE YOU ALL RIGHT?
STARFIRE... I AM NOT SOME PEST YOU CAN SIMPLY PLUCK OUT OF THE AIR, YOU ARROGANT--
WAIT! LISTEN--

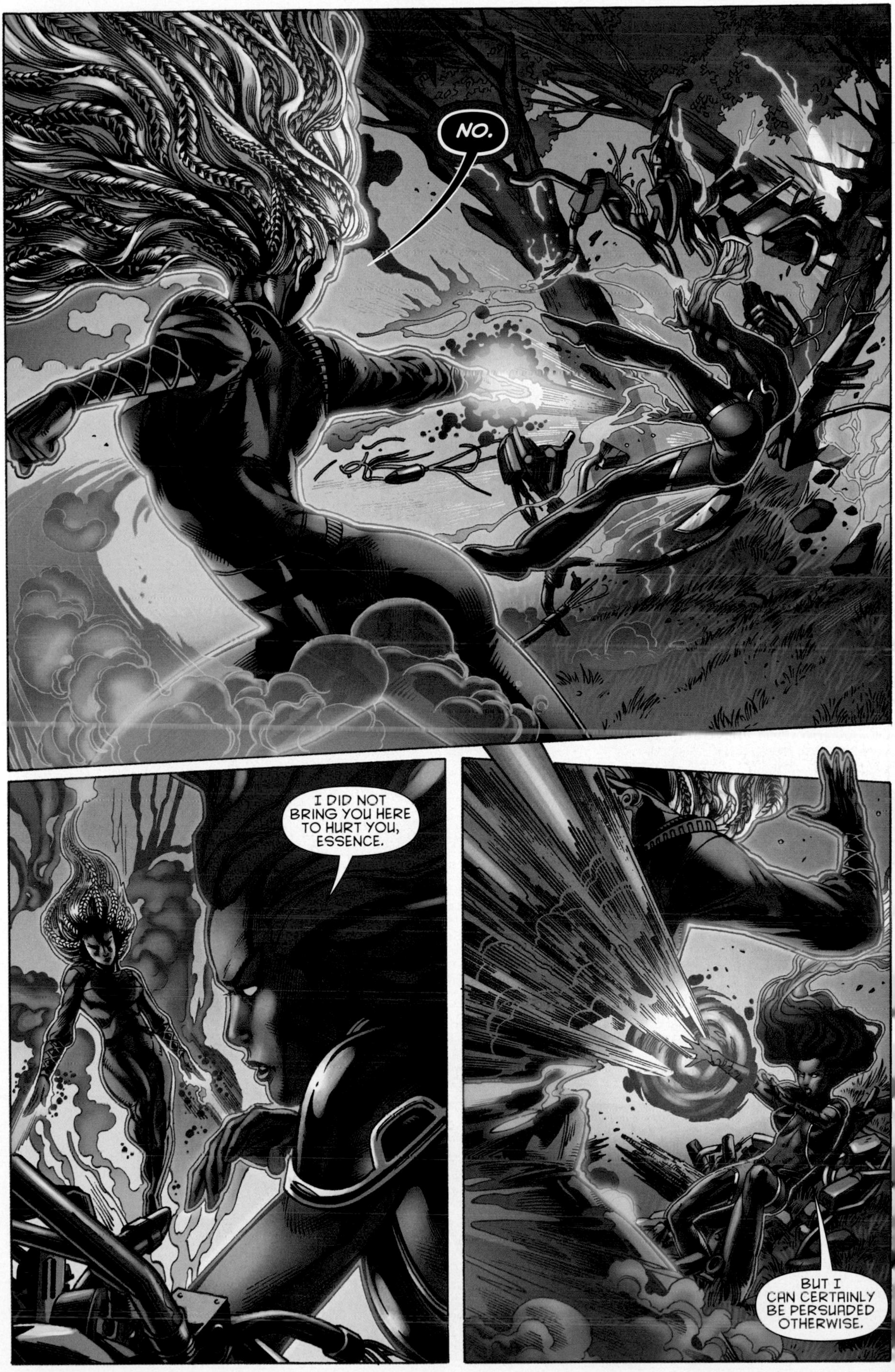
NO.
I DID NOT BRING YOU HERE TO HURT YOU, ESSENCE.
BUT I CAN CERTAINLY BE PERSUADED OTHERWISE.

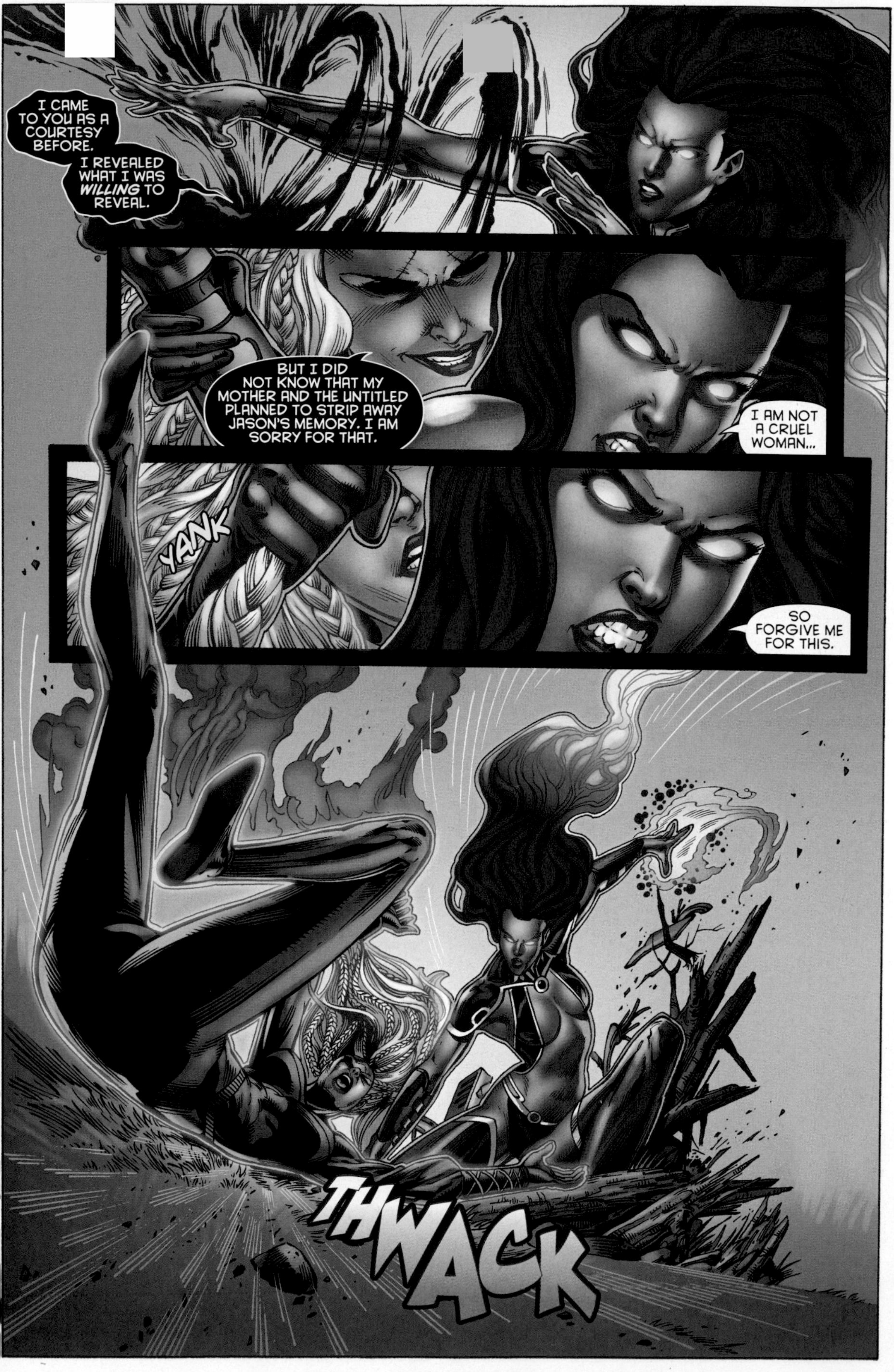
I CAME TO YOU AS A COURTESY BEFORE.
I REVEALED WHAT I WAS *WILLING* TO REVEAL.
BUT I DID NOT KNOW THAT MY MOTHER AND THE UNTITLED PLANNED TO STRIP AWAY JASON'S MEMORY. I AM SORRY FOR THAT.
I AM NOT A CRUEL WOMAN...
YANK
SO FORGIVE ME FOR THIS.
THWACK

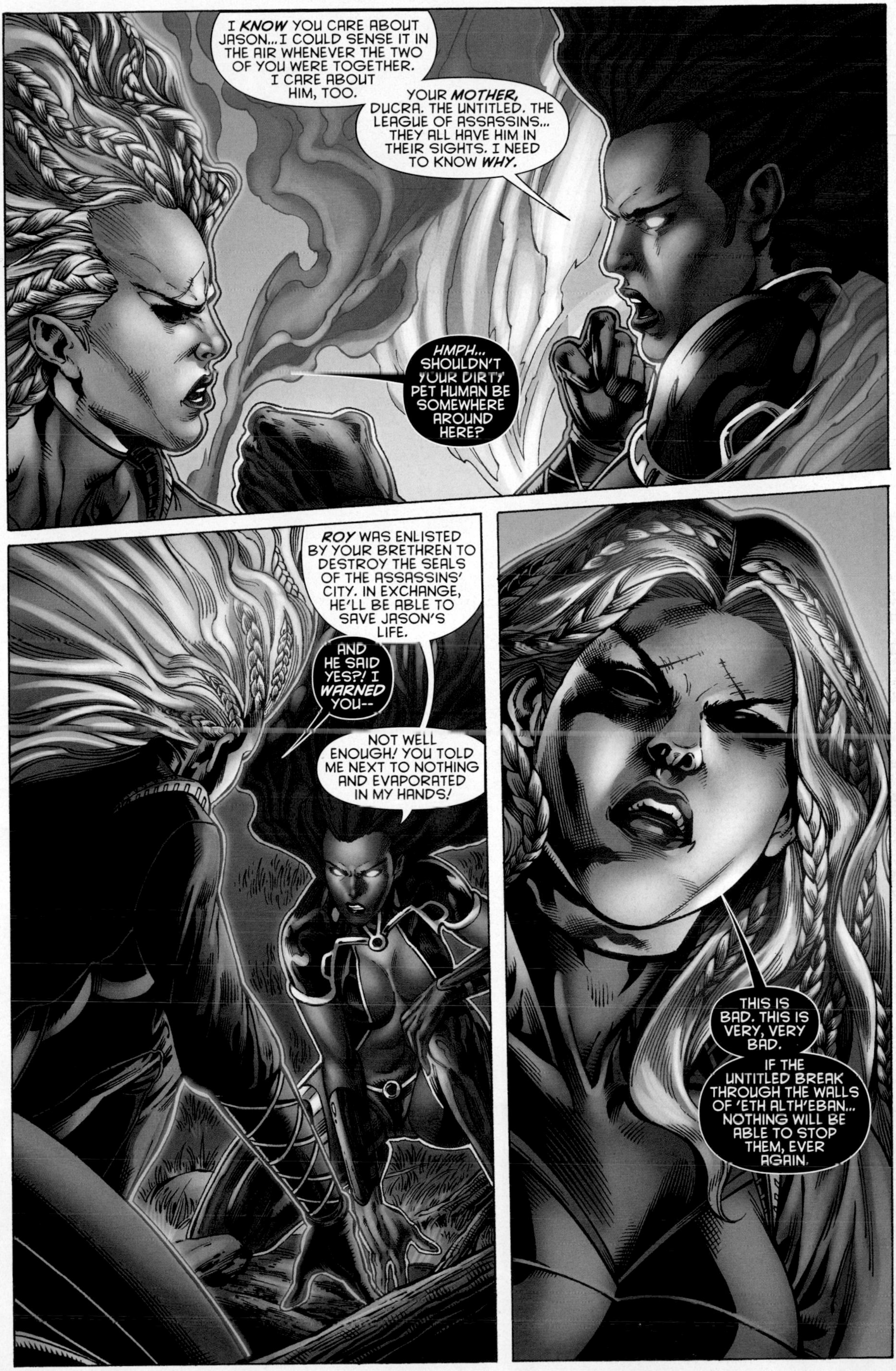
I KNOW YOU CARE ABOUT JASON... I COULD SENSE IT IN THE AIR WHENEVER THE TWO OF YOU WERE TOGETHER. I CARE ABOUT HIM, TOO.
YOUR MOTHER, DUCRA. THE UNTITLED. THE LEAGUE OF ASSASSINS... THEY ALL HAVE HIM IN THEIR SIGHTS. I NEED TO KNOW WHY.
HMPH... SHOULDN'T YOUR DIRTY PET HUMAN BE SOMEWHERE AROUND HERE?
ROY WAS ENLISTED BY YOUR BRETHREN TO DESTROY THE SEALS OF THE ASSASSINS' CITY. IN EXCHANGE, HE'LL BE ABLE TO SAVE JASON'S LIFE.
AND HE SAID YES?! I WARNED YOU--
NOT WELL ENOUGH! YOU TOLD ME NEXT TO NOTHING AND EVAPORATED IN MY HANDS!
THIS IS BAD. THIS IS VERY, VERY BAD.
IF THE UNTITLED BREAK THROUGH THE WALLS OF 'ETH ALTH'EBAN... NOTHING WILL BE ABLE TO STOP THEM, EVER AGAIN.

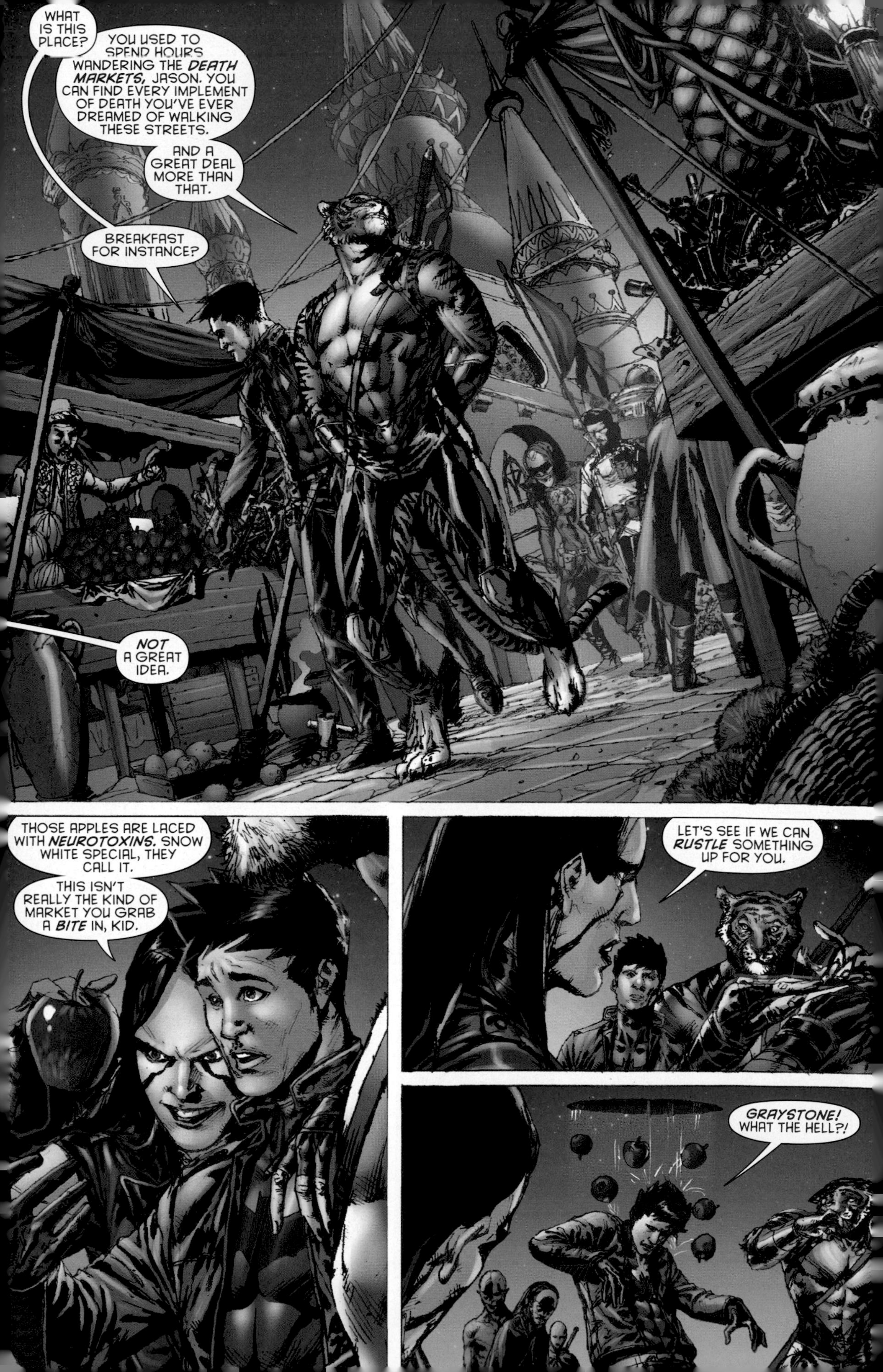
WHAT IS THIS PLACE?
YOU USED TO SPEND HOURS WANDERING THE *DEATH MARKETS,* JASON. YOU CAN FIND EVERY IMPLEMENT OF DEATH YOU'VE EVER DREAMED OF WALKING THESE STREETS.
AND A GREAT DEAL MORE THAN THAT.
BREAKFAST FOR INSTANCE?
NOT A GREAT IDEA.
THOSE APPLES ARE LACED WITH *NEUROTOXINS.* SNOW WHITE SPECIAL, THEY CALL IT.
THIS ISN'T REALLY THE KIND OF MARKET YOU GRAB A *BITE* IN, KID.
LET'S SEE IF WE CAN *RUSTLE* SOMETHING UP FOR YOU.
GRAYSTONE! WHAT THE HELL?!

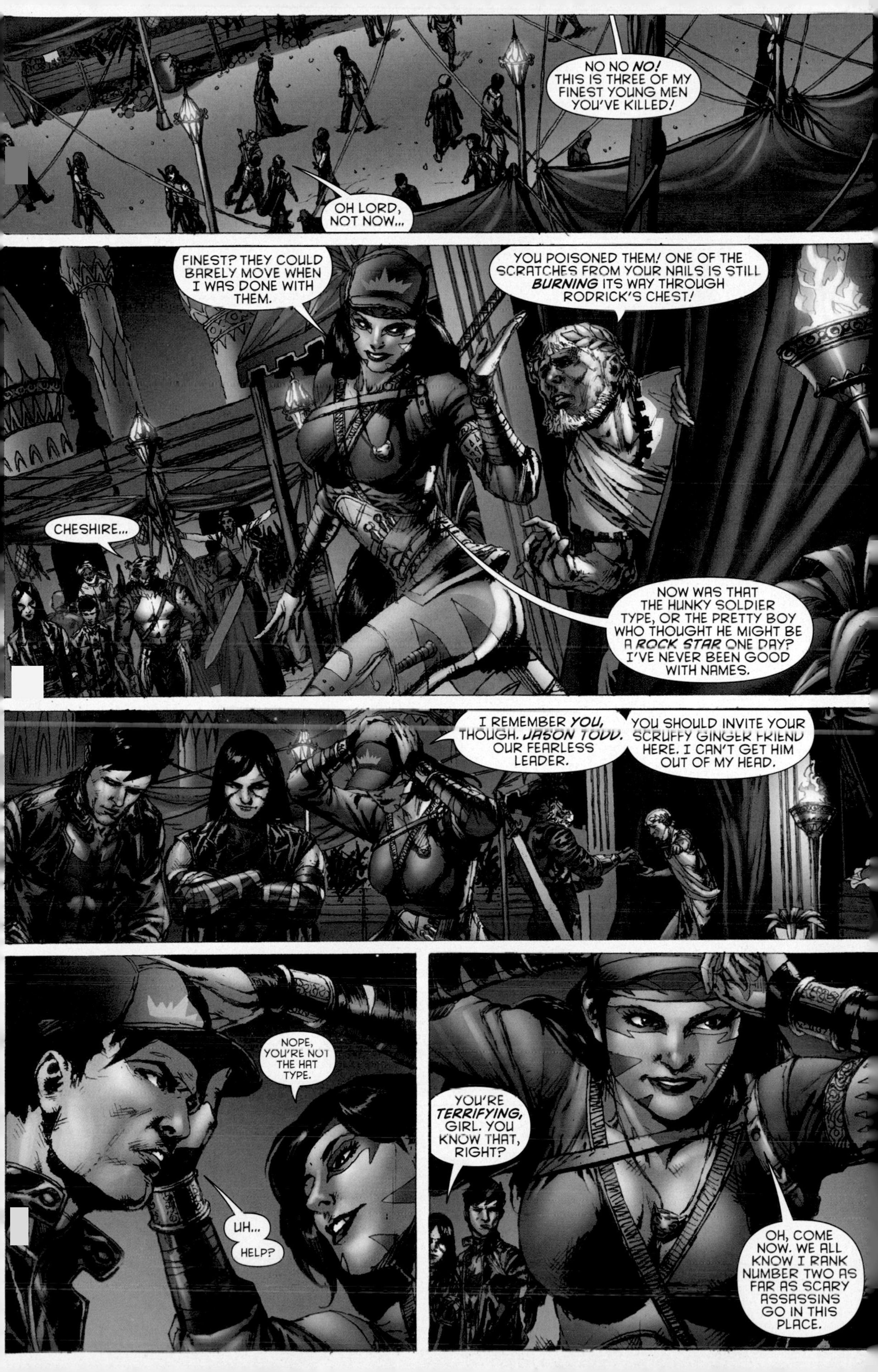
NO NO *NO!* THIS IS THREE OF MY FINEST YOUNG MEN YOU'VE KILLED!
OH LORD, NOT NOW...
FINEST? THEY COULD BARELY MOVE WHEN I WAS DONE WITH THEM.
YOU POISONED THEM! ONE OF THE SCRATCHES FROM YOUR NAILS IS STILL *BURNING* ITS WAY THROUGH RODRICK'S CHEST!
CHESHIRE...
NOW WAS THAT THE HUNKY SOLDIER TYPE, OR THE PRETTY BOY WHO THOUGHT HE MIGHT BE A *ROCK STAR* ONE DAY? I'VE NEVER BEEN GOOD WITH NAMES.
I REMEMBER *YOU,* THOUGH. *JASON TODD.* OUR FEARLESS LEADER.
YOU SHOULD INVITE YOUR SCRUFFY GINGER FRIEND HERE. I CAN'T GET HIM OUT OF MY HEAD.
NOPE, YOU'RE NOT THE HAT TYPE.
UH...
HELP?
YOU'RE *TERRIFYING,* GIRL. YOU KNOW THAT, RIGHT?
OH, COME NOW. WE ALL KNOW I RANK NUMBER TWO AS FAR AS SCARY ASSASSINS GO IN THIS PLACE.

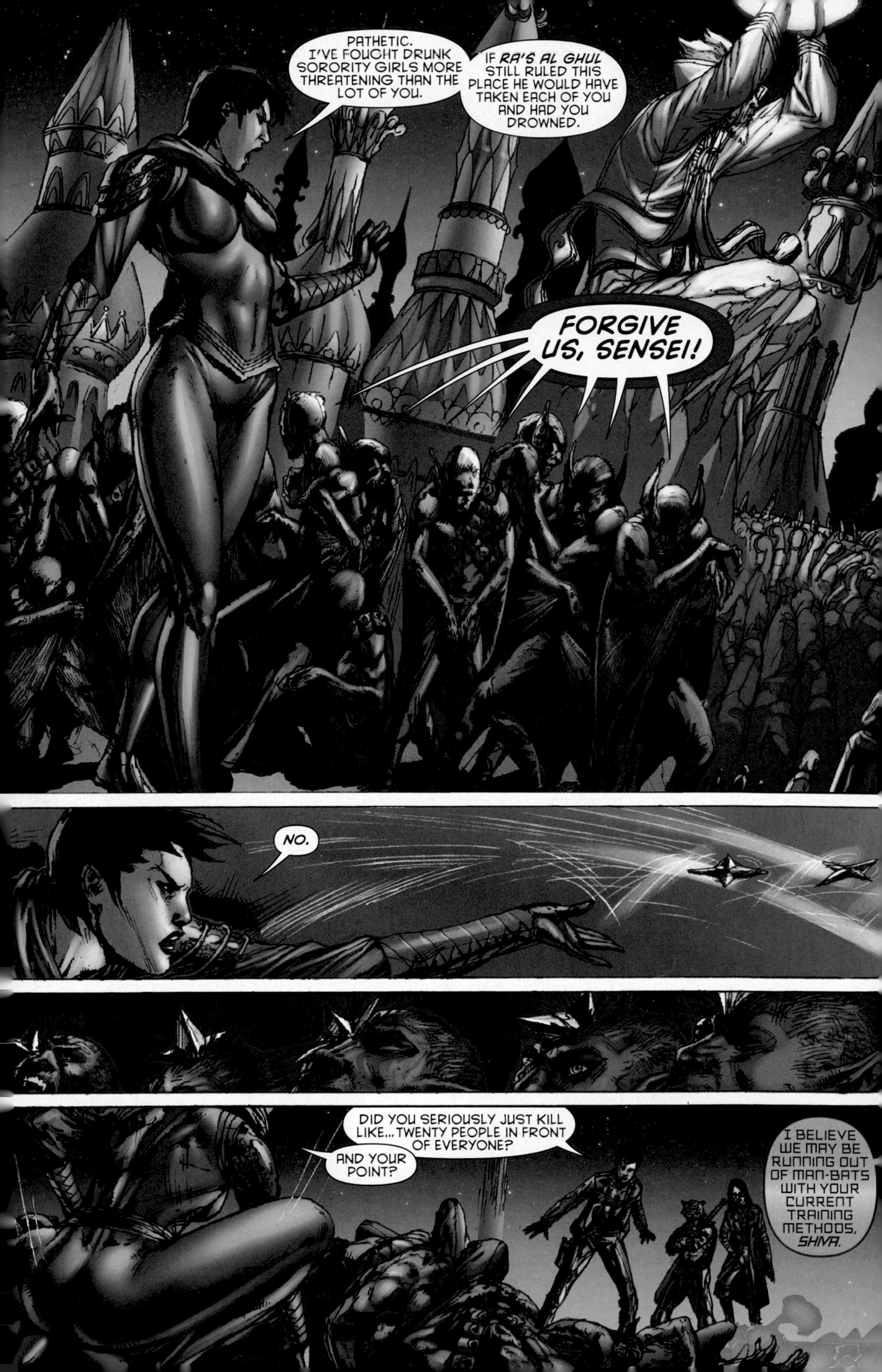
PATHETIC. I'VE FOUGHT DRUNK SORORITY GIRLS MORE THREATENING THAN THE LOT OF YOU.
IF RA'S AL GHUL STILL RULED THIS PLACE HE WOULD HAVE TAKEN EACH OF YOU AND HAD YOU DROWNED.
FORGIVE US, SENSEI!
NO.
DID YOU SERIOUSLY JUST KILL LIKE... TWENTY PEOPLE IN FRONT OF EVERYONE?
AND YOUR POINT?
I BELIEVE WE MAY BE RUNNING OUT OF MAN-BATS WITH YOUR CURRENT TRAINING METHODS, SHIVA.

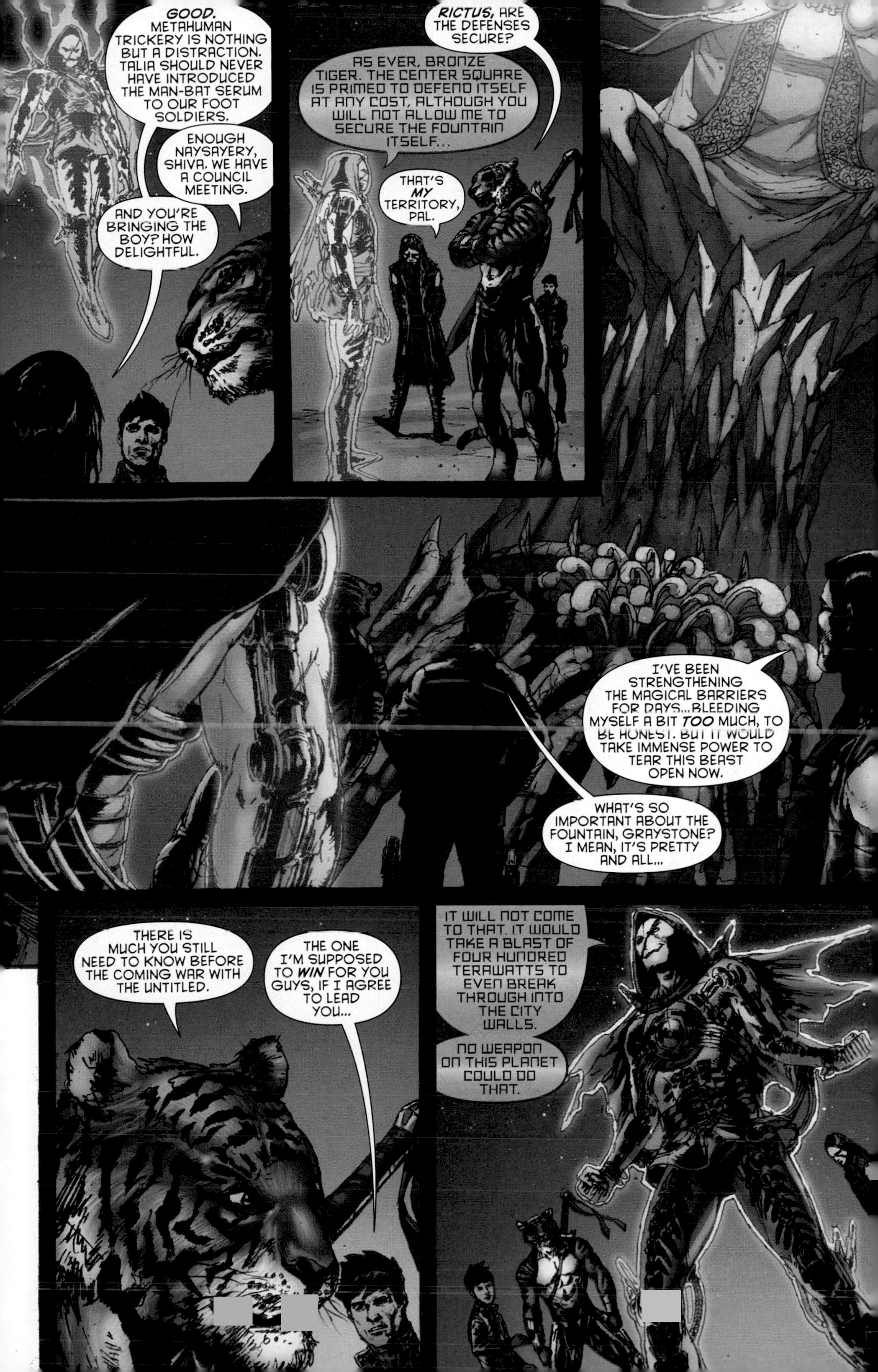
GOOD. METAHUMAN TRICKERY IS NOTHING BUT A DISTRACTION. TALIA SHOULD NEVER HAVE INTRODUCED THE MAN-BAT SERUM TO OUR FOOT SOLDIERS.
ENOUGH NAYSAYERY, SHIVA. WE HAVE A COUNCIL MEETING.
AND YOU'RE BRINGING THE BOY? HOW DELIGHTFUL.
RICTUS, ARE THE DEFENSES SECURE?
AS EVER, BRONZE TIGER. THE CENTER SQUARE IS PRIMED TO DEFEND ITSELF AT ANY COST, ALTHOUGH YOU WILL NOT ALLOW ME TO SECURE THE FOUNTAIN ITSELF...
THAT'S MY TERRITORY, PAL.
I'VE BEEN STRENGTHENING THE MAGICAL BARRIERS FOR DAYS...BLEEDING MYSELF A BIT TOO MUCH, TO BE HONEST. BUT IT WOULD TAKE IMMENSE POWER TO TEAR THIS BEAST OPEN NOW.
WHAT'S SO IMPORTANT ABOUT THE FOUNTAIN, GRAYSTONE? I MEAN, IT'S PRETTY AND ALL...
THERE IS MUCH YOU STILL NEED TO KNOW BEFORE THE COMING WAR WITH THE UNTITLED.
THE ONE I'M SUPPOSED TO WIN FOR YOU GUYS, IF I AGREE TO LEAD YOU...
IT WILL NOT COME TO THAT. IT WOULD TAKE A BLAST OF FOUR HUNDRED TERAWATTS TO EVEN BREAK THROUGH INTO THE CITY WALLS.
NO WEAPON ON THIS PLANET COULD DO THAT.

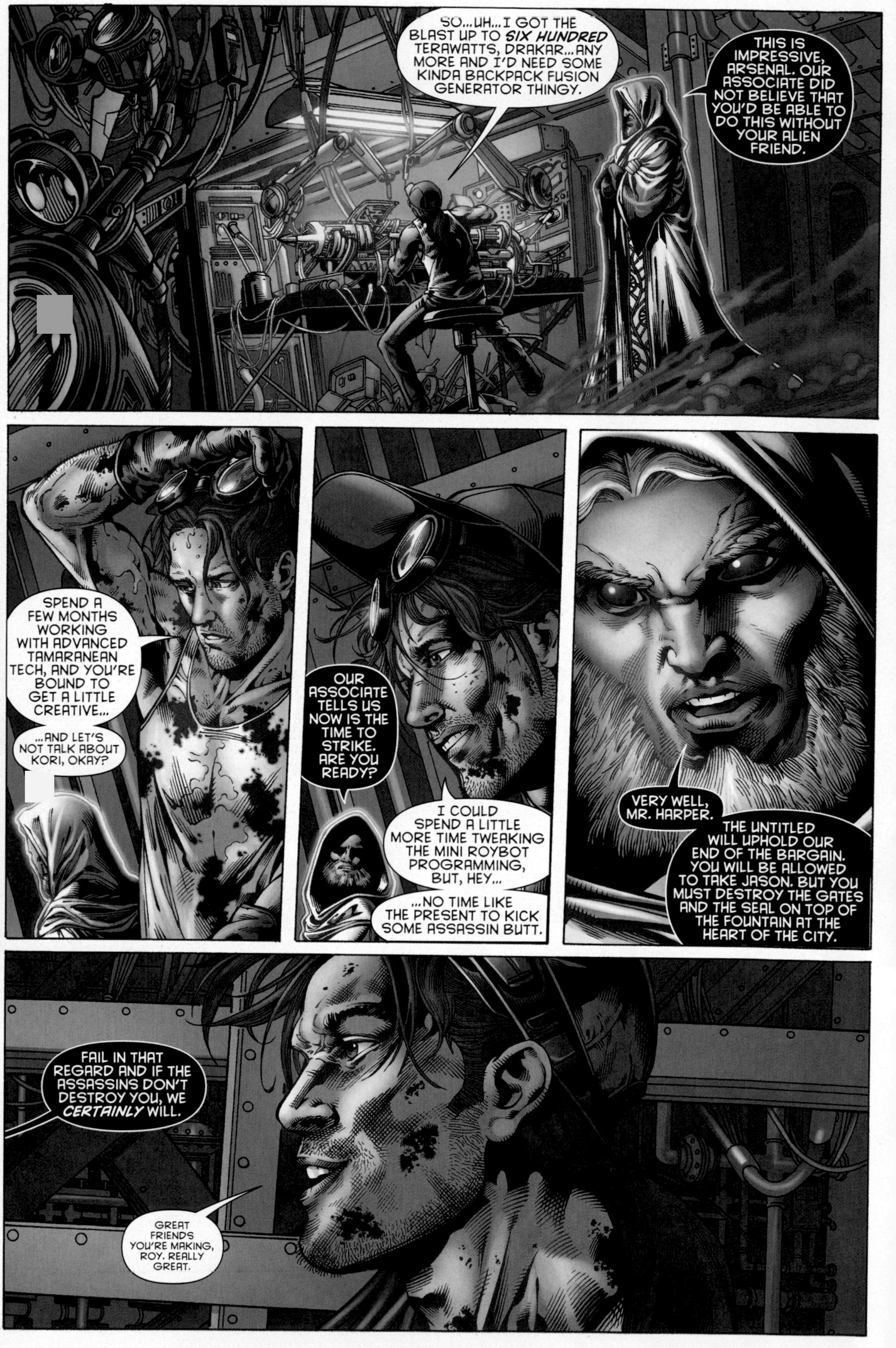
SO...UH...I GOT THE BLAST UP TO SIX HUNDRED TERAWATTS, DRAKAR...ANY MORE AND I'D NEED SOME KINDA BACKPACK FUSION GENERATOR THINGY.
THIS IS IMPRESSIVE, ARSENAL. OUR ASSOCIATE DID NOT BELIEVE THAT YOU'D BE ABLE TO DO THIS WITHOUT YOUR ALIEN FRIEND.
SPEND A FEW MONTHS WORKING WITH ADVANCED TAMARANEAN TECH, AND YOU'RE BOUND TO GET A LITTLE CREATIVE...
...AND LET'S NOT TALK ABOUT KORI, OKAY?
OUR ASSOCIATE TELLS US NOW IS THE TIME TO STRIKE. ARE YOU READY?
I COULD SPEND A LITTLE MORE TIME TWEAKING THE MINI ROYBOT PROGRAMMING, BUT, HEY...
...NO TIME LIKE THE PRESENT TO KICK SOME ASSASSIN BUTT.
VERY WELL, MR. HARPER.
THE UNTITLED WILL UPHOLD OUR END OF THE BARGAIN. YOU WILL BE ALLOWED TO TAKE JASON. BUT YOU MUST DESTROY THE GATES AND THE SEAL ON TOP OF THE FOUNTAIN AT THE HEART OF THE CITY.
FAIL IN THAT REGARD AND IF THE ASSASSINS DON'T DESTROY YOU, WE CERTAINLY WILL.
GREAT FRIENDS YOU'RE MAKING, ROY. REALLY GREAT.

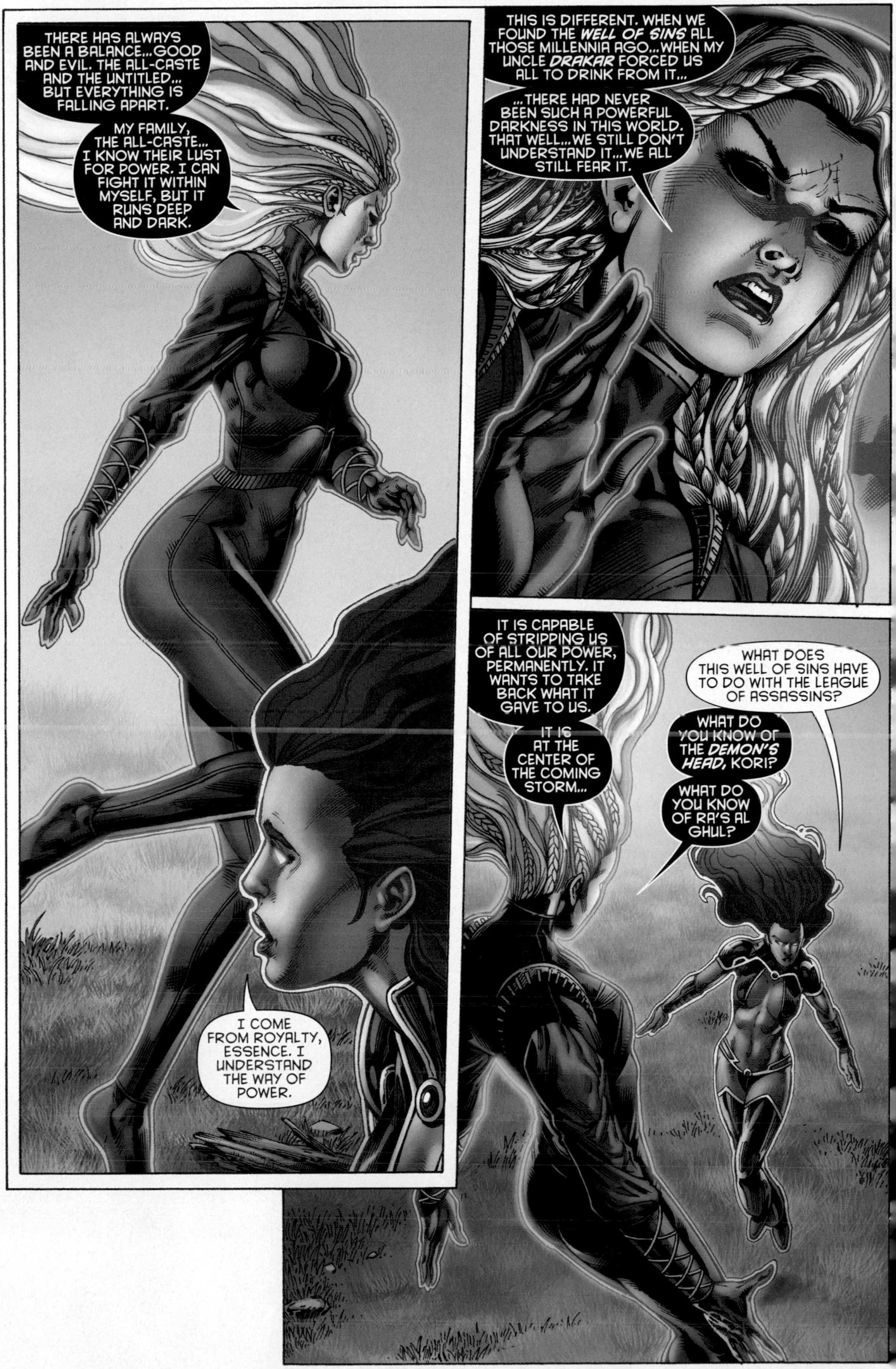

THERE HAS ALWAYS BEEN A BALANCE...GOOD AND EVIL. THE ALL-CASTE AND THE UNTITLED... BUT EVERYTHING IS FALLING APART.
MY FAMILY, THE ALL-CASTE... I KNOW THEIR LUST FOR POWER. I CAN FIGHT IT WITHIN MYSELF, BUT IT RUNS DEEP AND DARK.
I COME FROM ROYALTY, ESSENCE. I UNDERSTAND THE WAY OF POWER.
THIS IS DIFFERENT. WHEN WE FOUND THE WELL OF SINS ALL THOSE MILLENNIA AGO...WHEN MY UNCLE DRAKAR FORCED US ALL TO DRINK FROM IT...
...THERE HAD NEVER BEEN SUCH A POWERFUL DARKNESS IN THIS WORLD. THAT WELL...WE STILL DON'T UNDERSTAND IT...WE ALL STILL FEAR IT.
IT IS CAPABLE OF STRIPPING US OF ALL OUR POWER, PERMANENTLY. IT WANTS TO TAKE BACK WHAT IT GAVE TO US.
IT IS AT THE CENTER OF THE COMING STORM...
WHAT DOES THIS WELL OF SINS HAVE TO DO WITH THE LEAGUE OF ASSASSINS?
WHAT DO YOU KNOW OF THE DEMON'S HEAD, KORI?
WHAT DO YOU KNOW OF RA'S AL GHUL?

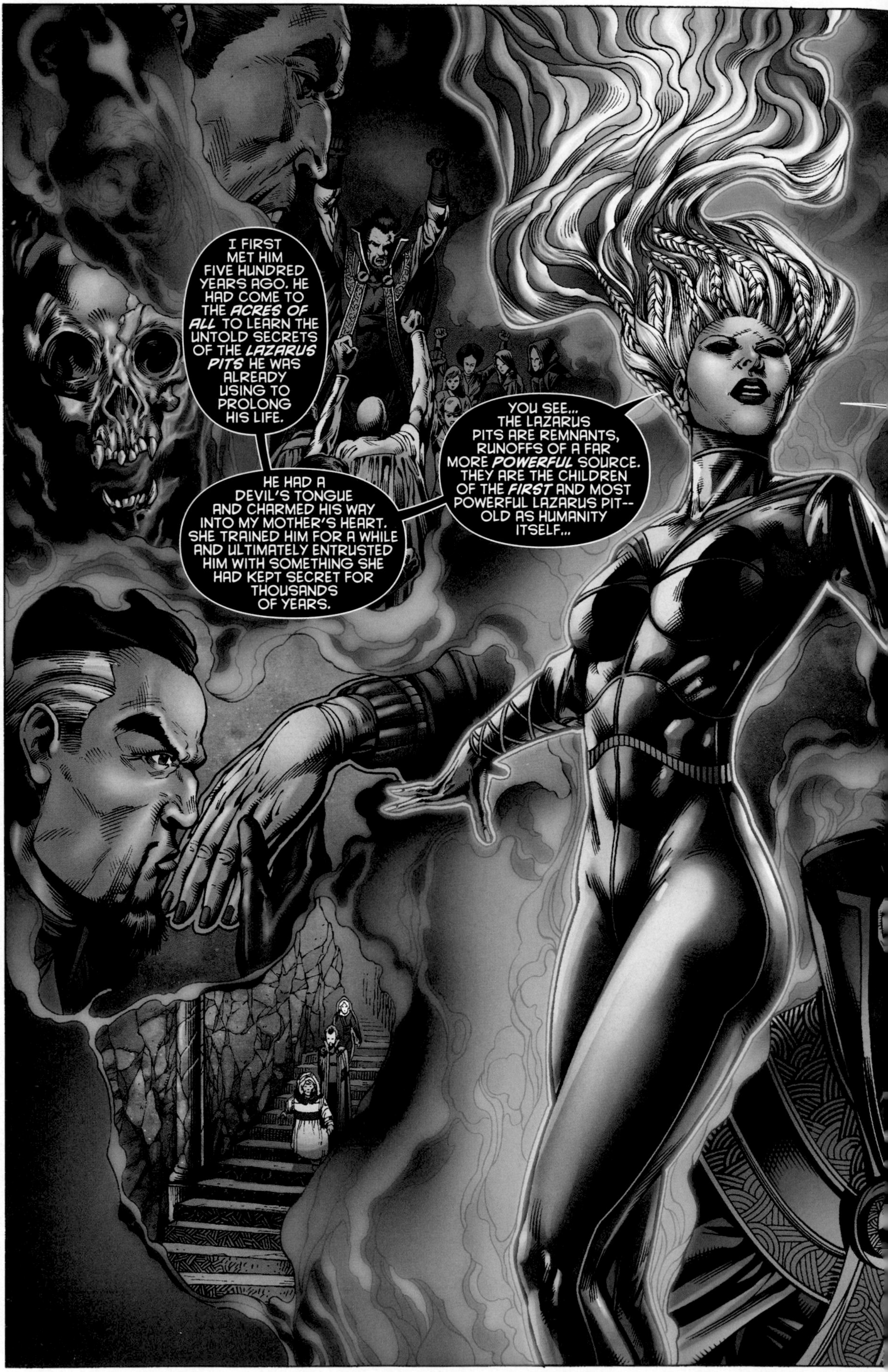
I FIRST MET HIM FIVE HUNDRED YEARS AGO. HE HAD COME TO THE ACRES OF ALL TO LEARN THE UNTOLD SECRETS OF THE LAZARUS PITS HE WAS ALREADY USING TO PROLONG HIS LIFE.
HE HAD A DEVIL'S TONGUE AND CHARMED HIS WAY INTO MY MOTHER'S HEART. SHE TRAINED HIM FOR A WHILE AND ULTIMATELY ENTRUSTED HIM WITH SOMETHING SHE HAD KEPT SECRET FOR THOUSANDS OF YEARS.
YOU SEE... THE LAZARUS PITS ARE REMNANTS, RUNOFFS OF A FAR MORE POWERFUL SOURCE. THEY ARE THE CHILDREN OF THE FIRST AND MOST POWERFUL LAZARUS PIT--OLD AS HUMANITY ITSELF...

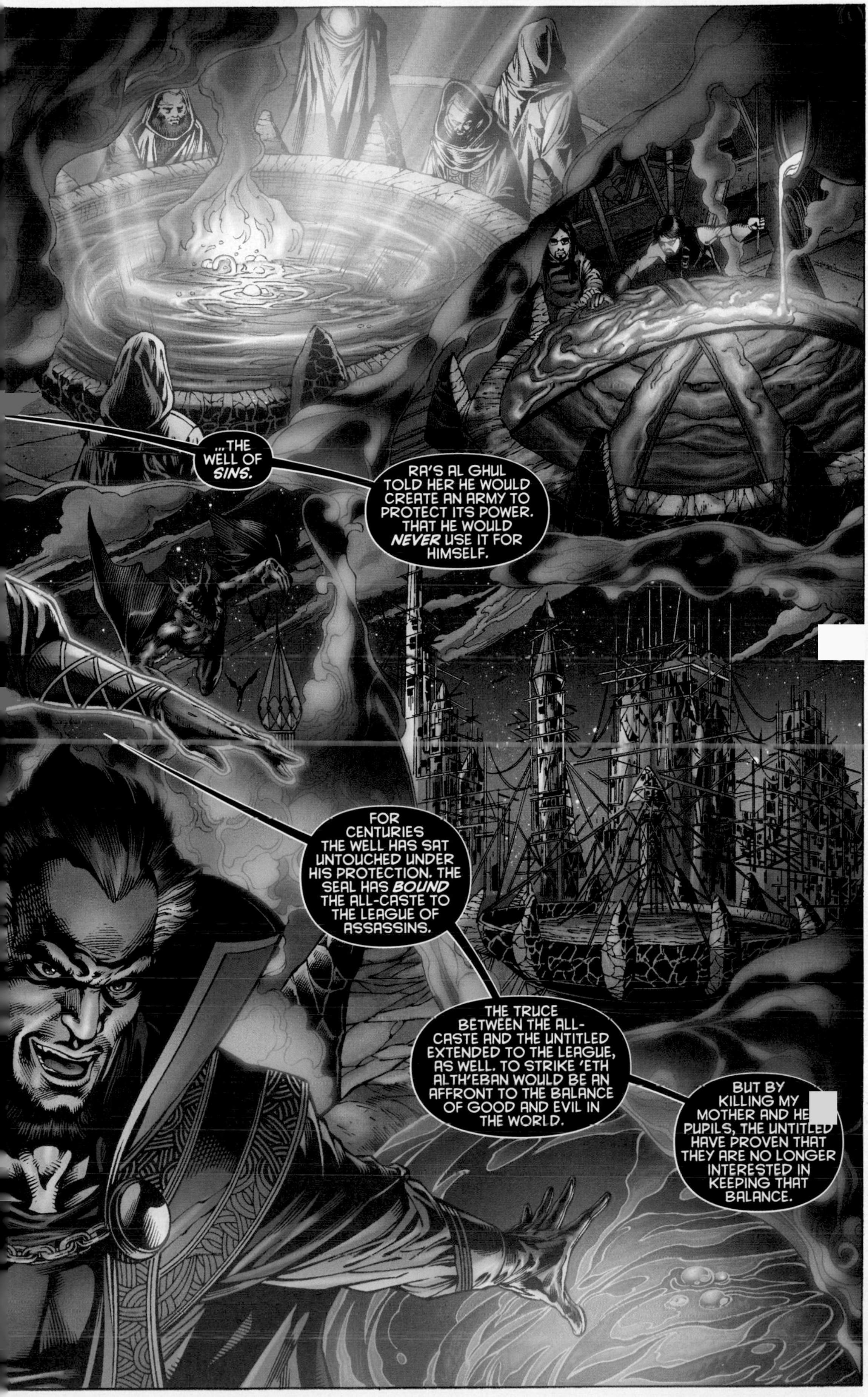
...THE WELL OF *SINS.*
RA'S AL GHUL TOLD HER HE WOULD CREATE AN ARMY TO PROTECT ITS POWER. THAT HE WOULD *NEVER* USE IT FOR HIMSELF.
FOR CENTURIES THE WELL HAS SAT UNTOUCHED UNDER HIS PROTECTION. THE SEAL HAS *BOUND* THE ALL-CASTE TO THE LEAGUE OF ASSASSINS.
THE TRUCE BETWEEN THE ALL-CASTE AND THE UNTITLED EXTENDED TO THE LEAGUE, AS WELL. TO STRIKE 'ETH ALTH'EBAN WOULD BE AN AFFRONT TO THE BALANCE OF GOOD AND EVIL IN THE WORLD.
BUT BY KILLING MY MOTHER AND HE
PUPILS, THE UNTITLED HAVE PROVEN THAT THEY ARE NO LONGER INTERESTED IN KEEPING THAT BALANCE.

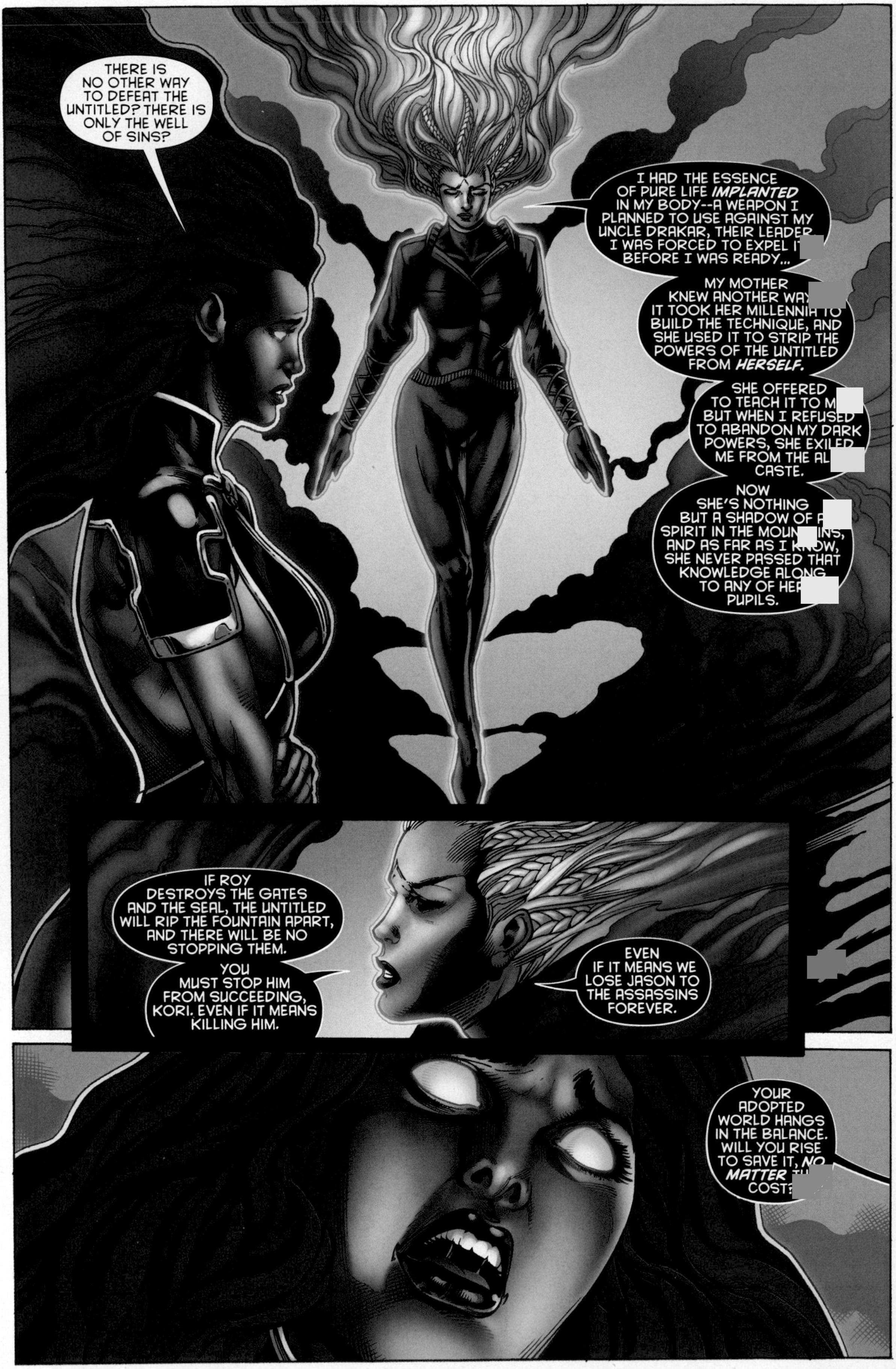
THERE IS NO OTHER WAY TO DEFEAT THE UNTITLED? THERE IS ONLY THE WELL OF SINS?
I HAD THE ESSENCE OF PURE LIFE *IMPLANTED* IN MY BODY--A WEAPON I PLANNED TO USE AGAINST MY UNCLE DRAKAR, THEIR LEADER. I WAS FORCED TO EXPEL I BEFORE I WAS READY...
MY MOTHER KNEW ANOTHER WA IT TOOK HER MILLENNIA TO BUILD THE TECHNIQUE, AND SHE USED IT TO STRIP THE POWERS OF THE UNTITLED FROM *HERSELF.*
SHE OFFERED TO TEACH IT TO M BUT WHEN I REFUSED TO ABANDON MY DARK POWERS, SHE EXILED ME FROM THE AL CASTE.
NOW SHE'S NOTHING BUT A SHADOW OF A SPIRIT IN THE MOUN INS, AND AS FAR AS I KNOW, SHE NEVER PASSED THAT KNOWLEDGE ALONG TO ANY OF HER PUPILS.
IF ROY DESTROYS THE GATES AND THE SEAL, THE UNTITLED WILL RIP THE FOUNTAIN APART, AND THERE WILL BE NO STOPPING THEM.
YOU MUST STOP HIM FROM SUCCEEDING, KORI. EVEN IF IT MEANS KILLING HIM.
EVEN IF IT MEANS WE LOSE JASON TO THE ASSASSINS FOREVER.
YOUR ADOPTED WORLD HANGS IN THE BALANCE. WILL YOU RISE TO SAVE IT, *NO MATTER* TH COST?

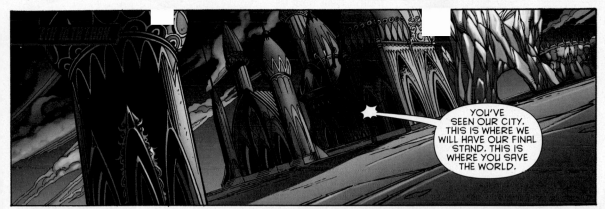

YOU'VE SEEN OUR CITY. THIS IS WHERE WE WILL HAVE OUR FINAL STAND. THIS IS WHERE YOU SAVE THE WORLD.

OKAY, SO THE THING I DON'T UNDERSTAND...YOU'RE ALL THE MOST *DANGEROUS* PEOPLE ON THE PLANET. I WOULD BE HARD PRESSED TO DEFEAT ANY OF YOU ONE-ON-ONE...

HARD PRESSED?

DON'T STEP ON THE KID'S FLATTERY, SHIV. I'M BLUSHING.

BUT SERIOUSLY...YOU'RE ALL FREAKED OUT ABOUT THESE UNTITLED PEOPLE COMING HERE. BUT WHAT IS IT ABOUT ME THAT YOU'RE SO CERTAIN CAN *BEAT* THEM WHEN THE REST OF YOU *CAN'T?*

NO, GO ON. TELL HIM. THIS IS THE FUNNIEST PART.

IT'S A JOKE, ALL RIGHT.

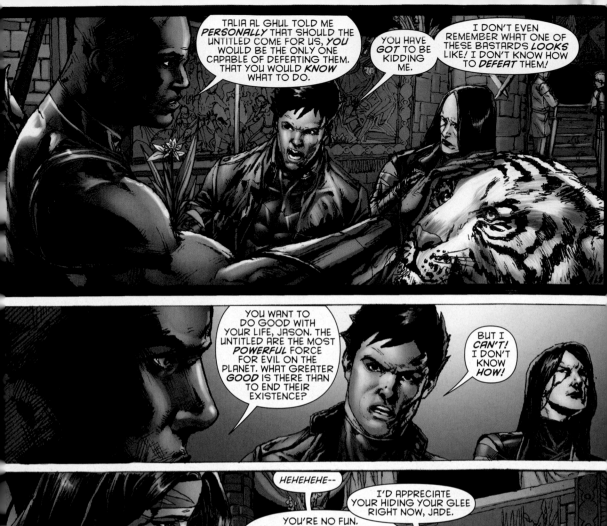

TALIA AL GHUL TOLD ME *PERSONALLY* THAT SHOULD THE UNTITLED COME FOR US, *YOU* WOULD BE THE ONLY ONE CAPABLE OF DEFEATING THEM. THAT YOU WOULD *KNOW* WHAT TO DO.

YOU HAVE *GOT* TO BE KIDDING ME.

I DON'T EVEN REMEMBER WHAT ONE OF THESE BASTARDS *LOOKS* LIKE! I DON'T KNOW HOW TO *DEFEAT* THEM!

YOU WANT TO DO GOOD WITH YOUR LIFE, JASON. THE UNTITLED ARE THE MOST *POWERFUL* FORCE FOR EVIL ON THE PLANET. WHAT GREATER *GOOD* IS THERE THAN TO END THEIR EXISTENCE?

BUT I *CAN'T!* I DON'T KNOW *HOW!*

HEHEHEHE--

I'D APPRECIATE YOUR HIDING YOUR GLEE RIGHT NOW, JADE.

YOU'RE NO FUN. THIS IS ALL SO SILLY. WE'RE ALL GOING TO DIE AT THE HANDS OF WEIRD SMOKEY CAVEMEN AND THERE'S NOTHING WE CAN DO ABOUT IT.

I'VE KILLED THOSE WHO'VE CLAIMED IMMORTALITY BEFORE. I CAN DO IT AGAIN.

WITHOUT THE HELP OF A PATHETIC, FAILED *BOY* SUPERHERO.

BADEEP BADEEP BADEEP

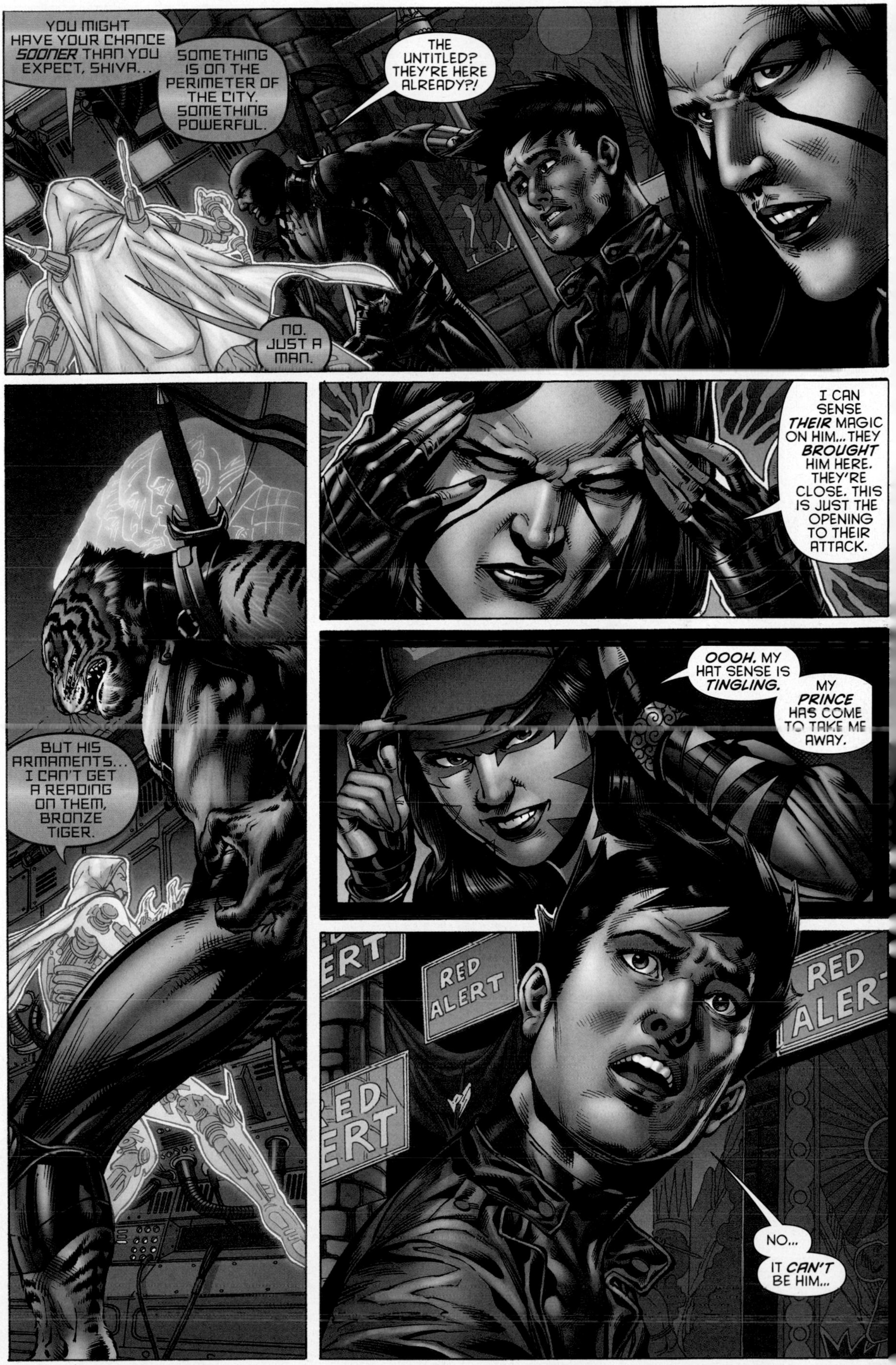
YOU MIGHT HAVE YOUR CHANCE SOONER THAN YOU EXPECT, SHIVA...
SOMETHING IS ON THE PERIMETER OF THE CITY. SOMETHING POWERFUL.
THE UNTITLED? THEY'RE HERE ALREADY?!
NO. JUST A MAN.
BUT HIS ARMAMENTS... I CAN'T GET A READING ON THEM, BRONZE TIGER.
I CAN SENSE THEIR MAGIC ON HIM... THEY BROUGHT HIM HERE. THEY'RE CLOSE. THIS IS JUST THE OPENING TO THEIR ATTACK.
OOOH. MY HAT SENSE IS TINGLING.
MY PRINCE HAS COME TO TAKE ME AWAY.
RED ALERT
RED ALERT
NO...
IT CAN'T BE HIM...

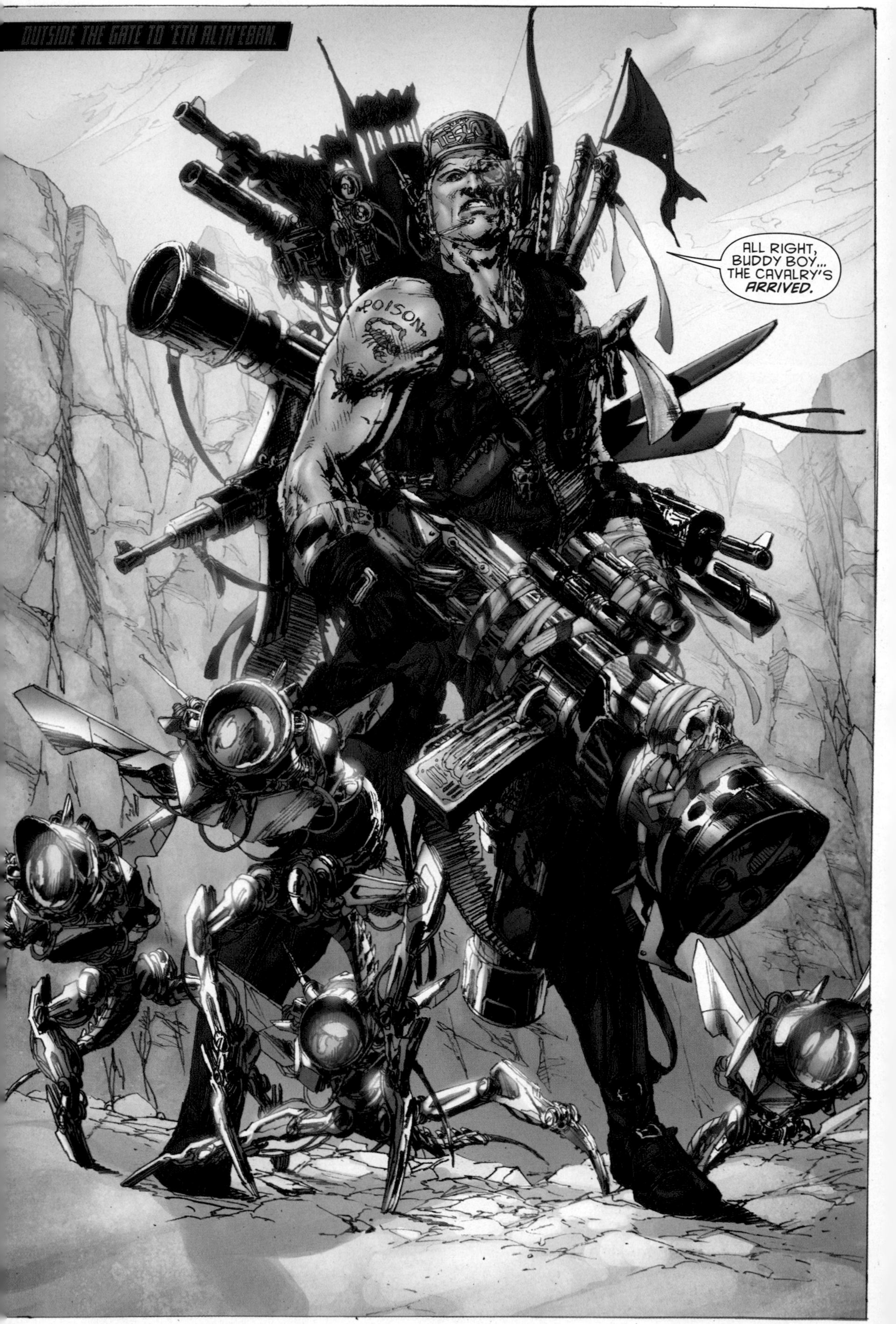
OUTSIDE THE GATE TO 'ETH ALTH'EBAN.
ALL RIGHT, BUDDY BOY... THE CAVALRY'S ARRIVED.
POISON

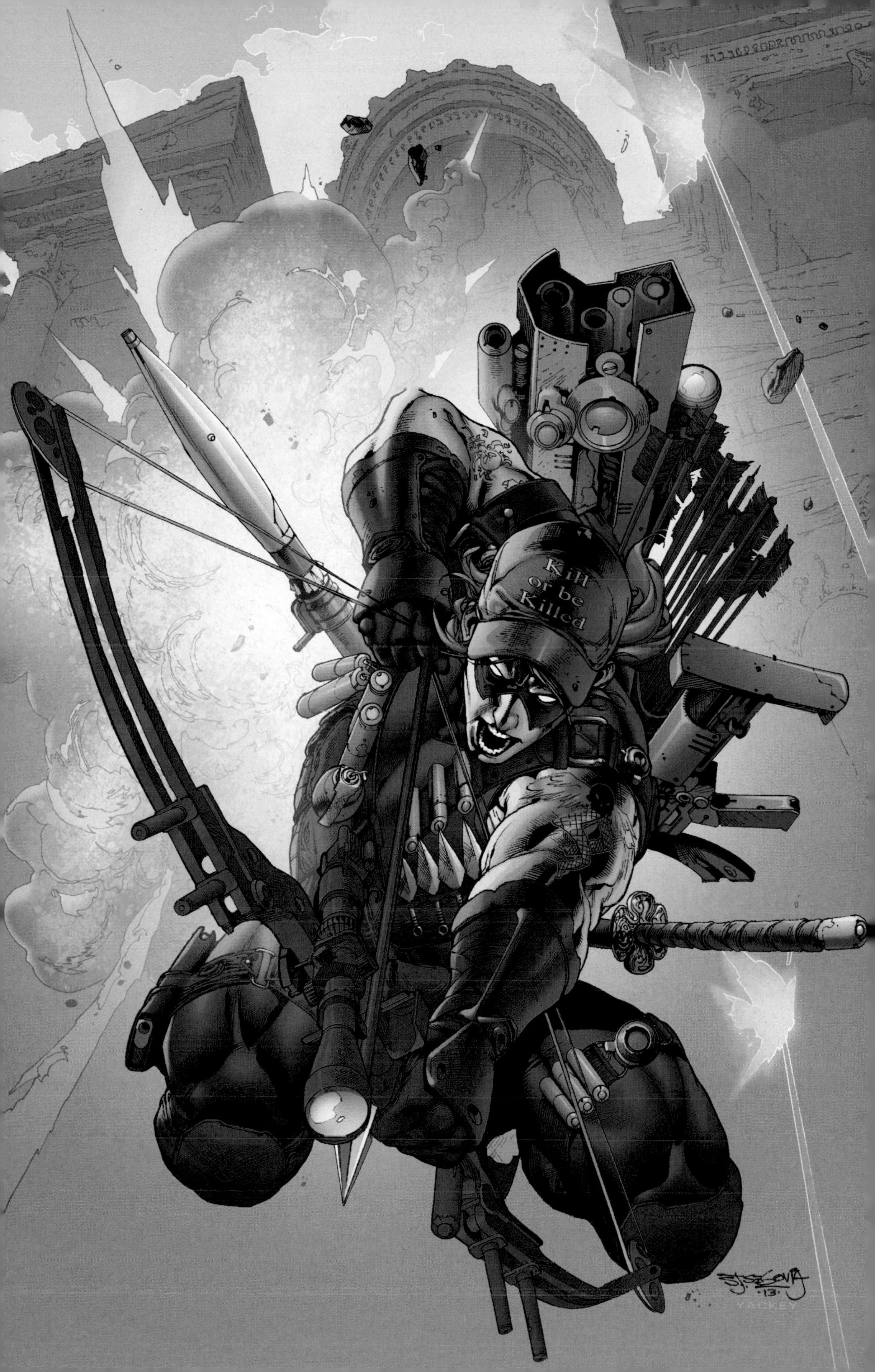
Kill or be Killed

JAMES TYNION IV writer **JULIUS GOPEZ** penciller **RAY McCARTHY, WALDEN WONG & WAYNE FAUCHER** inkers
IAN CHURCHILL thumbnail artist **NEI RUFFINO & DANIEL BROWN** colorists **STEPHEN SEGOVIA** with **MATT YACKEY** cover artists

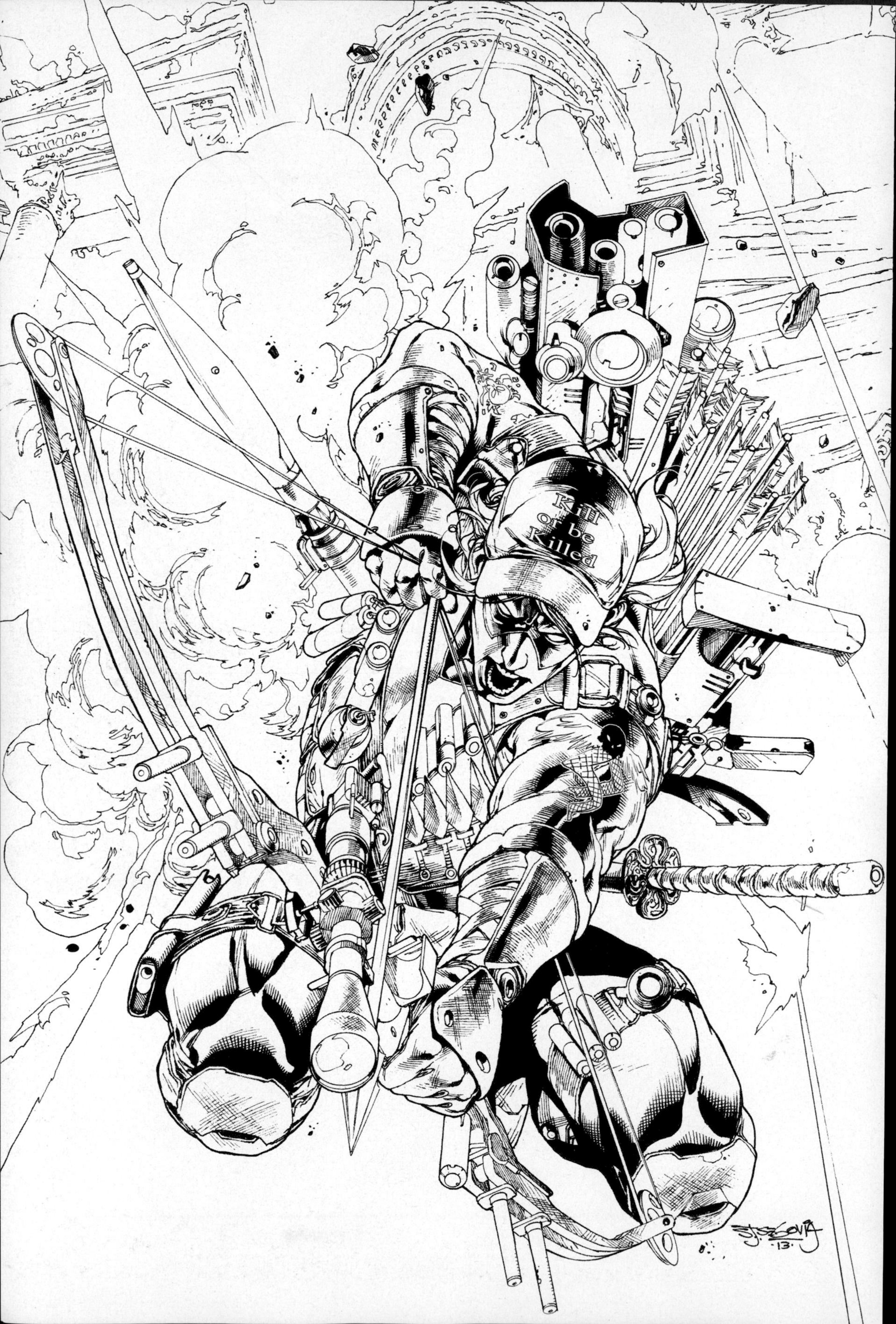
Kill or be Killed

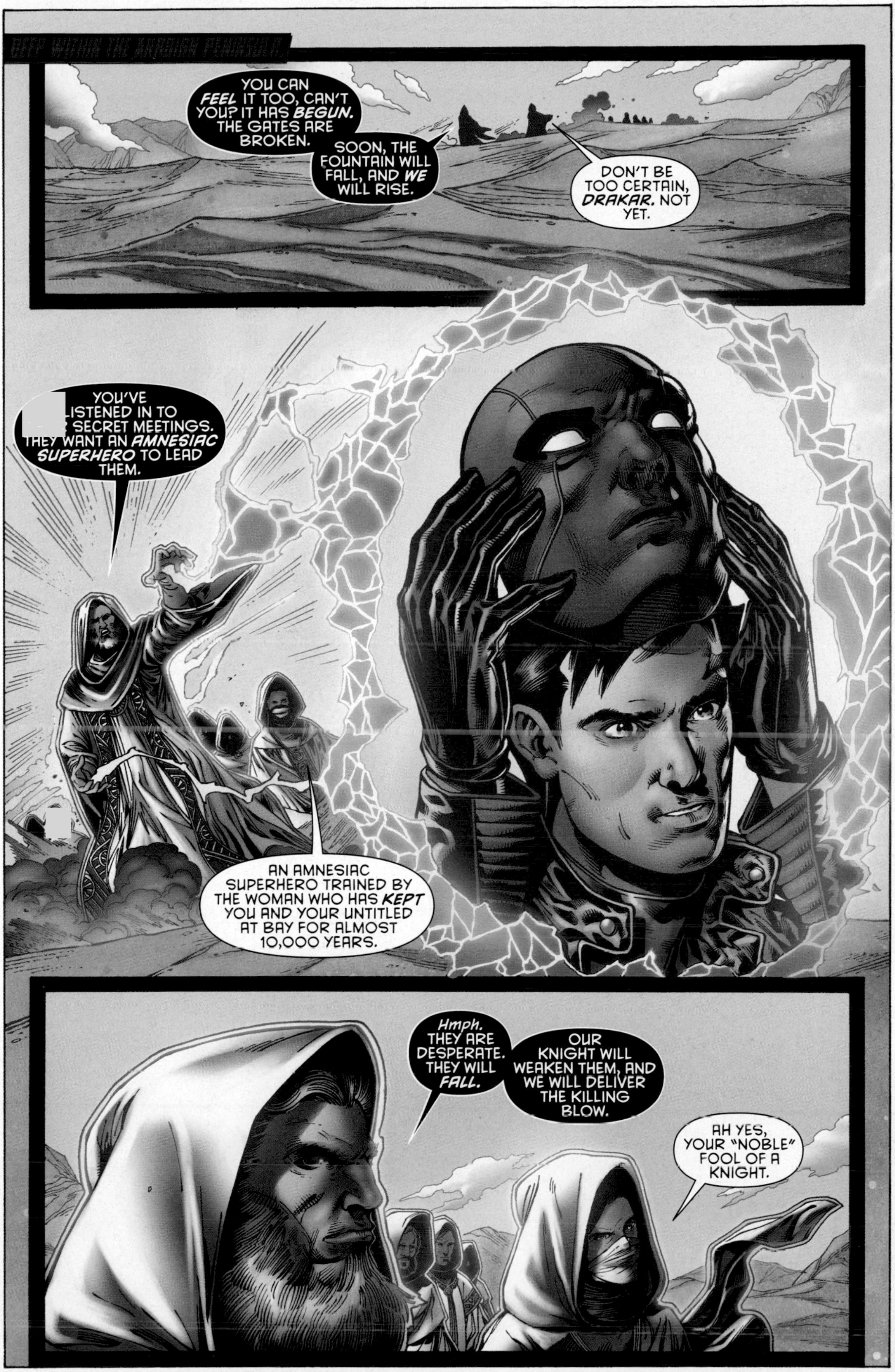
DEEP WITHIN THE ARABIAN PENINSULA.
YOU CAN FEEL IT TOO, CAN'T YOU? IT HAS BEGUN. THE GATES ARE BROKEN.
SOON, THE FOUNTAIN WILL FALL, AND WE WILL RISE.
DON'T BE TOO CERTAIN, DRAKAR. NOT YET.
YOU'VE LISTENED IN TO SECRET MEETINGS. THEY WANT AN AMNESIAC SUPERHERO TO LEAD THEM.
AN AMNESIAC SUPERHERO TRAINED BY THE WOMAN WHO HAS KEPT YOU AND YOUR UNTITLED AT BAY FOR ALMOST 10,000 YEARS.
Hmph. THEY ARE DESPERATE. THEY WILL FALL.
OUR KNIGHT WILL WEAKEN THEM, AND WE WILL DELIVER THE KILLING BLOW.
AH YES, YOUR "NOBLE" FOOL OF A KNIGHT.

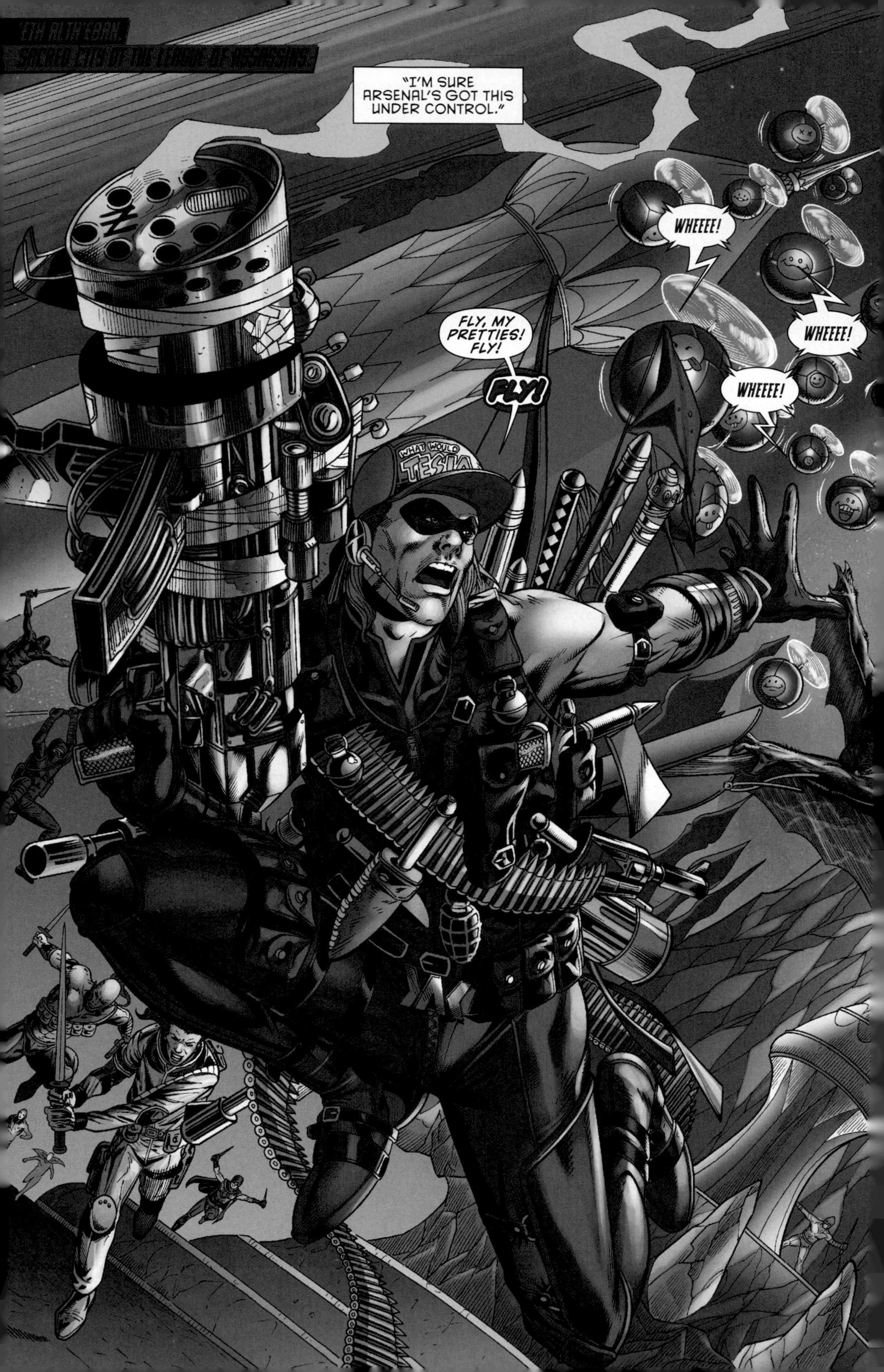
SACRED CITY OF THE LEAGUE OF ASSASSINS
"I'M SURE ARSENAL'S GOT THIS UNDER CONTROL."
FLY, MY PRETTIES! FLY!
FLY!
WHAT WOULD TESLA
WHEEEE!
WHEEEE!
WHEEEE!

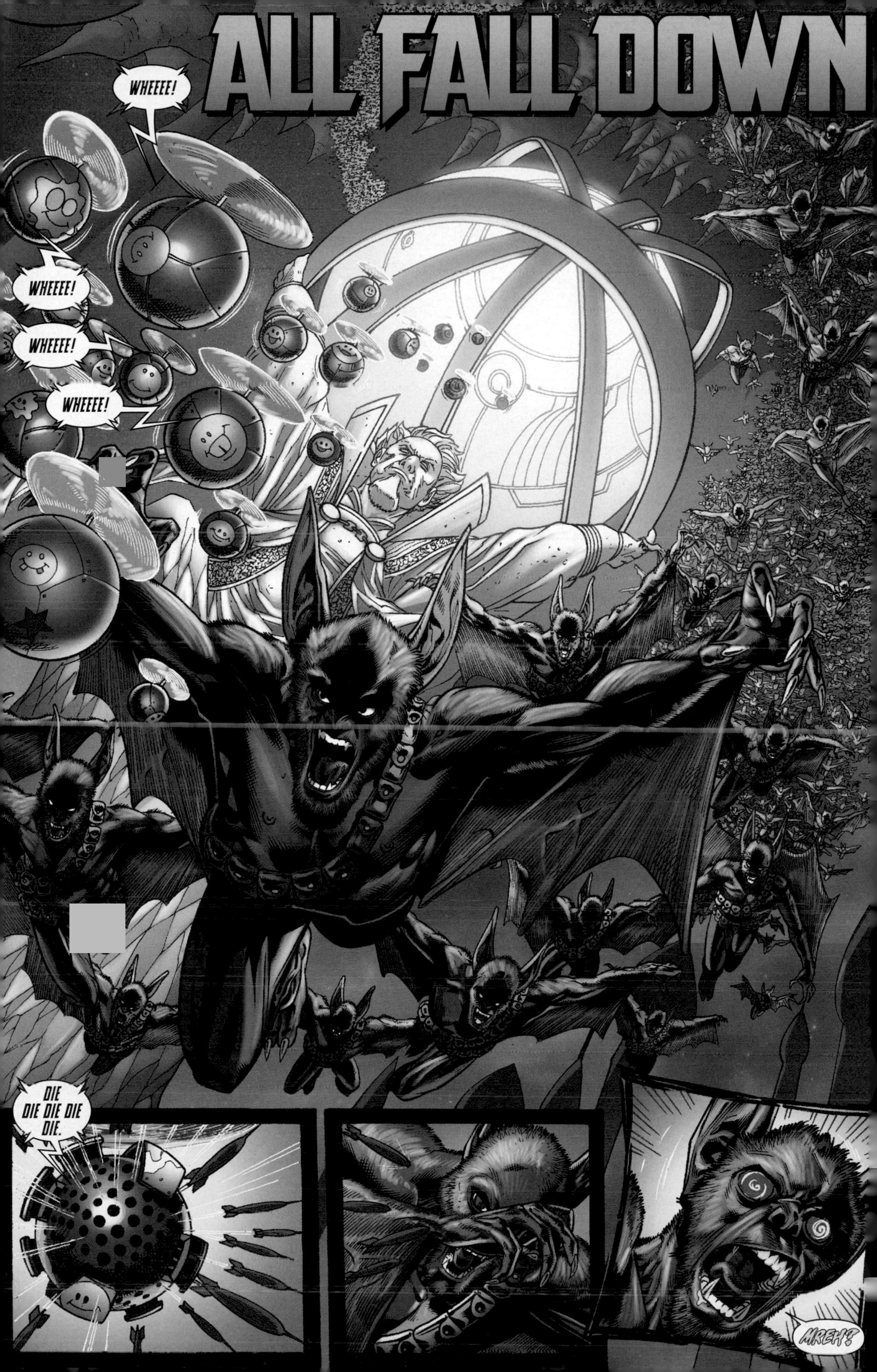

ALL FALL DOWN
WHEEEE!
WHEEEE!
WHEEEE!
WHEEEE!
DIE DIE DIE DIE DIE.
MREH?

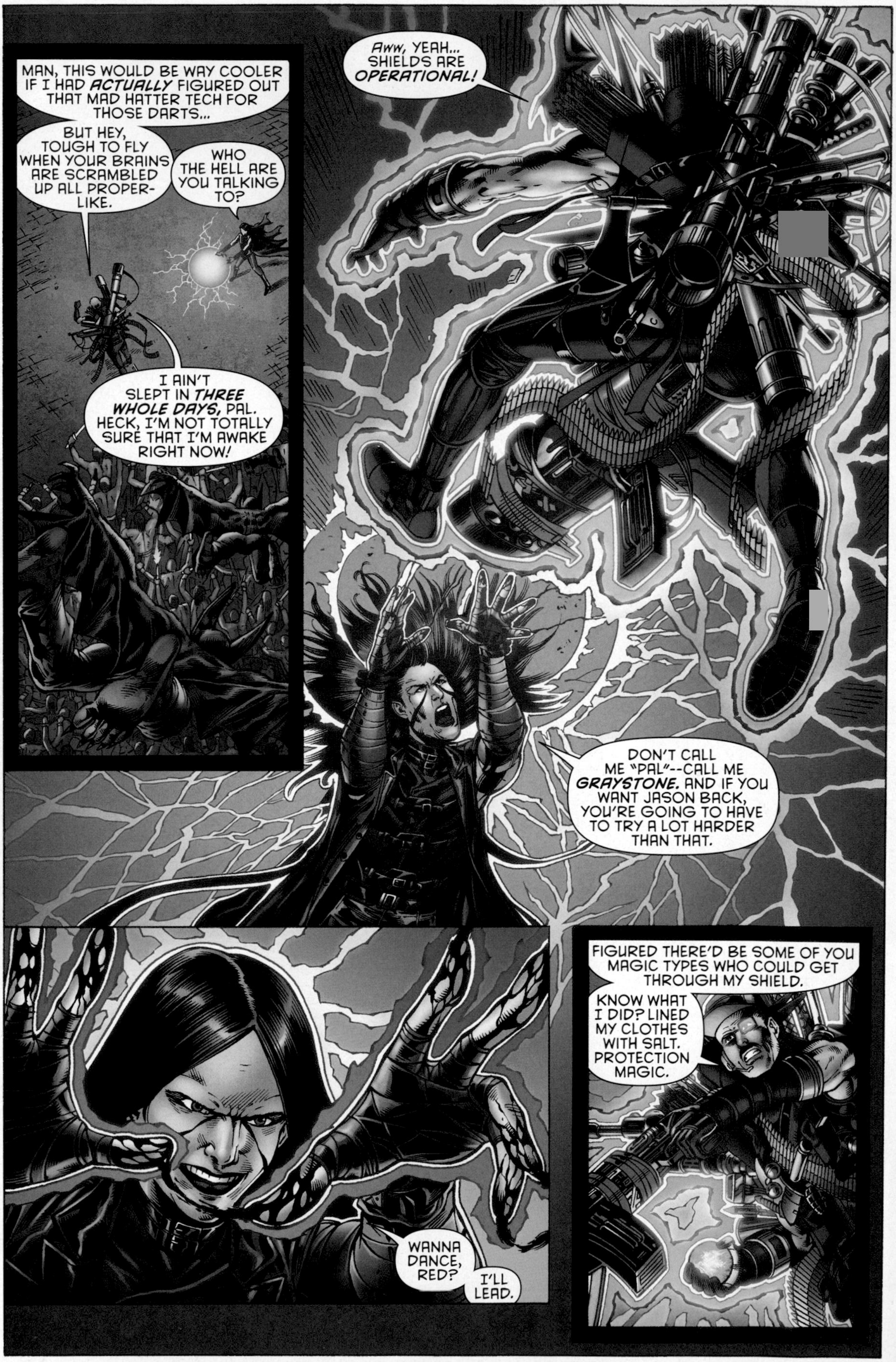

MAN, THIS WOULD BE WAY COOLER IF I HAD *ACTUALLY* FIGURED OUT THAT MAD HATTER TECH FOR THOSE DARTS...
BUT HEY, TOUGH TO FLY WHEN YOUR BRAINS ARE SCRAMBLED UP ALL PROPER-LIKE.
WHO THE HELL ARE YOU TALKING TO?
I AIN'T SLEPT IN *THREE WHOLE DAYS,* PAL. HECK, I'M NOT TOTALLY SURE THAT I'M AWAKE RIGHT NOW!
AWW, YEAH... SHIELDS ARE *OPERATIONAL!*
DON'T CALL ME "PAL"--CALL ME *GRAYSTONE.* AND IF YOU WANT JASON BACK, YOU'RE GOING TO HAVE TO TRY A LOT HARDER THAN THAT.
WANNA DANCE, RED?
I'LL LEAD.
FIGURED THERE'D BE SOME OF YOU MAGIC TYPES WHO COULD GET THROUGH MY SHIELD.
KNOW WHAT I DID? LINED MY CLOTHES WITH SALT. PROTECTION MAGIC.

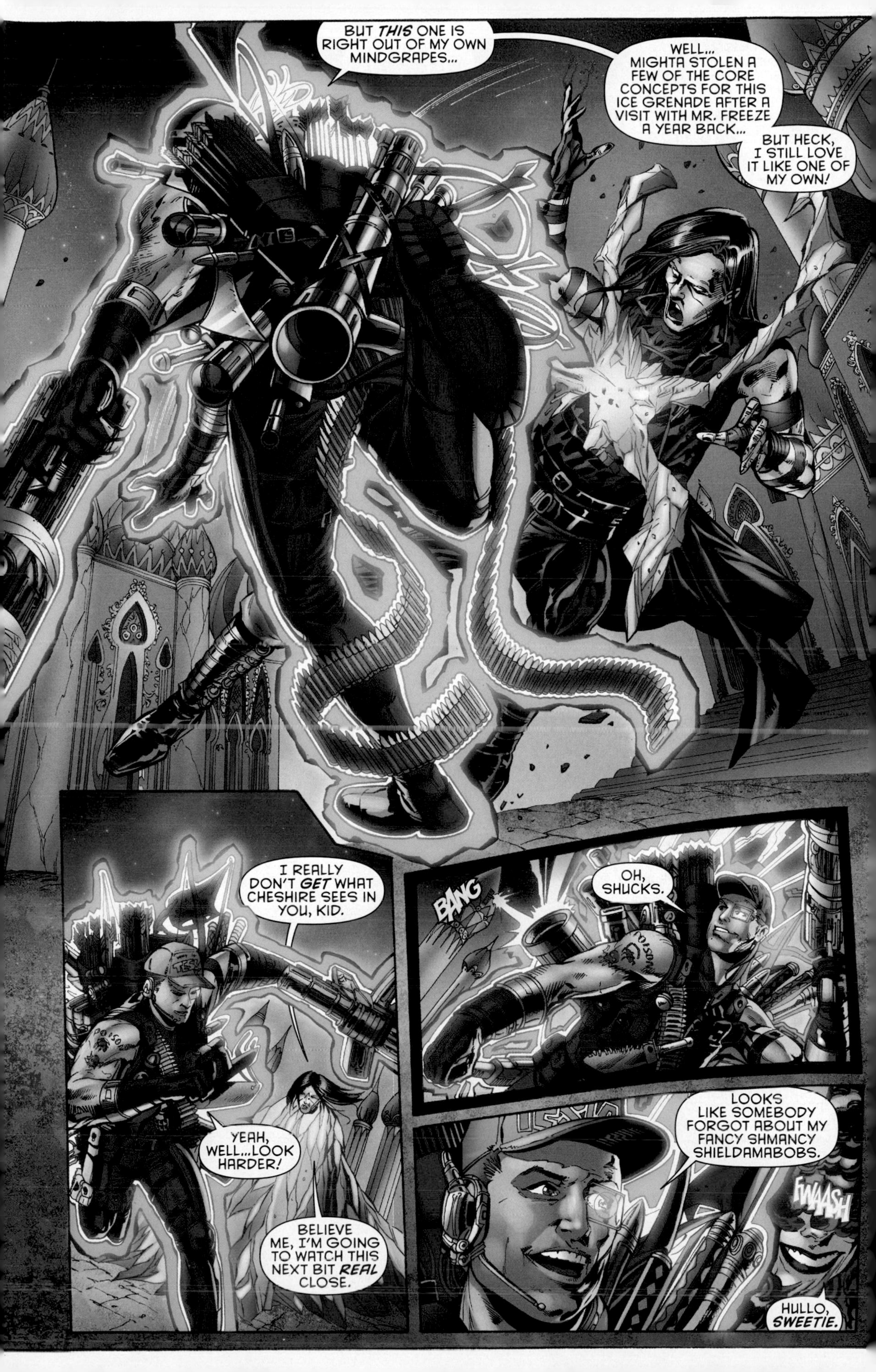
BUT THIS ONE IS RIGHT OUT OF MY OWN MINDGRAPES...
WELL... MIGHTA STOLEN A FEW OF THE CORE CONCEPTS FOR THIS ICE GRENADE AFTER A VISIT WITH MR. FREEZE A YEAR BACK...
BUT HECK, I STILL LOVE IT LIKE ONE OF MY OWN!
I REALLY DON'T GET WHAT CHESHIRE SEES IN YOU, KID.
YEAH, WELL...LOOK HARDER!
BELIEVE ME, I'M GOING TO WATCH THIS NEXT BIT REAL CLOSE.
BANG
OH, SHUCKS.
LOOKS LIKE SOMEBODY FORGOT ABOUT MY FANCY SHMANCY SHIELDAMABOBS.
FWAASH
HULLO, SWEETIE.

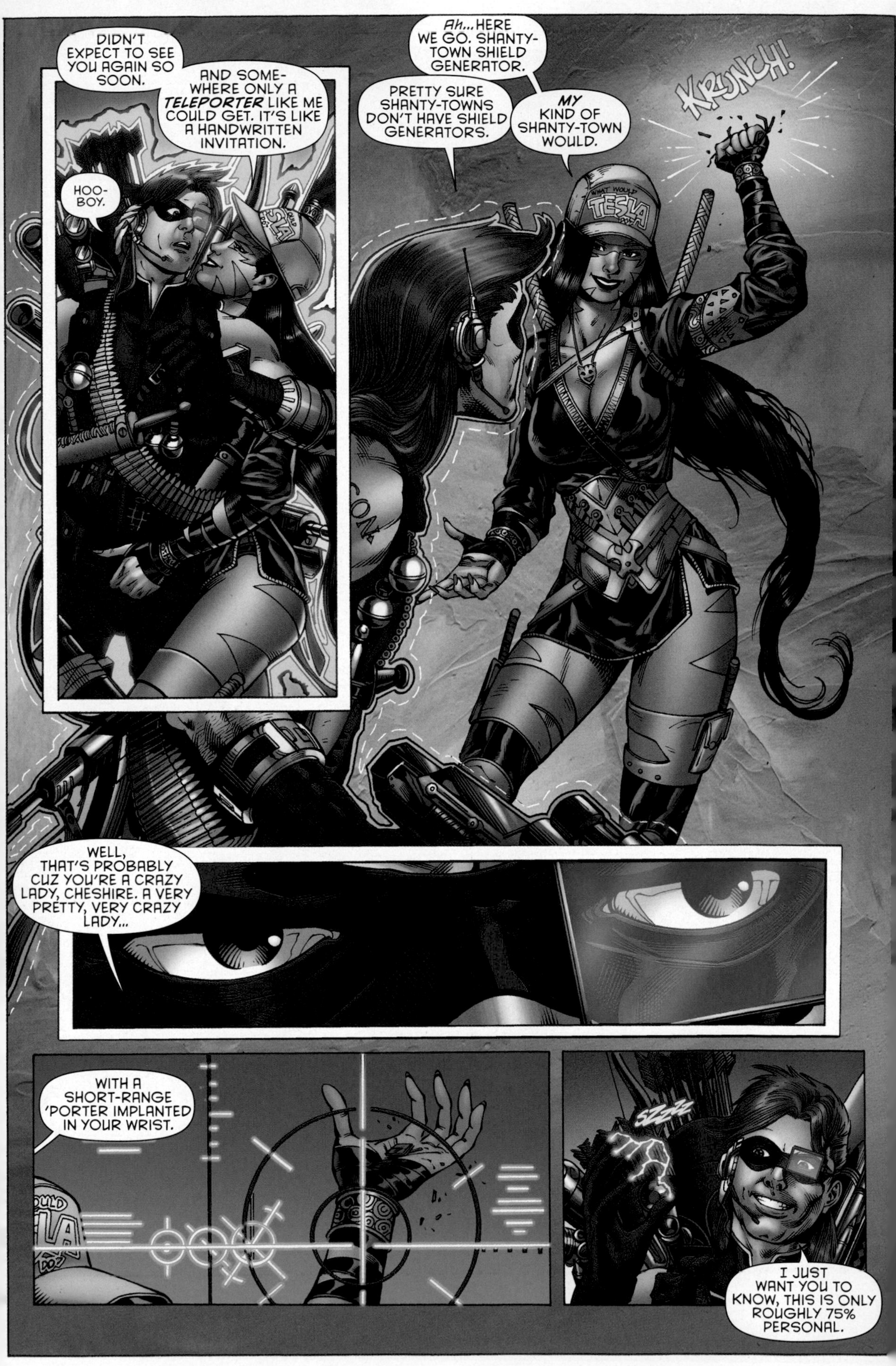
DIDN'T EXPECT TO SEE YOU AGAIN SO SOON.
AND SOMEWHERE ONLY A TELEPORTER LIKE ME COULD GET. IT'S LIKE A HANDWRITTEN INVITATION.
HOO-BOY.
AH... HERE WE GO. SHANTY-TOWN SHIELD GENERATOR.
PRETTY SURE SHANTY-TOWNS DON'T HAVE SHIELD GENERATORS.
MY KIND OF SHANTY-TOWN WOULD.
KRUNCH!
WHAT WOULD TESLA DO?
WELL, THAT'S PROBABLY CUZ YOU'RE A CRAZY LADY, CHESHIRE. A VERY PRETTY, VERY CRAZY LADY...
WITH A SHORT-RANGE 'PORTER IMPLANTED IN YOUR WRIST.
SZZZ
I JUST WANT YOU TO KNOW, THIS IS ONLY ROUGHLY 75% PERSONAL.

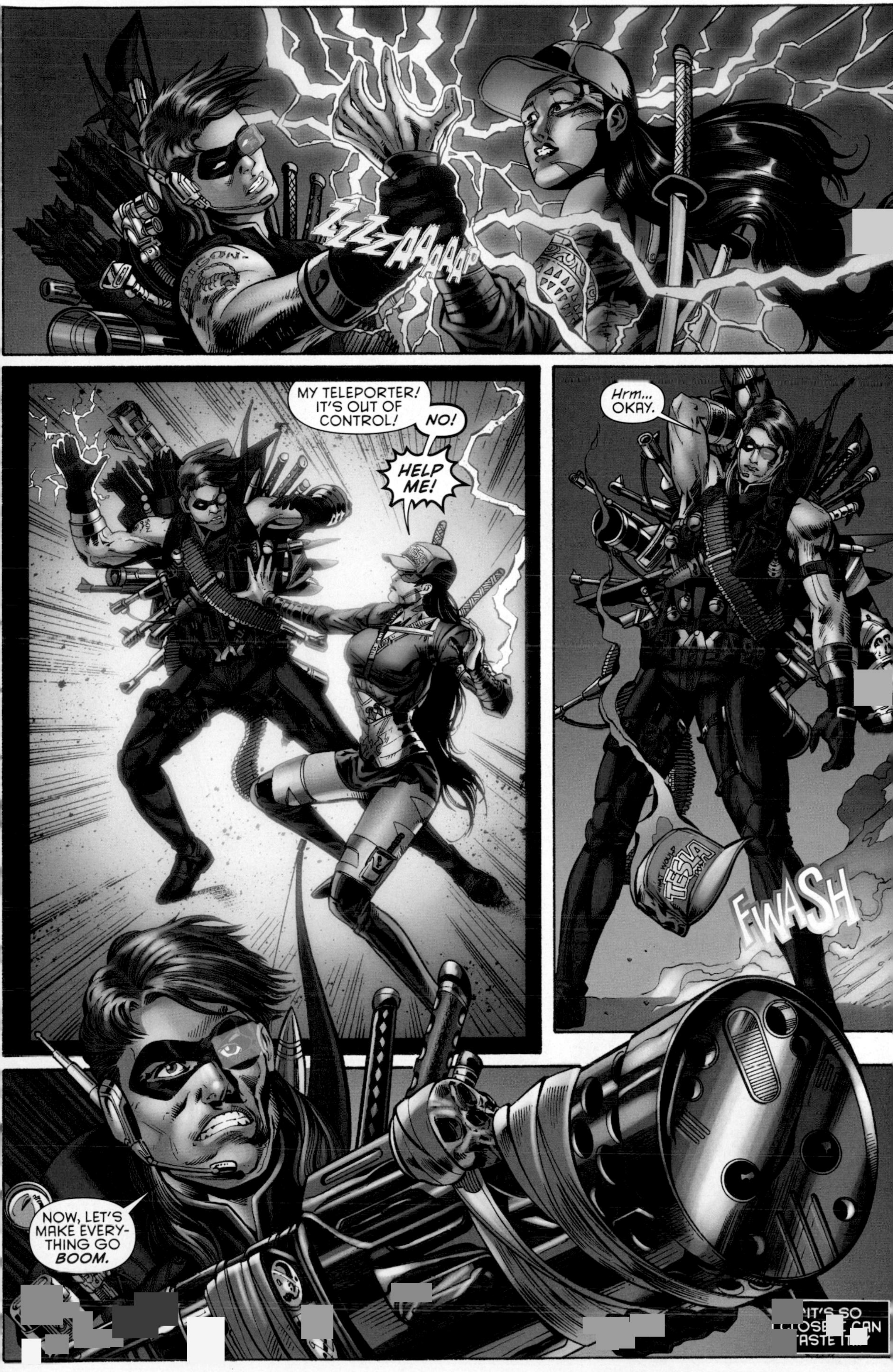
ZZZZAAAAAP
MY TELEPORTER! IT'S OUT OF CONTROL!
NO!
HELP ME!
Hrm... OKAY.
FWASH
NOW, LET'S MAKE EVERY-THING GO BOOM.
IT'S SO
CAN

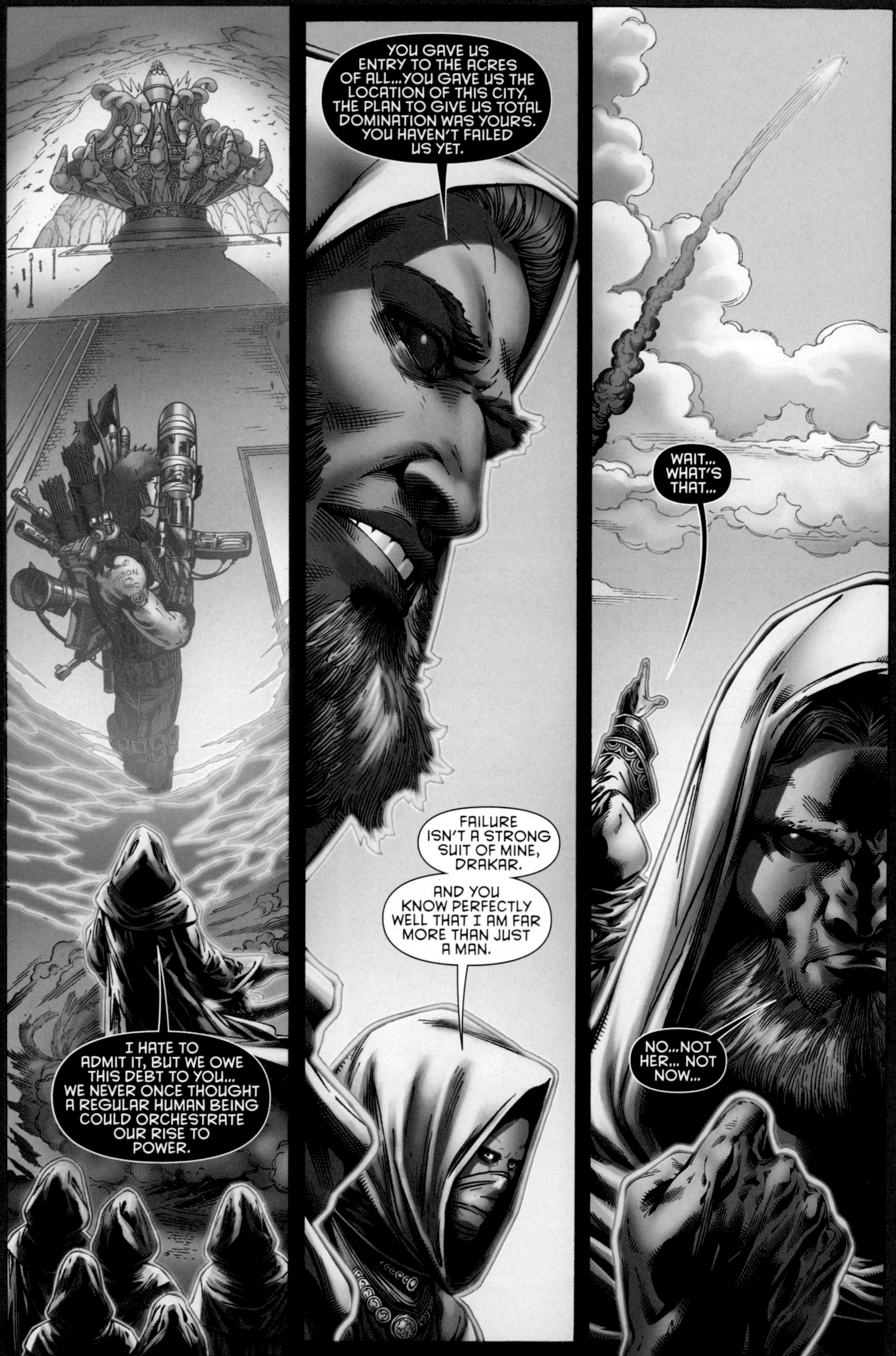
I HATE TO ADMIT IT, BUT WE OWE THIS DEBT TO YOU... WE NEVER ONCE THOUGHT A REGULAR HUMAN BEING COULD ORCHESTRATE OUR RISE TO POWER.
YOU GAVE US ENTRY TO THE ACRES OF ALL...YOU GAVE US THE LOCATION OF THIS CITY, THE PLAN TO GIVE US TOTAL DOMINATION WAS YOURS. YOU HAVEN'T FAILED US YET.
FAILURE ISN'T A STRONG SUIT OF MINE, DRAKAR.
AND YOU KNOW PERFECTLY WELL THAT I AM FAR MORE THAN JUST A MAN.
WAIT... WHAT'S THAT...
NO...NOT HER... NOT NOW...

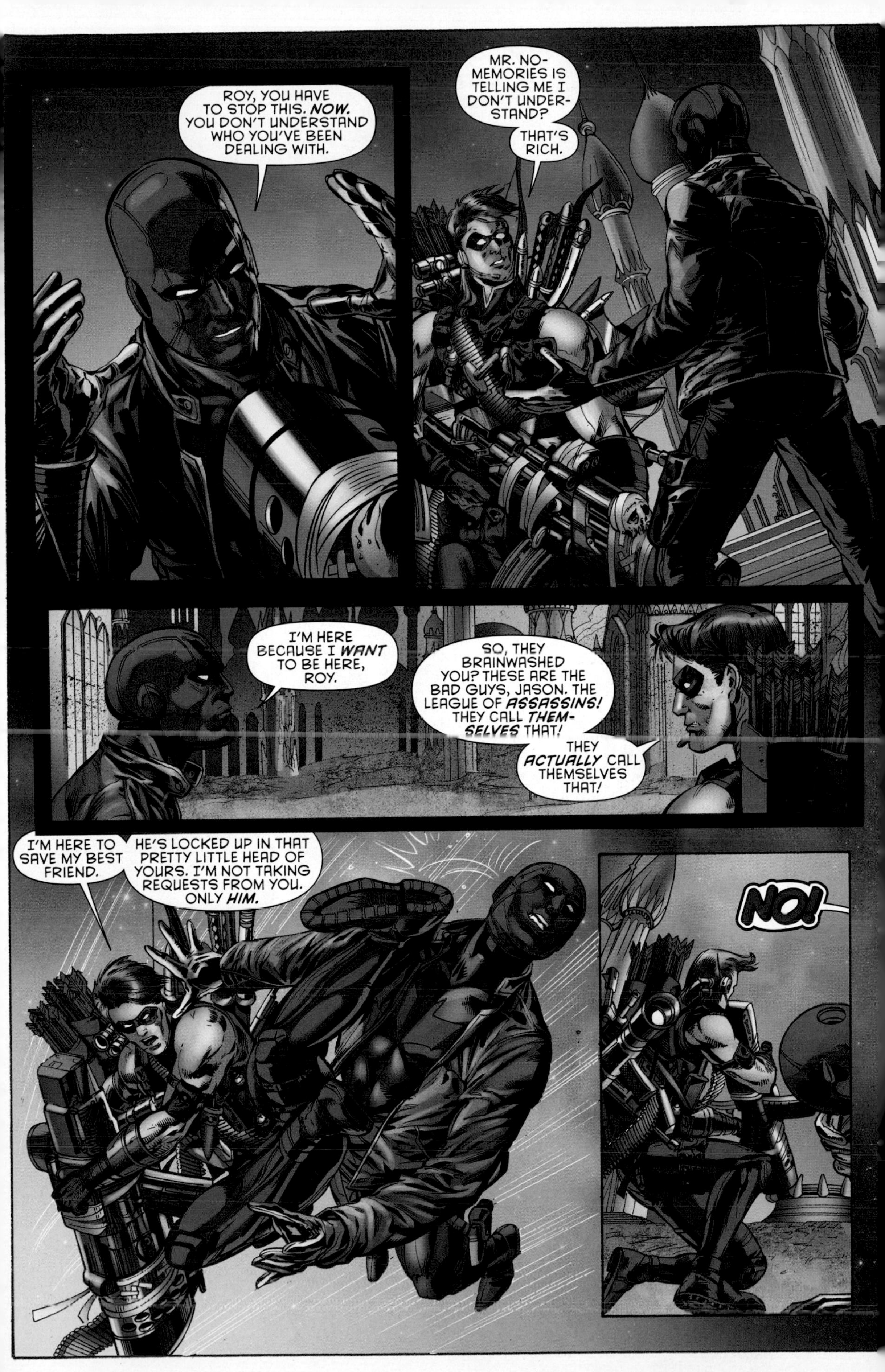
ROY, YOU HAVE TO STOP THIS. NOW. YOU DON'T UNDERSTAND WHO YOU'VE BEEN DEALING WITH.
MR. NO-MEMORIES IS TELLING ME I DON'T UNDER-STAND?
THAT'S RICH.
I'M HERE BECAUSE I WANT TO BE HERE, ROY.
SO, THEY BRAINWASHED YOU? THESE ARE THE BAD GUYS, JASON. THE LEAGUE OF ASSASSINS! THEY CALL THEM-SELVES THAT!
THEY ACTUALLY CALL THEMSELVES THAT!
I'M HERE TO SAVE MY BEST FRIEND.
HE'S LOCKED UP IN THAT PRETTY LITTLE HEAD OF YOURS. I'M NOT TAKING REQUESTS FROM YOU. ONLY HIM.
NO!

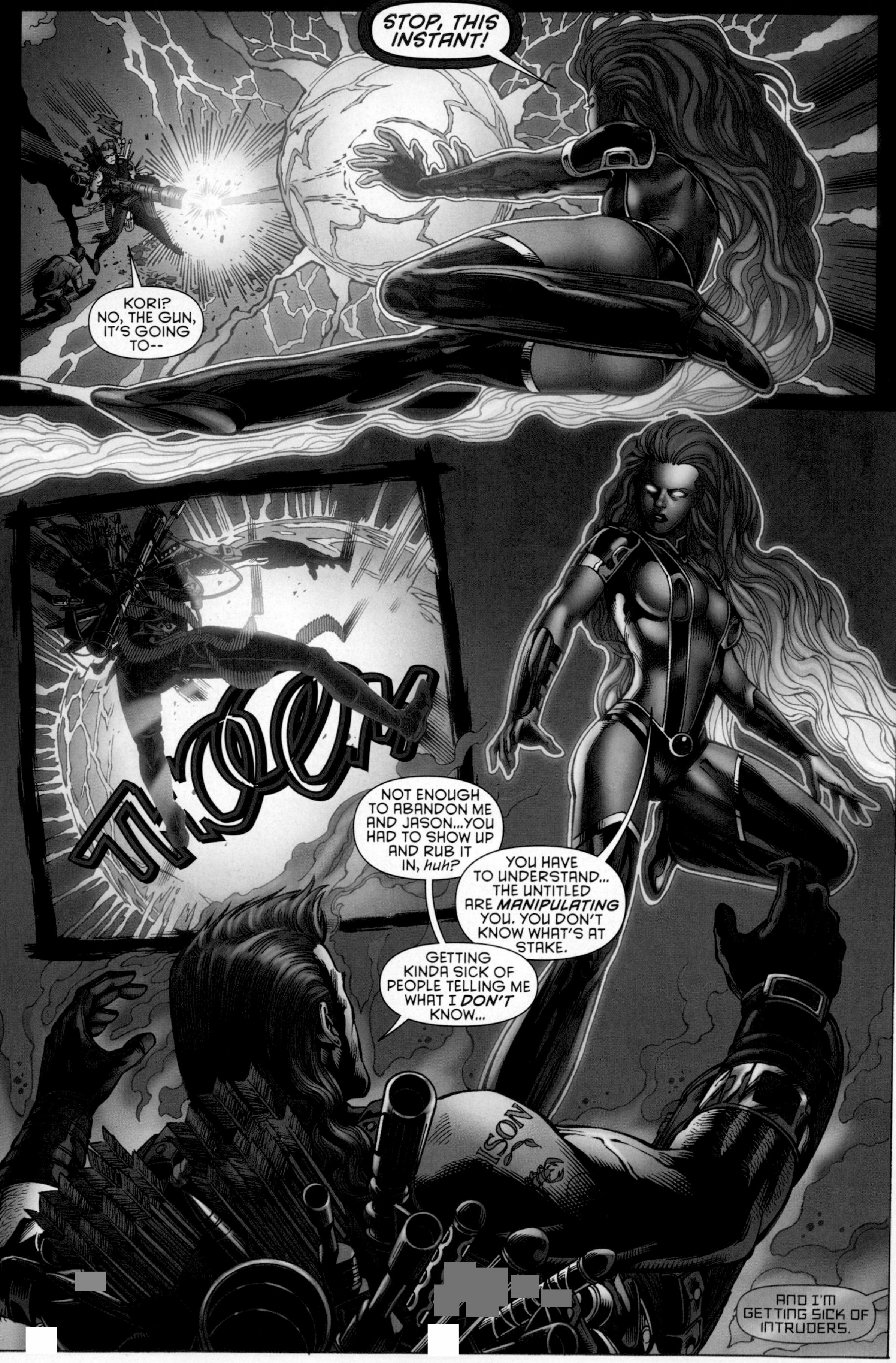
STOP, THIS INSTANT!
KORI? NO, THE GUN, IT'S GOING TO--
TWOOM
NOT ENOUGH TO ABANDON ME AND JASON...YOU HAD TO SHOW UP AND RUB IT IN, *huh?*
YOU HAVE TO UNDERSTAND... THE UNTITLED ARE ***MANIPULATING*** YOU. YOU DON'T KNOW WHAT'S AT STAKE.
GETTING KINDA SICK OF PEOPLE TELLING ME WHAT I ***DON'T*** KNOW...
AND I'M GETTING SICK OF INTRUDERS.

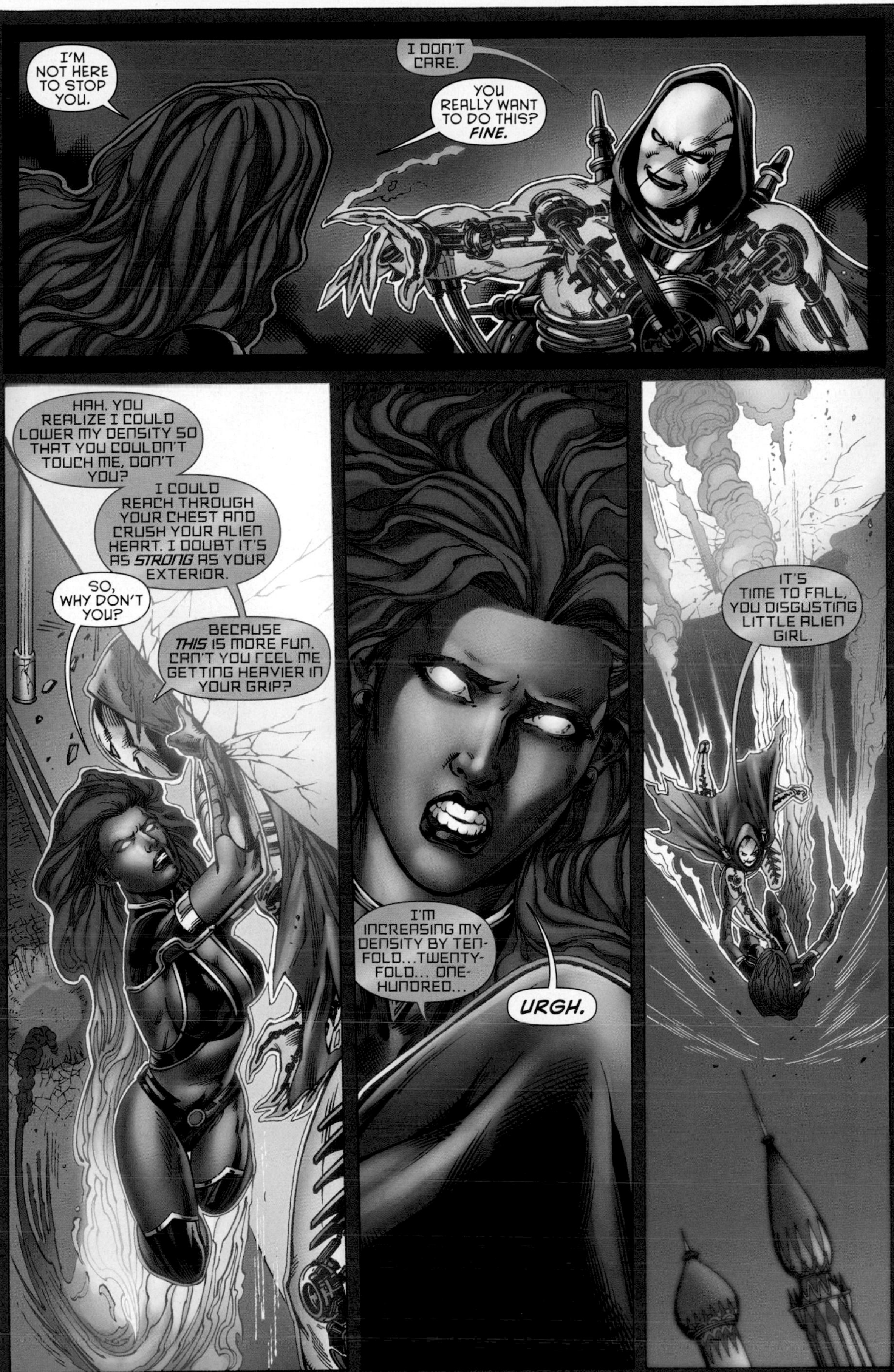
I'M NOT HERE TO STOP YOU.
I DON'T CARE.
YOU REALLY WANT TO DO THIS? FINE.
HAH. YOU REALIZE I COULD LOWER MY DENSITY SO THAT YOU COULDN'T TOUCH ME, DON'T YOU?
I COULD REACH THROUGH YOUR CHEST AND CRUSH YOUR ALIEN HEART. I DOUBT IT'S AS STRONG AS YOUR EXTERIOR.
SO, WHY DON'T YOU?
BECAUSE THIS IS MORE FUN. CAN'T YOU FEEL ME GETTING HEAVIER IN YOUR GRIP?
I'M INCREASING MY DENSITY BY TEN-FOLD...TWENTY-FOLD... ONE-HUNDRED...
URGH.
IT'S TIME TO FALL, YOU DISGUSTING LITTLE ALIEN GIRL.

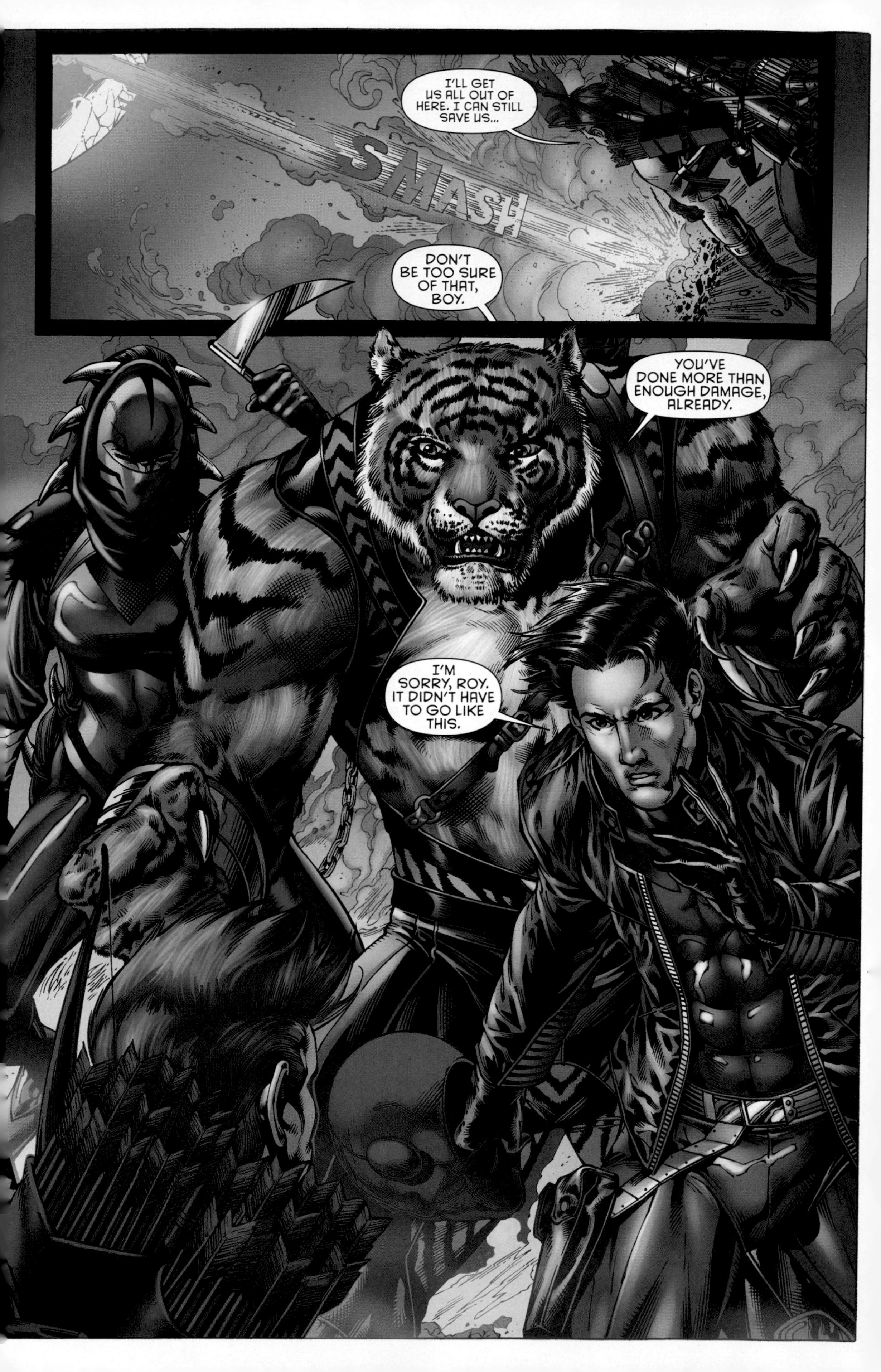
I'LL GET US ALL OUT OF HERE. I CAN STILL SAVE US...
SMASH
DON'T BE TOO SURE OF THAT, BOY.
YOU'VE DONE MORE THAN ENOUGH DAMAGE, ALREADY.
I'M SORRY, ROY. IT DIDN'T HAVE TO GO LIKE THIS.

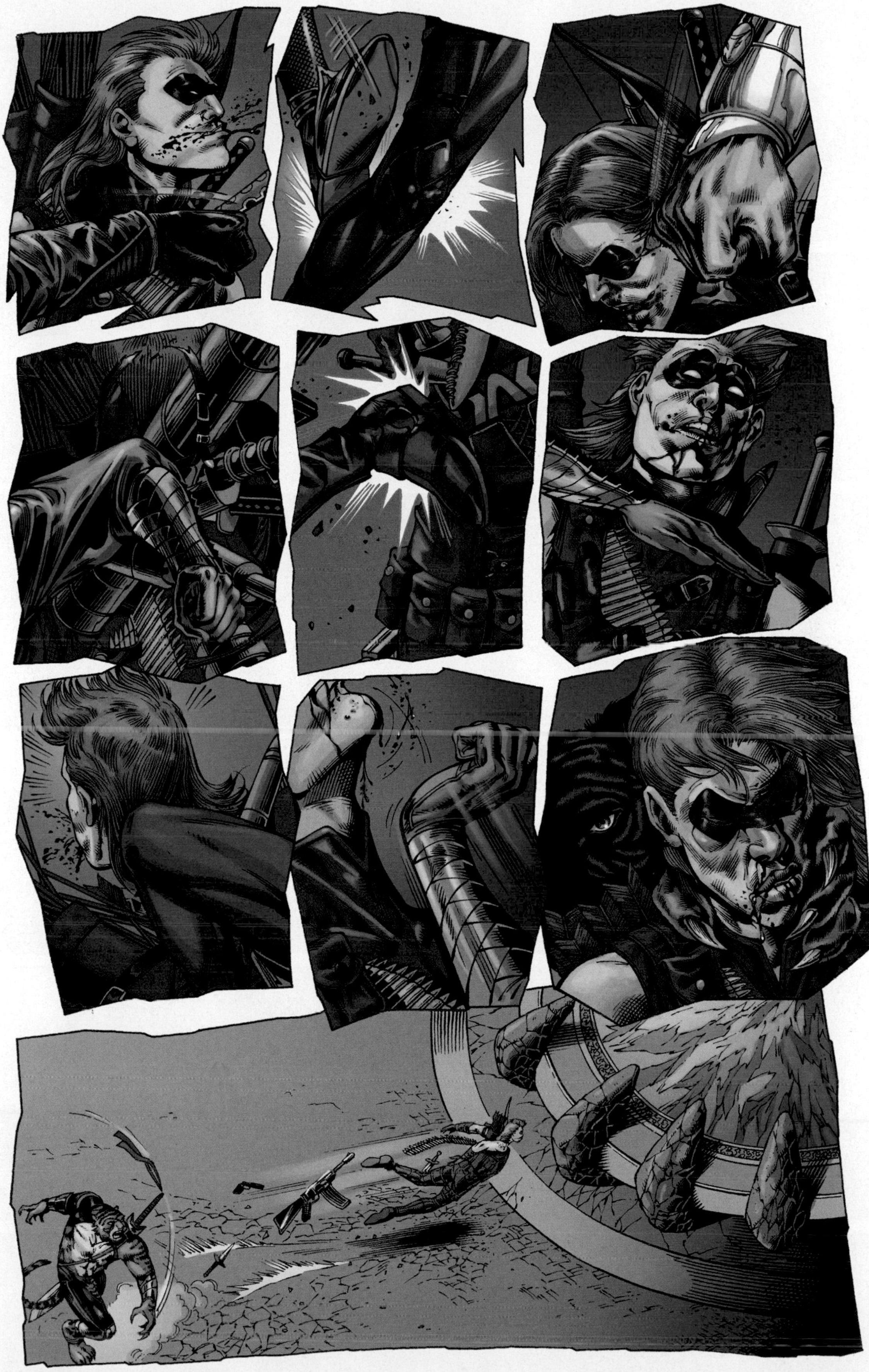

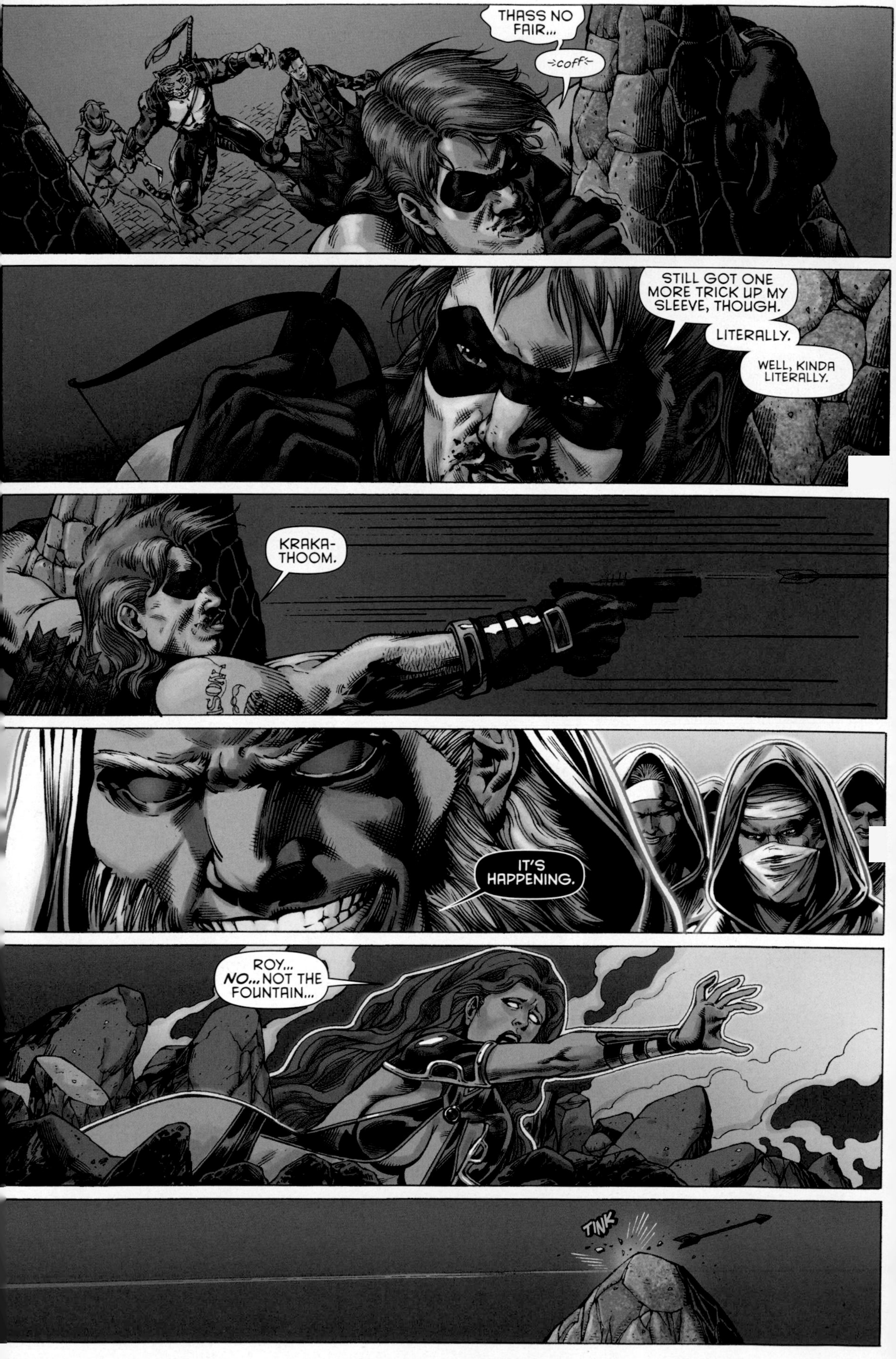
THASS NO FAIR...
coff
STILL GOT ONE MORE TRICK UP MY SLEEVE, THOUGH.
LITERALLY.
WELL, KINDA LITERALLY.
KRAKA-THOOM.
IT'S HAPPENING.
ROY... NO... NOT THE FOUNTAIN...
TINK

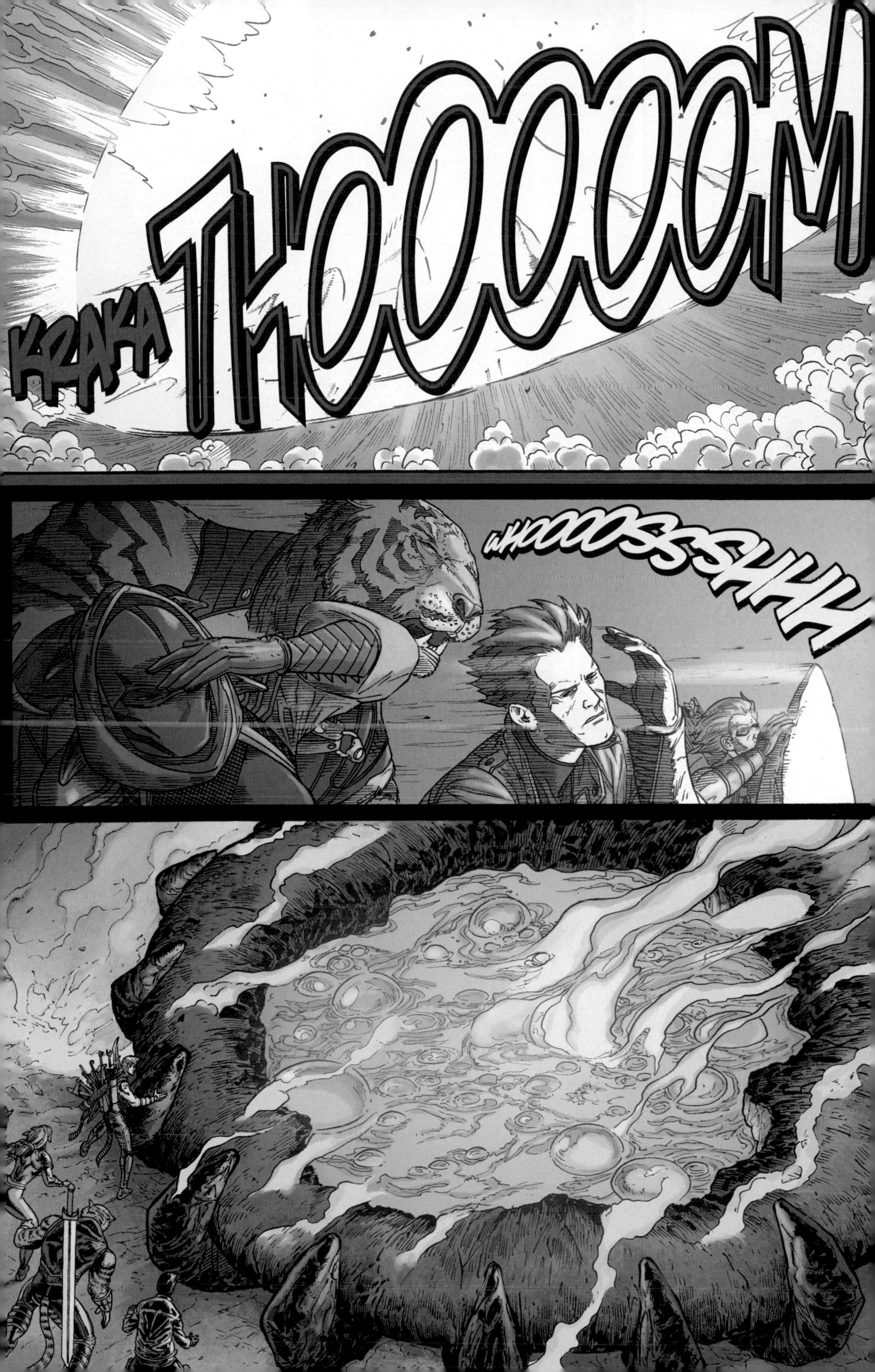
KRAKA THOOOOOM
WHOOOOSSSHHH

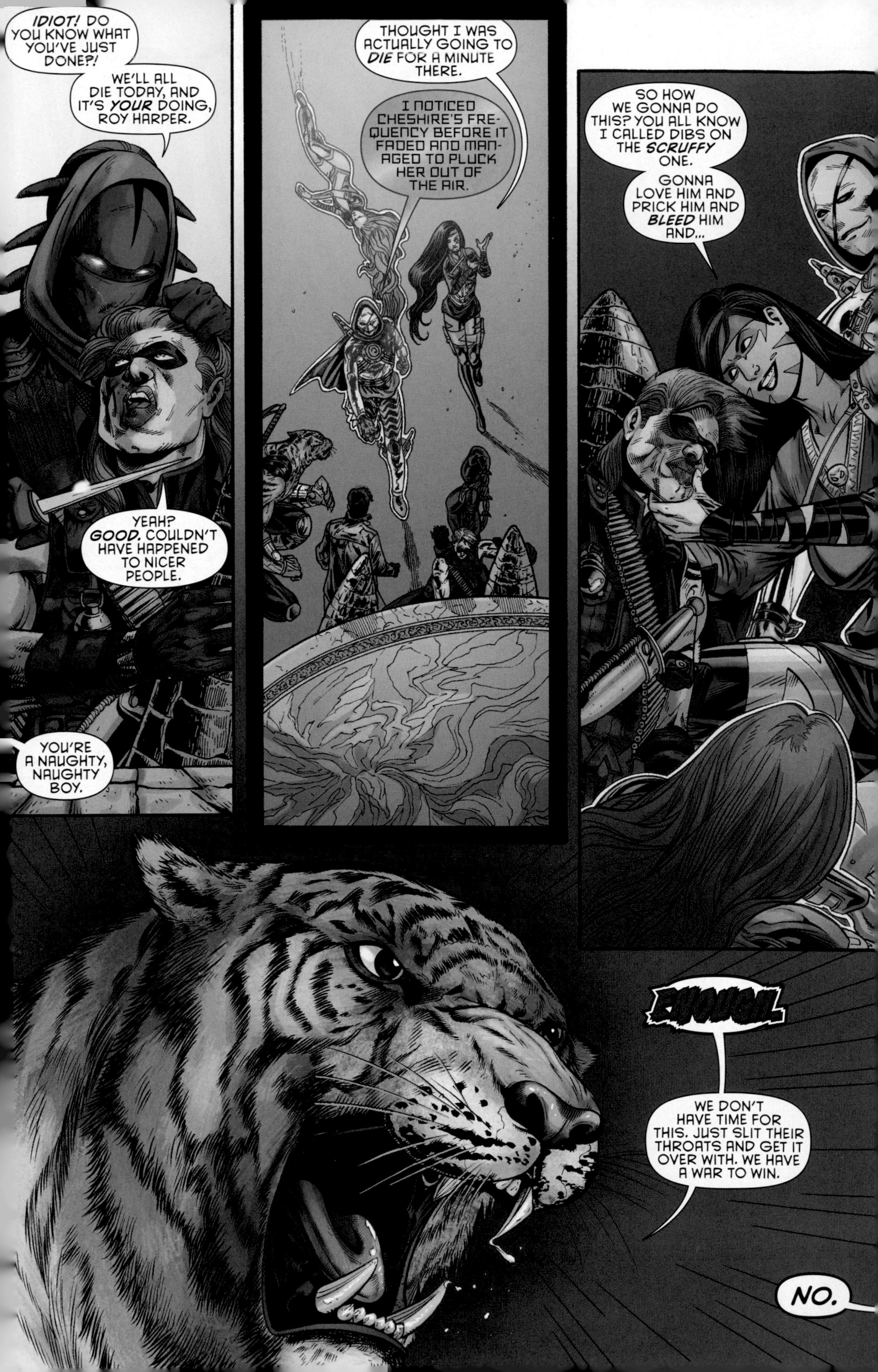

IDIOT! DO YOU KNOW WHAT YOU'VE JUST DONE?!
WE'LL ALL DIE TODAY, AND IT'S YOUR DOING, ROY HARPER.
YEAH? GOOD. COULDN'T HAVE HAPPENED TO NICER PEOPLE.
YOU'RE A NAUGHTY, NAUGHTY BOY.
THOUGHT I WAS ACTUALLY GOING TO DIE FOR A MINUTE THERE.
I NOTICED CHESHIRE'S FRE-QUENCY BEFORE IT FADED AND MAN-AGED TO PLUCK HER OUT OF THE AIR.
SO HOW WE GONNA DO THIS? YOU ALL KNOW I CALLED DIBS ON THE SCRUFFY ONE.
GONNA LOVE HIM AND PRICK HIM AND BLEED HIM AND...
ENOUGH.
WE DON'T HAVE TIME FOR THIS. JUST SLIT THEIR THROATS AND GET IT OVER WITH. WE HAVE A WAR TO WIN.
NO.

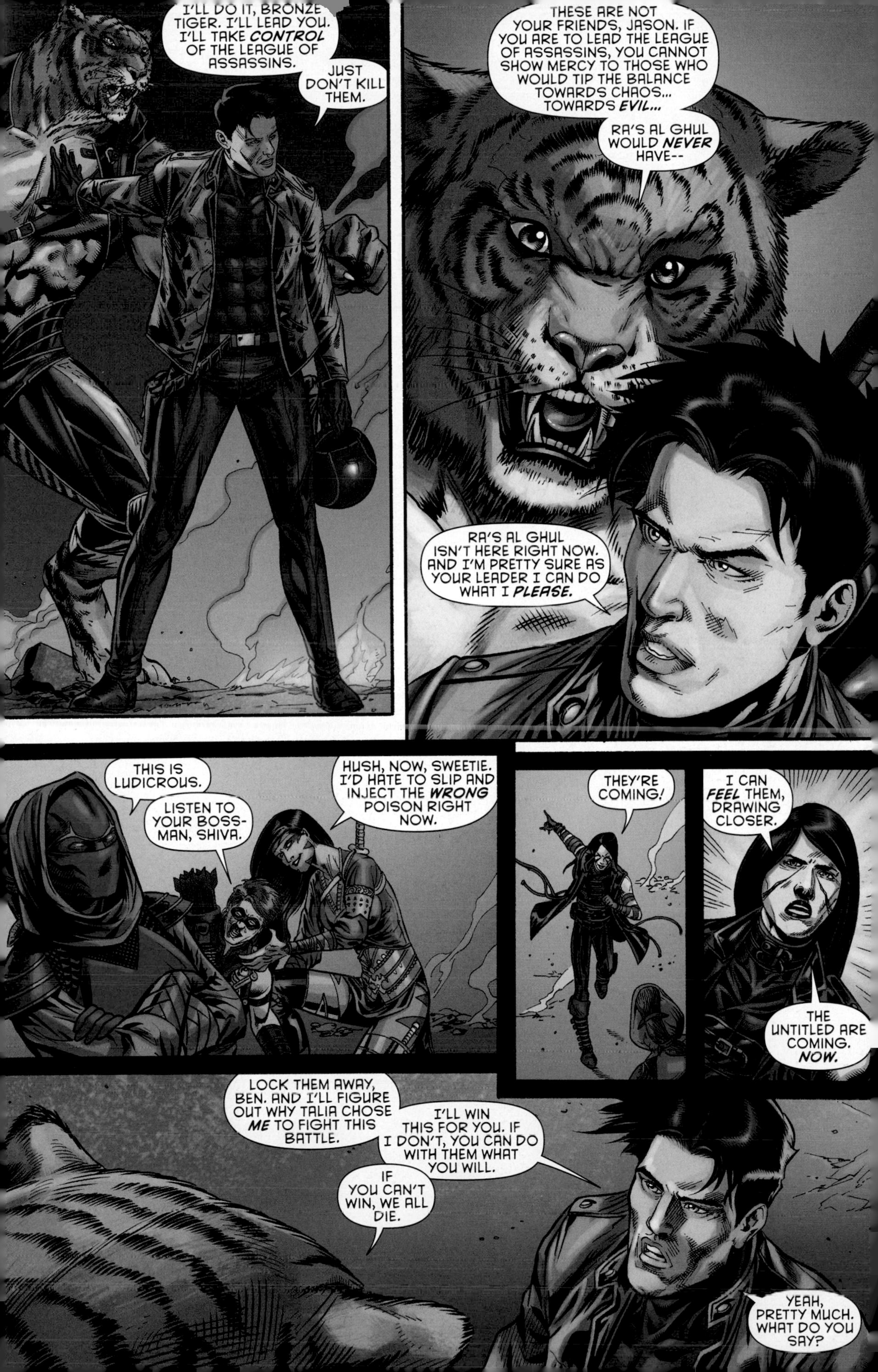
I'LL DO IT, BRONZE TIGER. I'LL LEAD YOU. I'LL TAKE CONTROL OF THE LEAGUE OF ASSASSINS.
JUST DON'T KILL THEM.
THESE ARE NOT YOUR FRIENDS, JASON. IF YOU ARE TO LEAD THE LEAGUE OF ASSASSINS, YOU CANNOT SHOW MERCY TO THOSE WHO WOULD TIP THE BALANCE TOWARDS CHAOS... TOWARDS EVIL...
RA'S AL GHUL WOULD NEVER HAVE--
RA'S AL GHUL ISN'T HERE RIGHT NOW. AND I'M PRETTY SURE AS YOUR LEADER I CAN DO WHAT I PLEASE.
THIS IS LUDICROUS.
LISTEN TO YOUR BOSS-MAN, SHIVA.
HUSH, NOW, SWEETIE. I'D HATE TO SLIP AND INJECT THE WRONG POISON RIGHT NOW.
THEY'RE COMING!
I CAN FEEL THEM, DRAWING CLOSER.
THE UNTITLED ARE COMING. NOW.
LOCK THEM AWAY, BEN. AND I'LL FIGURE OUT WHY TALIA CHOSE ME TO FIGHT THIS BATTLE.
I'LL WIN THIS FOR YOU. IF I DON'T, YOU CAN DO WITH THEM WHAT YOU WILL.
IF YOU CAN'T WIN, WE ALL DIE.
YEAH, PRETTY MUCH. WHAT DO YOU SAY?

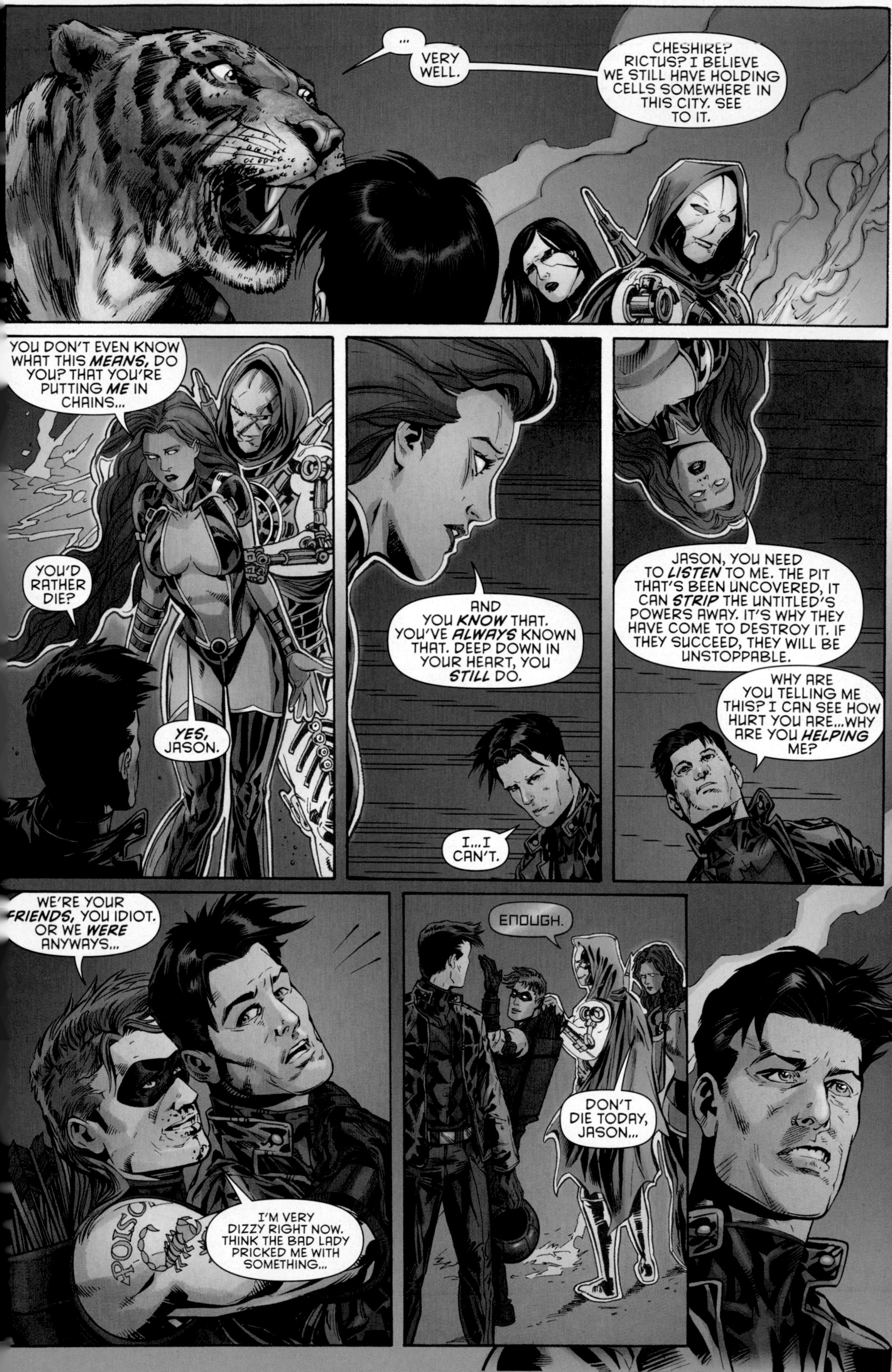
...
VERY WELL.
CHESHIRE? RICTUS? I BELIEVE WE STILL HAVE HOLDING CELLS SOMEWHERE IN THIS CITY. SEE TO IT.
YOU DON'T EVEN KNOW WHAT THIS MEANS, DO YOU? THAT YOU'RE PUTTING ME IN CHAINS...
YOU'D RATHER DIE?
YES, JASON.
AND YOU KNOW THAT. YOU'VE ALWAYS KNOWN THAT. DEEP DOWN IN YOUR HEART, YOU STILL DO.
I...I CAN'T.
JASON, YOU NEED TO LISTEN TO ME. THE PIT THAT'S BEEN UNCOVERED, IT CAN STRIP THE UNTITLED'S POWERS AWAY. IT'S WHY THEY HAVE COME TO DESTROY IT. IF THEY SUCCEED, THEY WILL BE UNSTOPPABLE.
WHY ARE YOU TELLING ME THIS? I CAN SEE HOW HURT YOU ARE...WHY ARE YOU HELPING ME?
WE'RE YOUR FRIENDS, YOU IDIOT. OR WE WERE ANYWAYS...
I'M VERY DIZZY RIGHT NOW. THINK THE BAD LADY PRICKED ME WITH SOMETHING...
ENOUGH.
DON'T DIE TODAY, JASON...

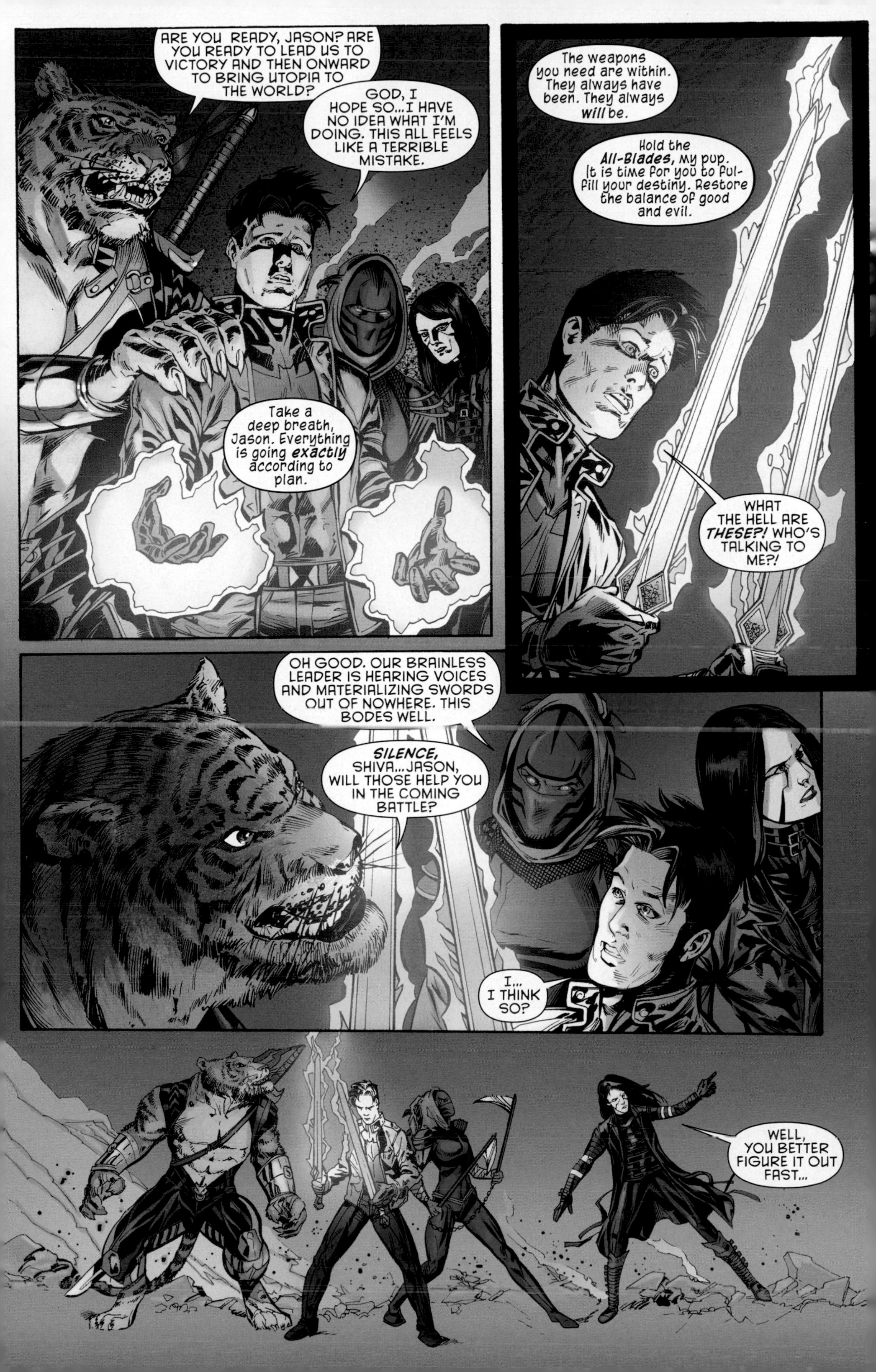
ARE YOU READY, JASON? ARE YOU READY TO LEAD US TO VICTORY AND THEN ONWARD TO BRING UTOPIA TO THE WORLD?
GOD, I HOPE SO...I HAVE NO IDEA WHAT I'M DOING. THIS ALL FEELS LIKE A TERRIBLE MISTAKE.
Take a deep breath, Jason. Everything is going exactly according to plan.
The weapons you need are within. They always have been. They always will be.
Hold the All-Blades, my pup. It is time for you to fulfill your destiny. Restore the balance of good and evil.
WHAT THE HELL ARE THESE?! WHO'S TALKING TO ME?!
OH GOOD. OUR BRAINLESS LEADER IS HEARING VOICES AND MATERIALIZING SWORDS OUT OF NOWHERE. THIS BODES WELL.
SILENCE, SHIVA...JASON, WILL THOSE HELP YOU IN THE COMING BATTLE?
I... I THINK SO?
WELL, YOU BETTER FIGURE IT OUT FAST...

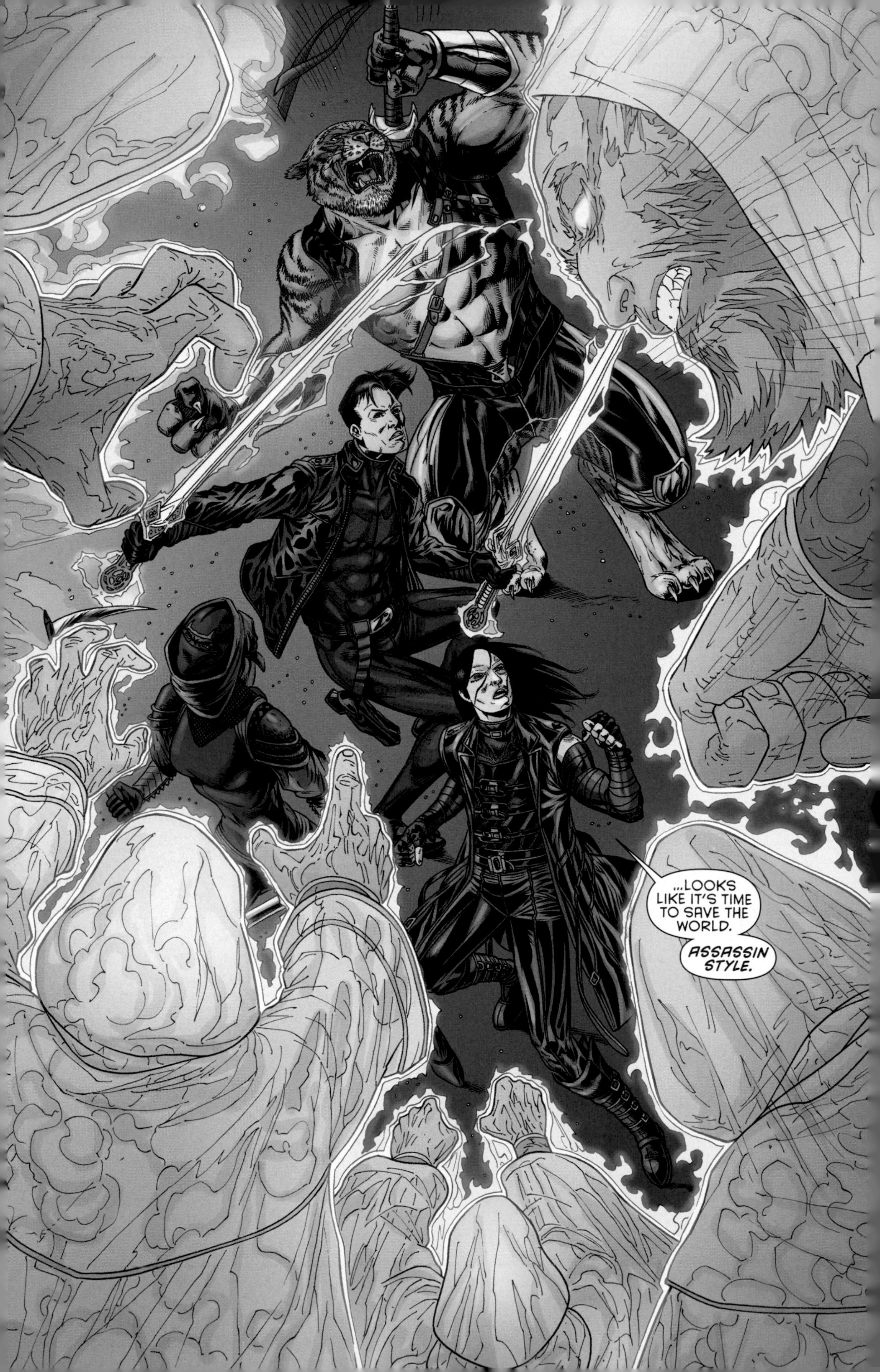
...LOOKS LIKE IT'S TIME TO SAVE THE WORLD.
ASSASSIN STYLE.

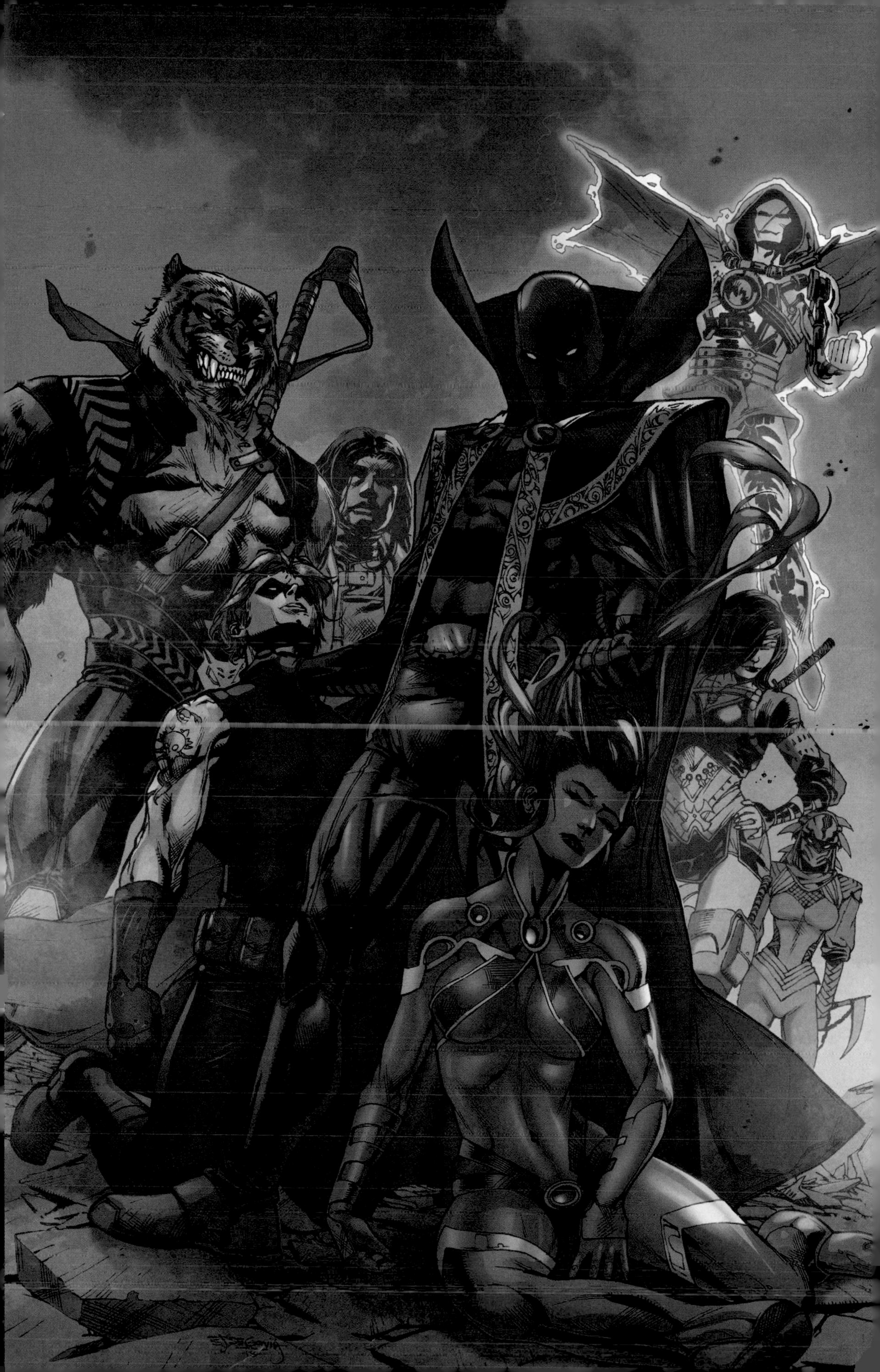

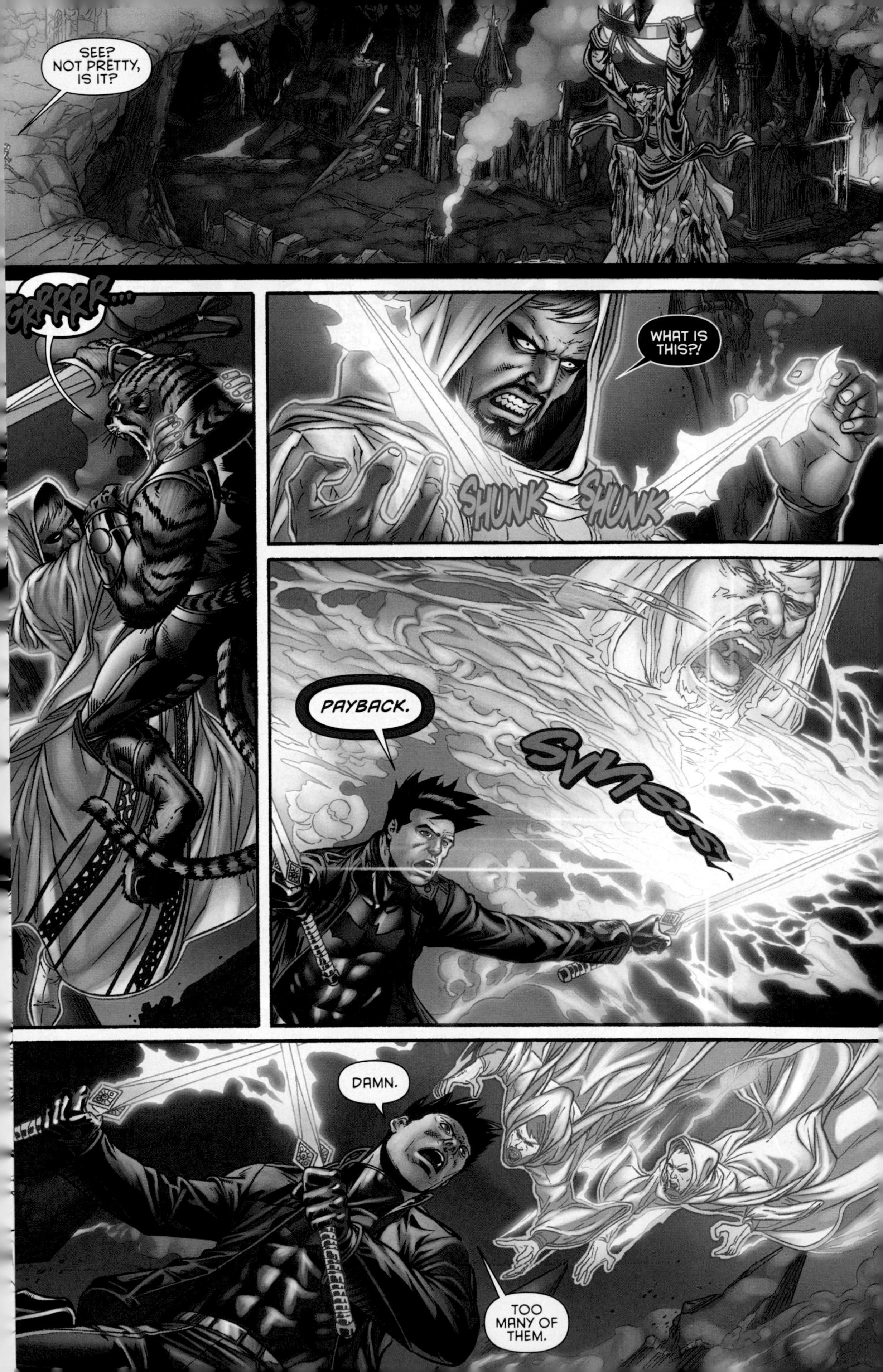
SEE? NOT PRETTY, IS IT?
GRRRRR...
WHAT IS THIS?!
SHUNK SHUNK
PAYBACK.
SVVISSS
DAMN.
TOO MANY OF THEM.

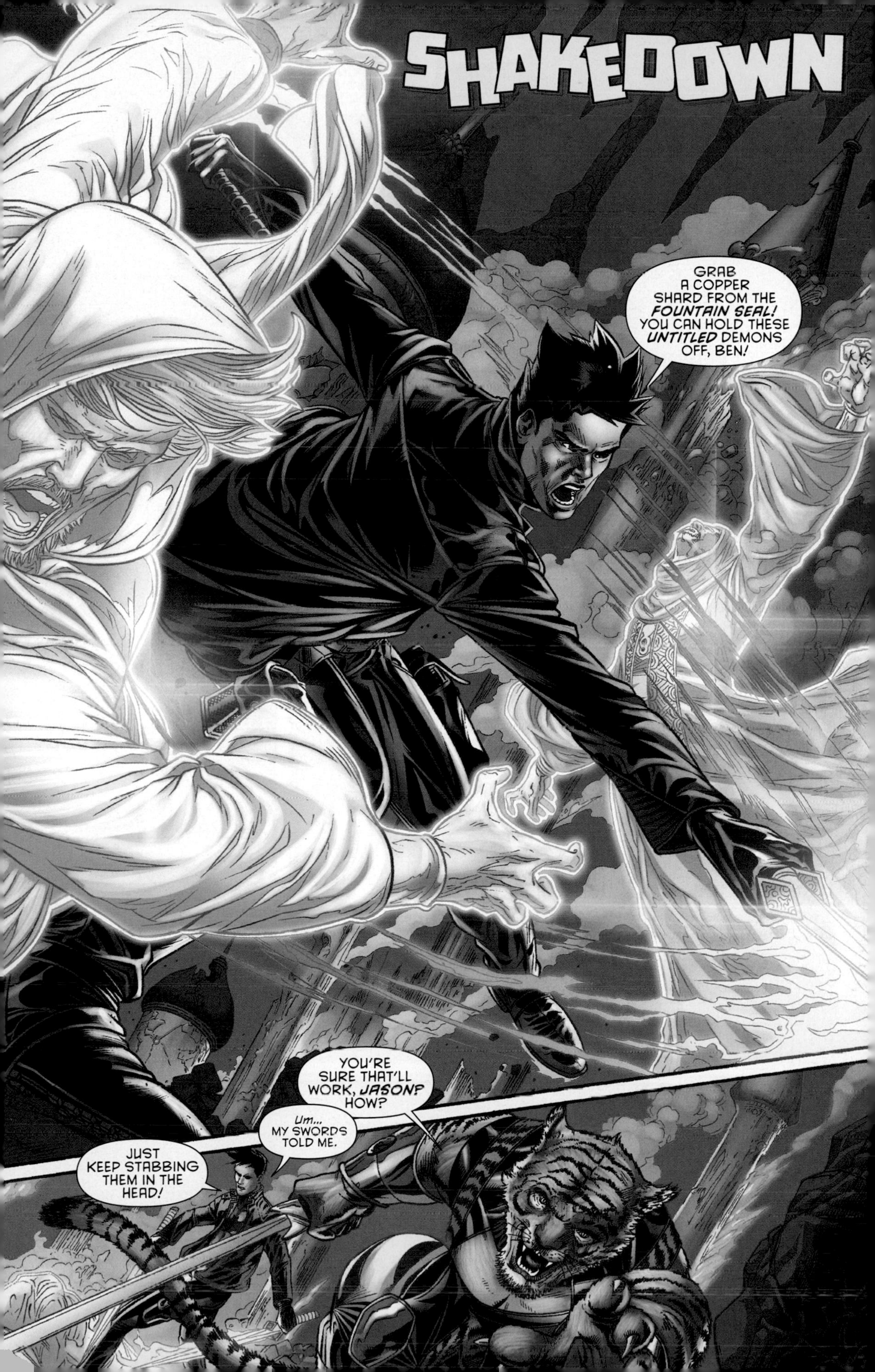
SHAKEDOWN
GRAB A COPPER SHARD FROM THE *FOUNTAIN SEAL!* YOU CAN HOLD THESE *UNTITLED* DEMONS OFF, BEN!
YOU'RE SURE THAT'LL WORK, *JASON?* HOW?
Um... MY SWORDS TOLD ME.
JUST KEEP STABBING THEM IN THE HEAD!

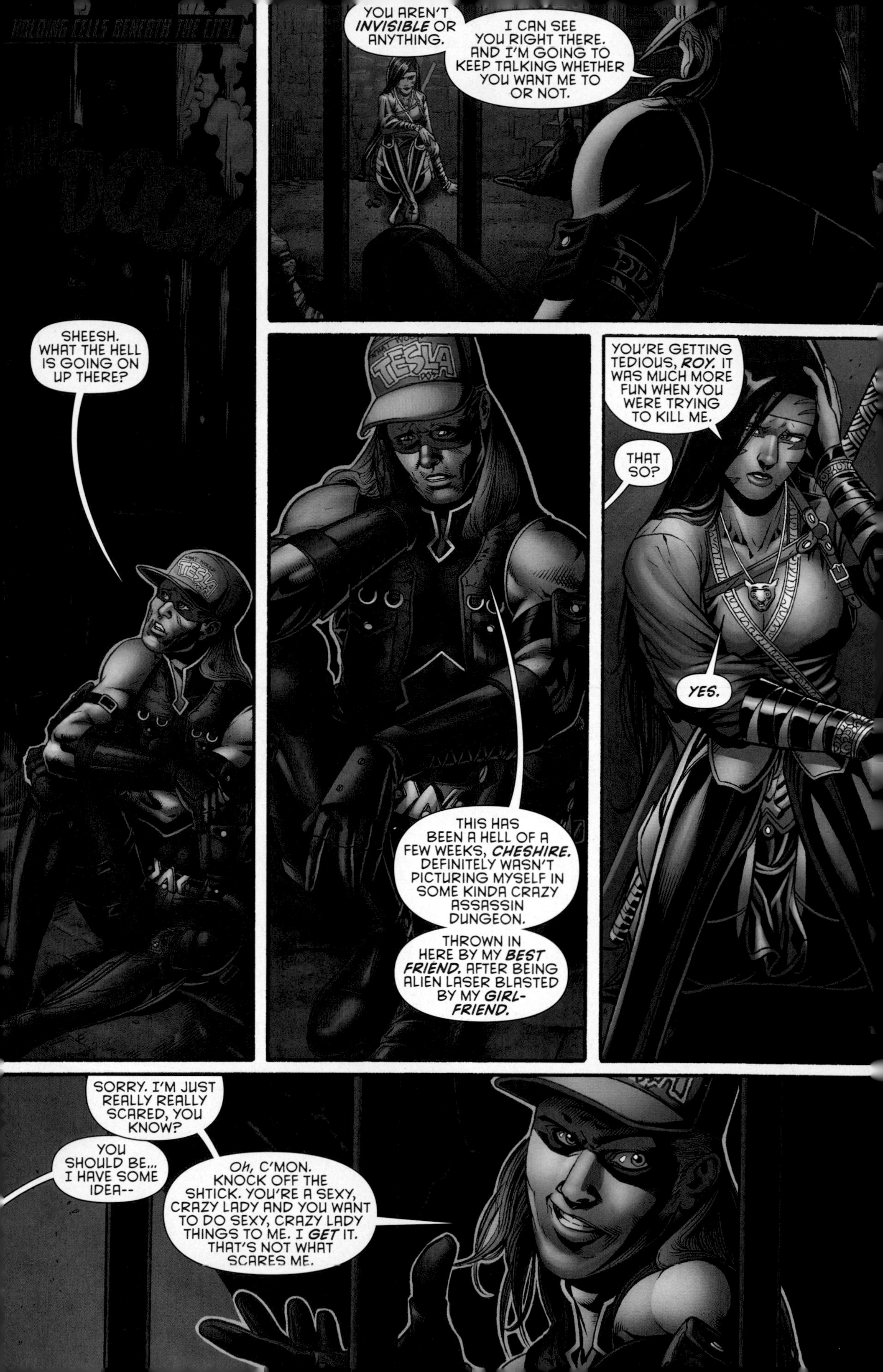
HOLDING CELLS BENEATH THE CITY.
YOU AREN'T *INVISIBLE* OR ANYTHING.
I CAN SEE YOU RIGHT THERE. AND I'M GOING TO KEEP TALKING WHETHER YOU WANT ME TO OR NOT.
SHEESH. WHAT THE HELL IS GOING ON UP THERE?
THIS HAS BEEN A HELL OF A FEW WEEKS, *CHESHIRE.* DEFINITELY WASN'T PICTURING MYSELF IN SOME KINDA CRAZY ASSASSIN DUNGEON.
THROWN IN HERE BY MY *BEST FRIEND.* AFTER BEING ALIEN LASER BLASTED BY MY *GIRL-FRIEND.*
YOU'RE GETTING TEDIOUS, *ROY.* IT WAS MUCH MORE FUN WHEN YOU WERE TRYING TO KILL ME.
THAT SO?
YES.
SORRY. I'M JUST REALLY REALLY SCARED, YOU KNOW?
YOU SHOULD BE... I HAVE SOME IDEA--
Oh, C'MON. KNOCK OFF THE SHTICK. YOU'RE A SEXY, CRAZY LADY AND YOU WANT TO DO SEXY, CRAZY LADY THINGS TO ME. I *GET* IT. THAT'S NOT WHAT SCARES ME.

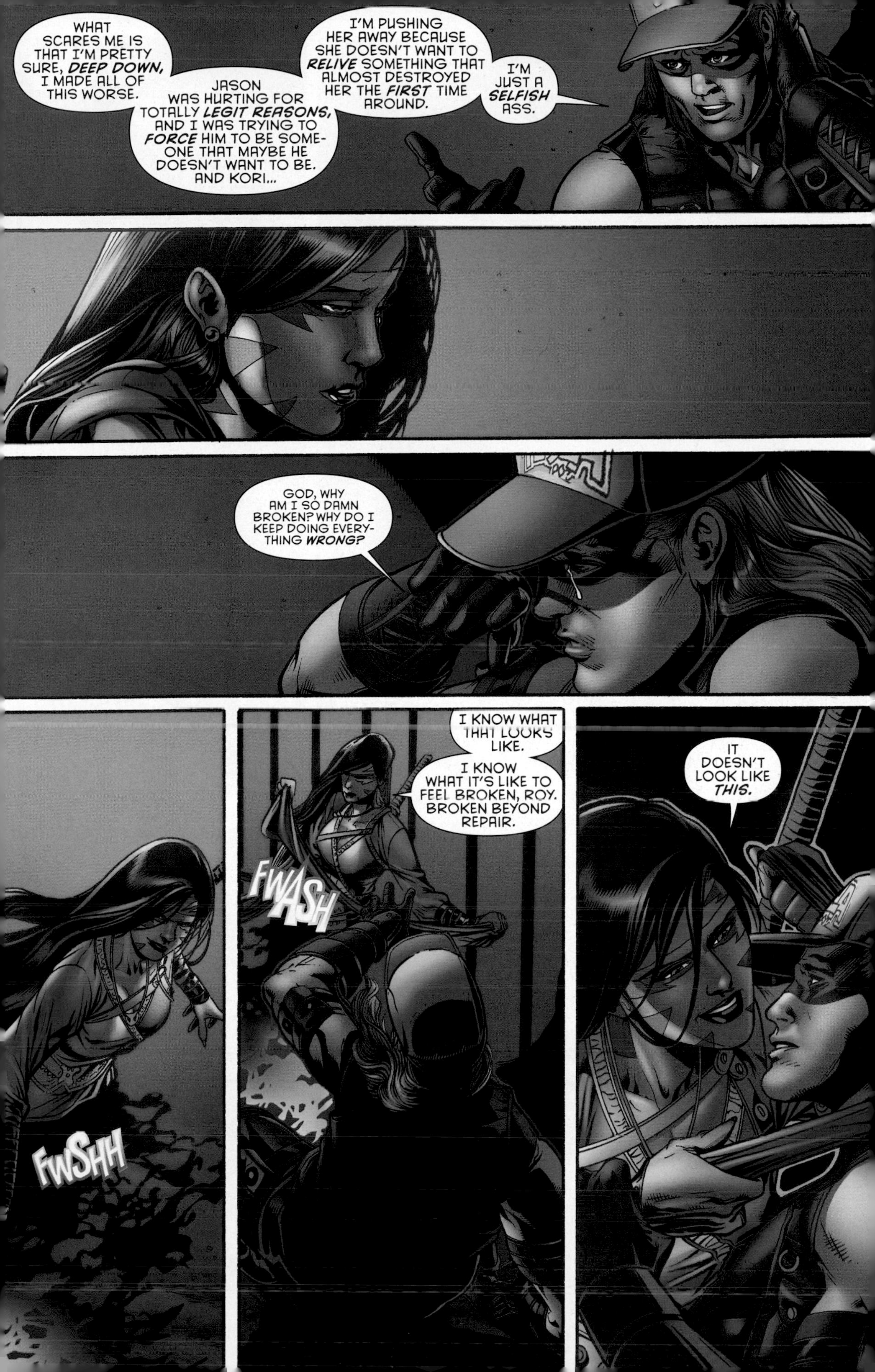
WHAT SCARES ME IS THAT I'M PRETTY SURE, DEEP DOWN, I MADE ALL OF THIS WORSE.
JASON WAS HURTING FOR TOTALLY LEGIT REASONS, AND I WAS TRYING TO FORCE HIM TO BE SOME-ONE THAT MAYBE HE DOESN'T WANT TO BE. AND KORI...
I'M PUSHING HER AWAY BECAUSE SHE DOESN'T WANT TO RELIVE SOMETHING THAT ALMOST DESTROYED HER THE FIRST TIME AROUND.
I'M JUST A SELFISH ASS.
GOD, WHY AM I SO DAMN BROKEN? WHY DO I KEEP DOING EVERY-THING WRONG?
FWSHH
FWASH
I KNOW WHAT THAT LOOKS LIKE.
I KNOW WHAT IT'S LIKE TO FEEL BROKEN, ROY. BROKEN BEYOND REPAIR.
IT DOESN'T LOOK LIKE THIS.

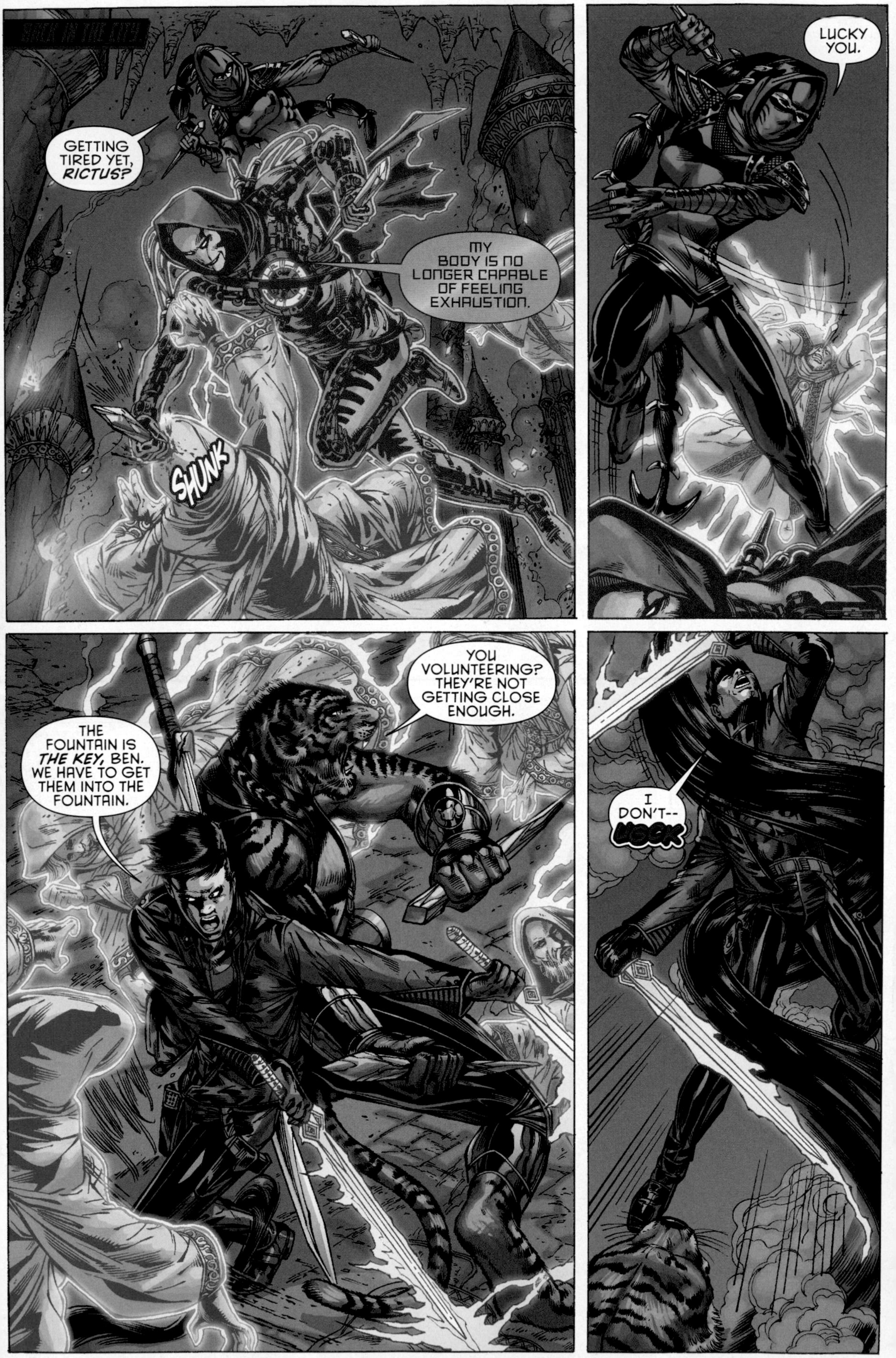
BACK IN THE CITY
GETTING TIRED YET, RICTUS?
MY BODY IS NO LONGER CAPABLE OF FEELING EXHAUSTION.
SHUNK
LUCKY YOU.
YOU VOLUNTEERING? THEY'RE NOT GETTING CLOSE ENOUGH.
THE FOUNTAIN IS THE KEY, BEN. WE HAVE TO GET THEM INTO THE FOUNTAIN.
I DON'T--

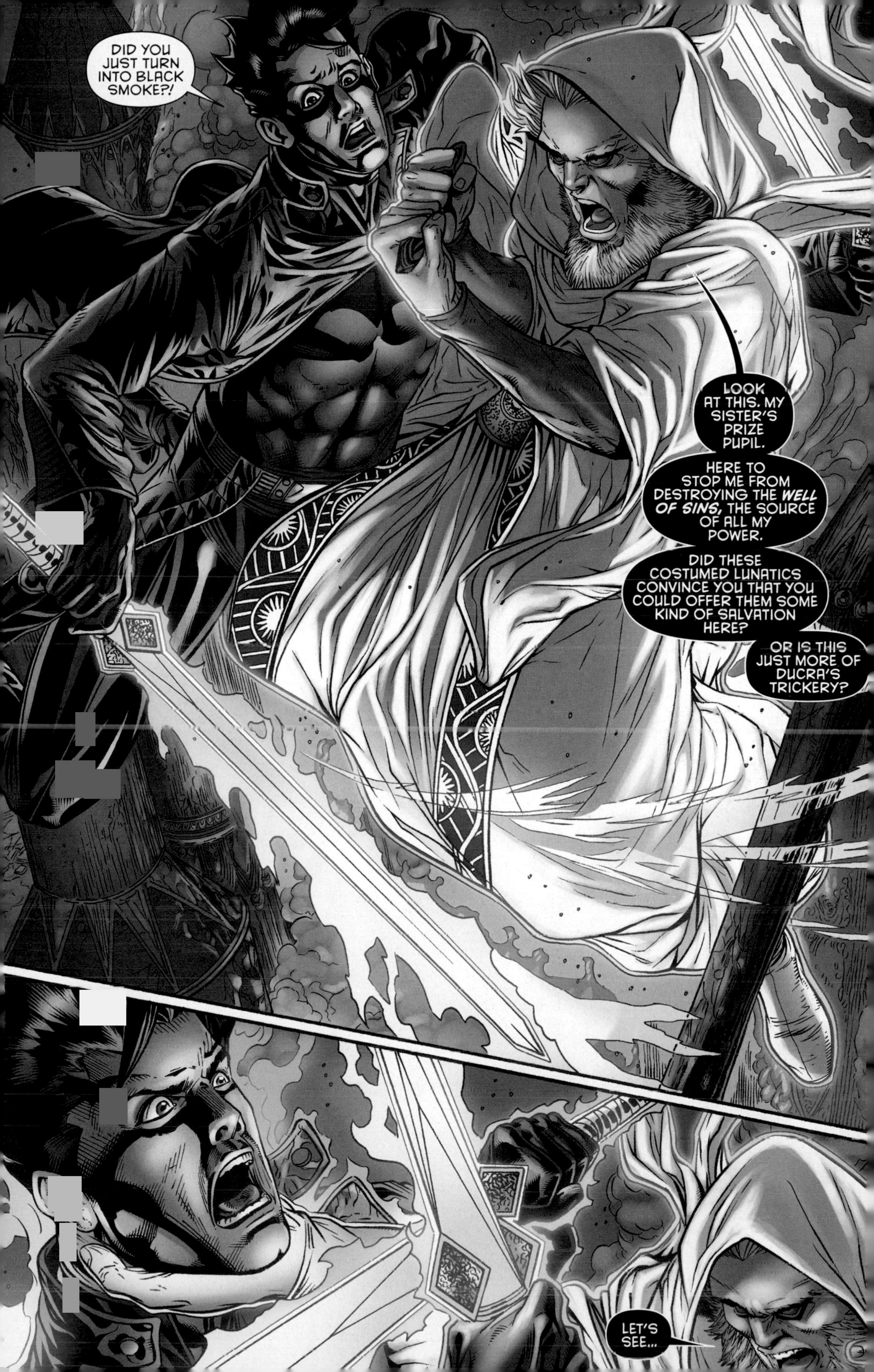
DID YOU JUST TURN INTO BLACK SMOKE?!
LOOK AT THIS. MY SISTER'S PRIZE PUPIL.
HERE TO STOP ME FROM DESTROYING THE *WELL OF SINS,* THE SOURCE OF ALL MY POWER.
DID THESE COSTUMED LUNATICS CONVINCE YOU THAT YOU COULD OFFER THEM SOME KIND OF SALVATION HERE?
OR IS THIS JUST MORE OF DUCRA'S TRICKERY?
LET'S SEE...

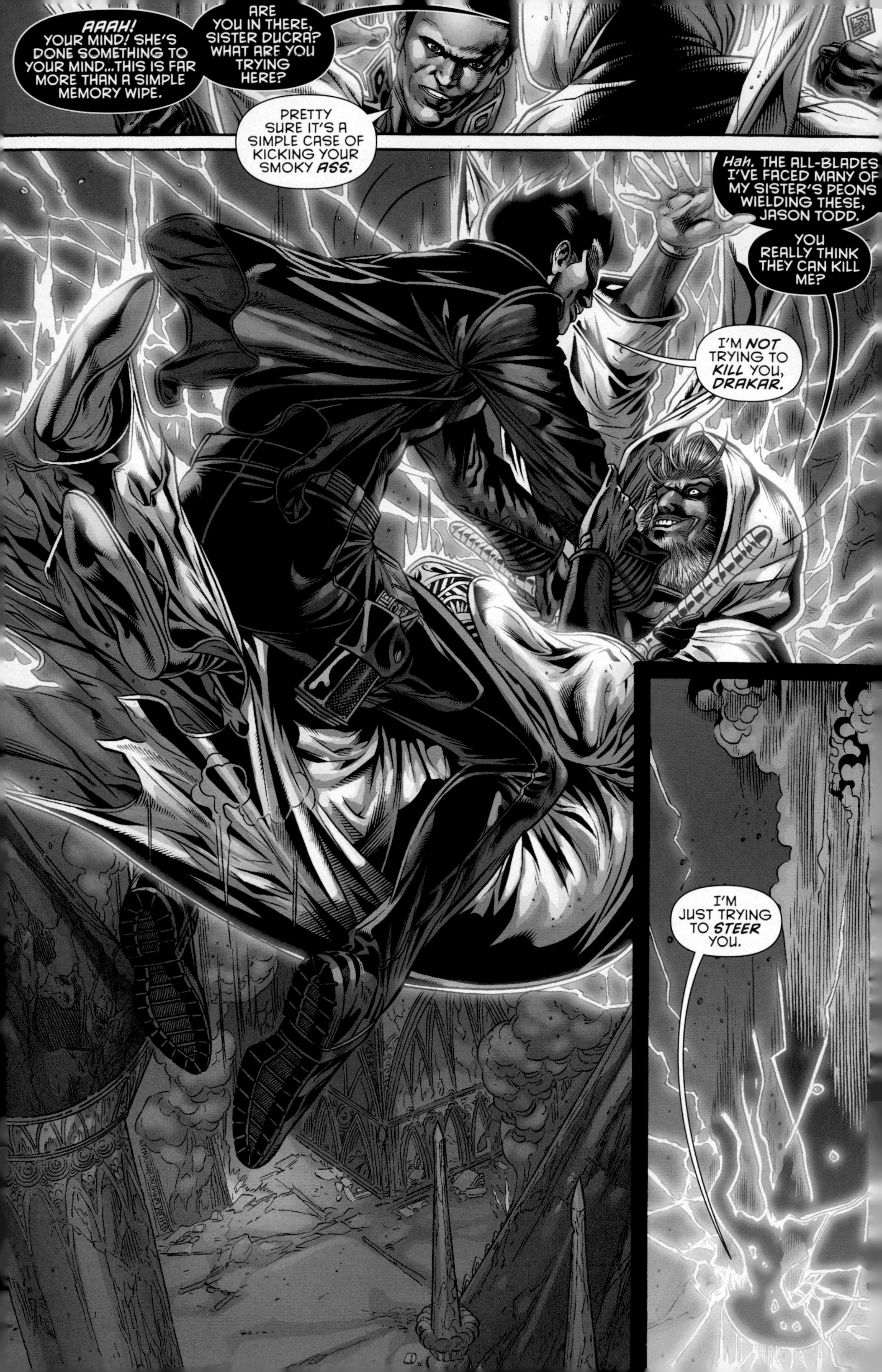

AAAH! YOUR MIND! SHE'S DONE SOMETHING TO YOUR MIND...THIS IS FAR MORE THAN A SIMPLE MEMORY WIPE.
ARE YOU IN THERE, SISTER DUCRA? WHAT ARE YOU TRYING HERE?
PRETTY SURE IT'S A SIMPLE CASE OF KICKING YOUR SMOKY ASS.
Hah. THE ALL-BLADES I'VE FACED MANY OF MY SISTER'S PEONS WIELDING THESE, JASON TODD.
YOU REALLY THINK THEY CAN KILL ME?
I'M NOT TRYING TO KILL YOU, DRAKAR.
I'M JUST TRYING TO STEER YOU.

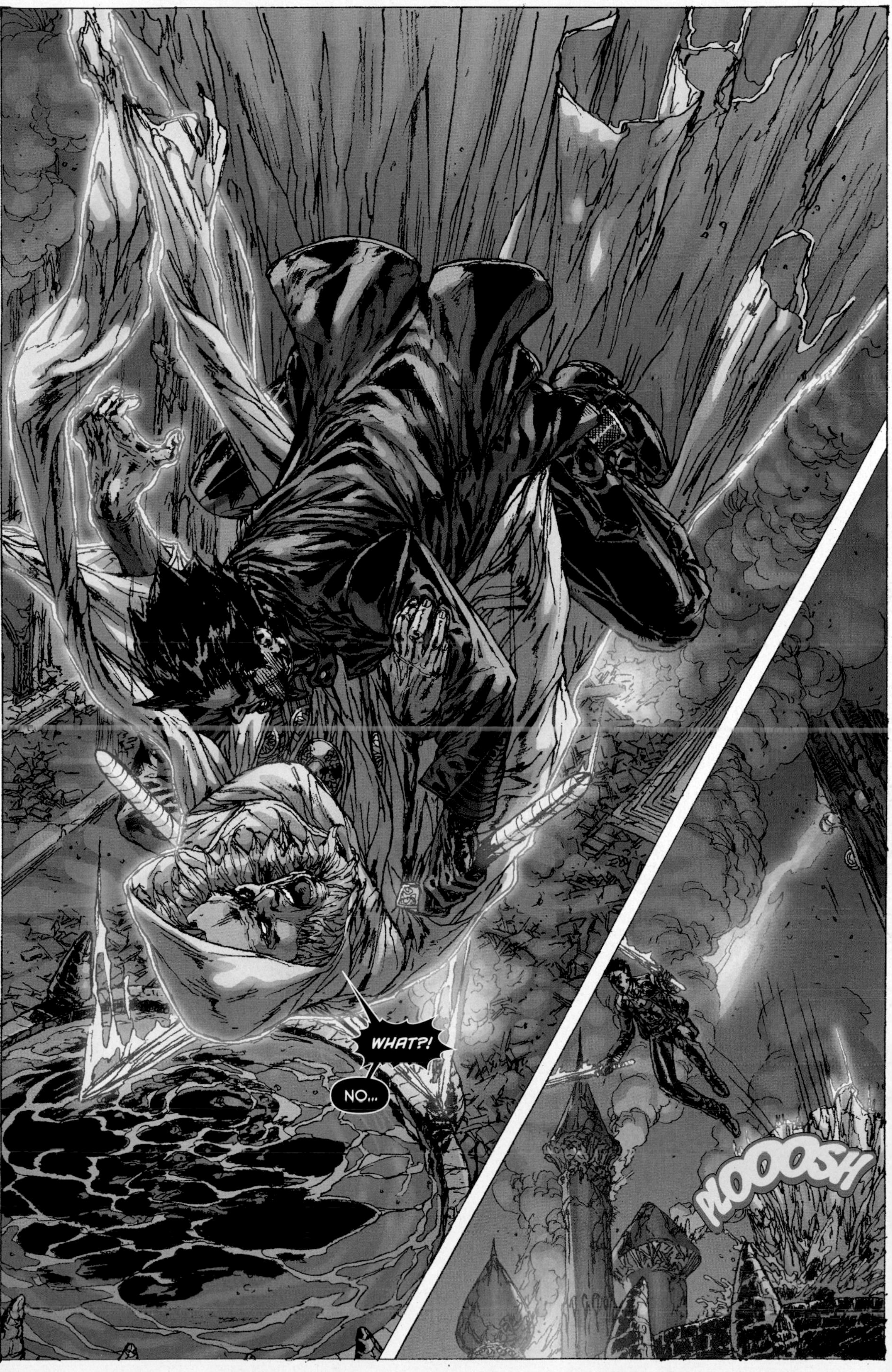
WHAT?!
NO...
PLOOOOSH

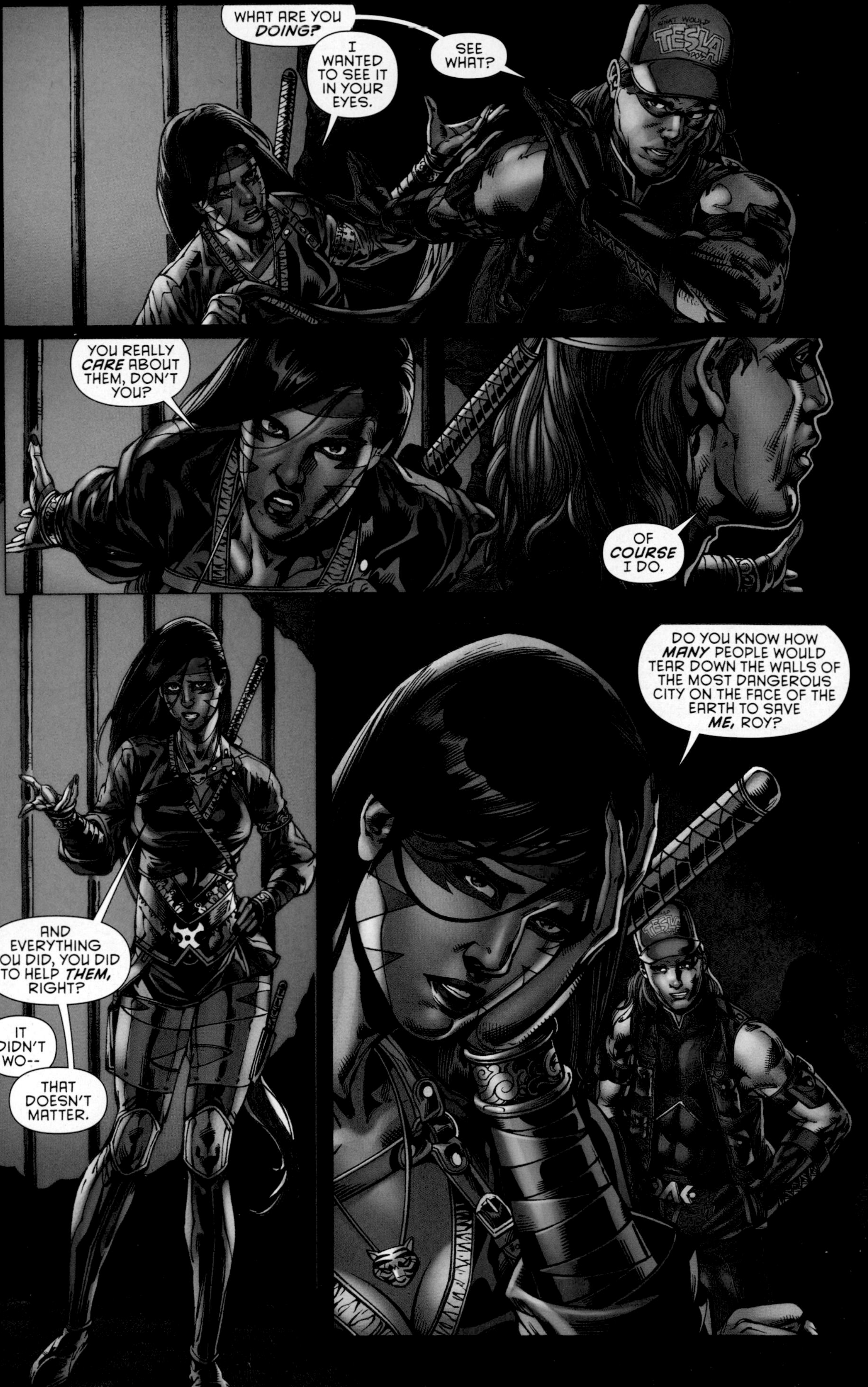
WHAT ARE YOU DOING?
SEE WHAT?
I WANTED TO SEE IT IN YOUR EYES.
YOU REALLY CARE ABOUT THEM, DON'T YOU?
OF COURSE I DO.
AND EVERYTHING YOU DID, YOU DID TO HELP THEM, RIGHT?
IT DIDN'T WO--
THAT DOESN'T MATTER.
DO YOU KNOW HOW MANY PEOPLE WOULD TEAR DOWN THE WALLS OF THE MOST DANGEROUS CITY ON THE FACE OF THE EARTH TO SAVE ME, ROY?
WHAT WOULD TESLA DO?

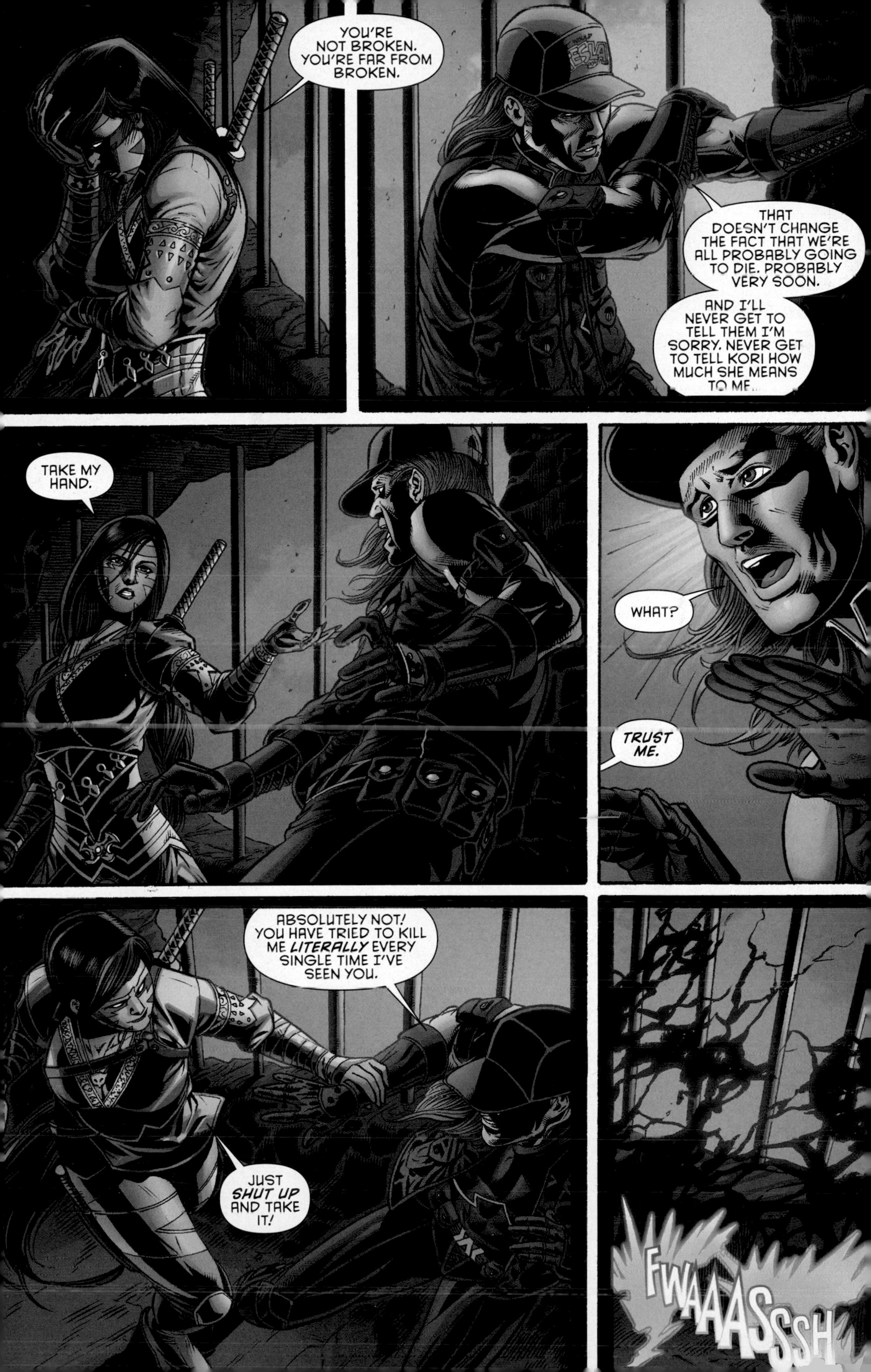

YOU'RE NOT BROKEN. YOU'RE FAR FROM BROKEN.
THAT DOESN'T CHANGE THE FACT THAT WE'RE ALL PROBABLY GOING TO DIE. PROBABLY VERY SOON.
AND I'LL NEVER GET TO TELL THEM I'M SORRY. NEVER GET TO TELL KORI HOW MUCH SHE MEANS TO ME...
TAKE MY HAND.
WHAT?
TRUST ME.
ABSOLUTELY NOT! YOU HAVE TRIED TO KILL ME LITERALLY EVERY SINGLE TIME I'VE SEEN YOU.
JUST SHUT UP AND TAKE IT!
FWAAASSSH

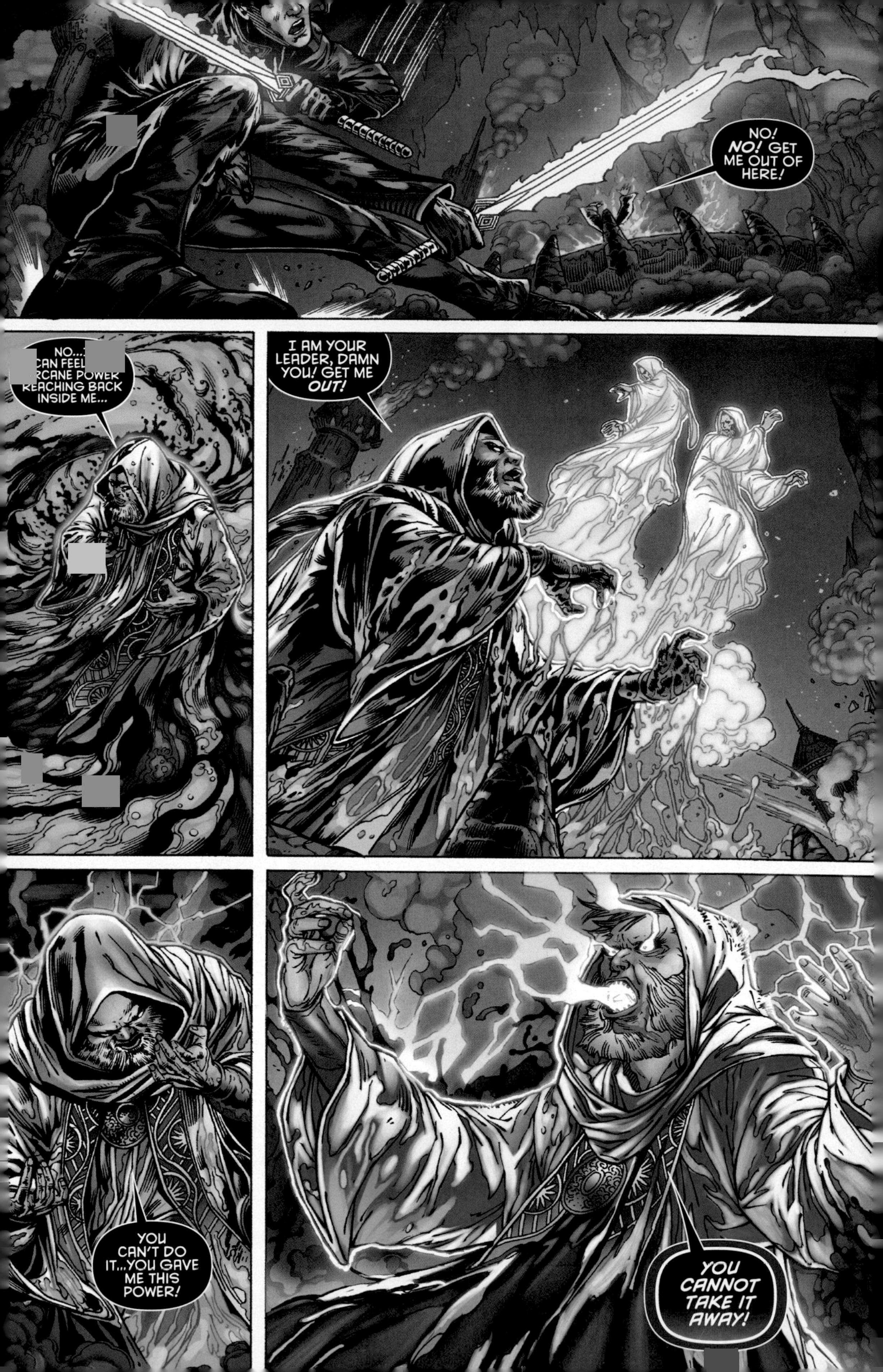
NO! NO! GET ME OUT OF HERE!
NO... CAN FEEL RCANE POWER REACHING BACK INSIDE ME...
I AM YOUR LEADER, DAMN YOU! GET ME OUT!
YOU CAN'T DO IT...YOU GAVE ME THIS POWER!
YOU CANNOT TAKE IT AWAY!

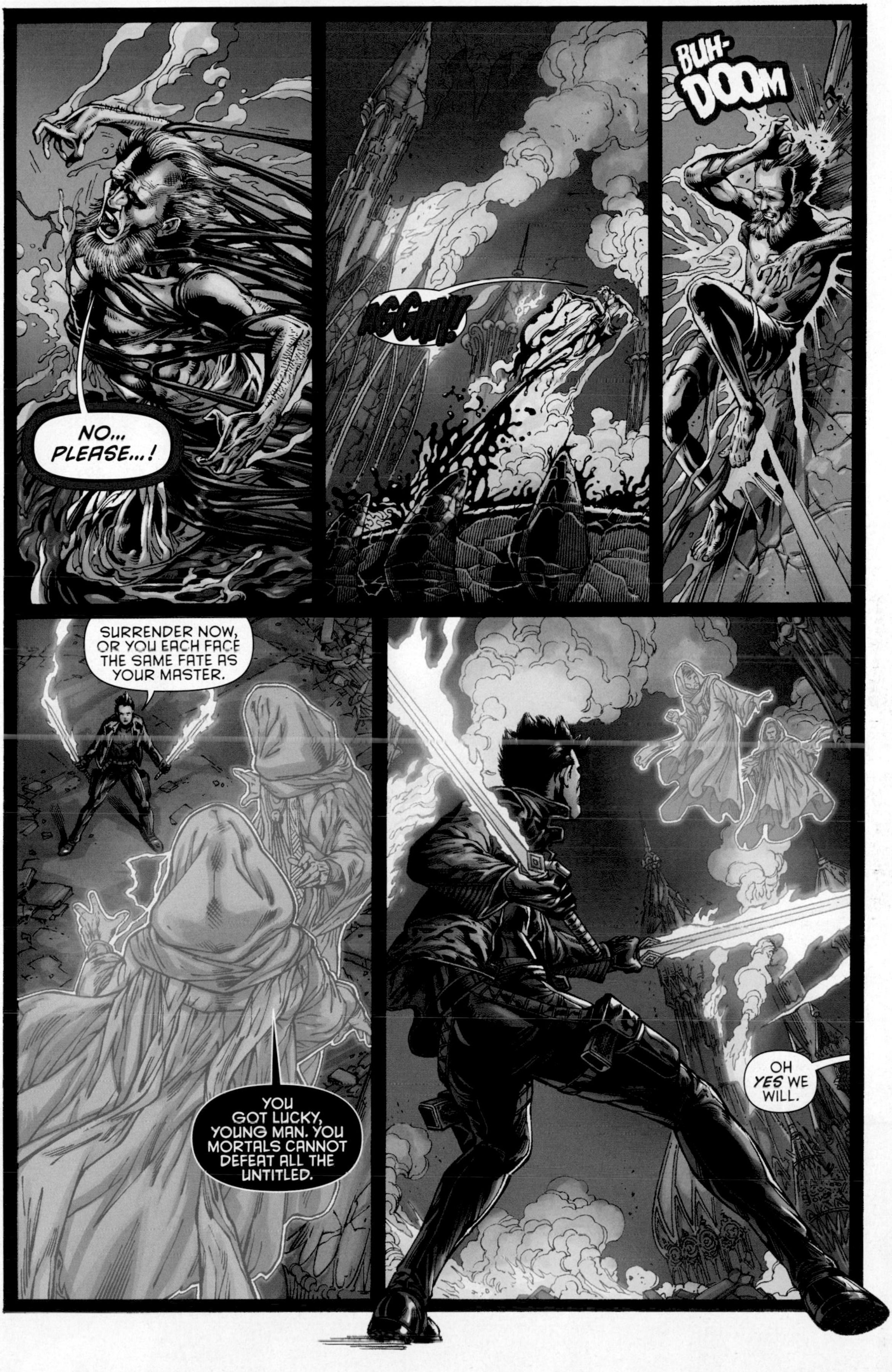
NO... PLEASE...!
AGGHH!
BUH-DOOM
SURRENDER NOW, OR YOU EACH FACE THE SAME FATE AS YOUR MASTER.
YOU GOT LUCKY, YOUNG MAN. YOU MORTALS CANNOT DEFEAT ALL THE UNTITLED.
OH YES WE WILL.

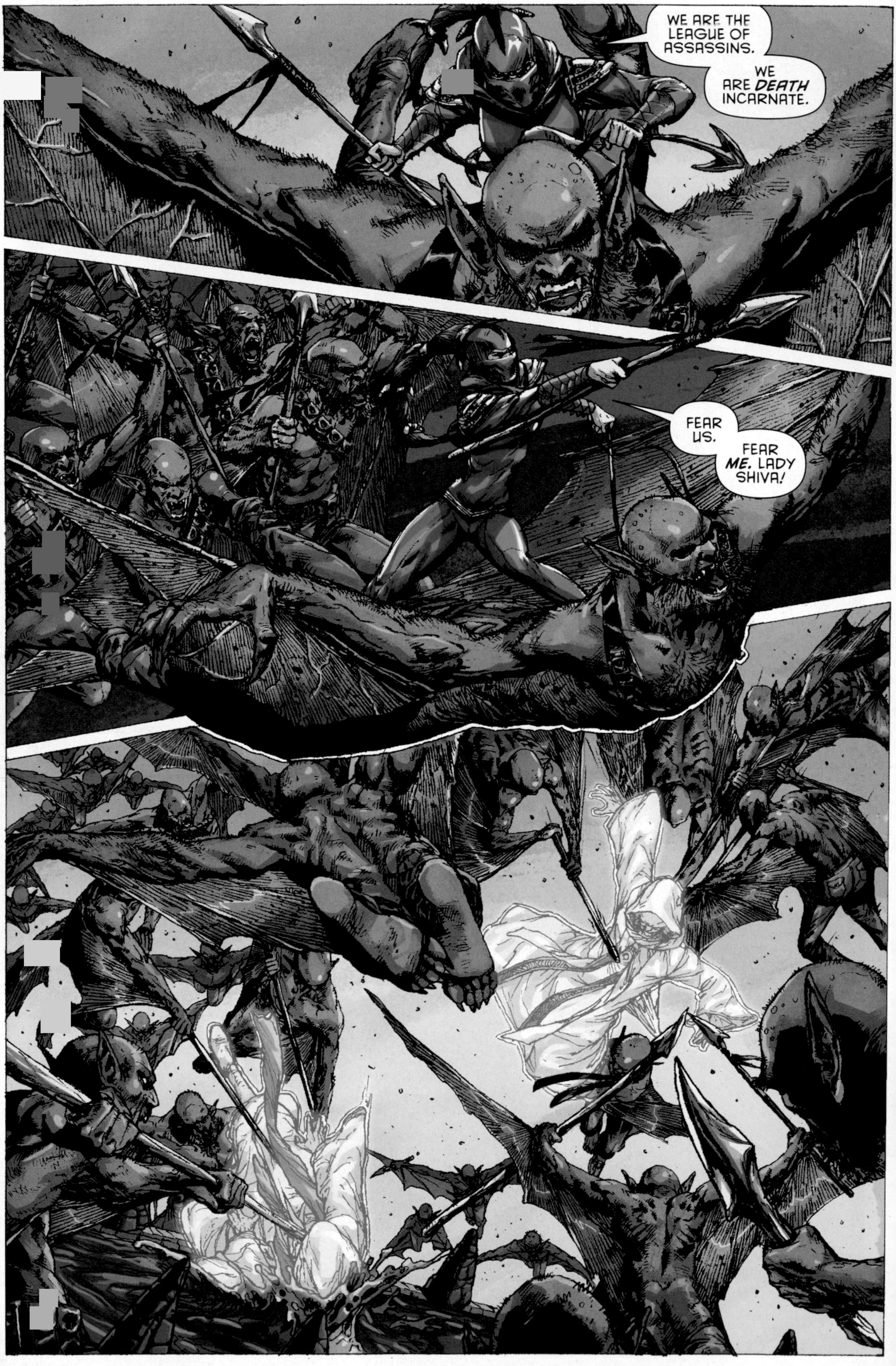
WE ARE THE LEAGUE OF ASSASSINS.
WE ARE *DEATH* INCARNATE.
FEAR US.
FEAR *ME.* LADY SHIVA!

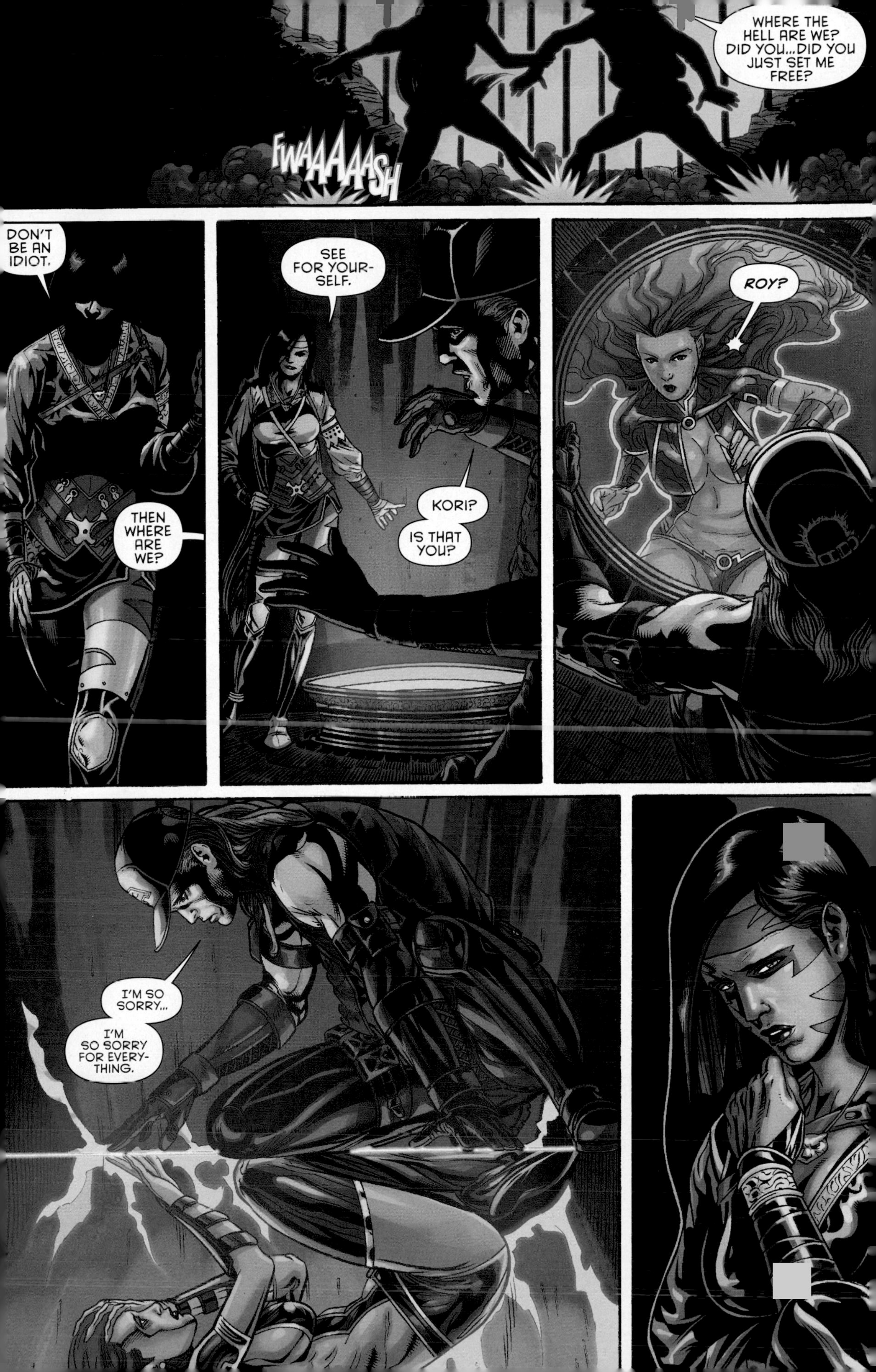
WHERE THE HELL ARE WE? DID YOU...DID YOU JUST SET ME FREE?
FWAAAAASH
DON'T BE AN IDIOT.
THEN WHERE ARE WE?
SEE FOR YOUR-SELF.
KORI?
IS THAT YOU?
ROY?
I'M SO SORRY...
I'M SO SORRY FOR EVERY-THING.

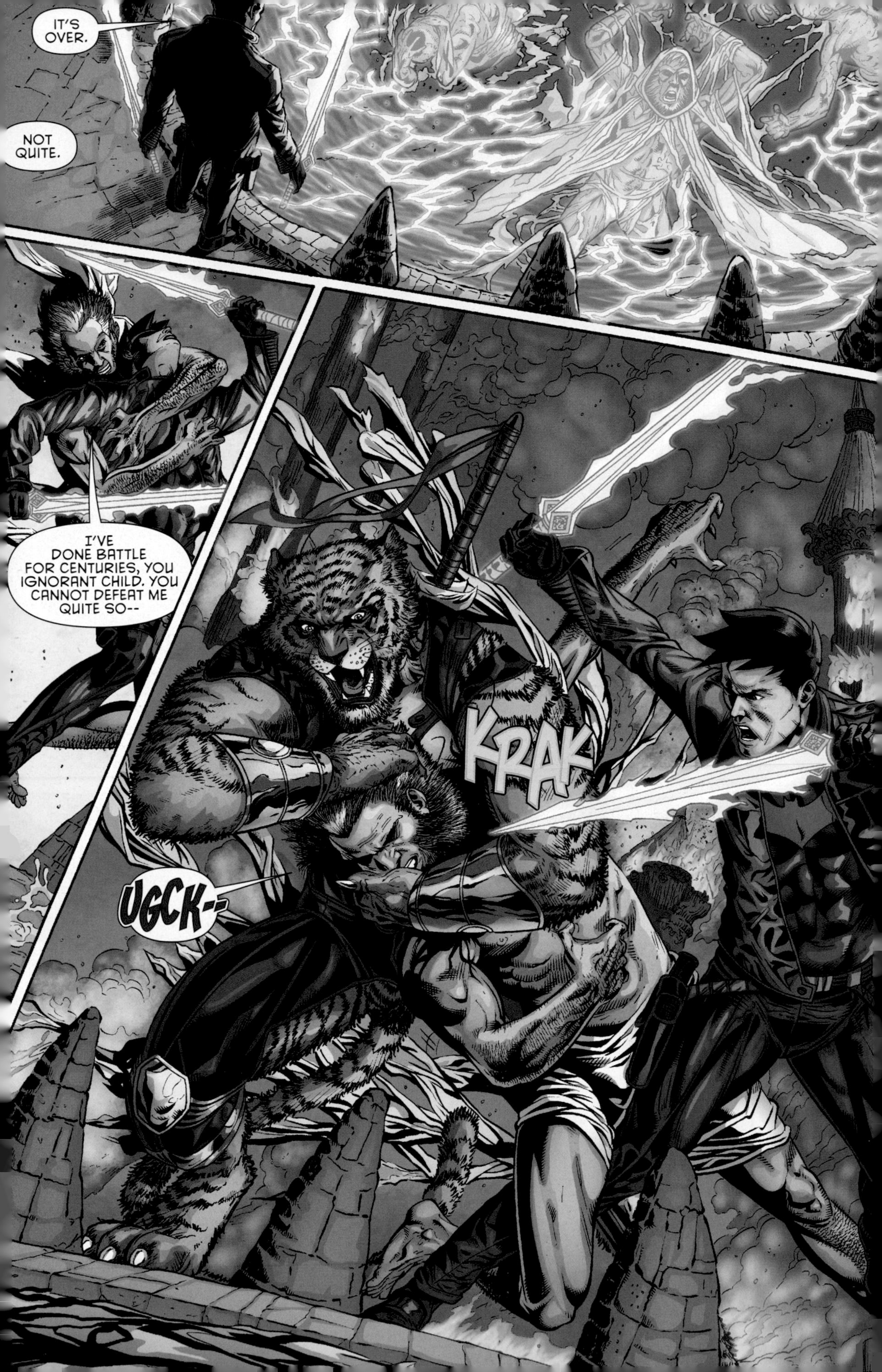
IT'S OVER.
NOT QUITE.
I'VE DONE BATTLE FOR CENTURIES, YOU IGNORANT CHILD. YOU CANNOT DEFEAT ME QUITE SO--
KRAK
UGCK--

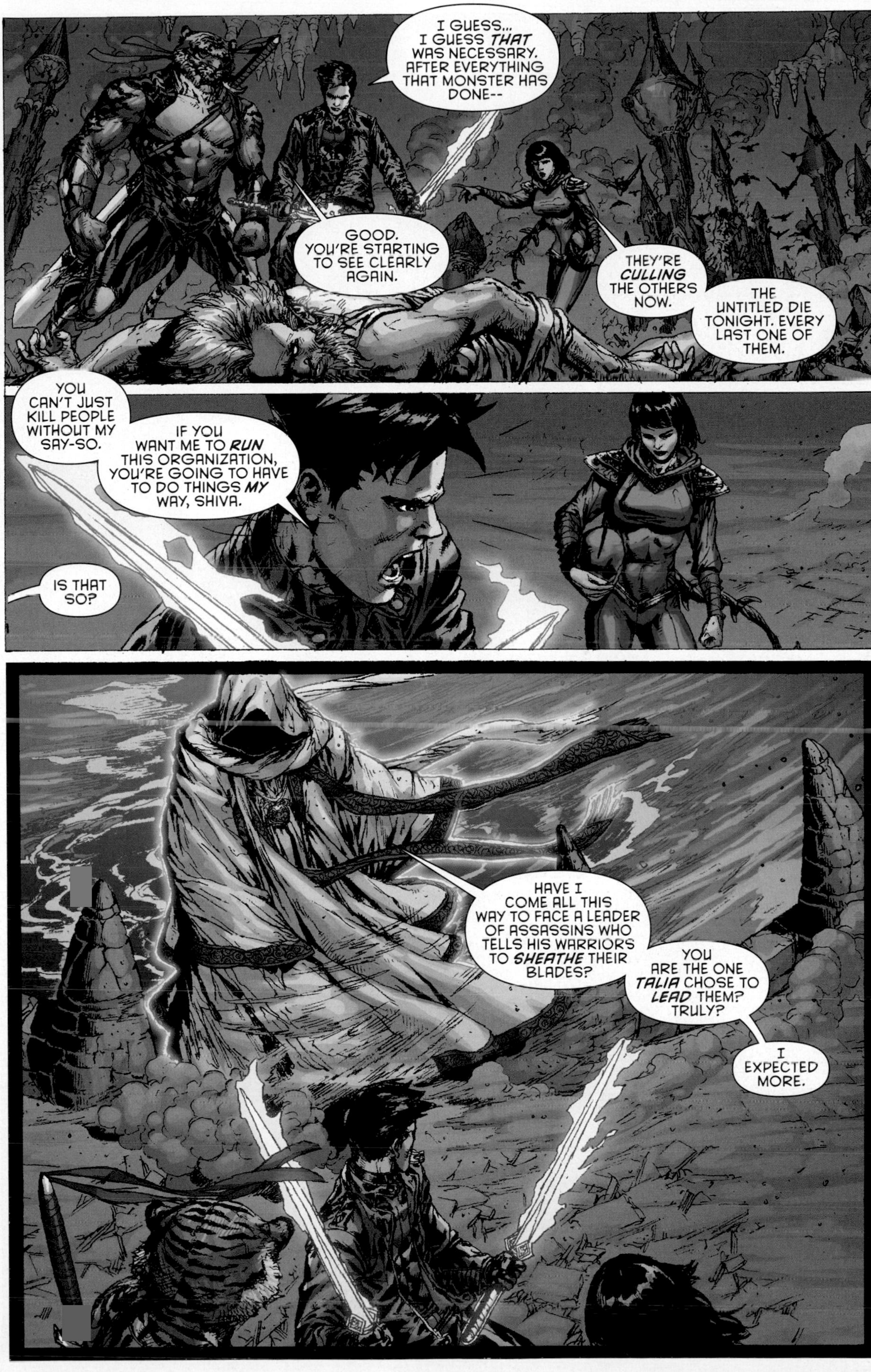

I GUESS... I GUESS *THAT* WAS NECESSARY. AFTER EVERYTHING THAT MONSTER HAS DONE--
GOOD. YOU'RE STARTING TO SEE CLEARLY AGAIN.
THEY'RE *CULLING* THE OTHERS NOW.
THE UNTITLED DIE TONIGHT. EVERY LAST ONE OF THEM.
YOU CAN'T JUST KILL PEOPLE WITHOUT MY SAY-SO.
IF YOU WANT ME TO *RUN* THIS ORGANIZATION, YOU'RE GOING TO HAVE TO DO THINGS *MY* WAY, SHIVA.
IS THAT SO?
HAVE I COME ALL THIS WAY TO FACE A LEADER OF ASSASSINS WHO TELLS HIS WARRIORS TO *SHEATHE* THEIR BLADES?
YOU ARE THE ONE *TALIA* CHOSE TO *LEAD* THEM? TRULY?
I EXPECTED MORE.

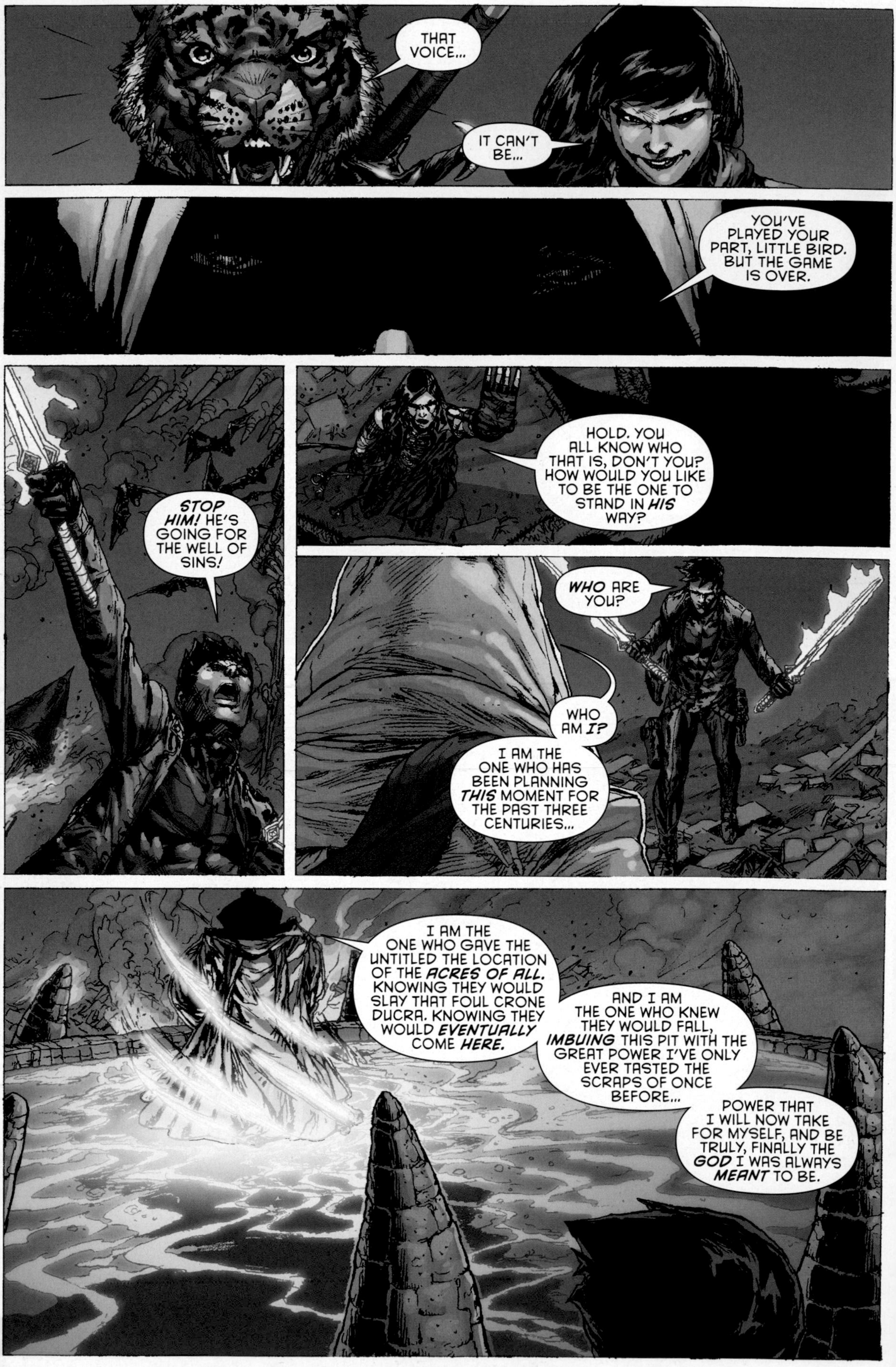

THAT VOICE...
IT CAN'T BE...
YOU'VE PLAYED YOUR PART, LITTLE BIRD. BUT THE GAME IS OVER.
STOP HIM! HE'S GOING FOR THE WELL OF SINS!
HOLD. YOU ALL KNOW WHO THAT IS, DON'T YOU? HOW WOULD YOU LIKE TO BE THE ONE TO STAND IN HIS WAY?
WHO ARE YOU?
WHO AM I?
I AM THE ONE WHO HAS BEEN PLANNING THIS MOMENT FOR THE PAST THREE CENTURIES...
I AM THE ONE WHO GAVE THE UNTITLED THE LOCATION OF THE ACRES OF ALL. KNOWING THEY WOULD SLAY THAT FOUL CRONE DUCRA. KNOWING THEY WOULD EVENTUALLY COME HERE.
AND I AM THE ONE WHO KNEW THEY WOULD FALL, IMBUING THIS PIT WITH THE GREAT POWER I'VE ONLY EVER TASTED THE SCRAPS OF ONCE BEFORE...
POWER THAT I WILL NOW TAKE FOR MYSELF, AND BE TRULY, FINALLY THE GOD I WAS ALWAYS MEANT TO BE.

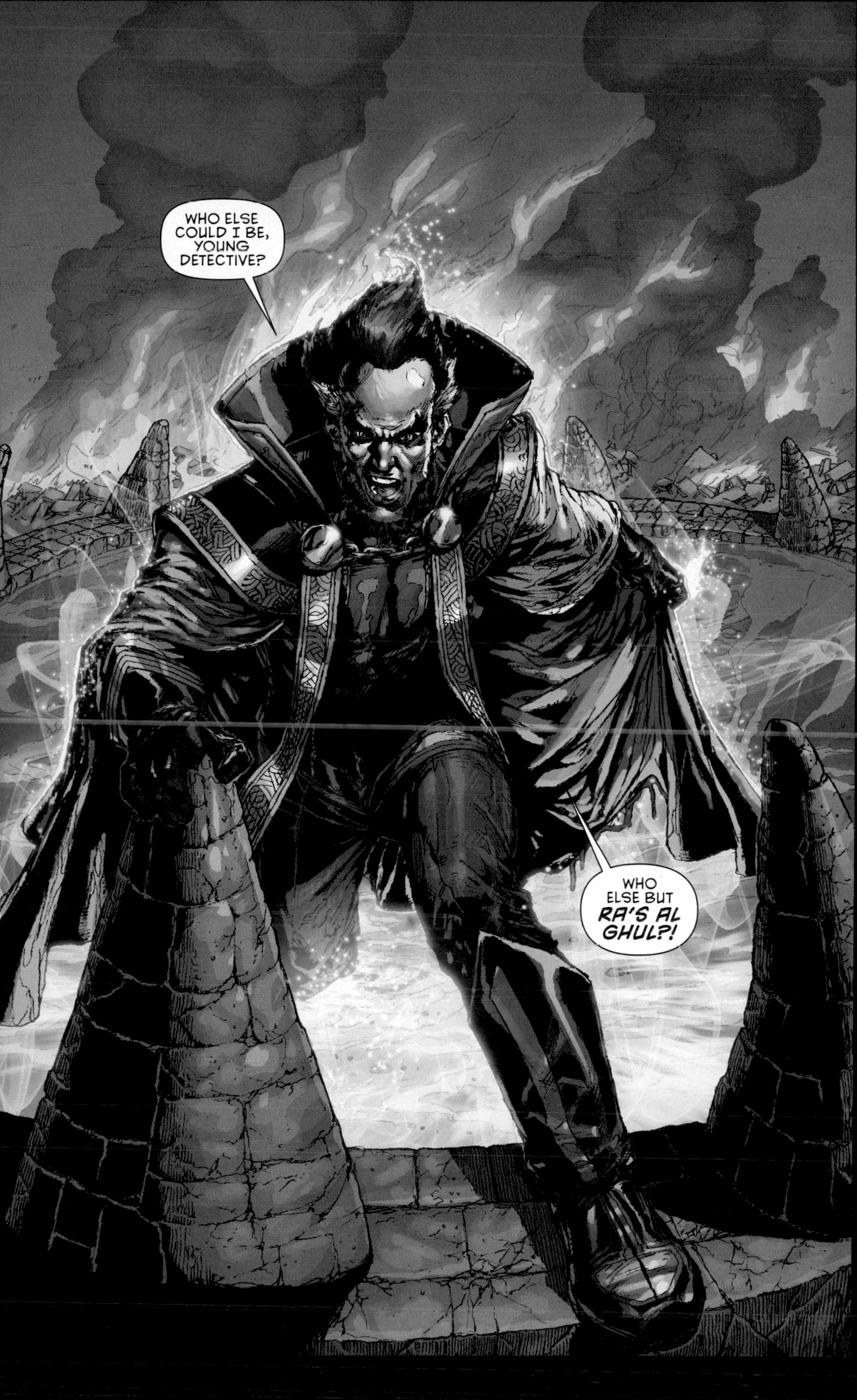
WHO ELSE COULD I BE, YOUNG DETECTIVE?
WHO ELSE BUT ***RA'S AL GHUL?!***

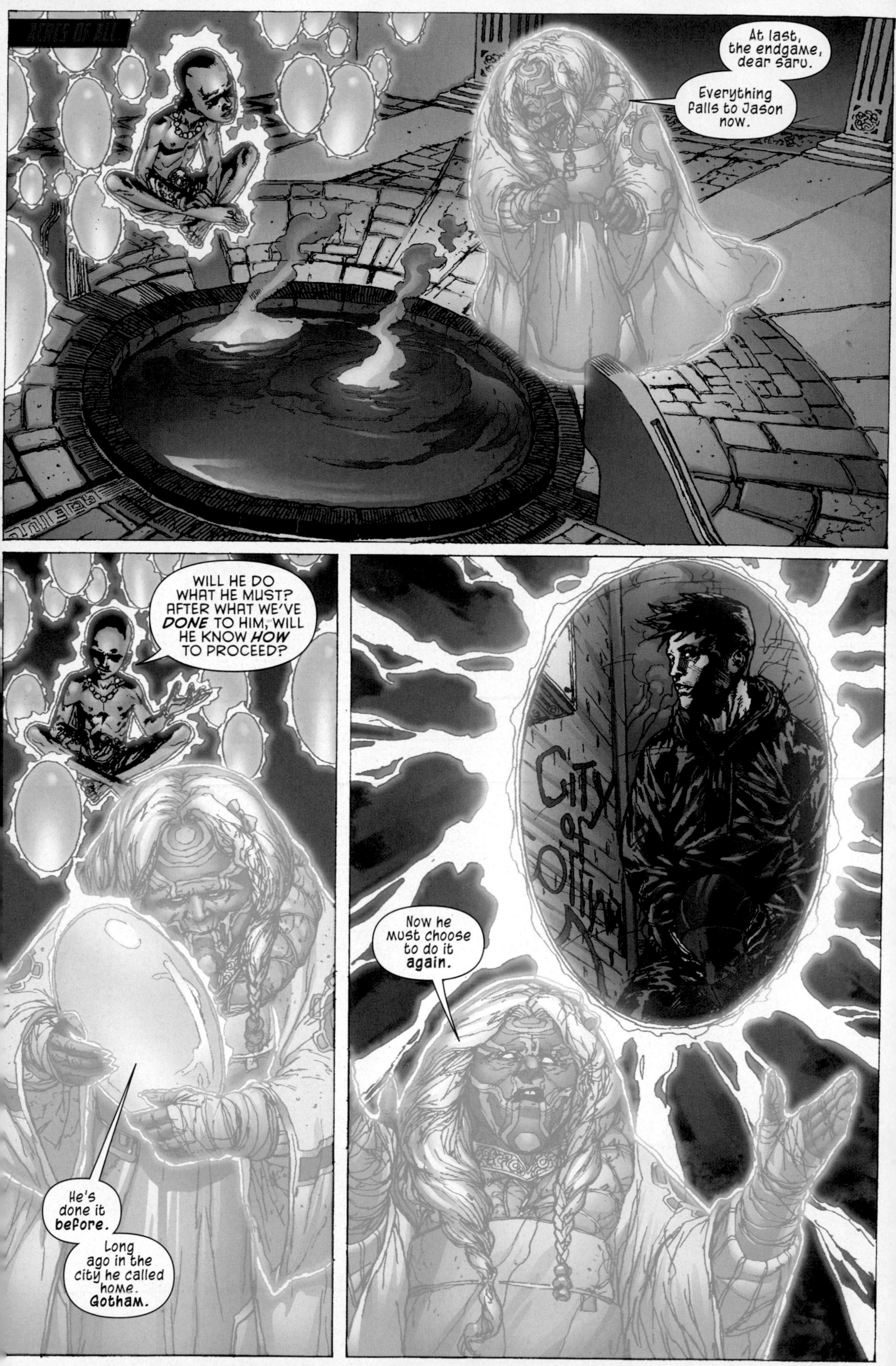
NEXUS OF ALL.
At last, the endgame, dear saru.
Everything falls to Jason now.
WILL HE DO WHAT HE MUST? AFTER WHAT WE'VE *DONE* TO HIM, WILL HE KNOW *HOW* TO PROCEED?
He's done it **before**.
Long ago in the city he called home. **Gotham.**
Now he must choose to do it **again**.

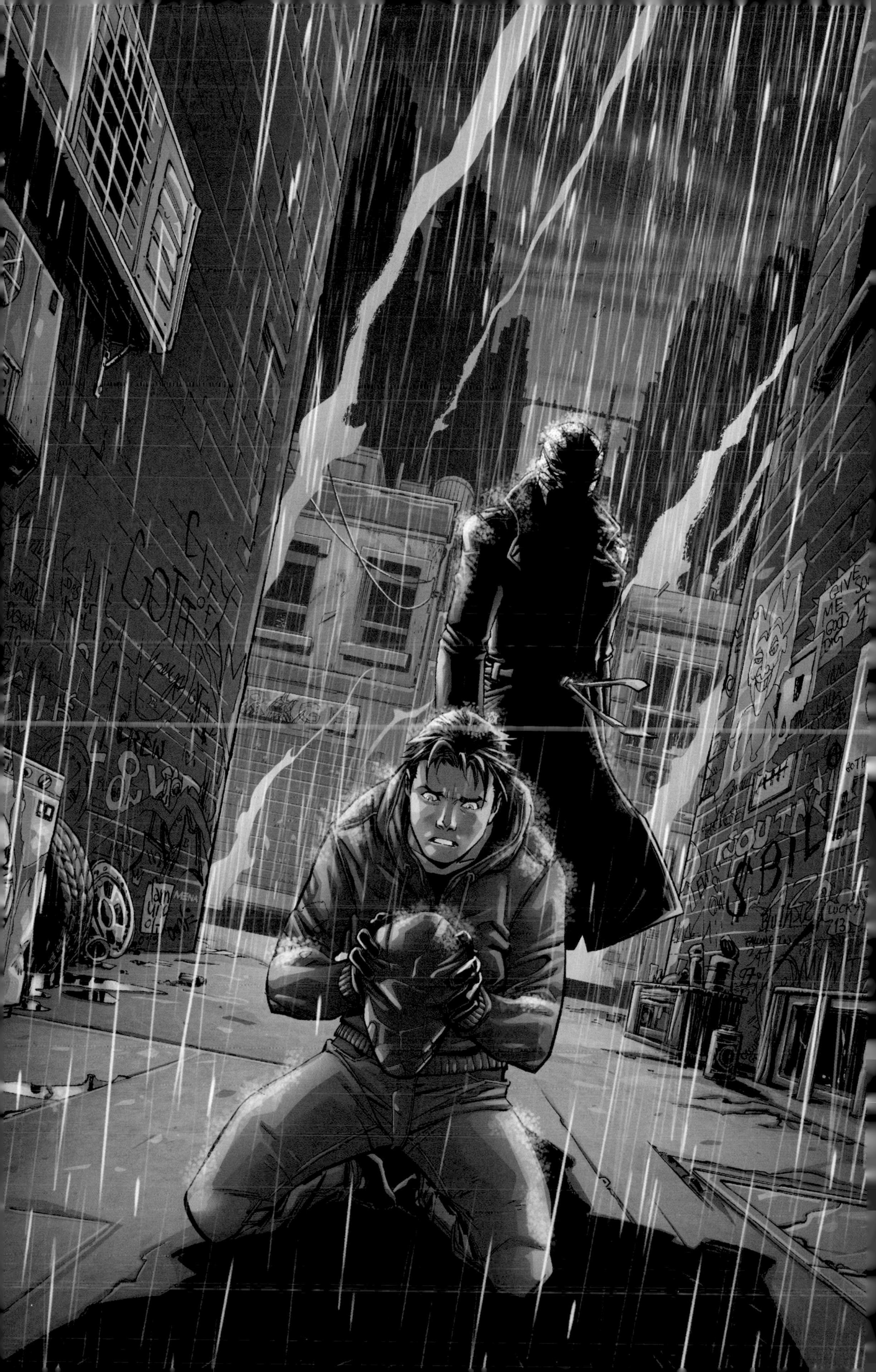
GIVE ME GOOD DOG
$ BIL
LUCKY 13

JAMES TYNION IV writer JEREMY HAUN artist JOHN KALISZ colorist
GIUSEPPE CAMUNCOLI & CAM SMITH with JAVIER MENA cover artists

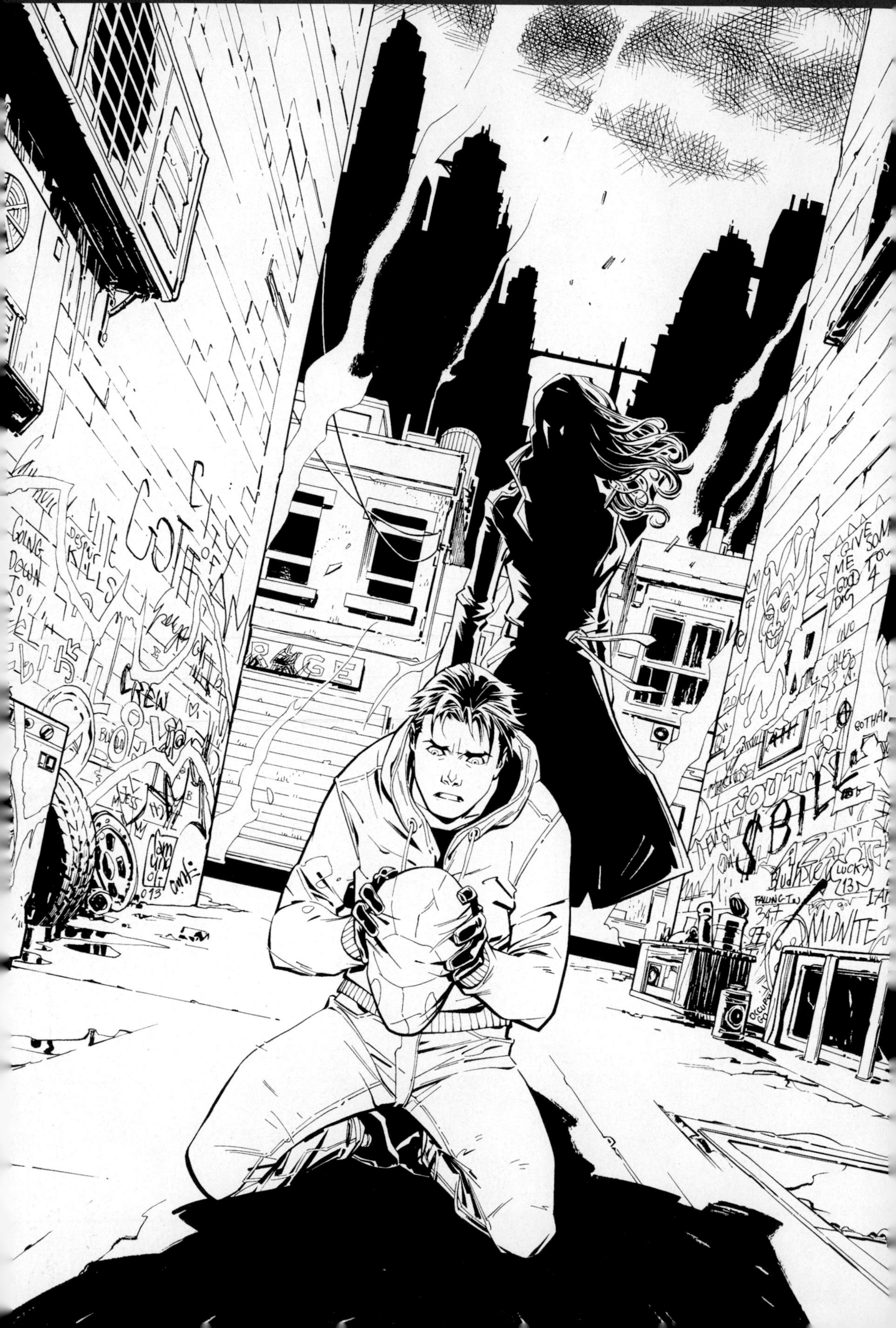
GOING DOWN TO
ELITE
despair KILLS
CITY OF GOTHAM
CREW
GIVE ME GOOD
SOUTH
$BILL
Bludhaven
LUCKY 13
MIDNITE
GOTHAM

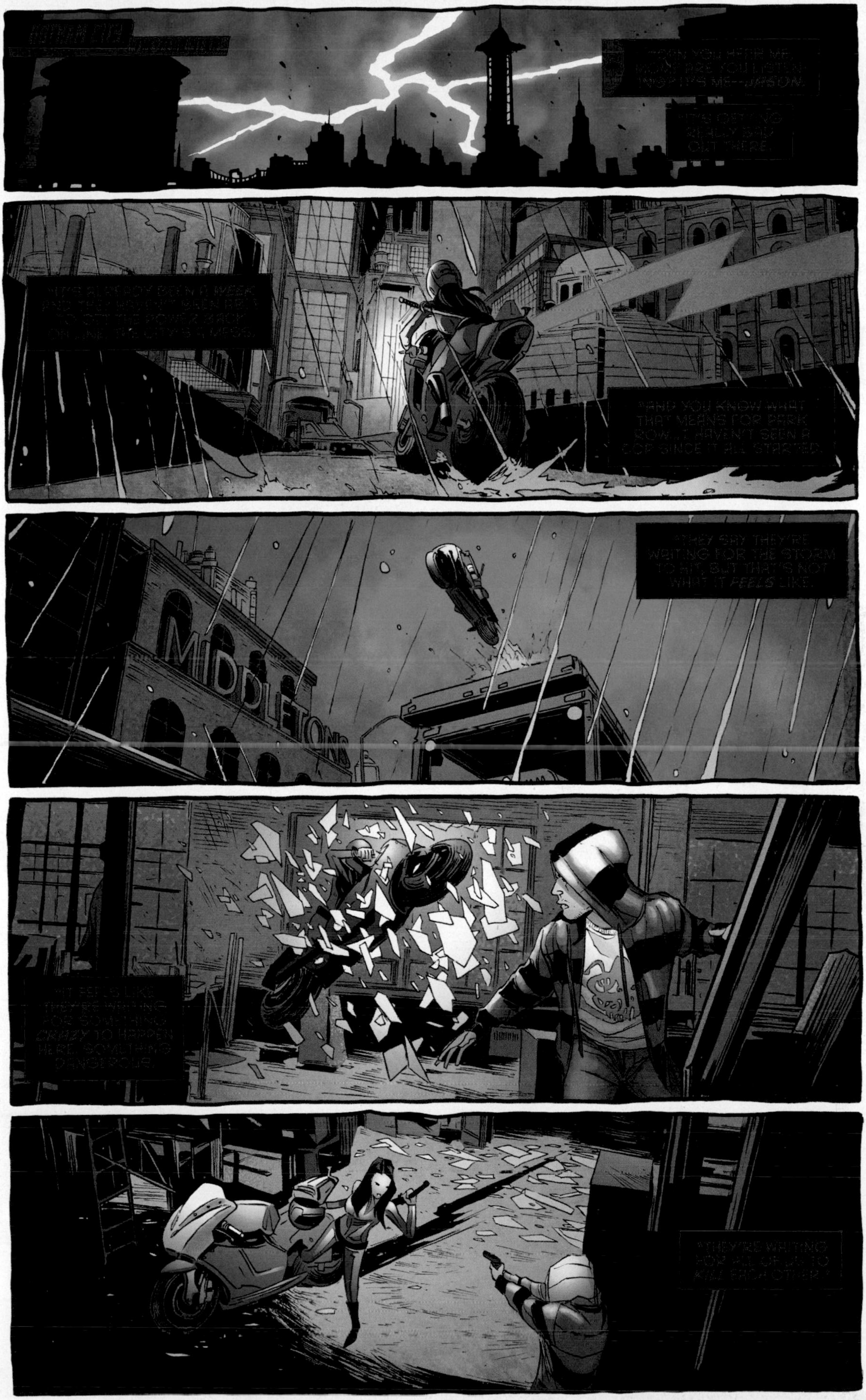
CAN YOU HEAR ME, MOM? ARE YOU LISTENING? IT'S ME—JASON.
IT'S GETTING REALLY BAD OUT THERE.
IT'S ALREADY BEEN A WEEK AND THEY HAVEN'T BEEN ABLE TO GET THE POWER BACK ONLINE. THE CITY'S A MESS.
AND YOU KNOW WHAT THAT MEANS FOR PARK ROW... I HAVEN'T SEEN A COP SINCE IT ALL STARTED.
MIDDLETON'S
THEY SAY THEY'RE WAITING FOR THE STORM TO HIT, BUT THAT'S NOT WHAT IT FEELS LIKE.
IT FEELS LIKE THEY'RE WAITING FOR SOMETHING CRAZY TO HAPPEN HERE. SOMETHING DANGEROUS.
THEY'RE WAITING FOR ALL OF US TO KILL EACH OTHER.

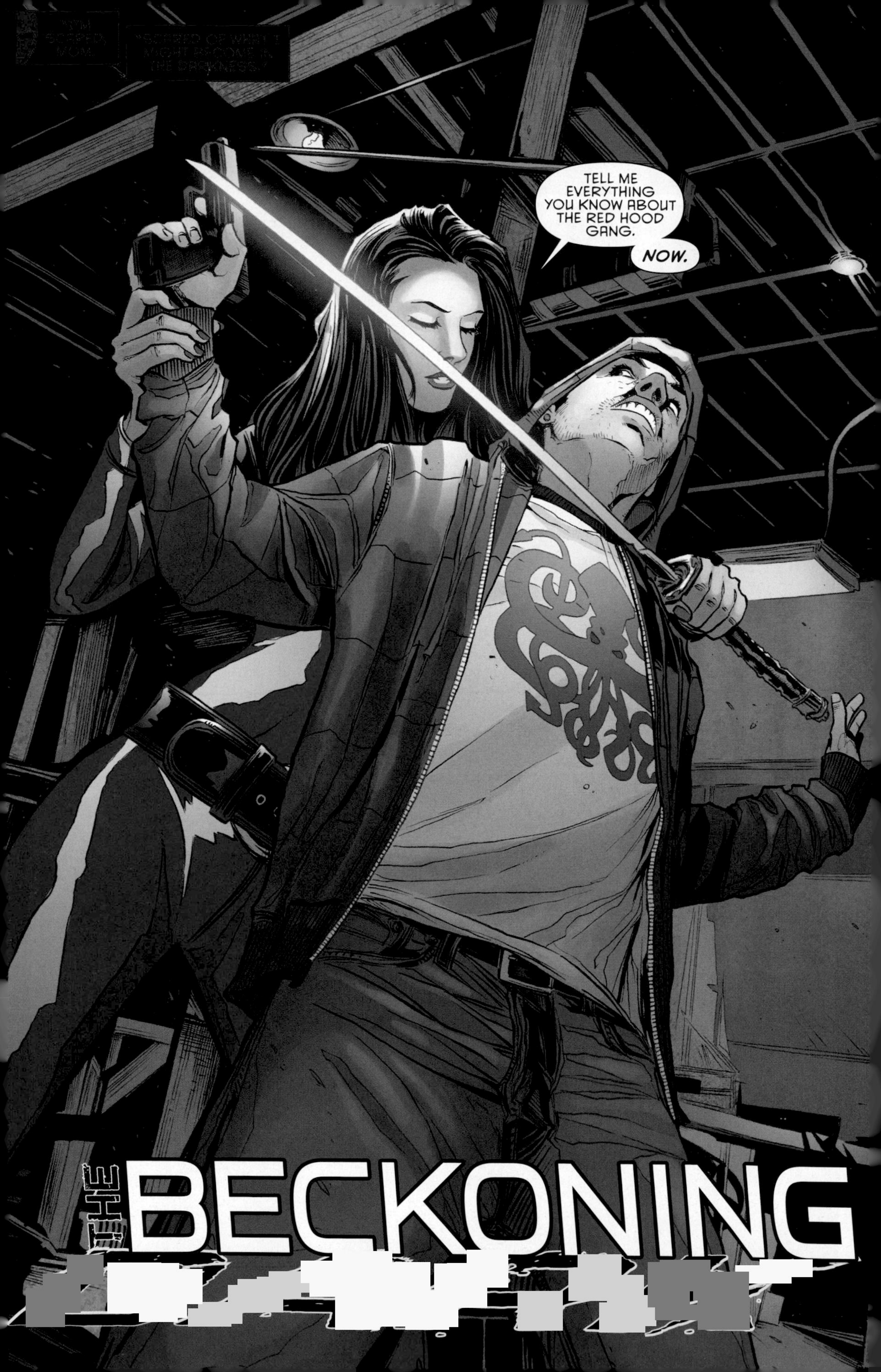

I'M SCARED, MOM.
"SCARED OF WHAT I MIGHT BECOME IN THE DARKNESS?"
TELL ME EVERYTHING YOU KNOW ABOUT THE RED HOOD GANG. NOW.
THE BECKONING

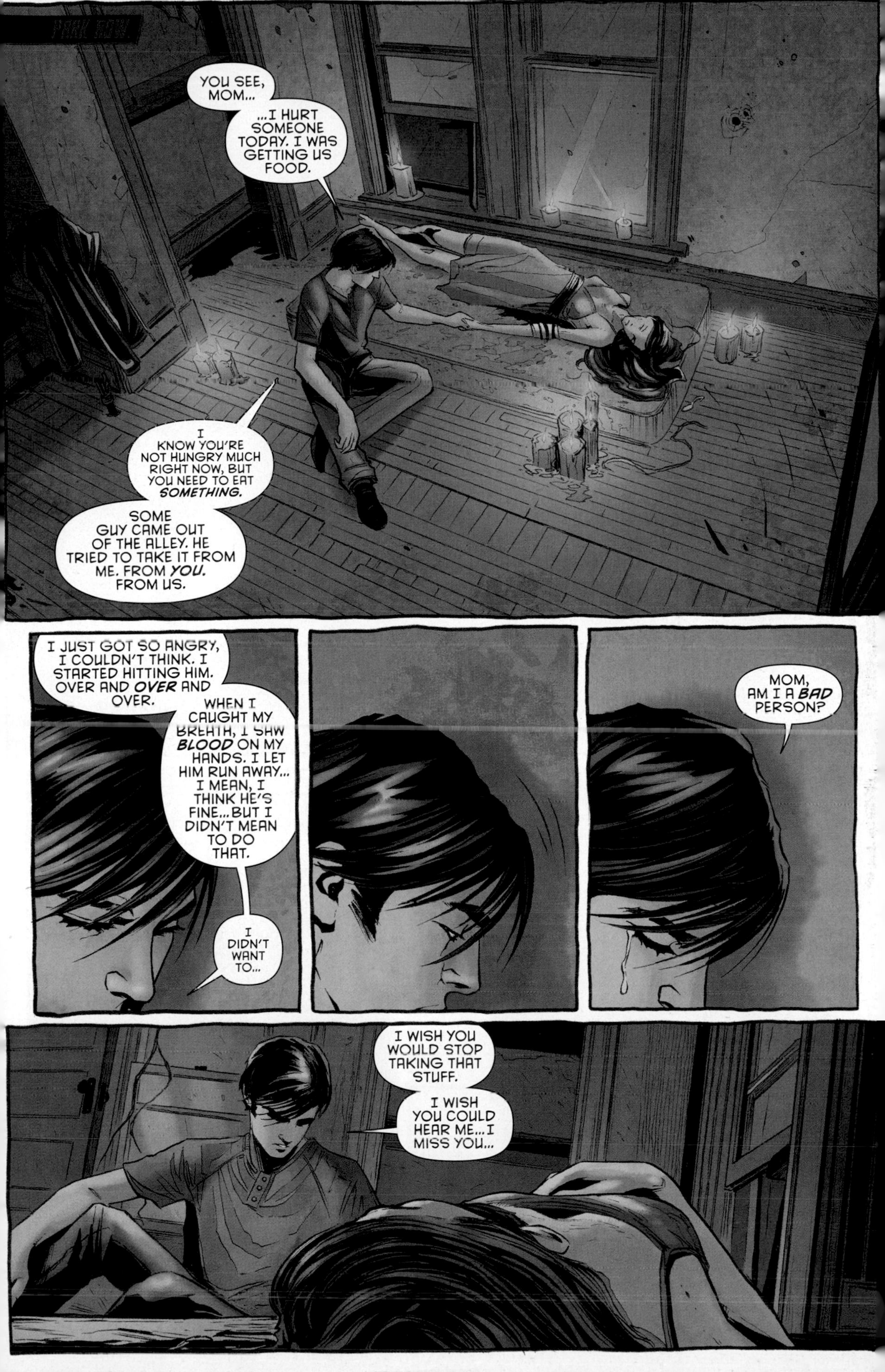
PARK ROW.
YOU SEE, MOM...
...I HURT SOMEONE TODAY. I WAS GETTING US FOOD.
I KNOW YOU'RE NOT HUNGRY MUCH RIGHT NOW, BUT YOU NEED TO EAT SOMETHING.
SOME GUY CAME OUT OF THE ALLEY. HE TRIED TO TAKE IT FROM ME. FROM YOU. FROM US.
I JUST GOT SO ANGRY, I COULDN'T THINK. I STARTED HITTING HIM. OVER AND OVER AND OVER.
WHEN I CAUGHT MY BREATH, I SAW BLOOD ON MY HANDS. I LET HIM RUN AWAY... I MEAN, I THINK HE'S FINE... BUT I DIDN'T MEAN TO DO THAT.
I DIDN'T WANT TO...
MOM, AM I A BAD PERSON?
I WISH YOU WOULD STOP TAKING THAT STUFF.
I WISH YOU COULD HEAR ME... I MISS YOU...

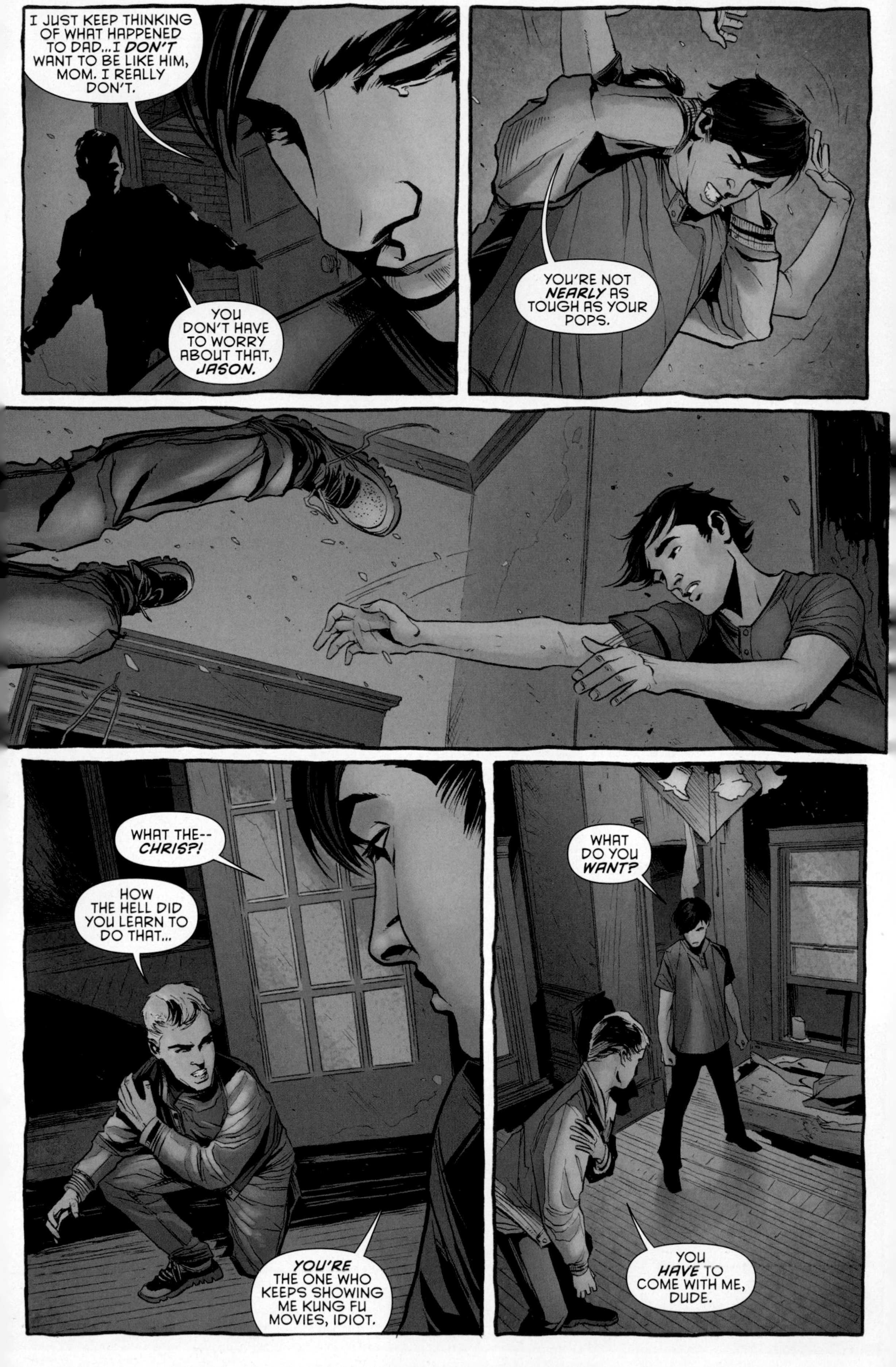
I JUST KEEP THINKING OF WHAT HAPPENED TO DAD...I DON'T WANT TO BE LIKE HIM, MOM. I REALLY DON'T.
YOU DON'T HAVE TO WORRY ABOUT THAT, JASON.
YOU'RE NOT NEARLY AS TOUGH AS YOUR POPS.
WHAT THE-- CHRIS?!
HOW THE HELL DID YOU LEARN TO DO THAT...
YOU'RE THE ONE WHO KEEPS SHOWING ME KUNG FU MOVIES, IDIOT.
WHAT DO YOU WANT?
YOU HAVE TO COME WITH ME, DUDE.

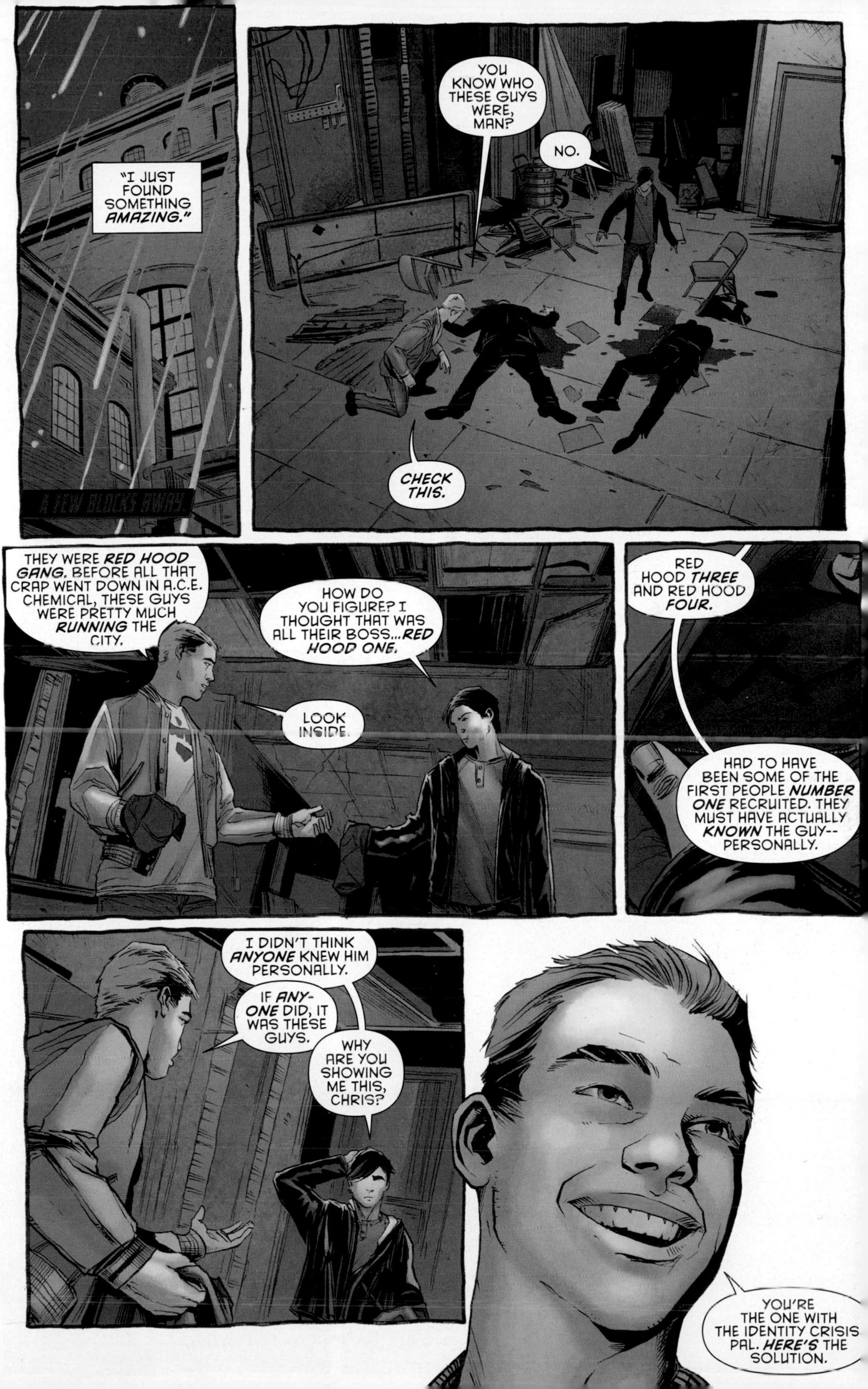
"I JUST FOUND SOMETHING *AMAZING.*"
A FEW BLOCKS AWAY.
YOU KNOW WHO THESE GUYS WERE, MAN?
NO.
CHECK THIS.
THEY WERE *RED HOOD GANG.* BEFORE ALL THAT CRAP WENT DOWN IN A.C.E. CHEMICAL, THESE GUYS WERE PRETTY MUCH *RUNNING* THE CITY.
HOW DO YOU FIGURE? I THOUGHT THAT WAS ALL THEIR BOSS... *RED HOOD ONE.*
LOOK INSIDE.
RED HOOD *THREE* AND RED HOOD *FOUR.*
HAD TO HAVE BEEN SOME OF THE FIRST PEOPLE *NUMBER ONE* RECRUITED. THEY MUST HAVE ACTUALLY *KNOWN* THE GUY-- PERSONALLY.
I DIDN'T THINK *ANYONE* KNEW HIM PERSONALLY.
IF *ANY-ONE* DID, IT WAS THESE GUYS.
WHY ARE YOU SHOWING ME THIS, CHRIS?
YOU'RE THE ONE WITH THE IDENTITY CRISIS PAL. *HERE'S* THE SOLUTION.

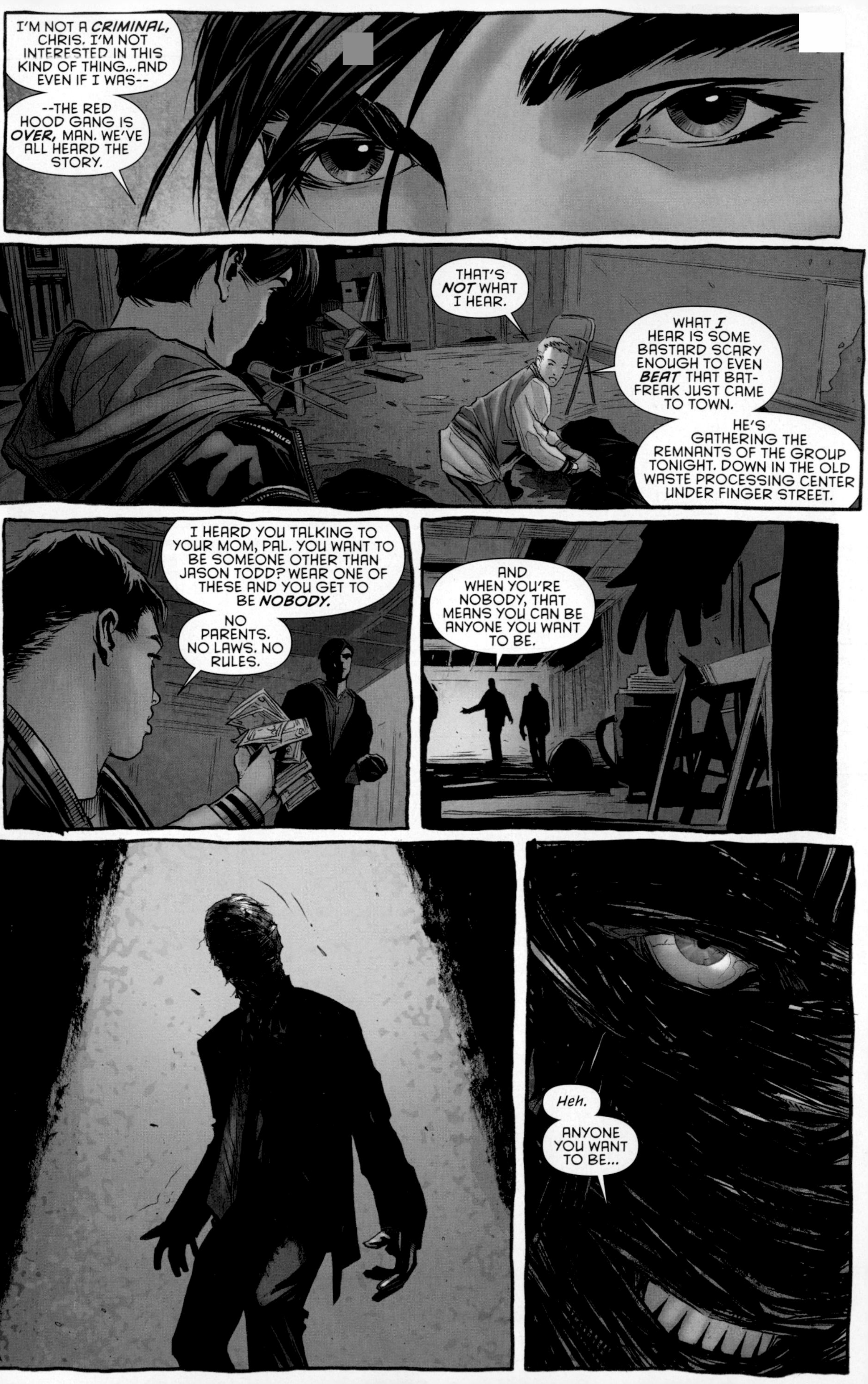
I'M NOT A *CRIMINAL,* CHRIS. I'M NOT INTERESTED IN THIS KIND OF THING...AND EVEN IF I WAS--
--THE RED HOOD GANG IS *OVER,* MAN. WE'VE ALL HEARD THE STORY.
THAT'S *NOT* WHAT I HEAR.
WHAT *I* HEAR IS SOME BASTARD SCARY ENOUGH TO EVEN *BEAT* THAT BAT-FREAK JUST CAME TO TOWN.
HE'S GATHERING THE REMNANTS OF THE GROUP TONIGHT. DOWN IN THE OLD WASTE PROCESSING CENTER UNDER FINGER STREET.
I HEARD YOU TALKING TO YOUR MOM, PAL. YOU WANT TO BE SOMEONE OTHER THAN JASON TODD? WEAR ONE OF THESE AND YOU GET TO BE *NOBODY.*
NO PARENTS. NO LAWS. NO RULES.
AND WHEN YOU'RE NOBODY, THAT MEANS YOU CAN BE ANYONE YOU WANT TO BE.
Heh.
ANYONE YOU WANT TO BE...

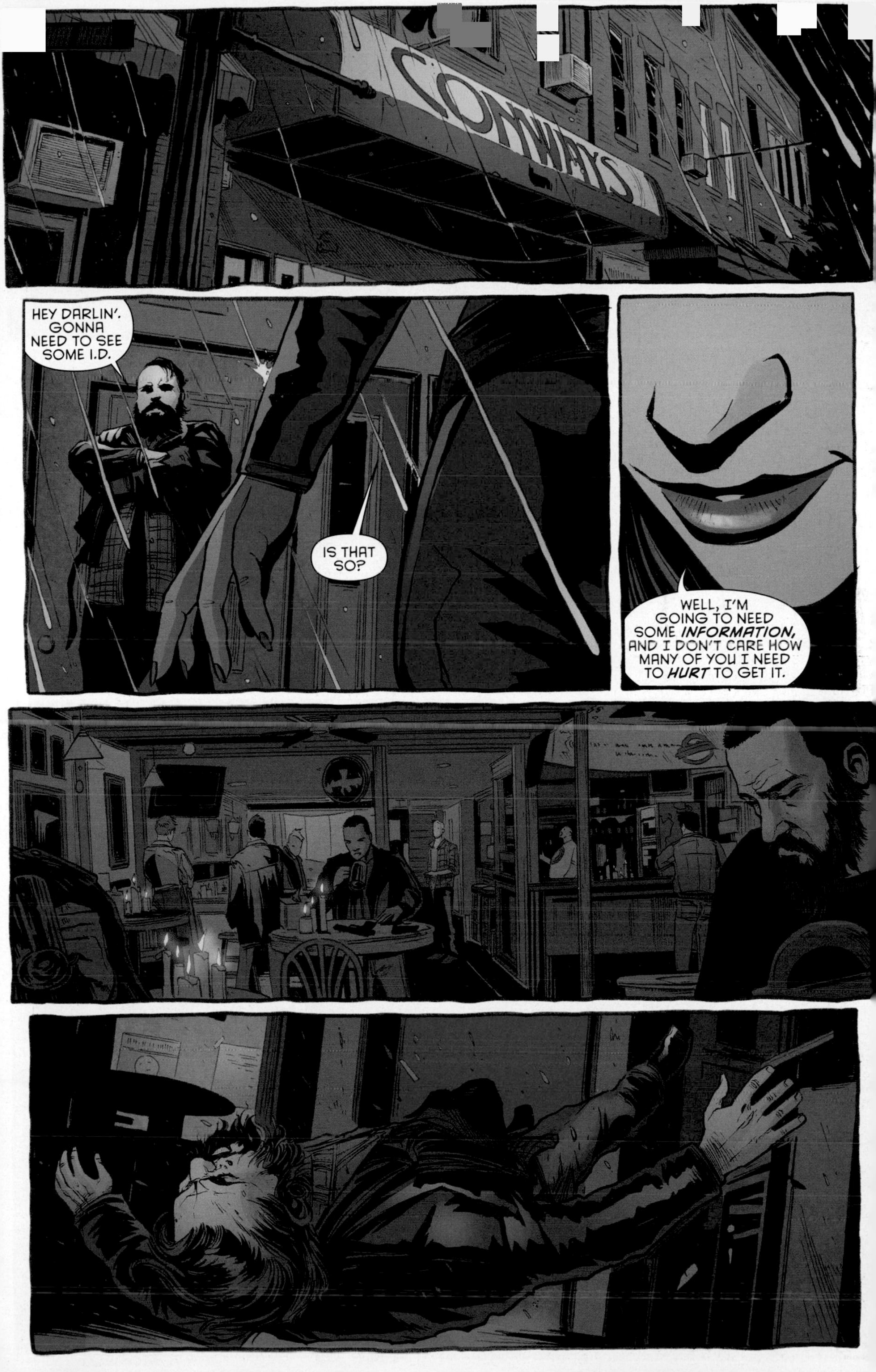
CONWAYS
HEY DARLIN'. GONNA NEED TO SEE SOME I.D.
IS THAT SO?
WELL, I'M GOING TO NEED SOME *INFORMATION,* AND I DON'T CARE HOW MANY OF YOU I NEED TO *HURT* TO GET IT.

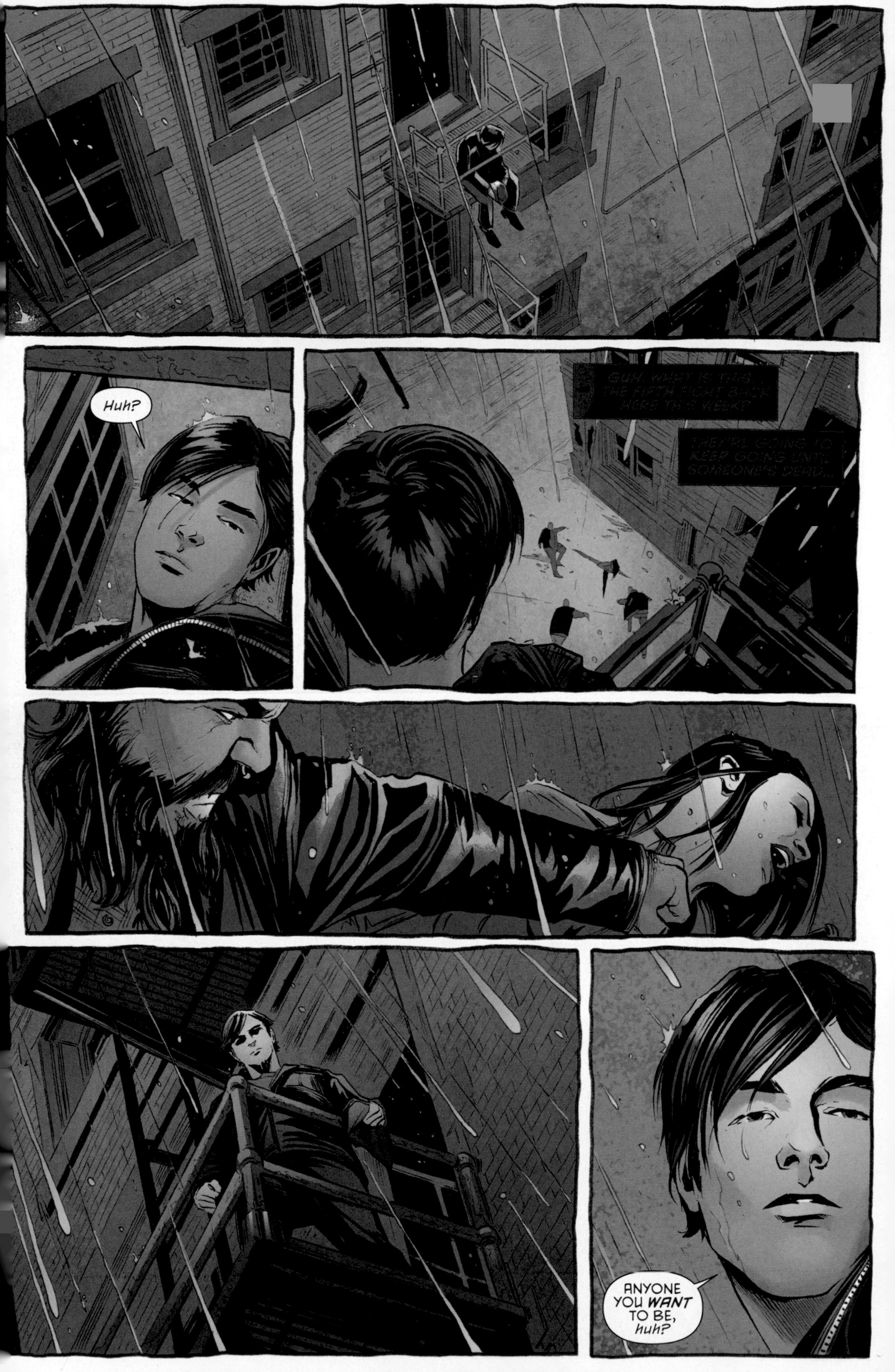
Huh?
GUH. WHAT IS THIS, THE FIFTH FIGHT BACK HERE THIS WEEK?
THEY'RE GOING TO KEEP GOING UNTIL SOMEONE'S DEAD...
ANYONE YOU *WANT* TO BE, *huh?*

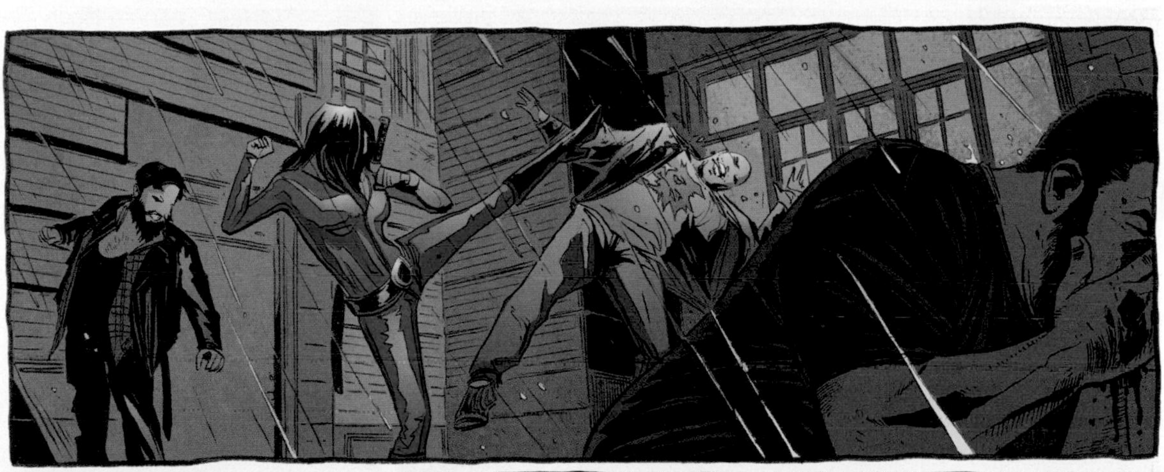

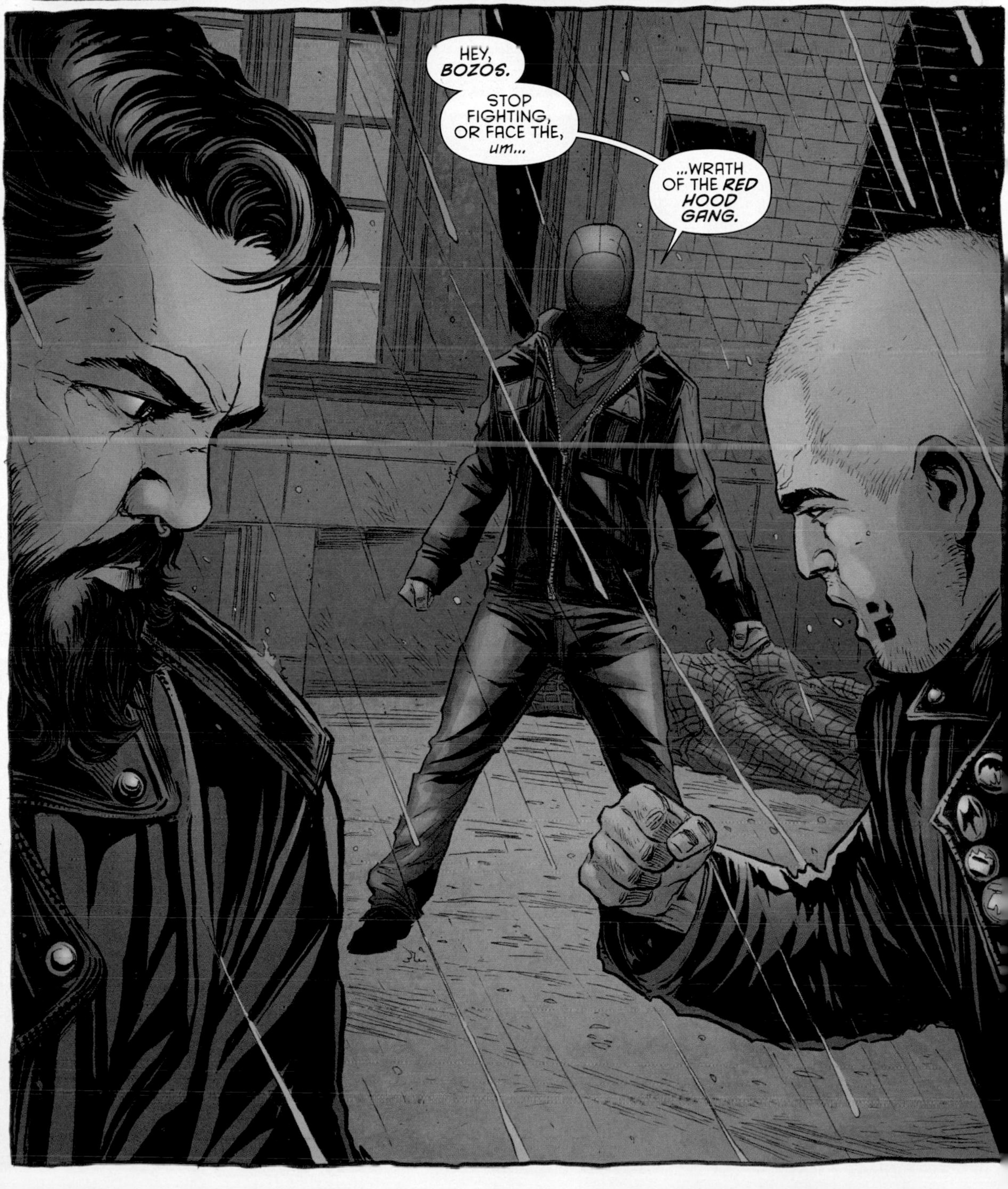
HEY, *BOZOS.*
STOP FIGHTING, OR FACE THE, *UM...*
...WRATH OF THE *RED HOOD GANG.*

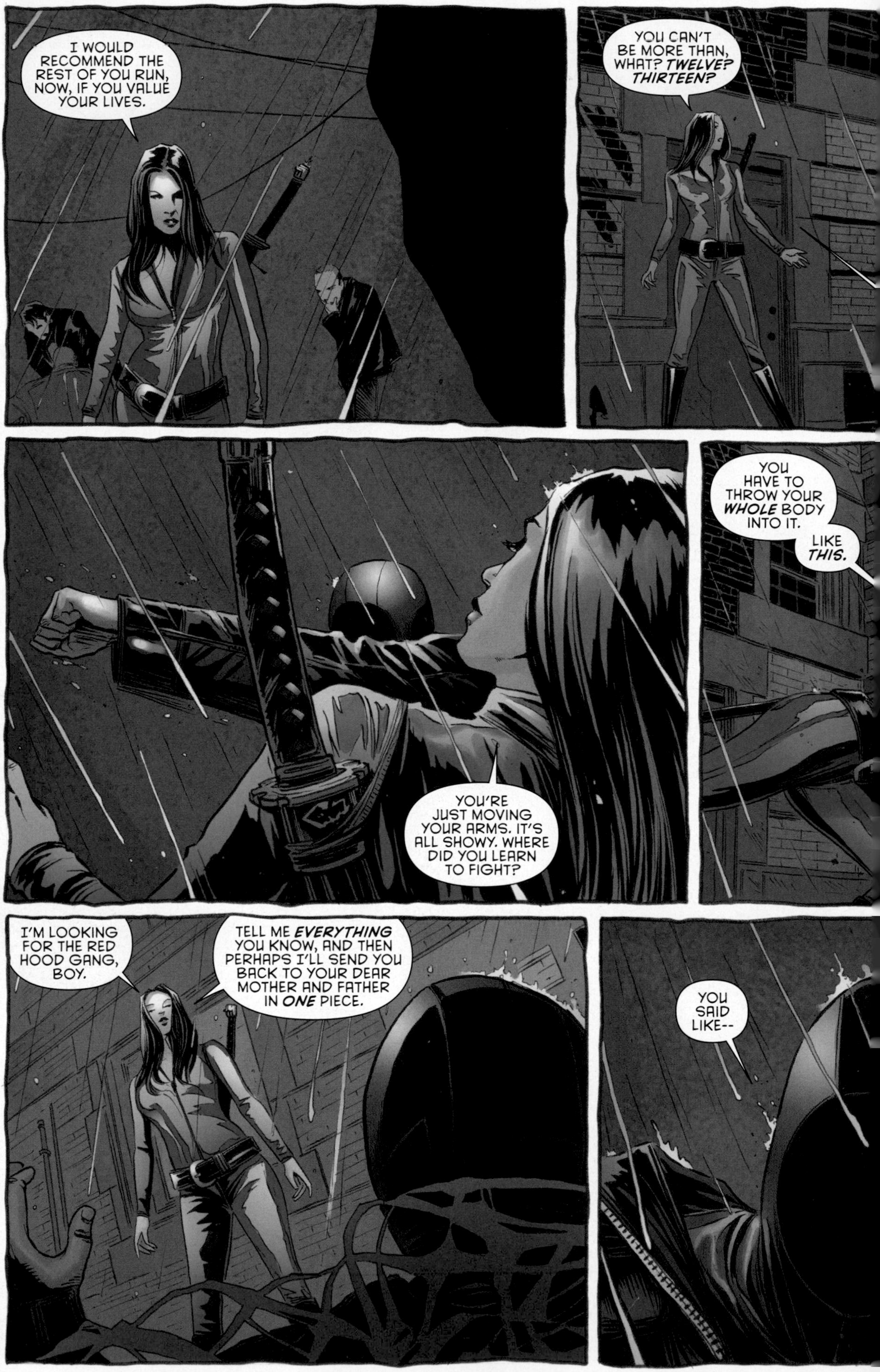
I WOULD RECOMMEND THE REST OF YOU RUN, NOW, IF YOU VALUE YOUR LIVES.
YOU CAN'T BE MORE THAN, WHAT? TWELVE? THIRTEEN?
YOU'RE JUST MOVING YOUR ARMS. IT'S ALL SHOWY. WHERE DID YOU LEARN TO FIGHT?
YOU HAVE TO THROW YOUR WHOLE BODY INTO IT.
LIKE THIS.
I'M LOOKING FOR THE RED HOOD GANG, BOY.
TELL ME EVERYTHING YOU KNOW, AND THEN PERHAPS I'LL SEND YOU BACK TO YOUR DEAR MOTHER AND FATHER IN ONE PIECE.
YOU SAID LIKE--

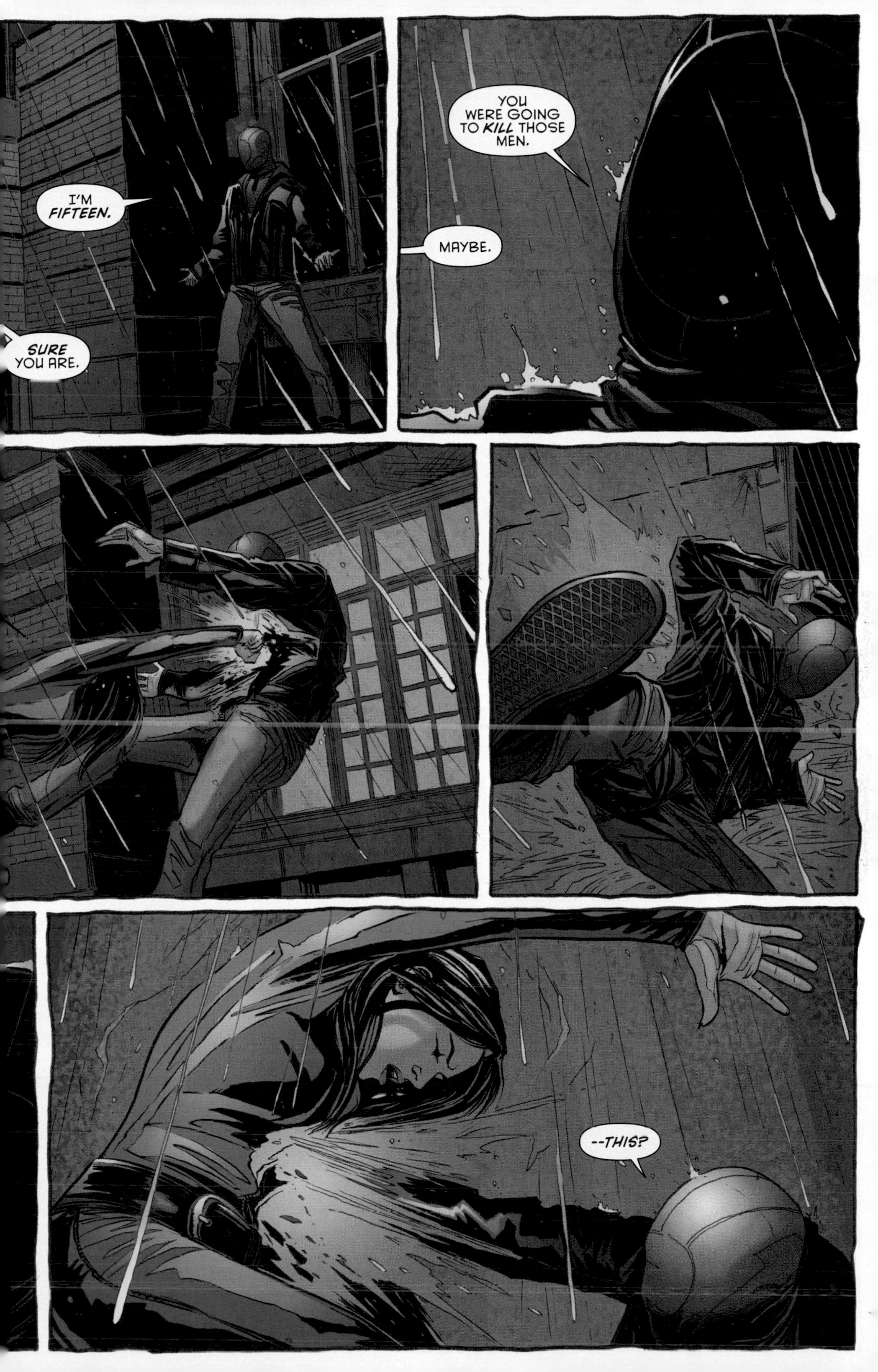
I'M FIFTEEN.
SURE YOU ARE.
YOU WERE GOING TO KILL THOSE MEN.
MAYBE.
--THIS?

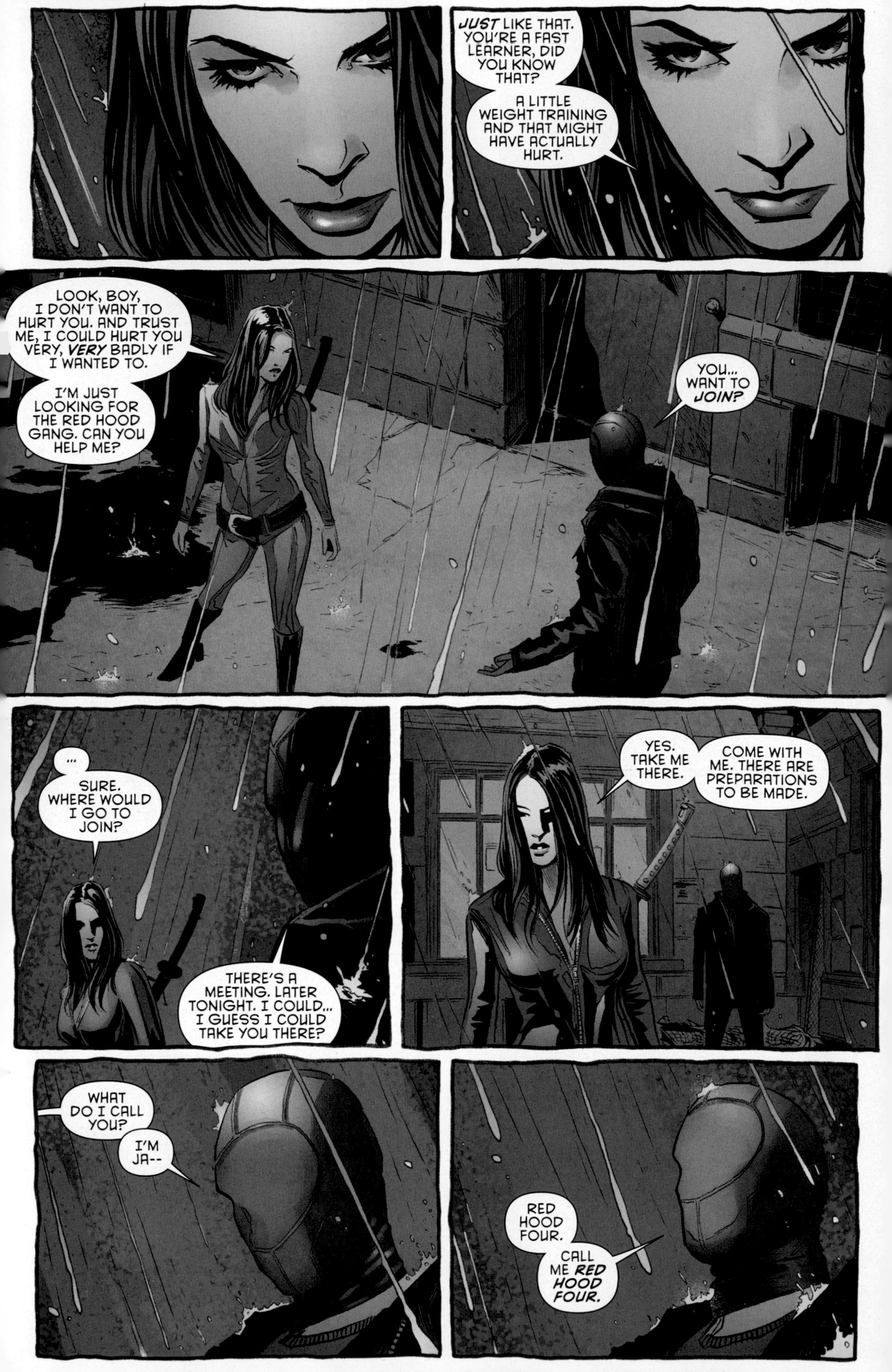
JUST LIKE THAT. YOU'RE A FAST LEARNER, DID YOU KNOW THAT?
A LITTLE WEIGHT TRAINING AND THAT MIGHT HAVE ACTUALLY HURT.
LOOK, BOY, I DON'T WANT TO HURT YOU. AND TRUST ME, I COULD HURT YOU VERY, VERY BADLY IF I WANTED TO.
I'M JUST LOOKING FOR THE RED HOOD GANG. CAN YOU HELP ME?
YOU... WANT TO JOIN?
...
SURE. WHERE WOULD I GO TO JOIN?
THERE'S A MEETING. LATER TONIGHT. I COULD... I GUESS I COULD TAKE YOU THERE?
YES. TAKE ME THERE.
COME WITH ME. THERE ARE PREPARATIONS TO BE MADE.
WHAT DO I CALL YOU?
I'M JA--
RED HOOD FOUR.
CALL ME RED HOOD FOUR.

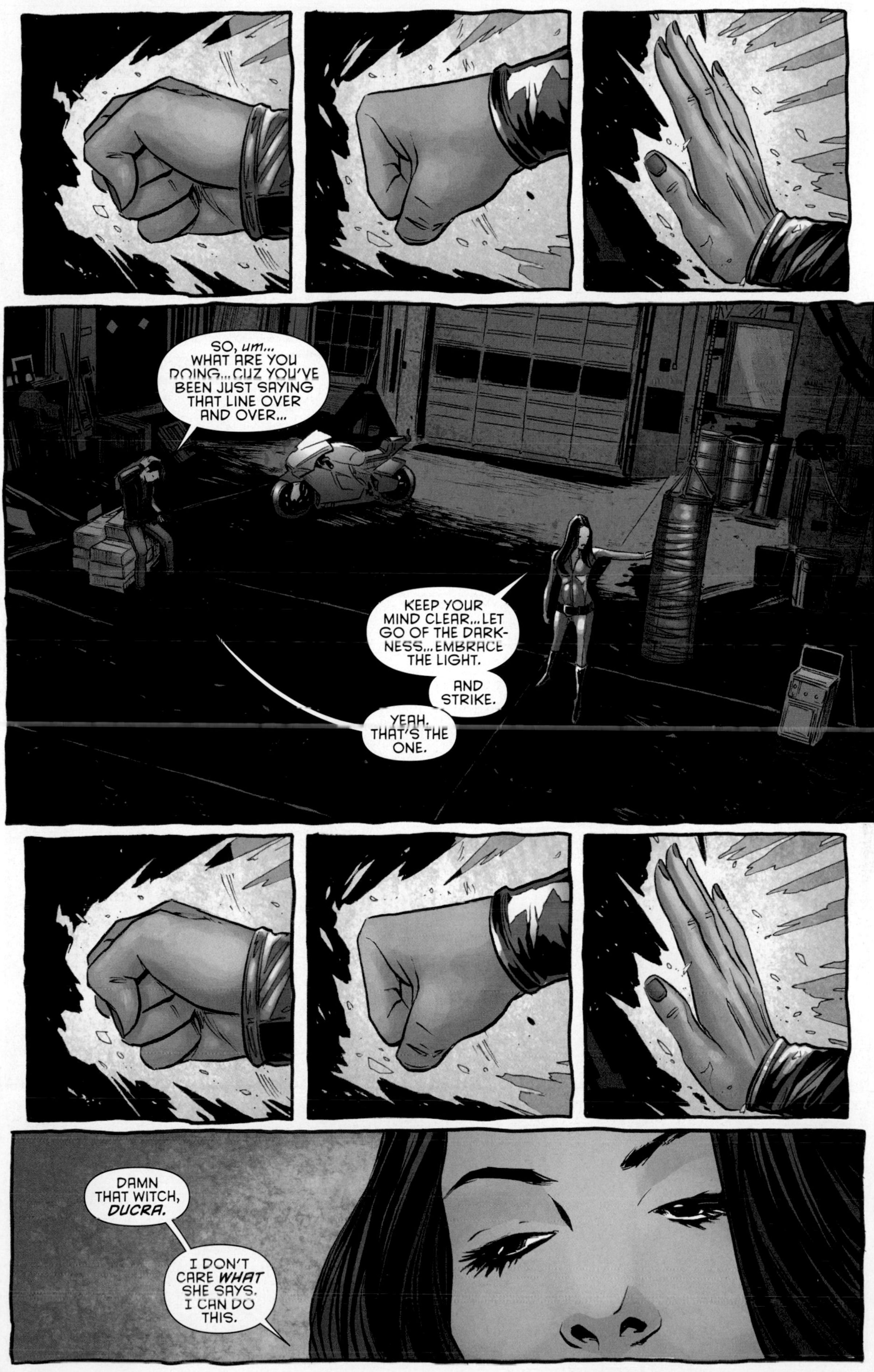
SO, *um*... WHAT ARE YOU DOING... CUZ YOU'VE BEEN JUST SAYING THAT LINE OVER AND OVER...
KEEP YOUR MIND CLEAR... LET GO OF THE DARK-NESS... EMBRACE THE LIGHT.
AND STRIKE.
YEAH. THAT'S THE ONE.
DAMN THAT WITCH, ***DUCRA.***
I DON'T CARE ***WHAT*** SHE SAYS. I CAN DO THIS.

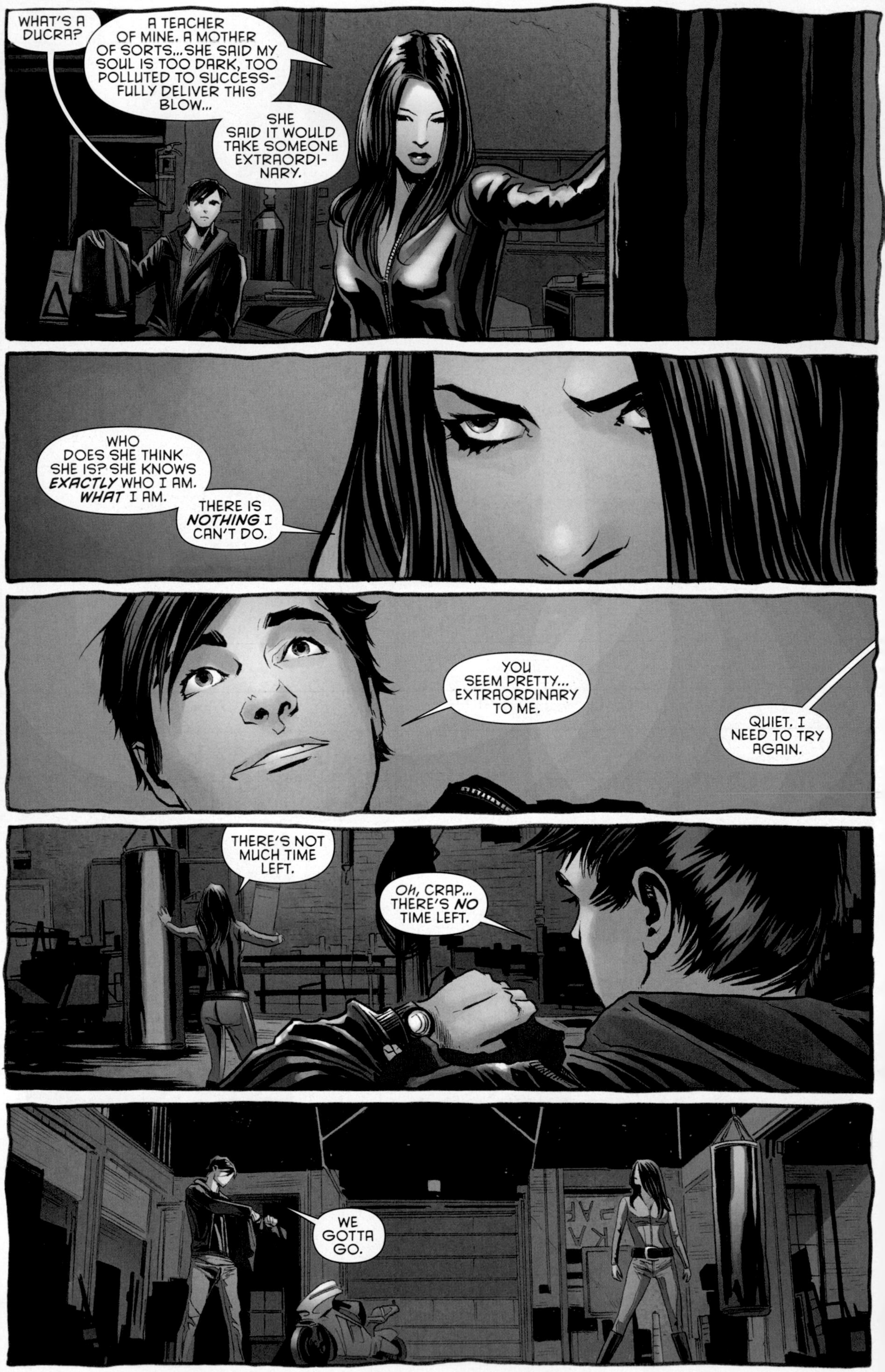
WHAT'S A DUCRA?
A TEACHER OF MINE. A MOTHER OF SORTS... SHE SAID MY SOUL IS TOO DARK, TOO POLLUTED TO SUCCESSFULLY DELIVER THIS BLOW...
SHE SAID IT WOULD TAKE SOMEONE EXTRAORDINARY.
WHO DOES SHE THINK SHE IS? SHE KNOWS *EXACTLY* WHO I AM. *WHAT* I AM.
THERE IS *NOTHING* I CAN'T DO.
YOU SEEM PRETTY... EXTRAORDINARY TO ME.
QUIET. I NEED TO TRY AGAIN.
THERE'S NOT MUCH TIME LEFT.
Oh, CRAP... THERE'S *NO* TIME LEFT.
WE GOTTA GO.

THIS IS THE BEST PLACE TO GET DOWN THERE...WELL, THERE ARE A FEW BETTER WAYS, BUT THEY INVOLVE *MANHOLES* AND USUALLY A COUPLE OF RATS...

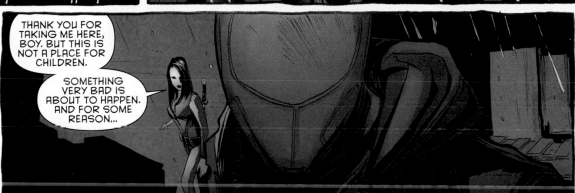

THANK YOU FOR TAKING ME HERE, BOY. BUT THIS IS NOT A PLACE FOR CHILDREN.

SOMETHING VERY BAD IS ABOUT TO HAPPEN. AND FOR SOME REASON...

...I'D PREFER YOU LIVE *THROUGH* TONIGHT.

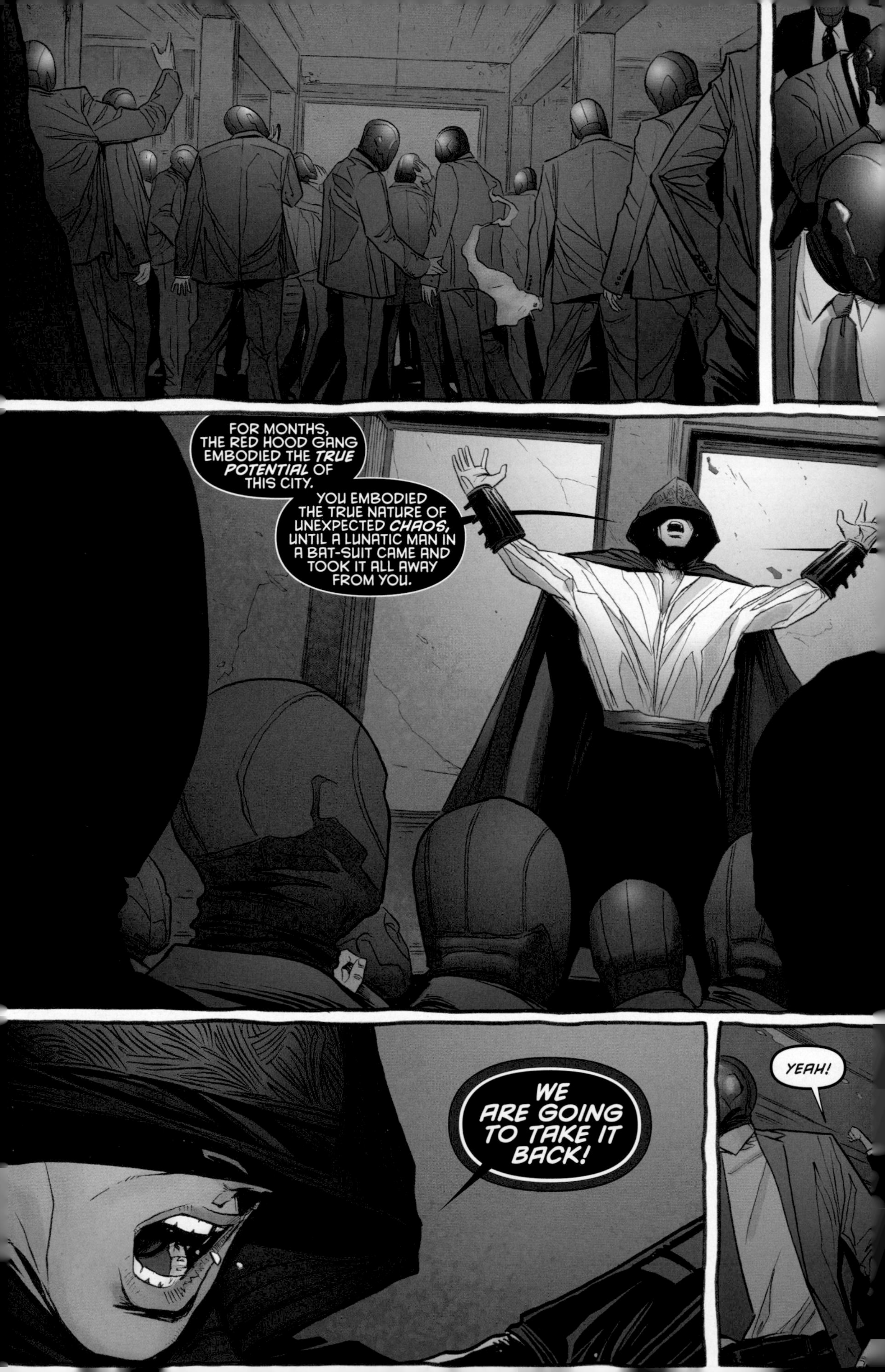
FOR MONTHS, THE RED HOOD GANG EMBODIED THE *TRUE POTENTIAL* OF THIS CITY.
YOU EMBODIED THE TRUE NATURE OF UNEXPECTED *CHAOS,* UNTIL A LUNATIC MAN IN A BAT-SUIT CAME AND TOOK IT ALL AWAY FROM YOU.
WE ARE GOING TO TAKE IT BACK!
YEAH!

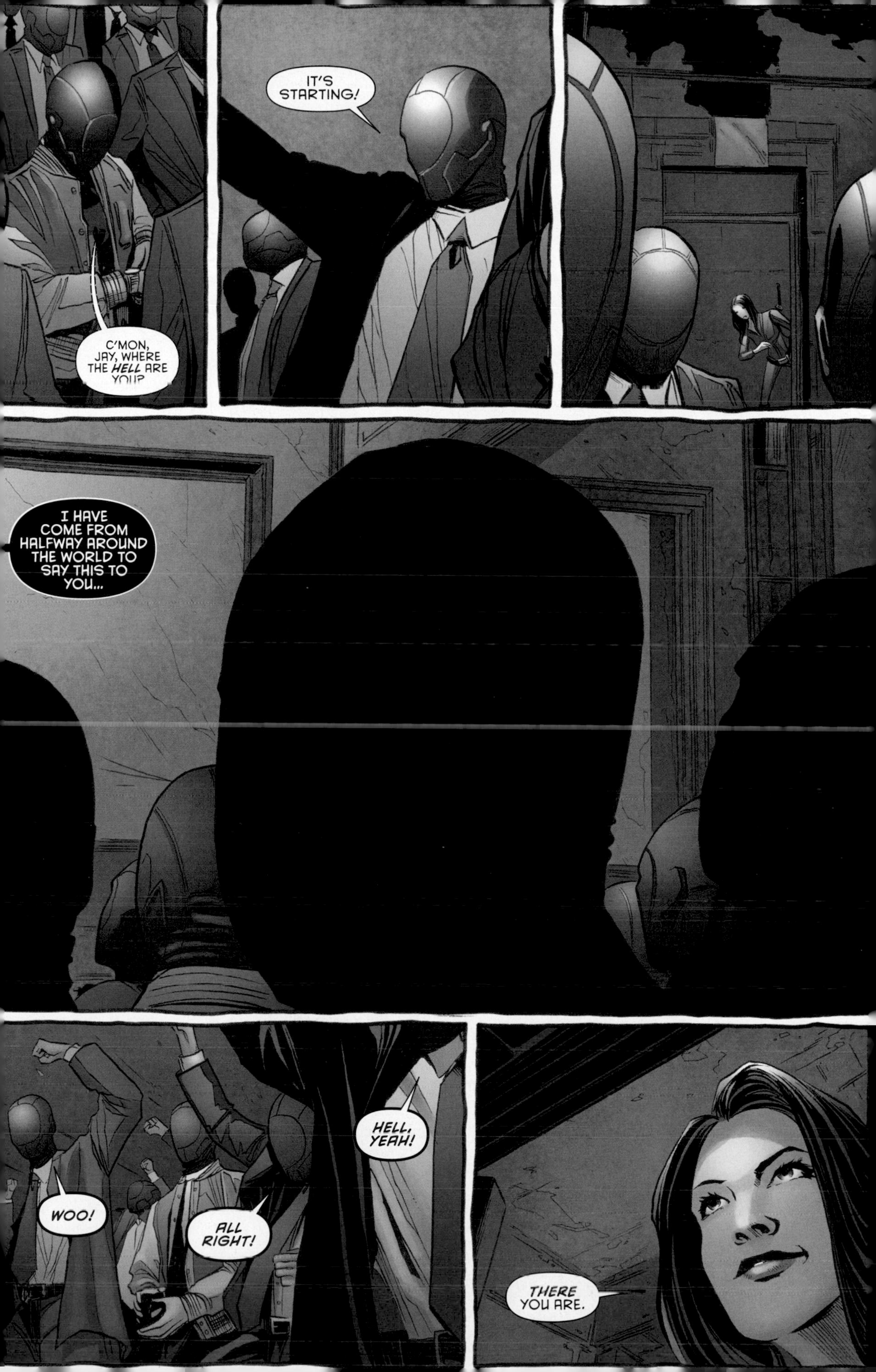
C'MON, JAY, WHERE THE HELL ARE YOU!?
IT'S STARTING!
I HAVE COME FROM HALFWAY AROUND THE WORLD TO SAY THIS TO YOU...
WOO!
ALL RIGHT!
HELL, YEAH!
THERE YOU ARE.

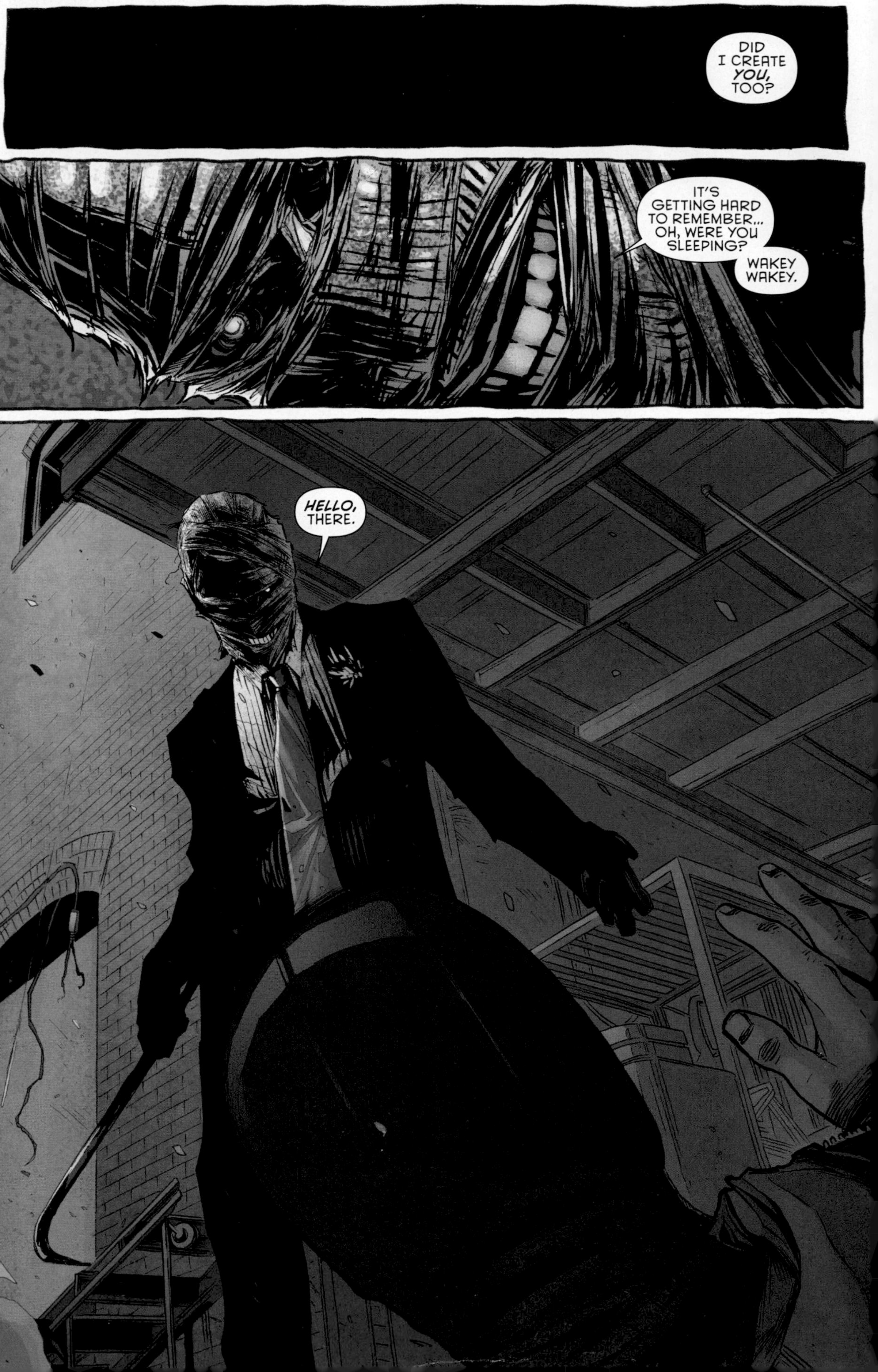
DID I CREATE *YOU,* TOO?
IT'S GETTING HARD TO REMEMBER... OH, WERE YOU SLEEPING?
WAKEY WAKEY.
HELLO, THERE.

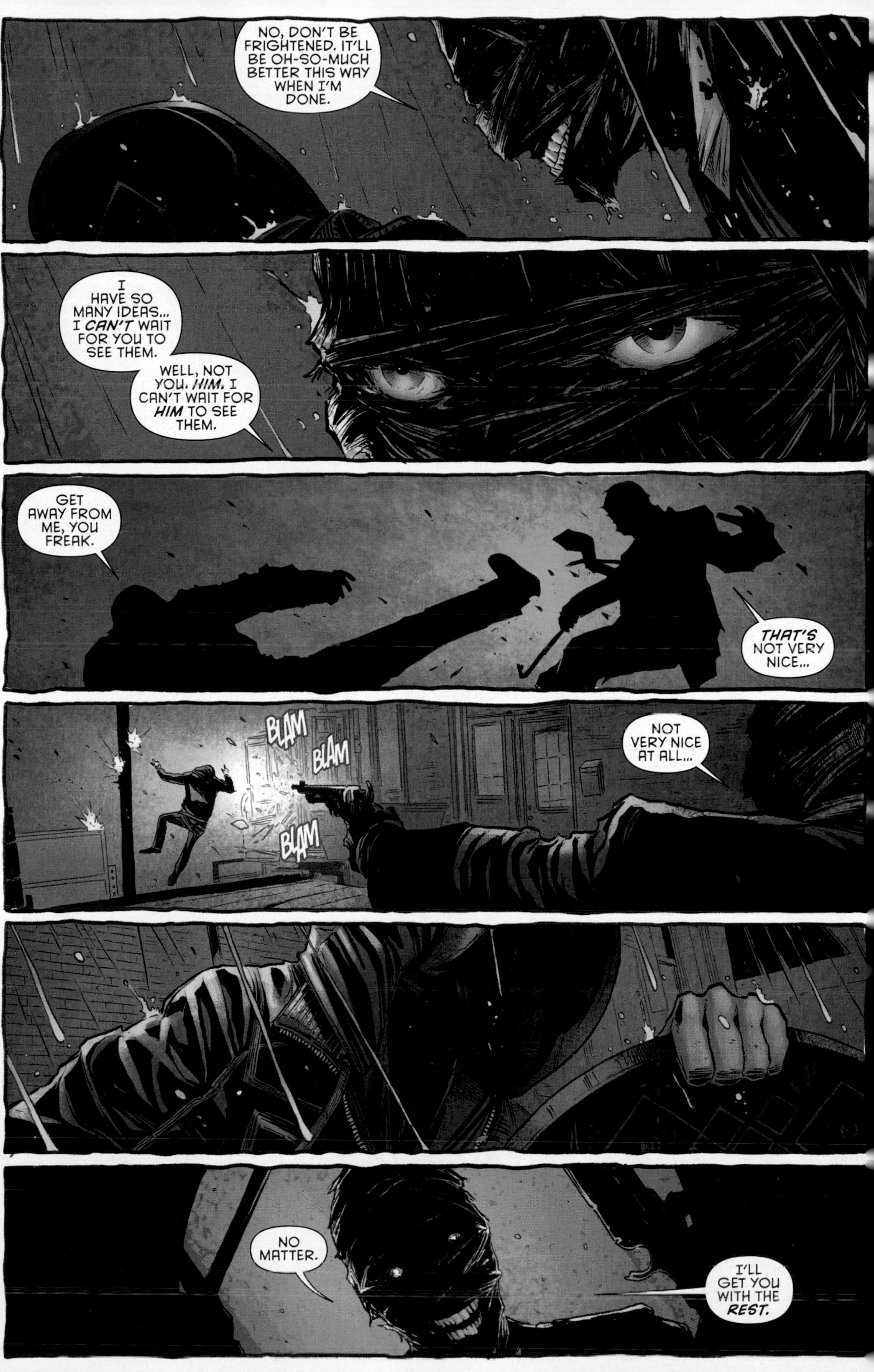
NO, DON'T BE FRIGHTENED. IT'LL BE OH-SO-MUCH BETTER THIS WAY WHEN I'M DONE.
I HAVE SO MANY IDEAS... I CAN'T WAIT FOR YOU TO SEE THEM.
WELL, NOT YOU. HIM. I CAN'T WAIT FOR HIM TO SEE THEM.
GET AWAY FROM ME, YOU FREAK.
THAT'S NOT VERY NICE...
BLAM
BLAM
BLAM
NOT VERY NICE AT ALL...
NO MATTER.
I'LL GET YOU WITH THE REST.

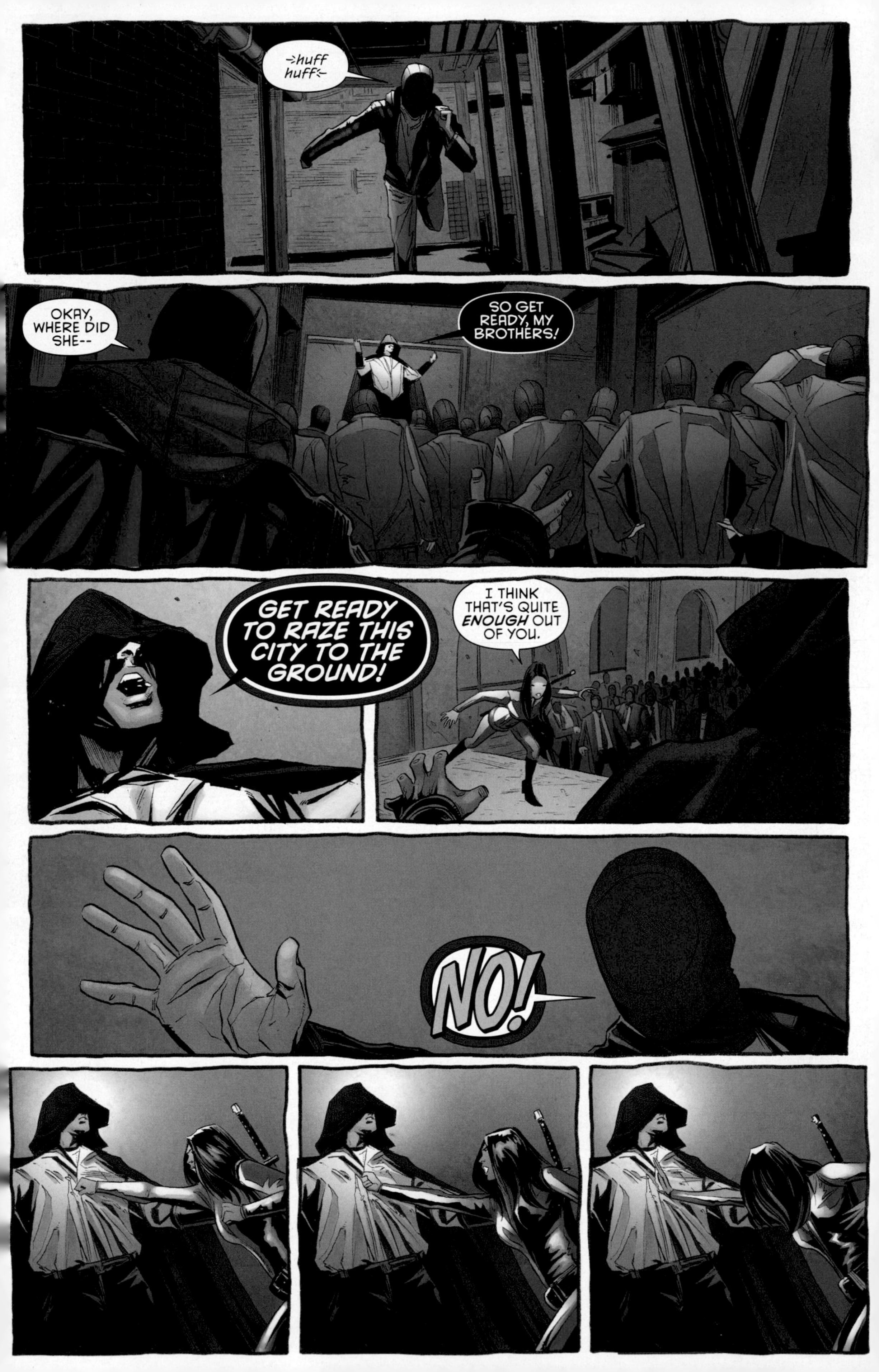

-huff huff-
OKAY, WHERE DID SHE--
SO GET READY, MY BROTHERS!
GET READY TO RAZE THIS CITY TO THE GROUND!
I THINK THAT'S QUITE ENOUGH OUT OF YOU.
NO!

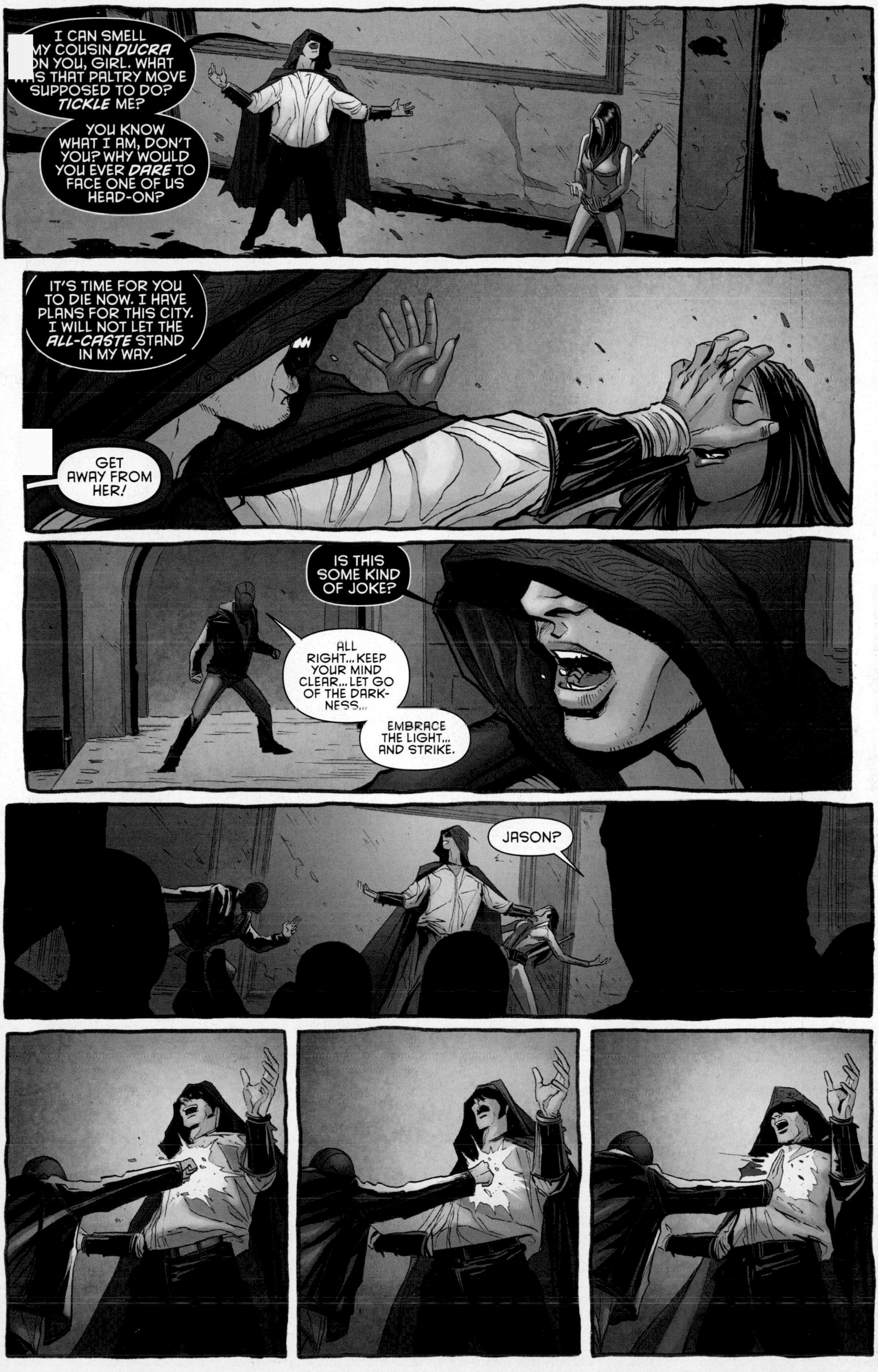
I CAN SMELL MY COUSIN DUCRA ON YOU, GIRL. WHAT WAS THAT PALTRY MOVE SUPPOSED TO DO? TICKLE ME?
YOU KNOW WHAT I AM, DON'T YOU? WHY WOULD YOU EVER DARE TO FACE ONE OF US HEAD-ON?
IT'S TIME FOR YOU TO DIE NOW. I HAVE PLANS FOR THIS CITY. I WILL NOT LET THE ALL-CASTE STAND IN MY WAY.
GET AWAY FROM HER!
IS THIS SOME KIND OF JOKE?
ALL RIGHT... KEEP YOUR MIND CLEAR... LET GO OF THE DARK-NESS...
EMBRACE THE LIGHT... AND STRIKE.
JASON?

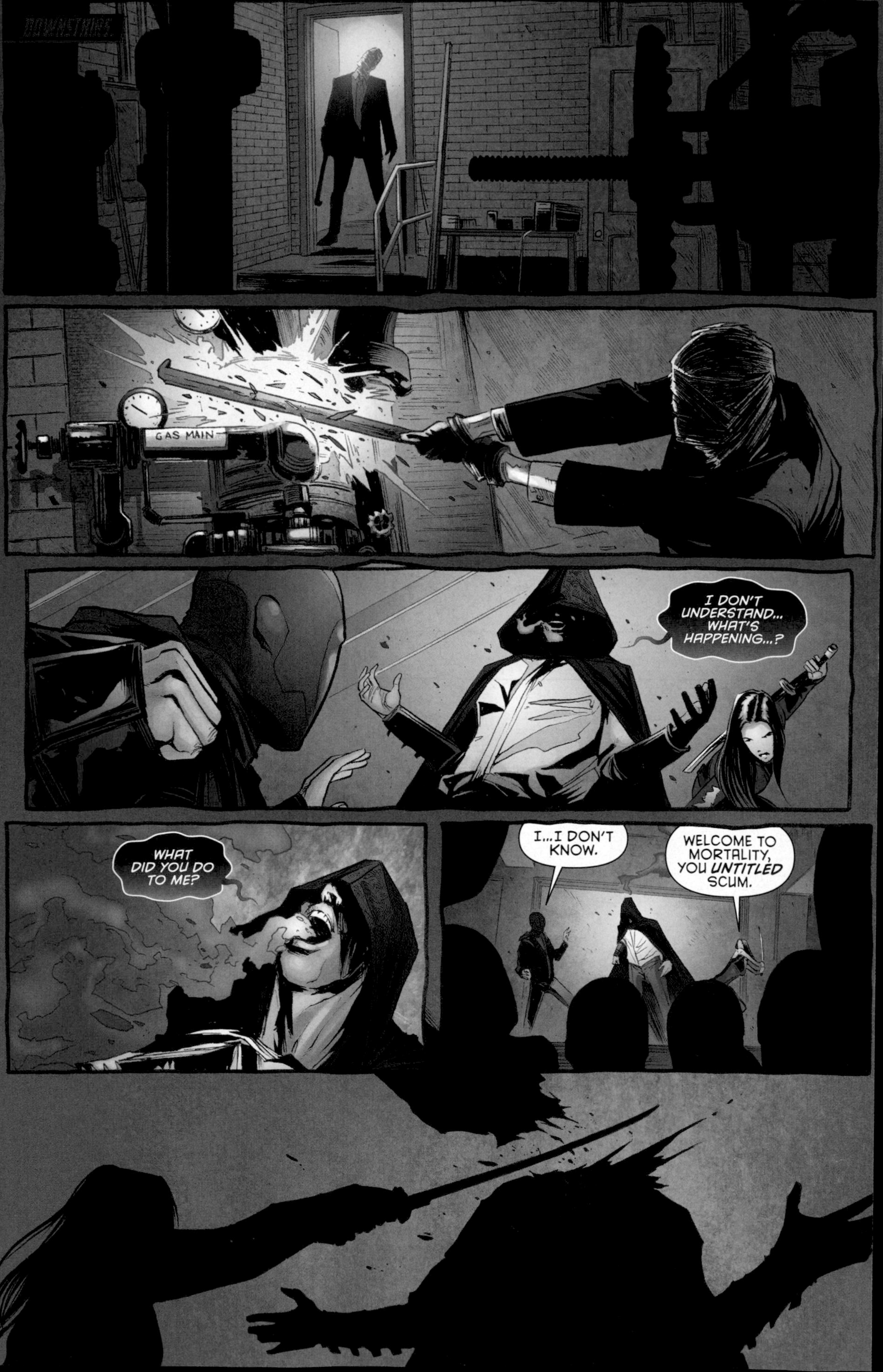
DOWNSTAIRS.
GAS MAIN
I DON'T UNDERSTAND... WHAT'S HAPPENING...?
WHAT DID YOU DO TO ME?
I...I DON'T KNOW.
WELCOME TO MORTALITY, YOU UNTITLED SCUM.

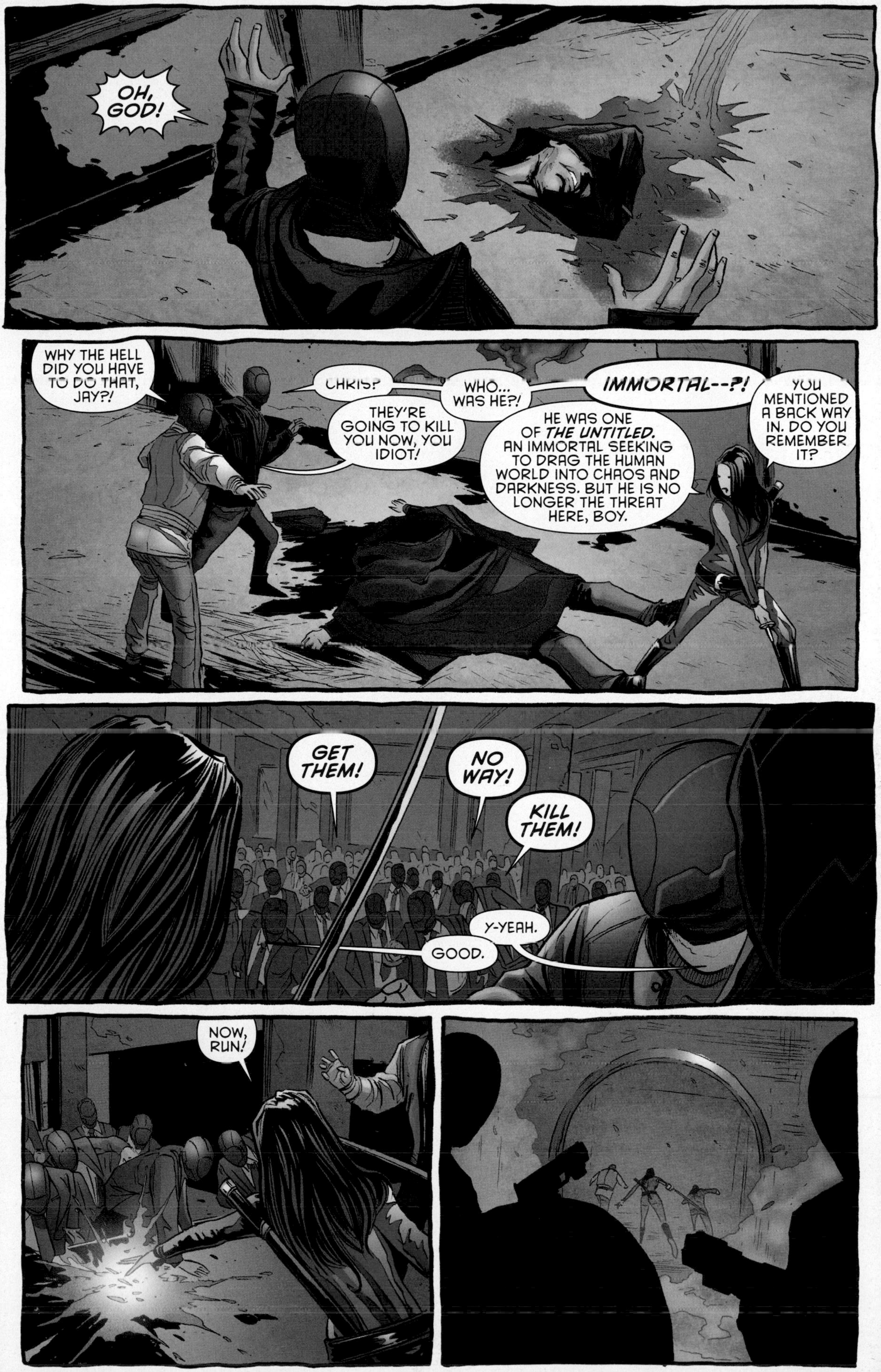
OH, GOD!
WHY THE HELL DID YOU HAVE TO DO THAT, JAY?!
CHRIS?
THEY'RE GOING TO KILL YOU NOW, YOU IDIOT!
WHO... WAS HE?!
IMMORTAL--?!
HE WAS ONE OF THE UNTITLED. AN IMMORTAL SEEKING TO DRAG THE HUMAN WORLD INTO CHAOS AND DARKNESS. BUT HE IS NO LONGER THE THREAT HERE, BOY.
YOU MENTIONED A BACK WAY IN. DO YOU REMEMBER IT?
GET THEM!
NO WAY!
KILL THEM!
Y-YEAH.
GOOD.
NOW, RUN!

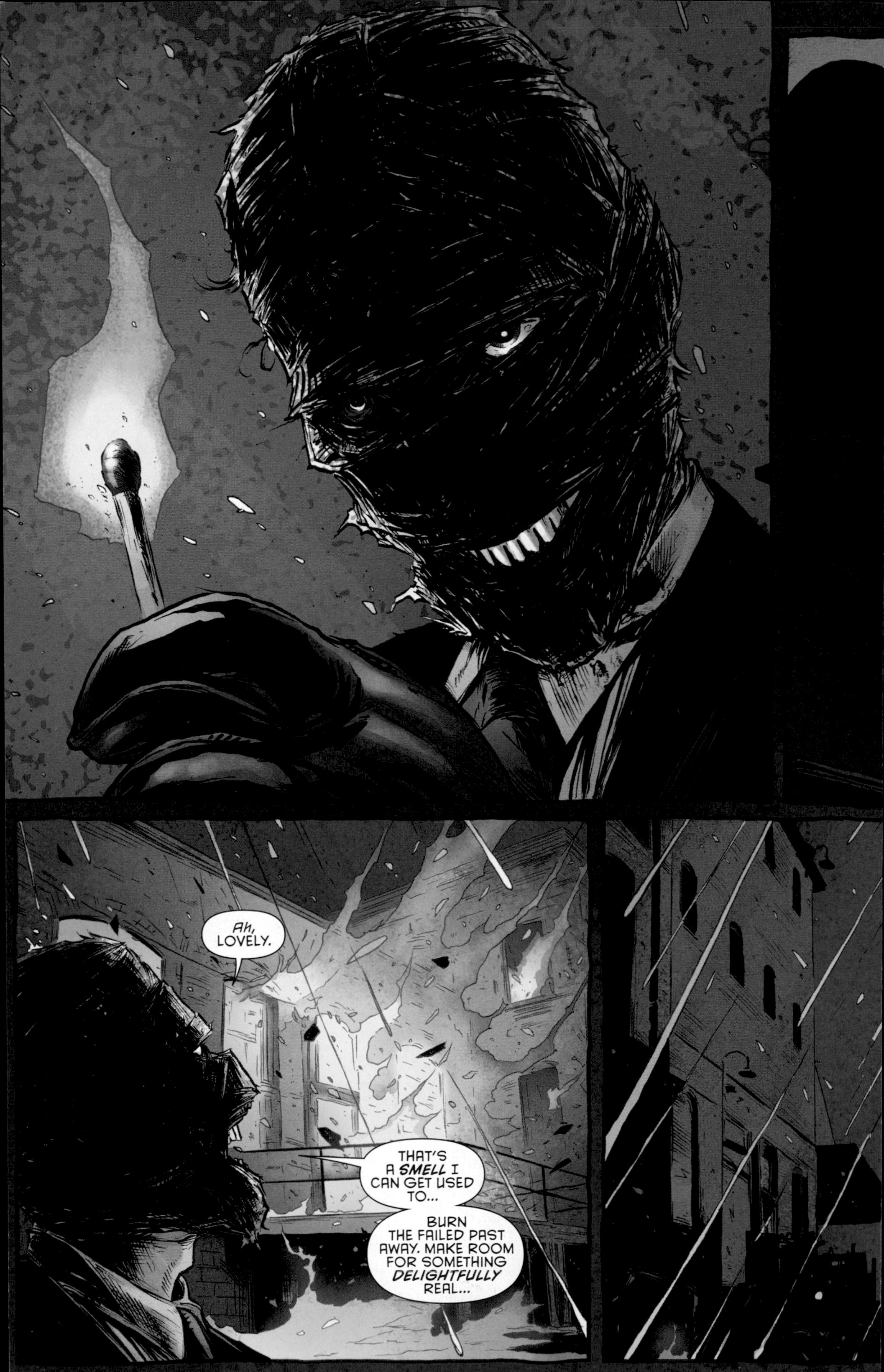
Ah, LOVELY.
THAT'S A SMELL I CAN GET USED TO...
BURN THE FAILED PAST AWAY. MAKE ROOM FOR SOMETHING DELIGHTFULLY REAL...

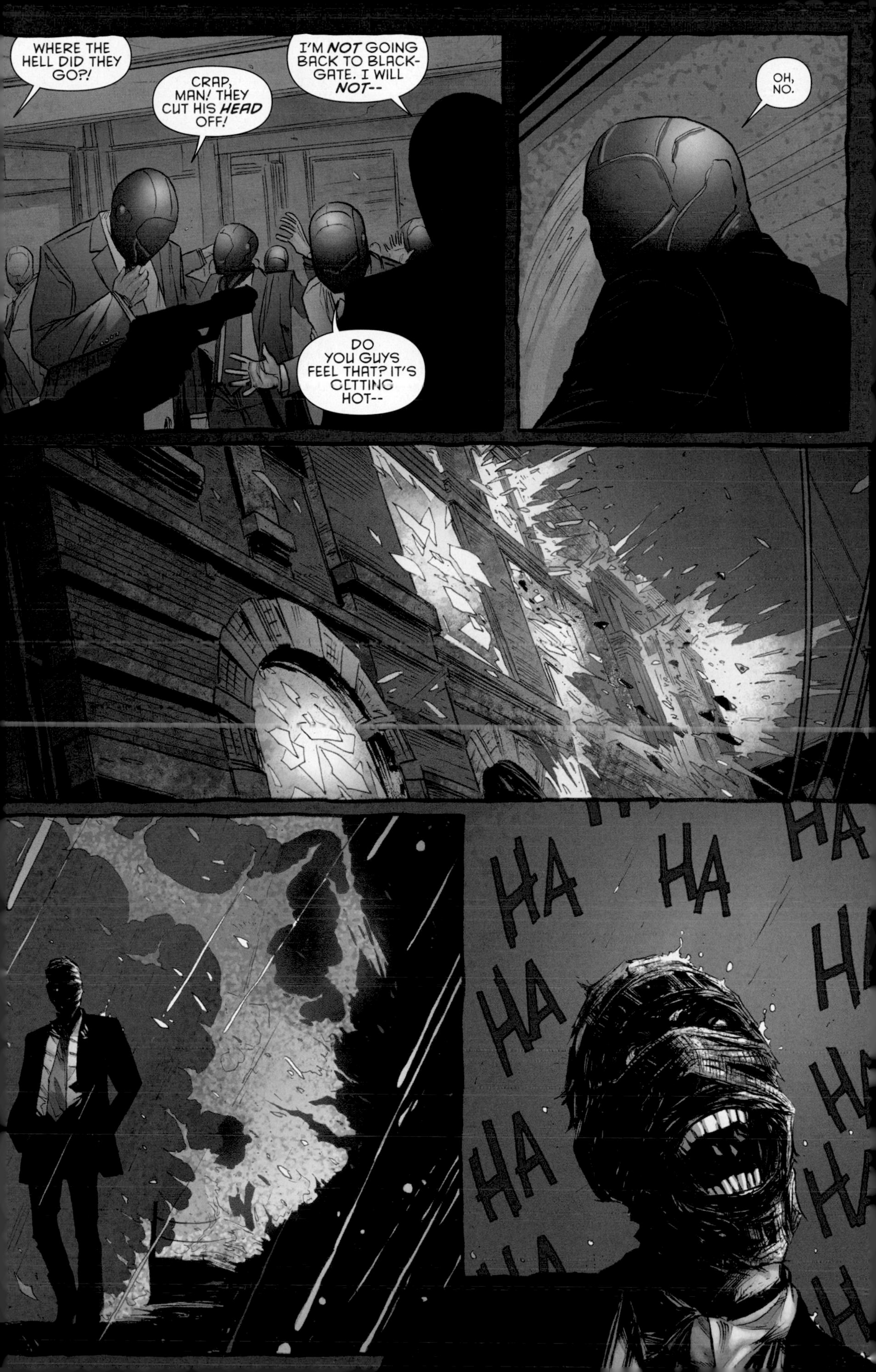
WHERE THE HELL DID THEY GO?!
CRAP, MAN! THEY CUT HIS HEAD OFF!
I'M NOT GOING BACK TO BLACKGATE. I WILL NOT--
DO YOU GUYS FEEL THAT? IT'S GETTING HOT--
OH, NO.
HA HA HA HA HA HA HA HA HA HA HA HA HA HA

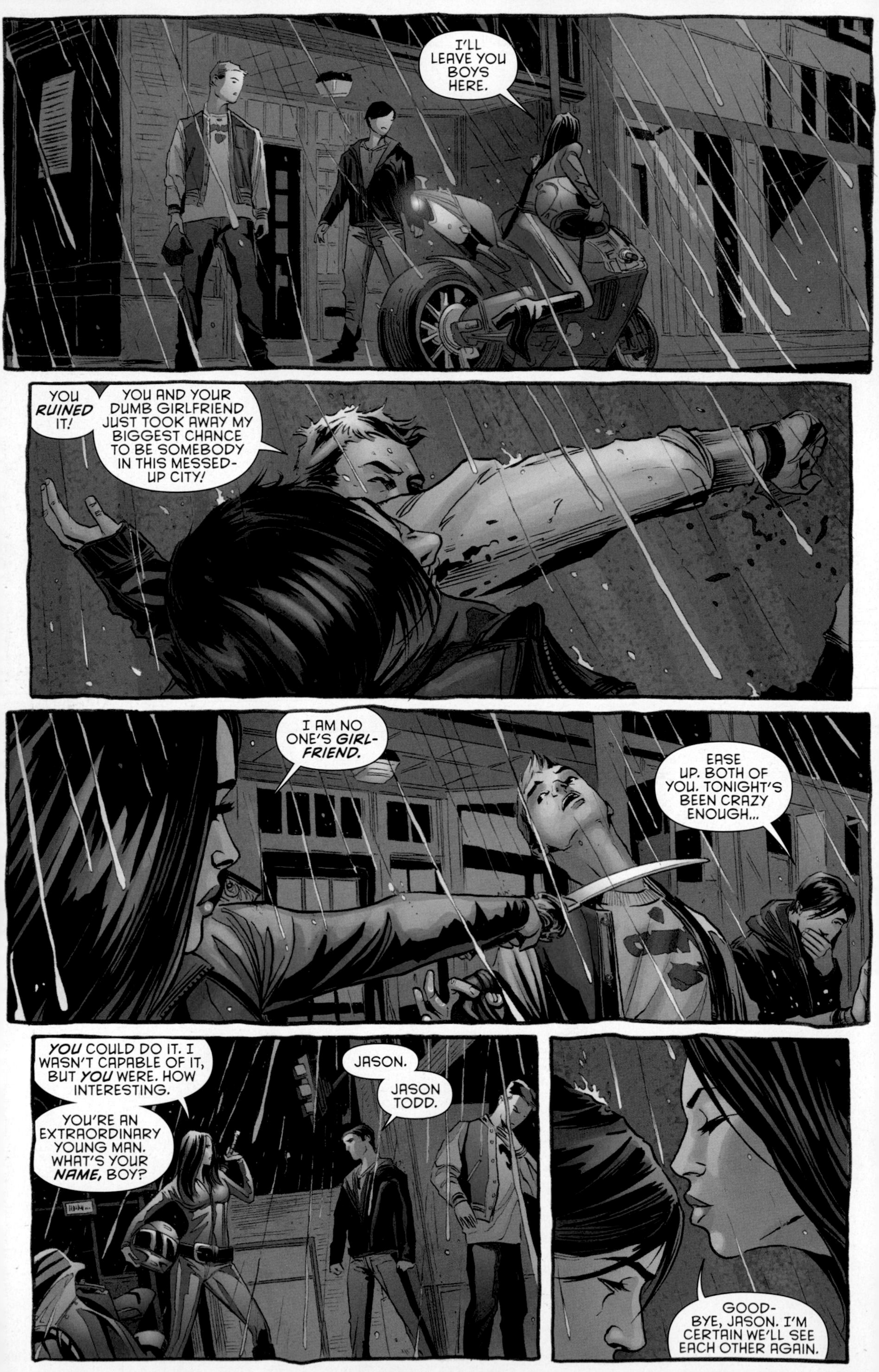

I'LL LEAVE YOU BOYS HERE.
YOU *RUINED* IT!
YOU AND YOUR DUMB GIRLFRIEND JUST TOOK AWAY MY BIGGEST CHANCE TO BE SOMEBODY IN THIS MESSED-UP CITY!
I AM NO ONE'S *GIRLFRIEND.*
EASE UP. BOTH OF YOU. TONIGHT'S BEEN CRAZY ENOUGH...
YOU COULD DO IT. I WASN'T CAPABLE OF IT, BUT *YOU* WERE. HOW INTERESTING.
YOU'RE AN EXTRAORDINARY YOUNG MAN. WHAT'S YOUR *NAME,* BOY?
JASON.
JASON TODD.
GOOD-BYE, JASON. I'M CERTAIN WE'LL SEE EACH OTHER AGAIN.

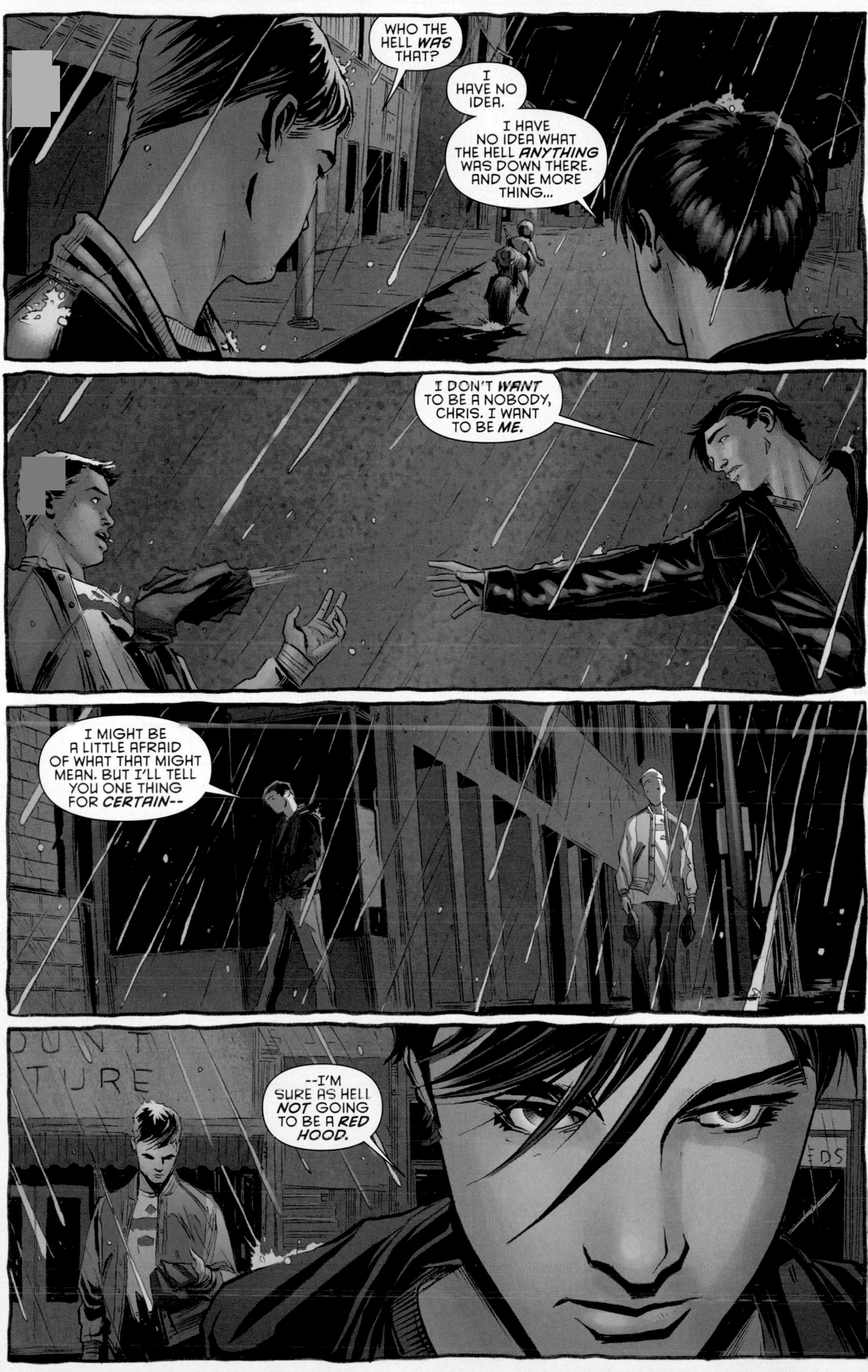
WHO THE HELL *WAS* THAT?
I HAVE NO IDEA.
I HAVE NO IDEA WHAT THE HELL *ANYTHING* WAS DOWN THERE. AND ONE MORE THING...
I DON'T *WANT* TO BE A NOBODY, CHRIS. I WANT TO BE *ME.*
I MIGHT BE A LITTLE AFRAID OF WHAT THAT MIGHT MEAN. BUT I'LL TELL YOU ONE THING FOR *CERTAIN*--
--I'M SURE AS HELL *NOT* GOING TO BE A *RED HOOD.*

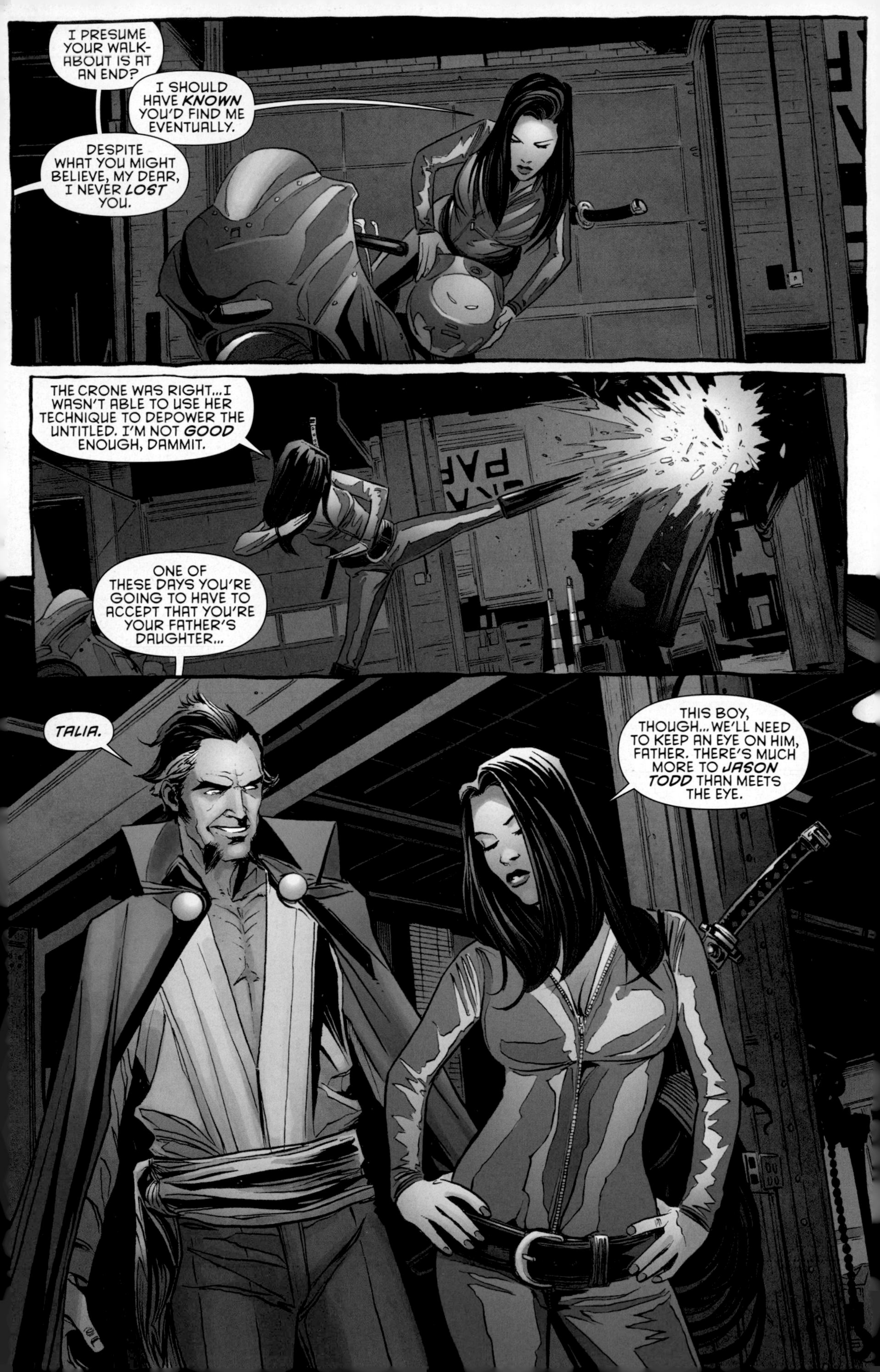
I PRESUME YOUR WALK-ABOUT IS AT AN END?
I SHOULD HAVE KNOWN YOU'D FIND ME EVENTUALLY.
DESPITE WHAT YOU MIGHT BELIEVE, MY DEAR, I NEVER LOST YOU.
THE CRONE WAS RIGHT... I WASN'T ABLE TO USE HER TECHNIQUE TO DEPOWER THE UNTITLED. I'M NOT GOOD ENOUGH, DAMMIT.
ONE OF THESE DAYS YOU'RE GOING TO HAVE TO ACCEPT THAT YOU'RE YOUR FATHER'S DAUGHTER...
TALIA.
THIS BOY, THOUGH... WE'LL NEED TO KEEP AN EYE ON HIM, FATHER. THERE'S MUCH MORE TO JASON TODD THAN MEETS THE EYE.

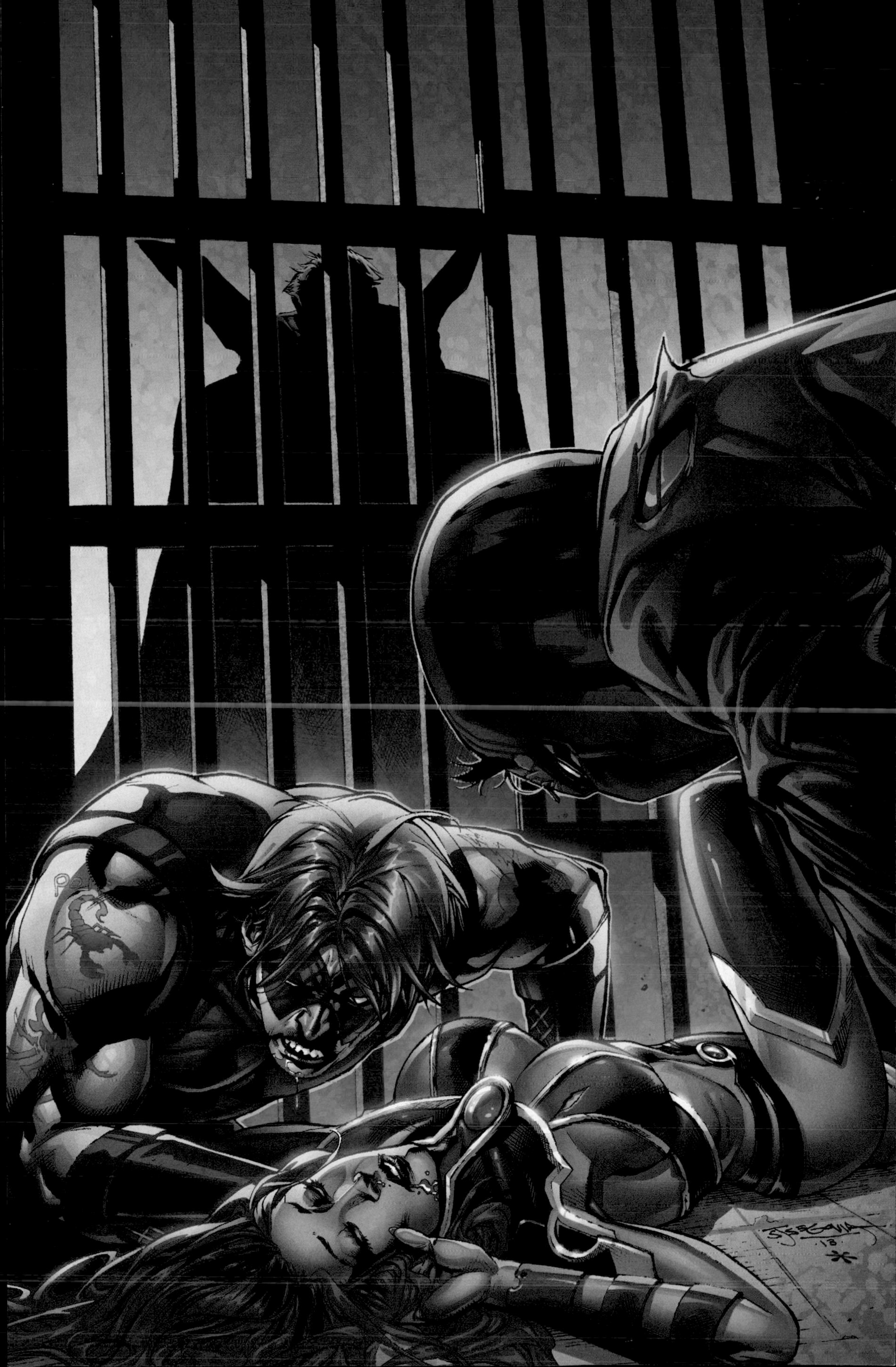

JAMES TYNION IV writer **JULIUS GOPEZ** penciller **SANDU FLOREA & WALDEN WONG** inkers
NEI RUFFINO colorist **STEPHEN SEGOVIA** with **HI-FI** cover artists

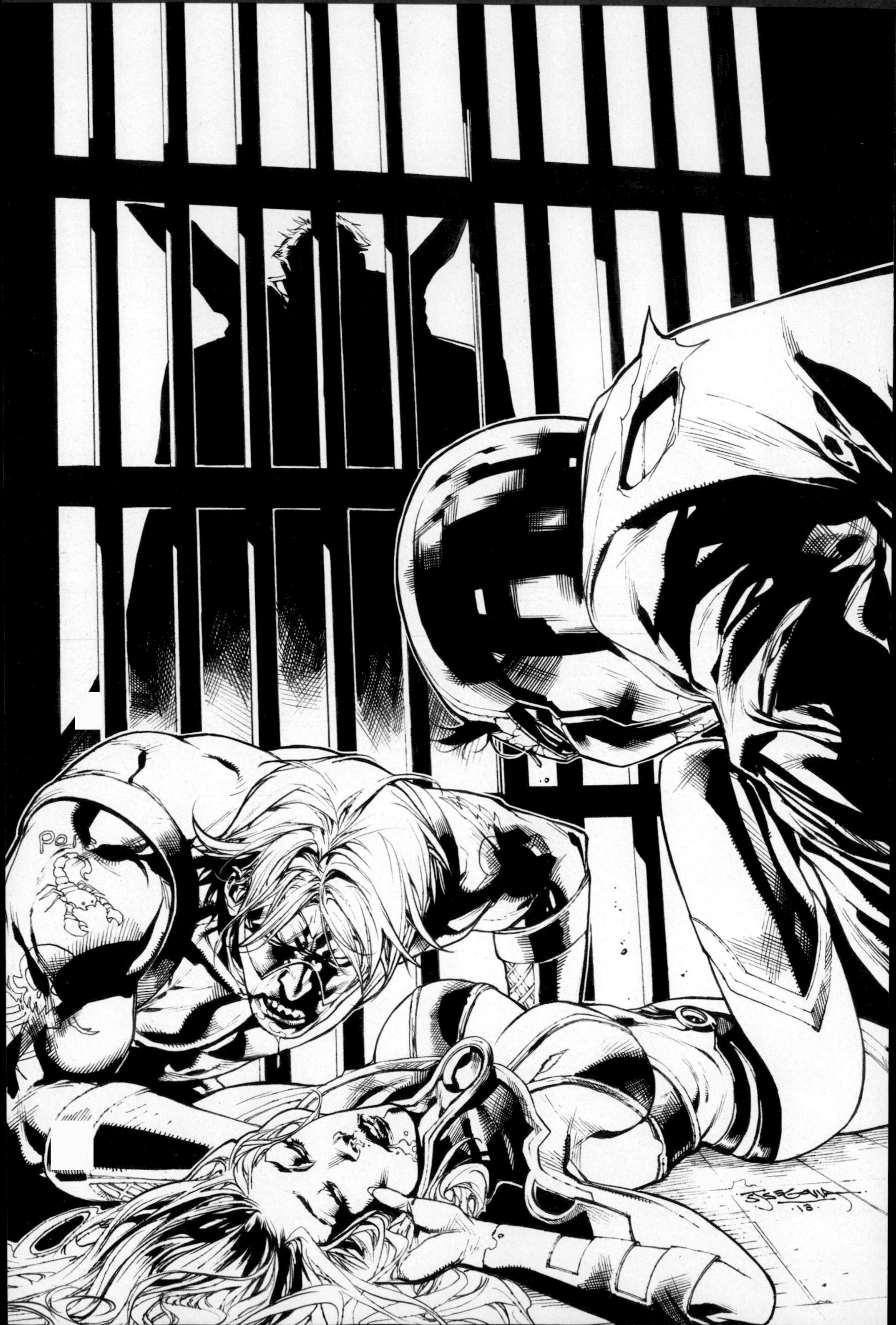

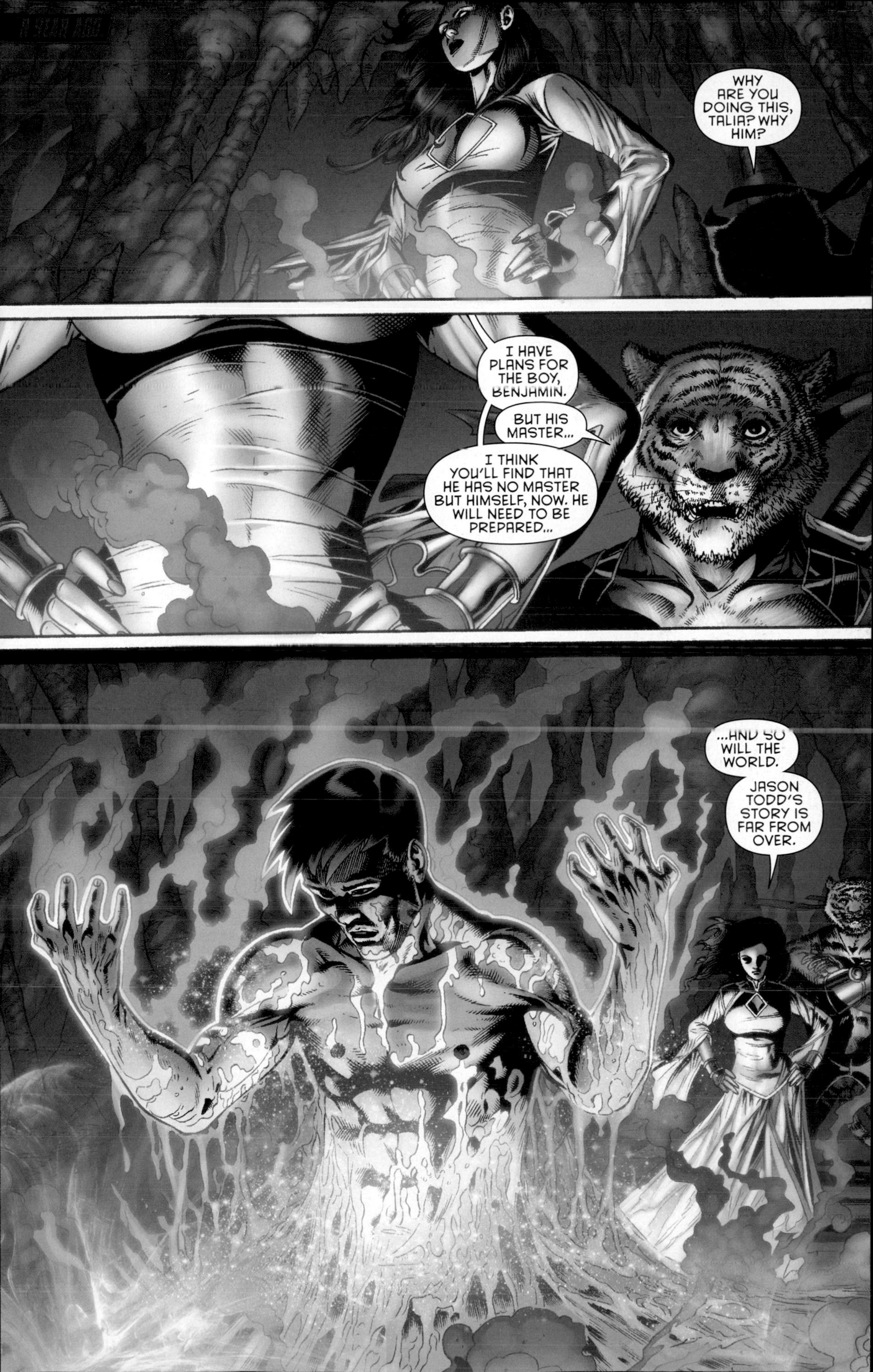
WHY ARE YOU DOING THIS, TALIA? WHY HIM?
I HAVE PLANS FOR THE BOY, BENJAMIN.
BUT HIS MASTER...
I THINK YOU'LL FIND THAT HE HAS NO MASTER BUT HIMSELF, NOW. HE WILL NEED TO BE PREPARED...
...AND SO WILL THE WORLD.
JASON TODD'S STORY IS FAR FROM OVER.

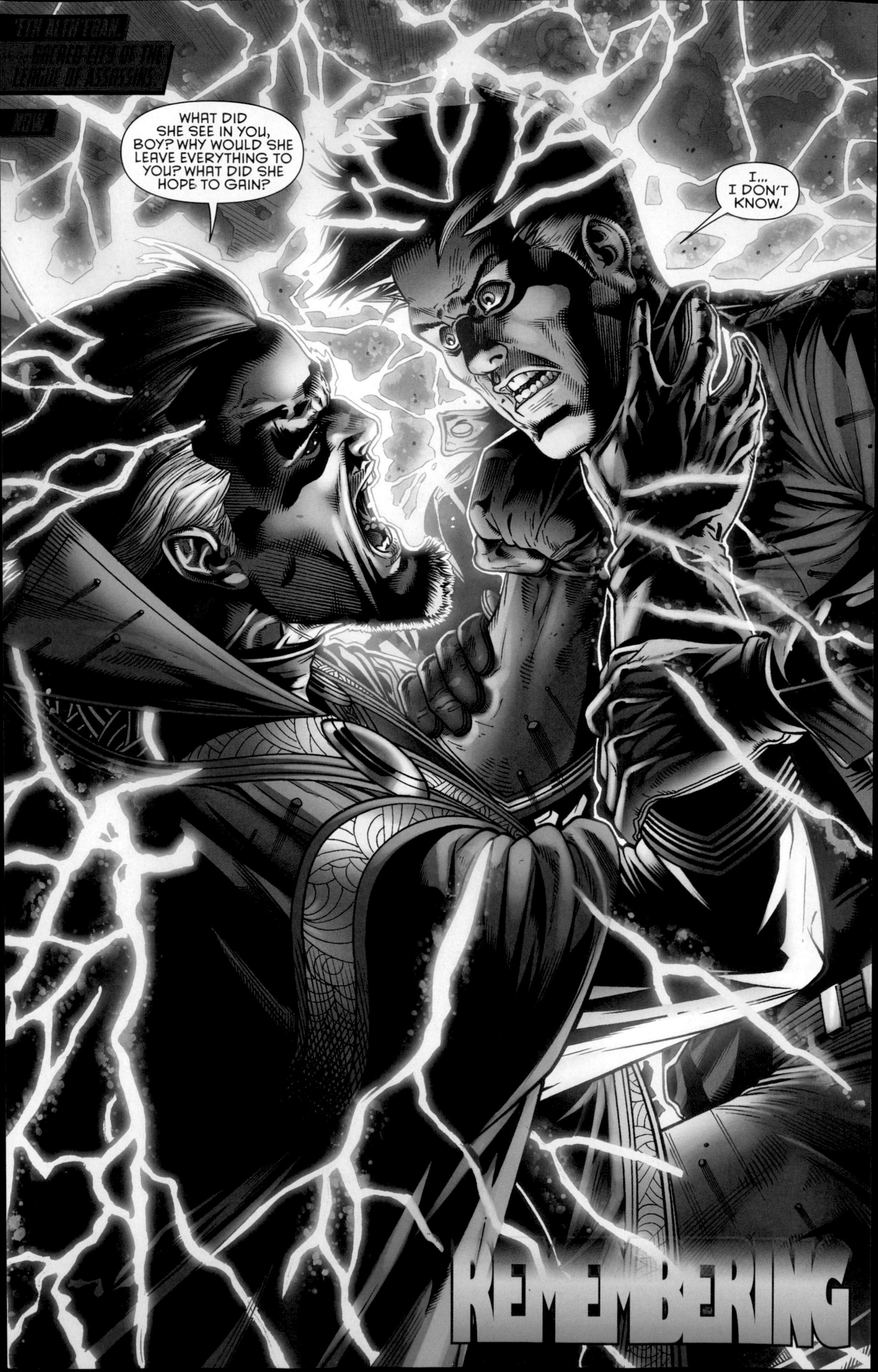
...SACRED CITY OF THE LEAGUE OF ASSASSINS.
NOW.
WHAT DID SHE SEE IN YOU, BOY? WHY WOULD SHE LEAVE EVERYTHING TO YOU? WHAT DID SHE HOPE TO GAIN?
I... I DON'T KNOW.
REMEMBERING

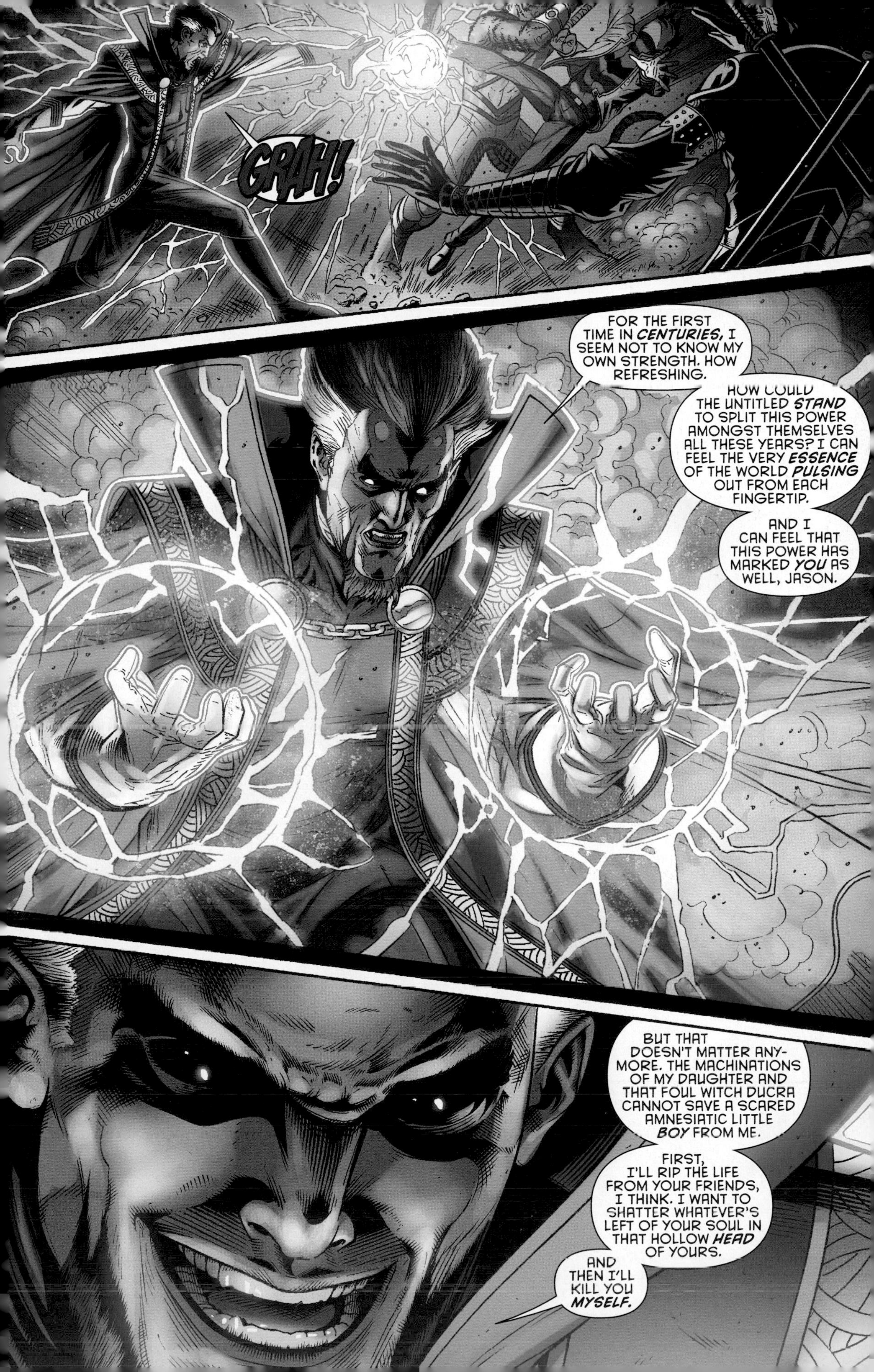
GRAH!
FOR THE FIRST TIME IN CENTURIES, I SEEM NOT TO KNOW MY OWN STRENGTH. HOW REFRESHING.
HOW COULD THE UNTITLED STAND TO SPLIT THIS POWER AMONGST THEMSELVES ALL THESE YEARS? I CAN FEEL THE VERY ESSENCE OF THE WORLD PULSING OUT FROM EACH FINGERTIP.
AND I CAN FEEL THAT THIS POWER HAS MARKED YOU AS WELL, JASON.
BUT THAT DOESN'T MATTER ANY-MORE. THE MACHINATIONS OF MY DAUGHTER AND THAT FOUL WITCH DUCRA CANNOT SAVE A SCARED AMNESIATIC LITTLE BOY FROM ME.
FIRST, I'LL RIP THE LIFE FROM YOUR FRIENDS, I THINK. I WANT TO SHATTER WHATEVER'S LEFT OF YOUR SOUL IN THAT HOLLOW HEAD OF YOURS.
AND THEN I'LL KILL YOU MYSELF.

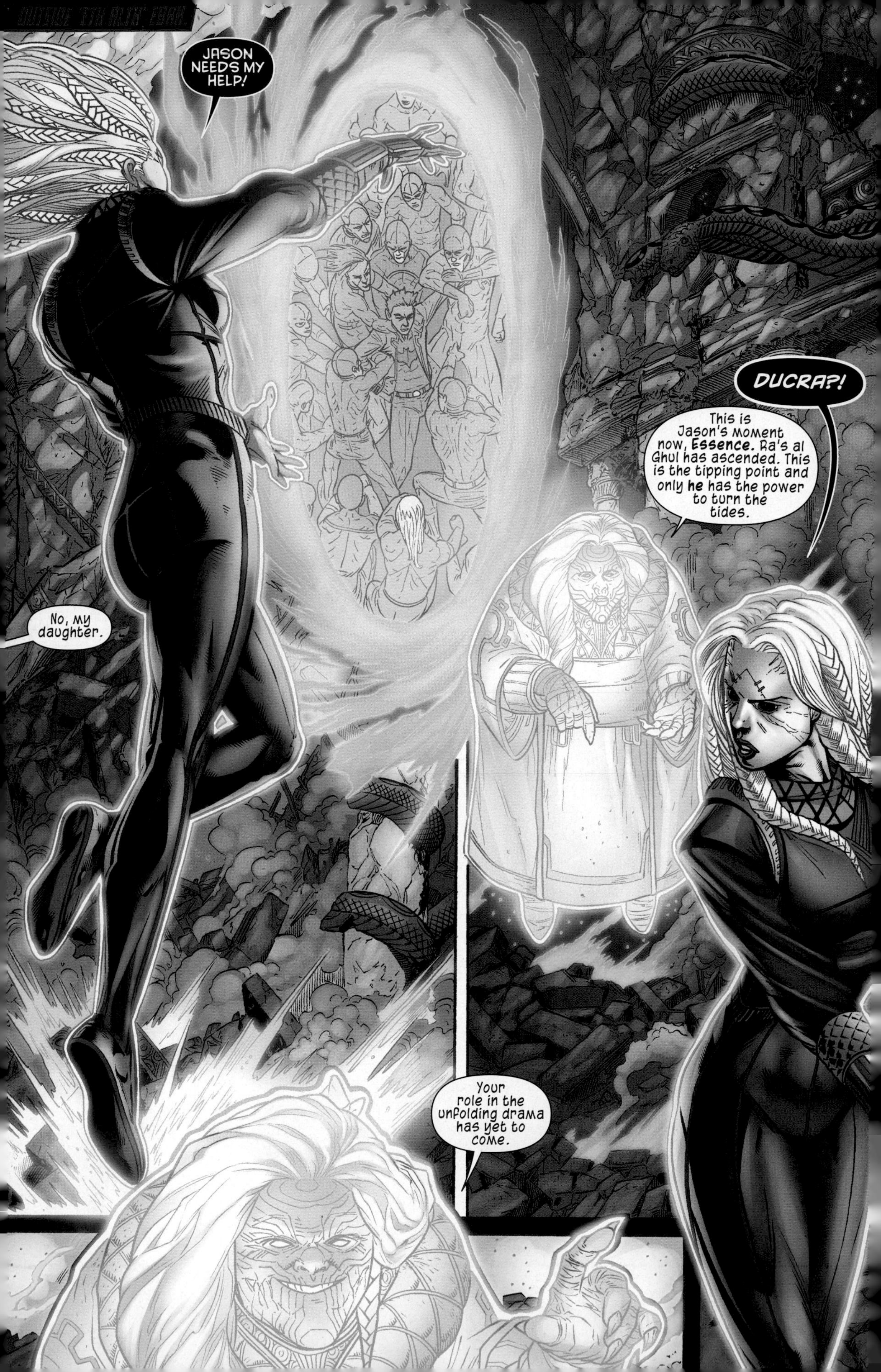
JASON NEEDS MY HELP!
DUCRA?!
This is Jason's moment now, **Essence.** Ra's al Ghul has ascended. This is the tipping point and only **he** has the power to turn the tides.
No, my daughter.
Your role in the unfolding drama has yet to come.

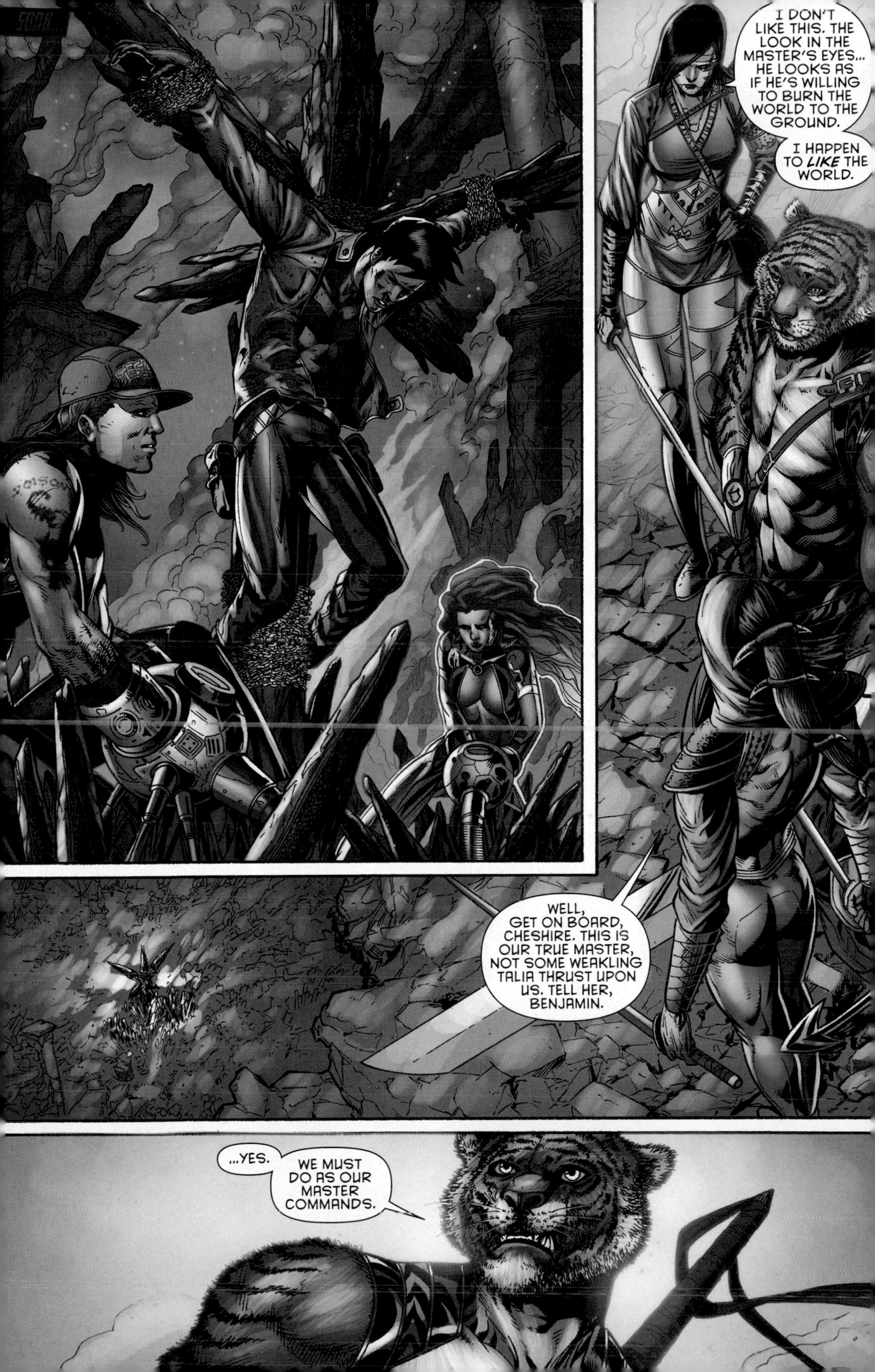
I DON'T LIKE THIS. THE LOOK IN THE MASTER'S EYES... HE LOOKS AS IF HE'S WILLING TO BURN THE WORLD TO THE GROUND.
I HAPPEN TO *LIKE* THE WORLD.
WELL, GET ON BOARD, CHESHIRE. THIS IS OUR TRUE MASTER, NOT SOME WEAKLING TALIA THRUST UPON US. TELL HER, BENJAMIN.
...YES.
WE MUST DO AS OUR MASTER COMMANDS.

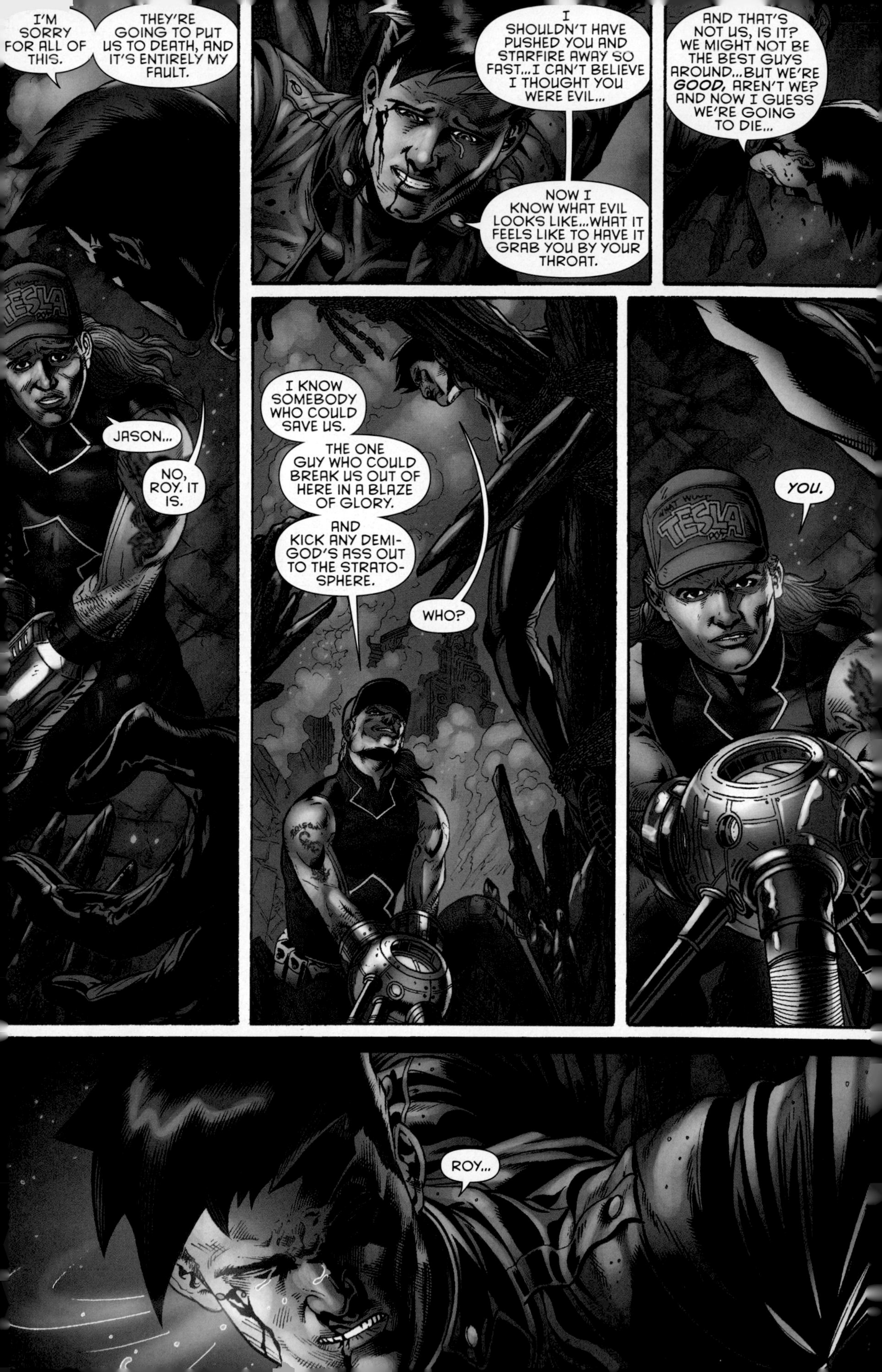

I'M SORRY FOR ALL OF THIS.
THEY'RE GOING TO PUT US TO DEATH, AND IT'S ENTIRELY MY FAULT.
I SHOULDN'T HAVE PUSHED YOU AND STARFIRE AWAY SO FAST...I CAN'T BELIEVE I THOUGHT YOU WERE EVIL...
NOW I KNOW WHAT EVIL LOOKS LIKE...WHAT IT FEELS LIKE TO HAVE IT GRAB YOU BY YOUR THROAT.
AND THAT'S NOT US, IS IT? WE MIGHT NOT BE THE BEST GUYS AROUND...BUT WE'RE *GOOD,* AREN'T WE? AND NOW I GUESS WE'RE GOING TO DIE...
JASON...
NO, ROY. IT IS.
I KNOW SOMEBODY WHO COULD SAVE US.
THE ONE GUY WHO COULD BREAK US OUT OF HERE IN A BLAZE OF GLORY.
AND KICK ANY DEMIGOD'S ASS OUT TO THE STRATOSPHERE.
WHO?
YOU.
ROY...

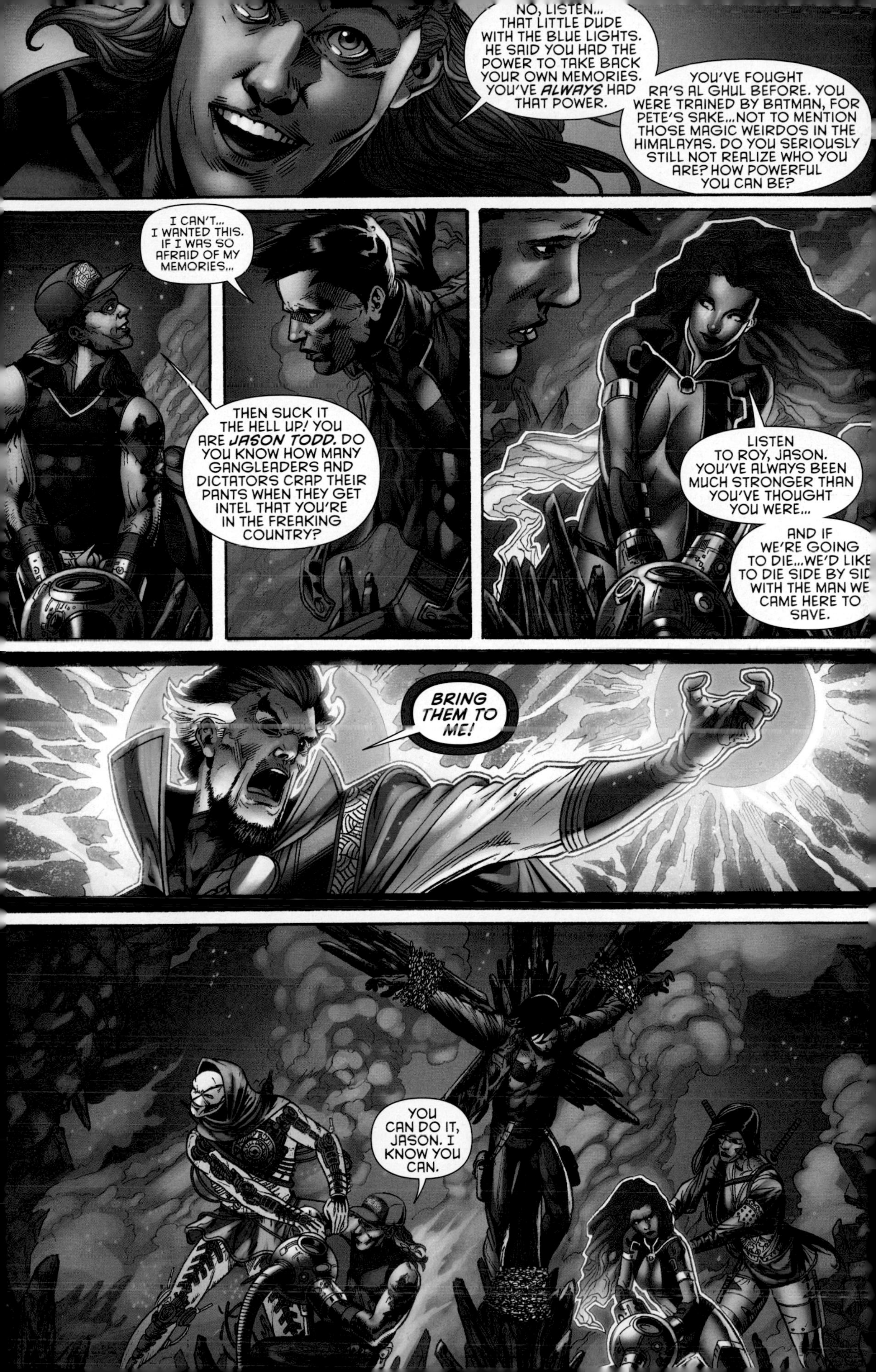
NO, LISTEN... THAT LITTLE DUDE WITH THE BLUE LIGHTS. HE SAID YOU HAD THE POWER TO TAKE BACK YOUR OWN MEMORIES. YOU'VE ALWAYS HAD THAT POWER.
YOU'VE FOUGHT RA'S AL GHUL BEFORE. YOU WERE TRAINED BY BATMAN, FOR PETE'S SAKE...NOT TO MENTION THOSE MAGIC WEIRDOS IN THE HIMALAYAS. DO YOU SERIOUSLY STILL NOT REALIZE WHO YOU ARE? HOW POWERFUL YOU CAN BE?
I CAN'T... I WANTED THIS. IF I WAS SO AFRAID OF MY MEMORIES...
THEN SUCK IT THE HELL UP! YOU ARE JASON TODD. DO YOU KNOW HOW MANY GANGLEADERS AND DICTATORS CRAP THEIR PANTS WHEN THEY GET INTEL THAT YOU'RE IN THE FREAKING COUNTRY?
LISTEN TO ROY, JASON. YOU'VE ALWAYS BEEN MUCH STRONGER THAN YOU'VE THOUGHT YOU WERE...
AND IF WE'RE GOING TO DIE...WE'D LIKE TO DIE SIDE BY SID WITH THE MAN WE CAME HERE TO SAVE.
BRING THEM TO ME!
YOU CAN DO IT, JASON. I KNOW YOU CAN.

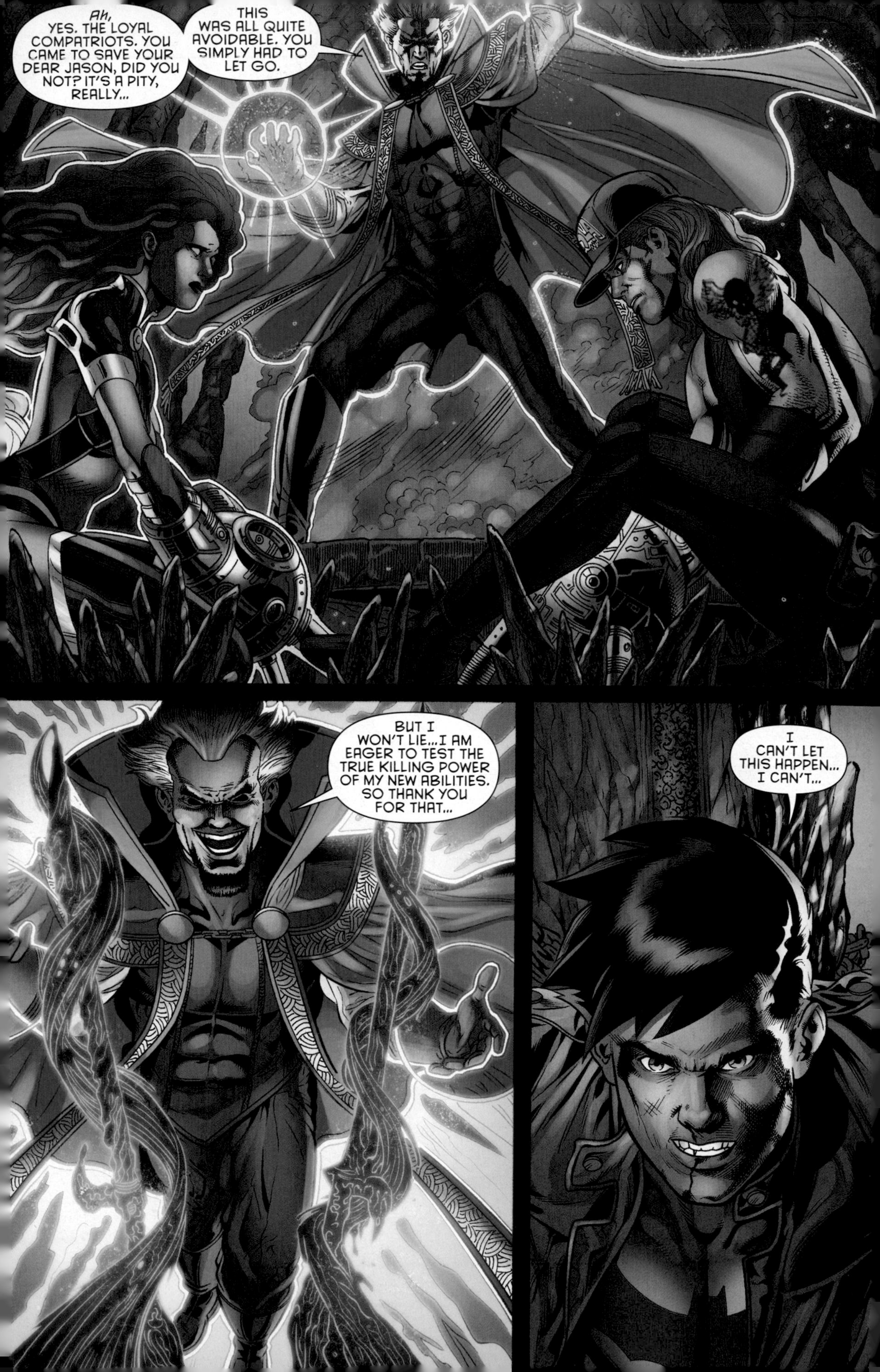
AH, YES. THE LOYAL COMPATRIOTS. YOU CAME TO SAVE YOUR DEAR JASON, DID YOU NOT? IT'S A PITY, REALLY...
THIS WAS ALL QUITE AVOIDABLE. YOU SIMPLY HAD TO LET GO.
BUT I WON'T LIE...I AM EAGER TO TEST THE TRUE KILLING POWER OF MY NEW ABILITIES. SO THANK YOU FOR THAT...
I CAN'T LET THIS HAPPEN... I CAN'T...

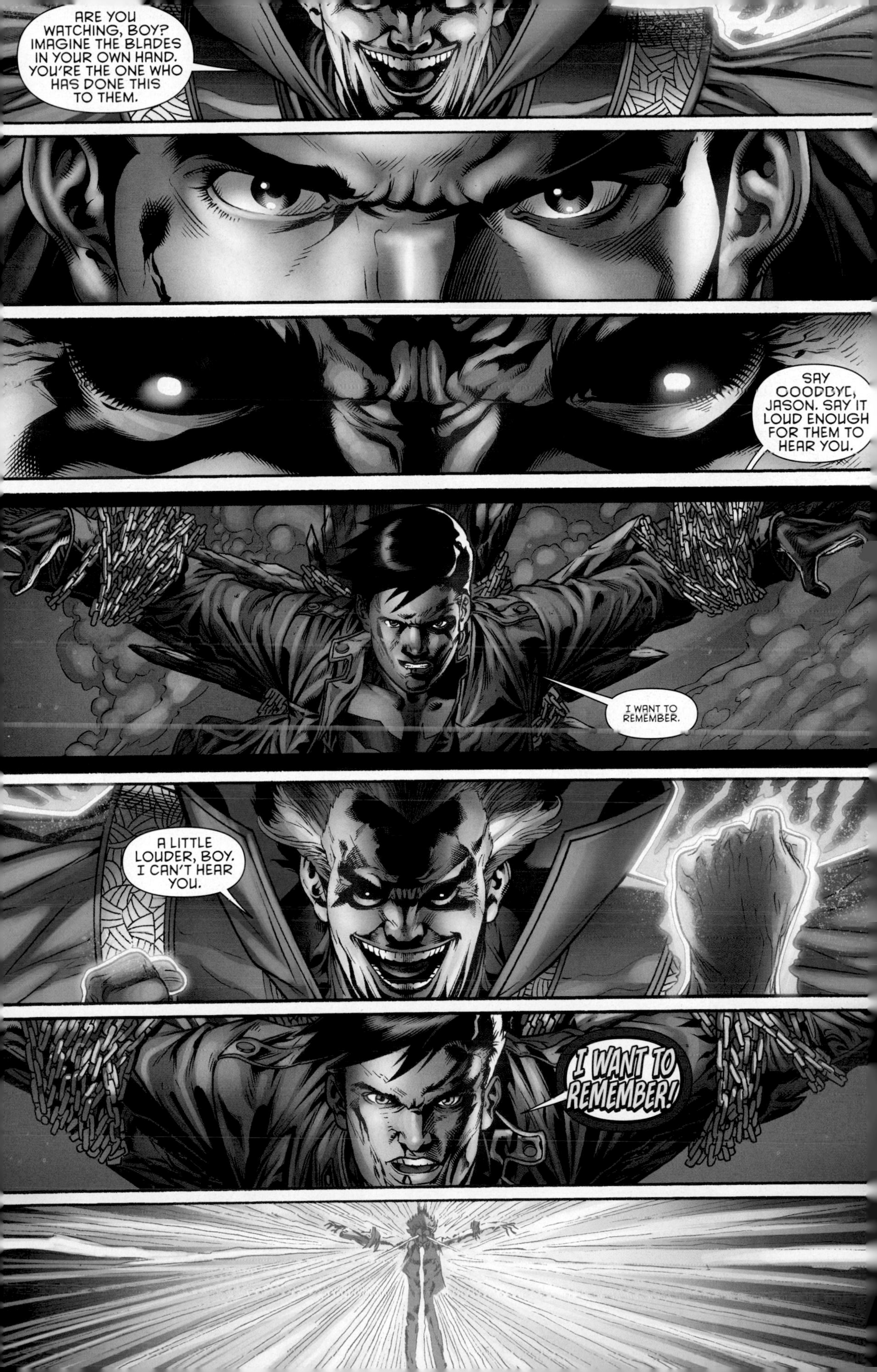
ARE YOU WATCHING, BOY? IMAGINE THE BLADES IN YOUR OWN HAND. YOU'RE THE ONE WHO HAS DONE THIS TO THEM.
SAY GOODBYE, JASON. SAY IT LOUD ENOUGH FOR THEM TO HEAR YOU.
I WANT TO REMEMBER.
A LITTLE LOUDER, BOY. I CAN'T HEAR YOU.
I WANT TO REMEMBER!

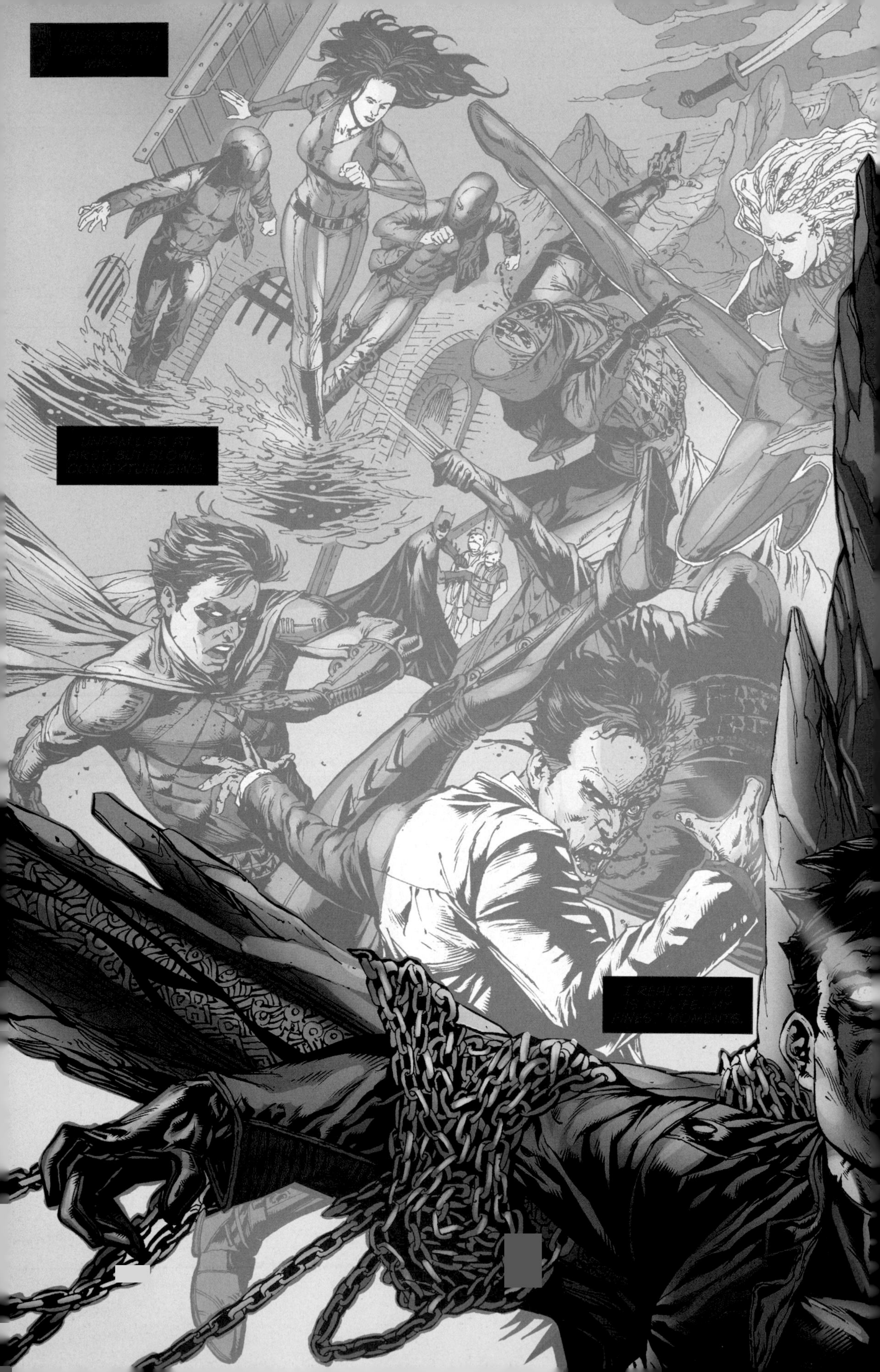
[redacted]
[redacted]
[redacted]

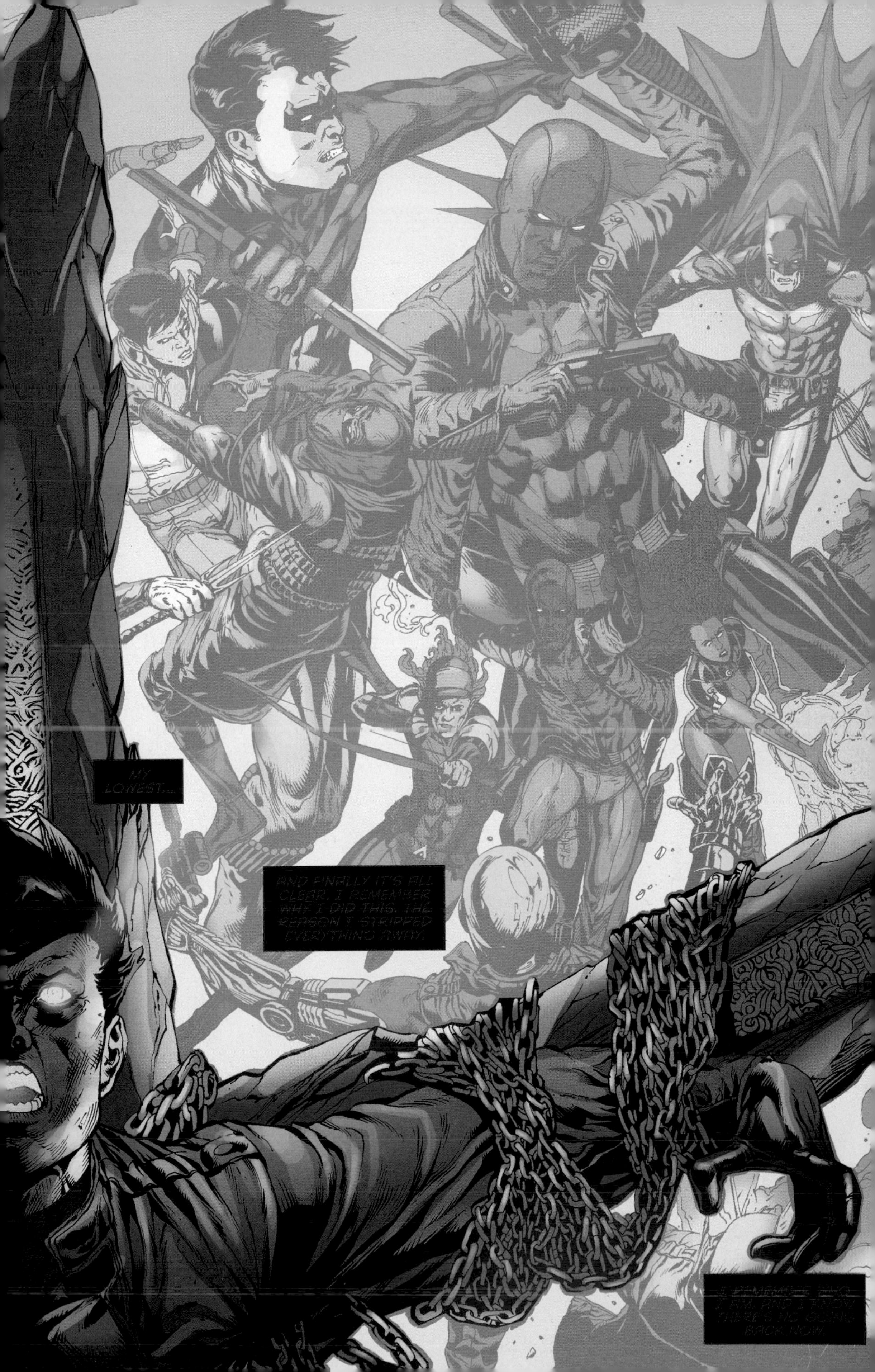
MY LOWEST...
AND FINALLY IT'S ALL CLEAR. I REMEMBER WHY I DID THIS. THE REASON I STRIPPED EVERYTHING AWAY.
I REMEMBER WHO I AM. AND I KNOW THERE'S NO GOING BACK NOW.

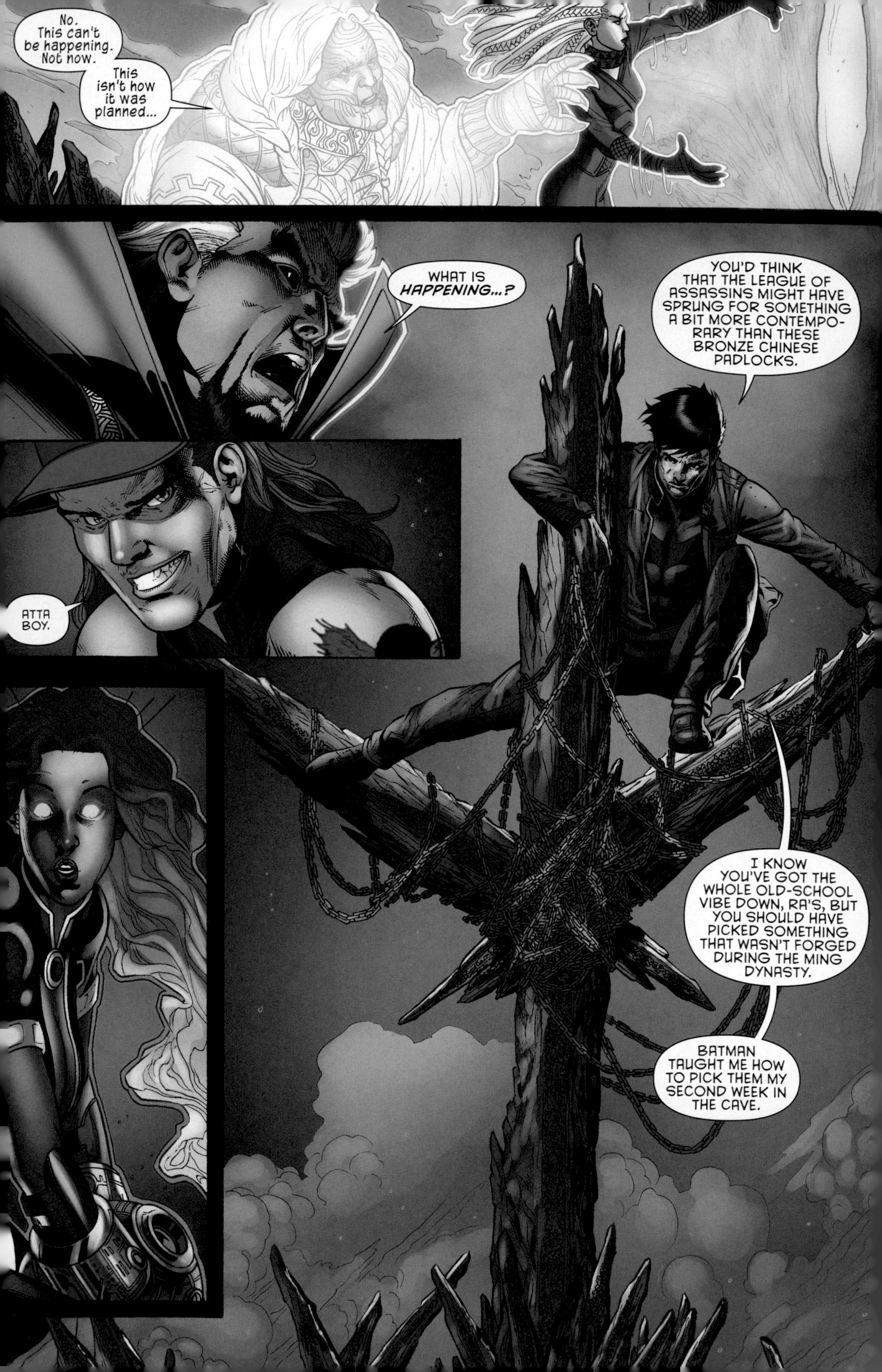
No. This can't be happening. Not now.
This isn't how it was planned...
WHAT IS *HAPPENING...?*
ATTA BOY.
YOU'D THINK THAT THE LEAGUE OF ASSASSINS MIGHT HAVE SPRUNG FOR SOMETHING A BIT MORE CONTEMPORARY THAN THESE BRONZE CHINESE PADLOCKS.
I KNOW YOU'VE GOT THE WHOLE OLD-SCHOOL VIBE DOWN, RA'S, BUT YOU SHOULD HAVE PICKED SOMETHING THAT WASN'T FORGED DURING THE MING DYNASTY.
BATMAN TAUGHT ME HOW TO PICK THEM MY SECOND WEEK IN THE CAVE.

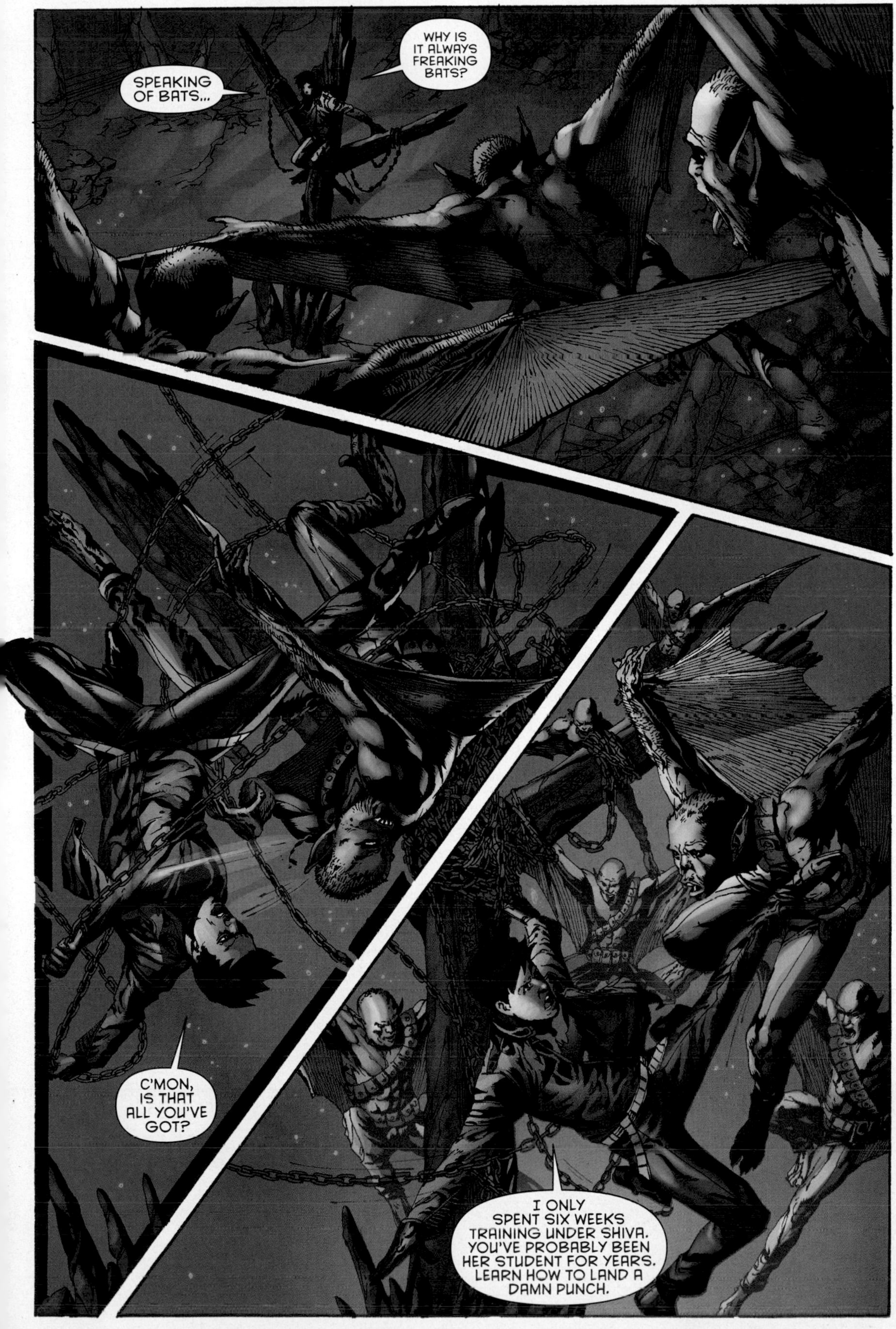
WHY IS IT ALWAYS FREAKING BATS?
SPEAKING OF BATS...
C'MON, IS THAT ALL YOU'VE GOT?
I ONLY SPENT SIX WEEKS TRAINING UNDER SHIVA. YOU'VE PROBABLY BEEN HER STUDENT FOR YEARS. LEARN HOW TO LAND A DAMN PUNCH.

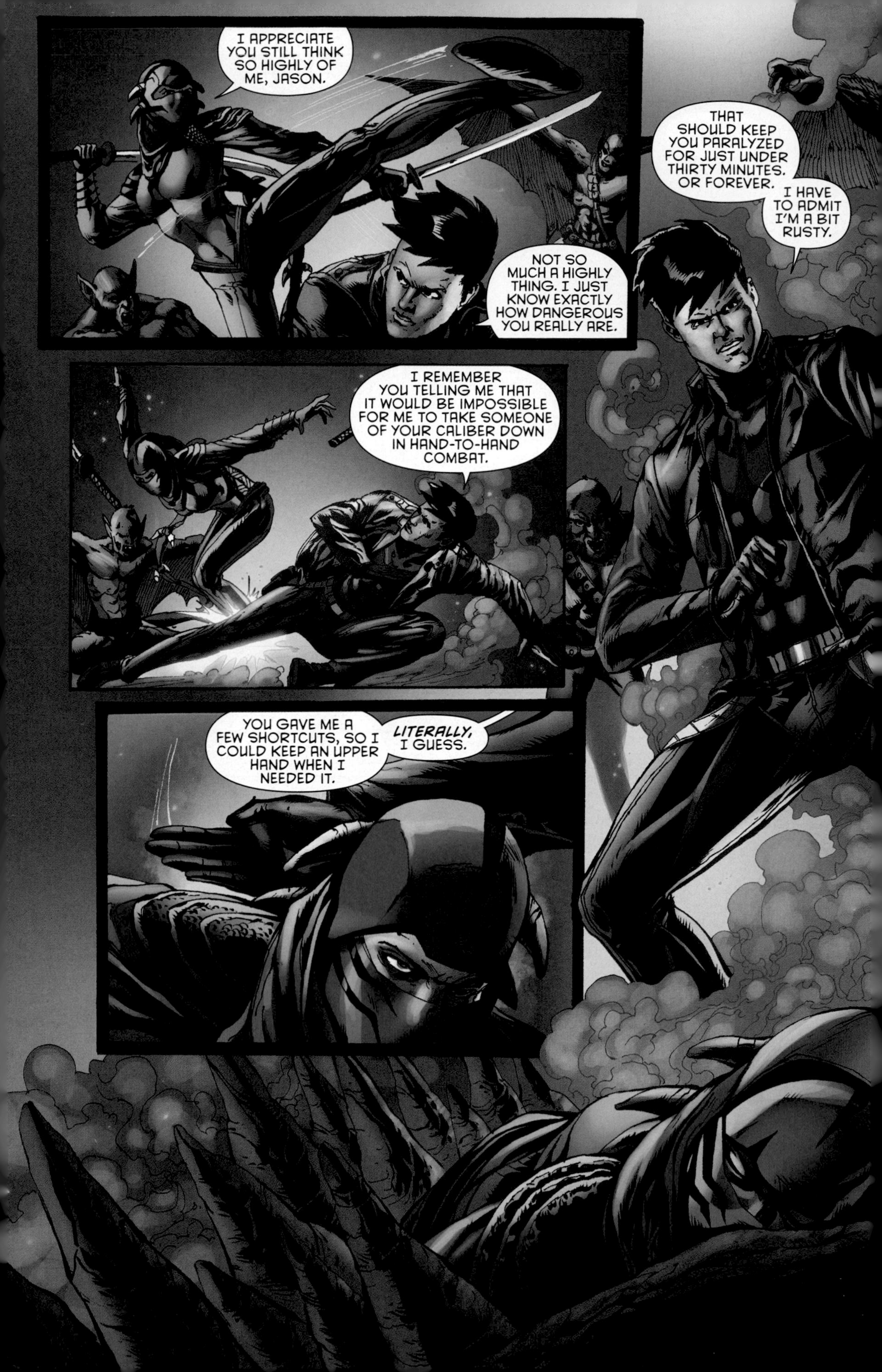
I APPRECIATE YOU STILL THINK SO HIGHLY OF ME, JASON.
NOT SO MUCH A HIGHLY THING. I JUST KNOW EXACTLY HOW DANGEROUS YOU REALLY ARE.
I REMEMBER YOU TELLING ME THAT IT WOULD BE IMPOSSIBLE FOR ME TO TAKE SOMEONE OF YOUR CALIBER DOWN IN HAND-TO-HAND COMBAT.
YOU GAVE ME A FEW SHORTCUTS, SO I COULD KEEP AN UPPER HAND WHEN I NEEDED IT.
LITERALLY, I GUESS.
THAT SHOULD KEEP YOU PARALYZED FOR JUST UNDER THIRTY MINUTES. OR FOREVER.
I HAVE TO ADMIT I'M A BIT RUSTY.

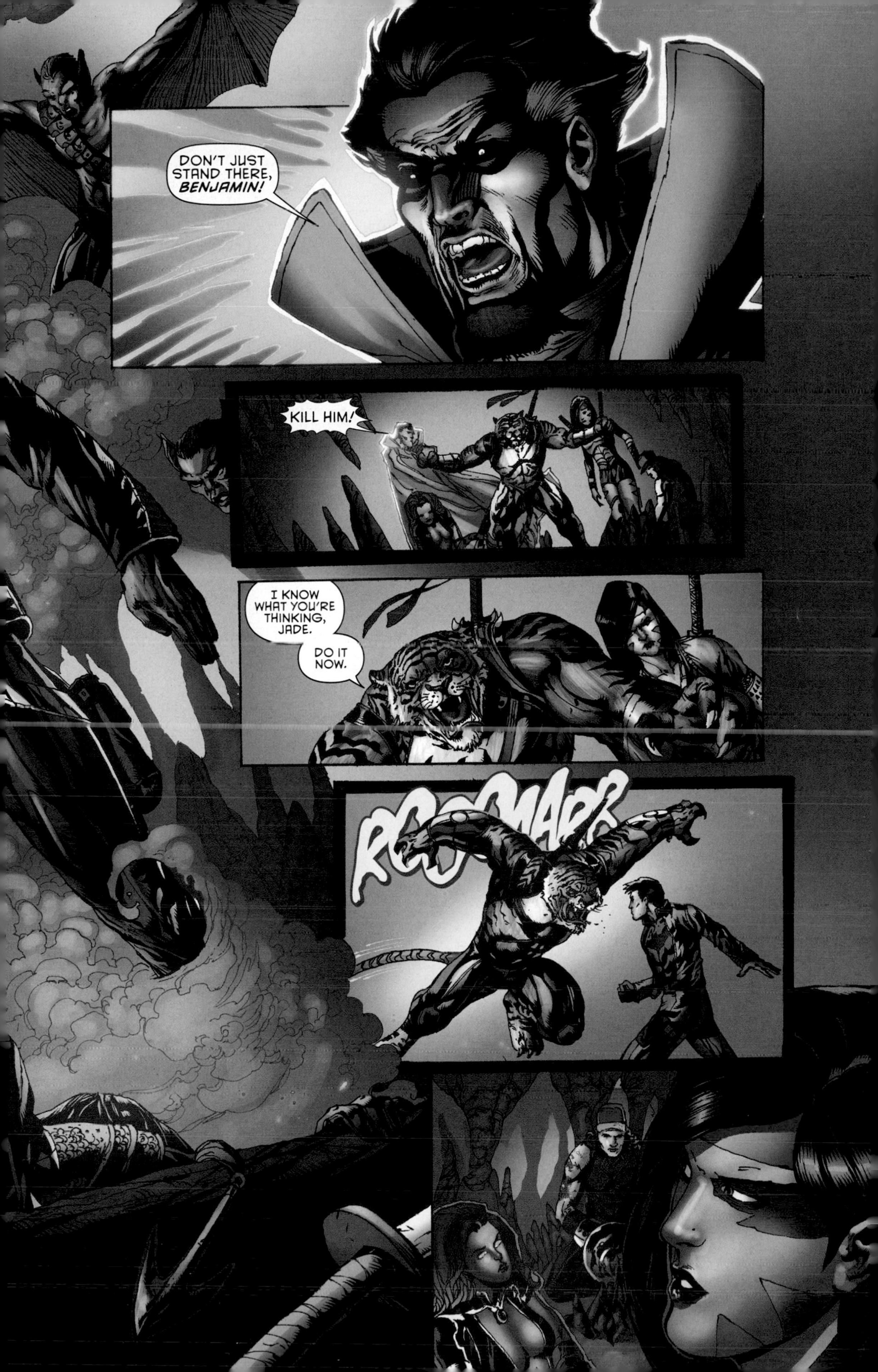
DON'T JUST STAND THERE, BENJAMIN!
KILL HIM!
I KNOW WHAT YOU'RE THINKING, JADE.
DO IT NOW.

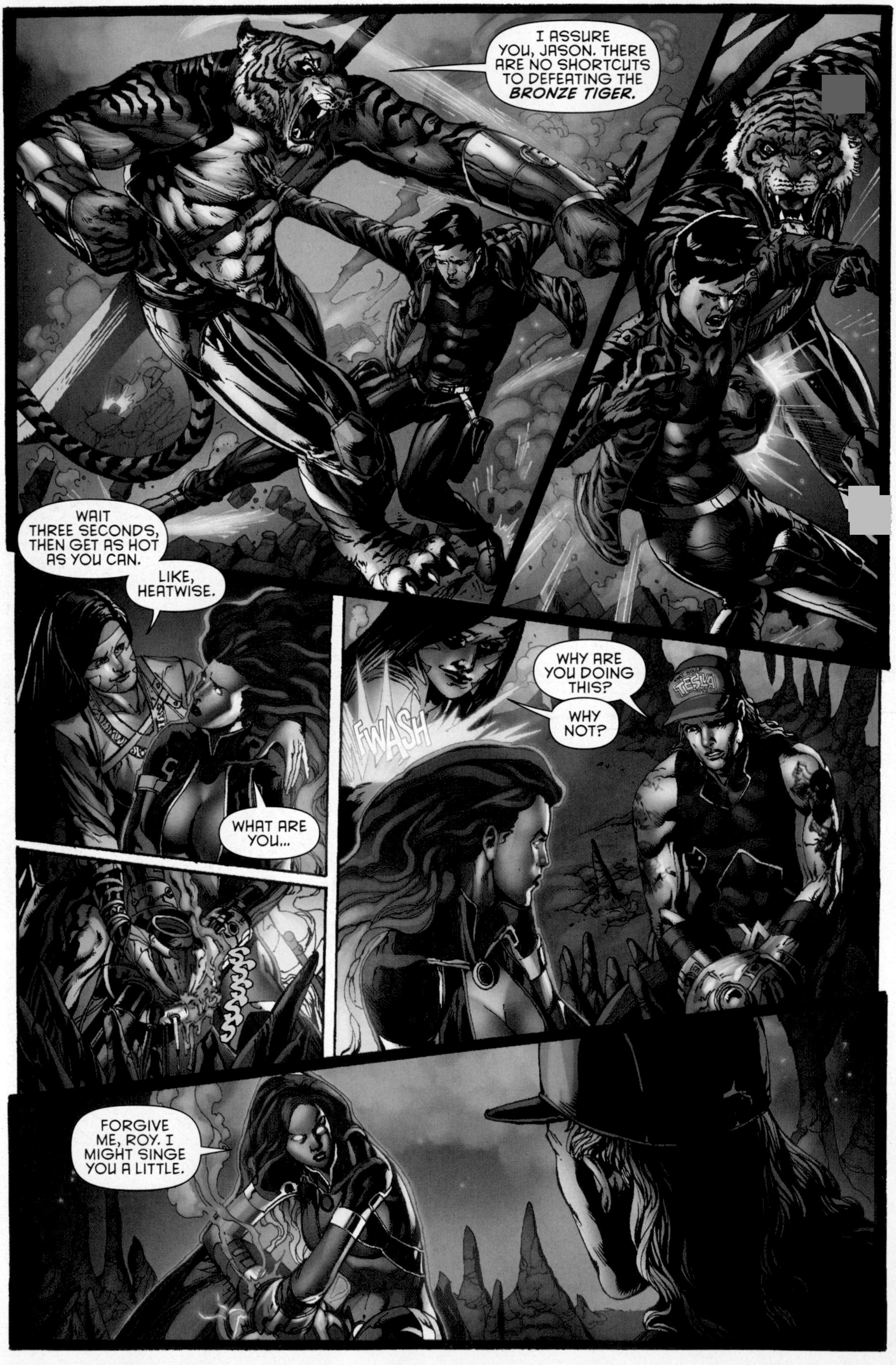
I ASSURE YOU, JASON. THERE ARE NO SHORTCUTS TO DEFEATING THE *BRONZE TIGER.*
WAIT THREE SECONDS, THEN GET AS HOT AS YOU CAN.
LIKE, HEATWISE.
WHAT ARE YOU...
FWASH
WHY ARE YOU DOING THIS?
WHY NOT?
TESLA
FORGIVE ME, ROY. I MIGHT SINGE YOU A LITTLE.

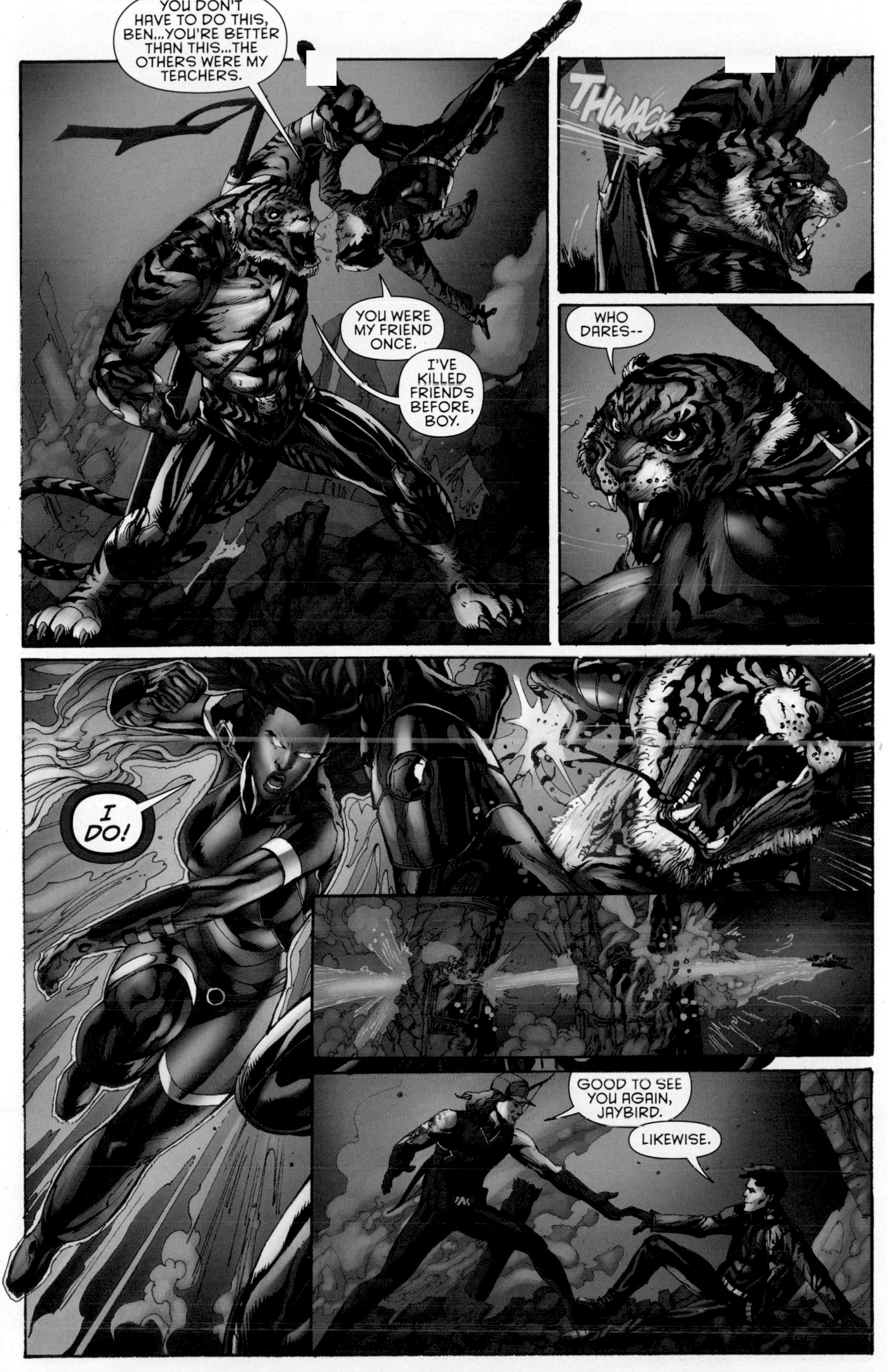
YOU DON'T HAVE TO DO THIS, BEN...YOU'RE BETTER THAN THIS...THE OTHERS WERE MY TEACHERS.
YOU WERE MY FRIEND ONCE.
I'VE KILLED FRIENDS BEFORE, BOY.
THWACK
WHO DARES--
I DO!
GOOD TO SEE YOU AGAIN, JAYBIRD.
LIKEWISE.

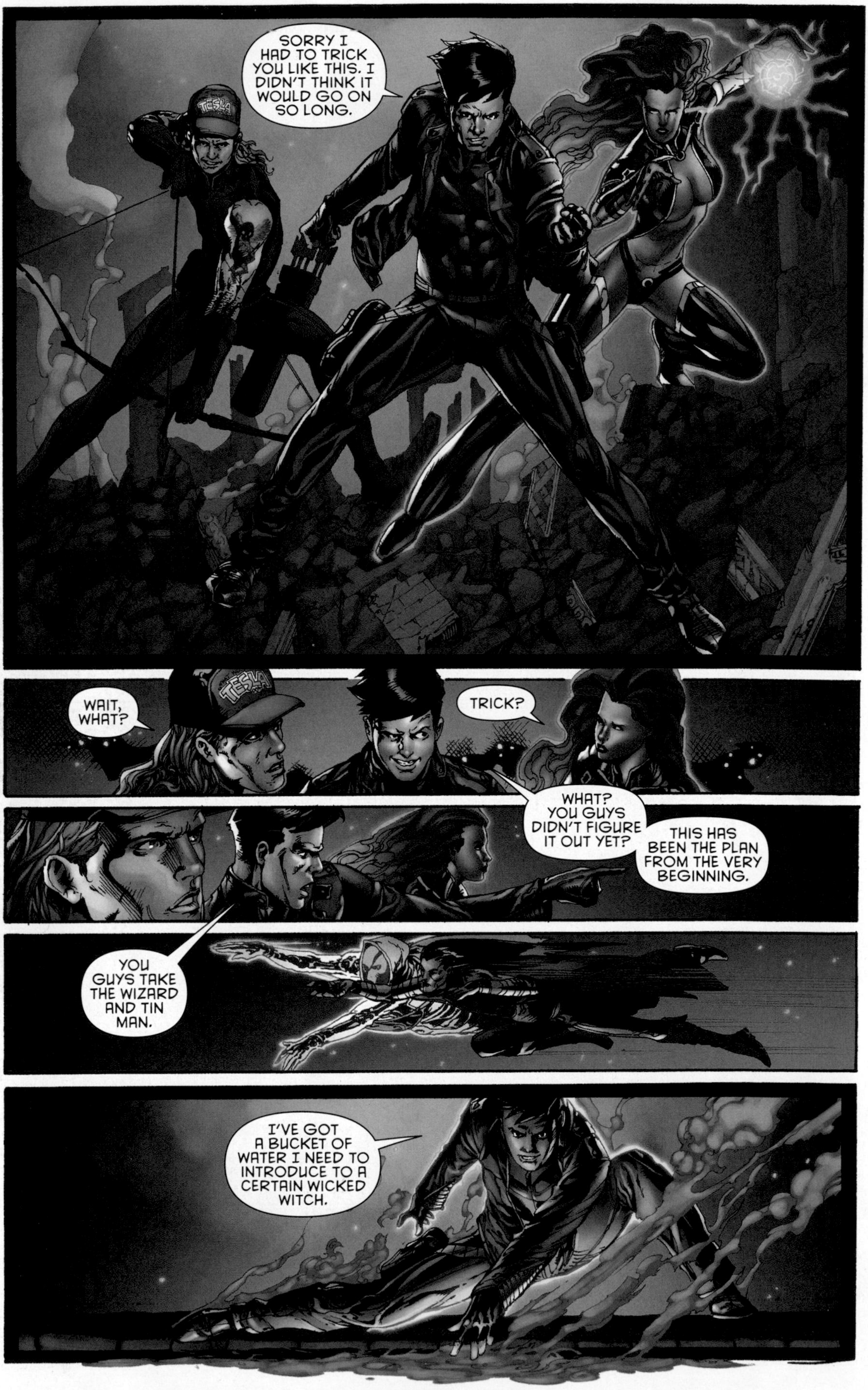
SORRY I HAD TO TRICK YOU LIKE THIS. I DIDN'T THINK IT WOULD GO ON SO LONG.
TESLA
TESLA
WAIT, WHAT?
TRICK?
WHAT? YOU GUYS DIDN'T FIGURE IT OUT YET?
THIS HAS BEEN THE PLAN FROM THE VERY BEGINNING.
YOU GUYS TAKE THE WIZARD AND TIN MAN.
I'VE GOT A BUCKET OF WATER I NEED TO INTRODUCE TO A CERTAIN WICKED WITCH.

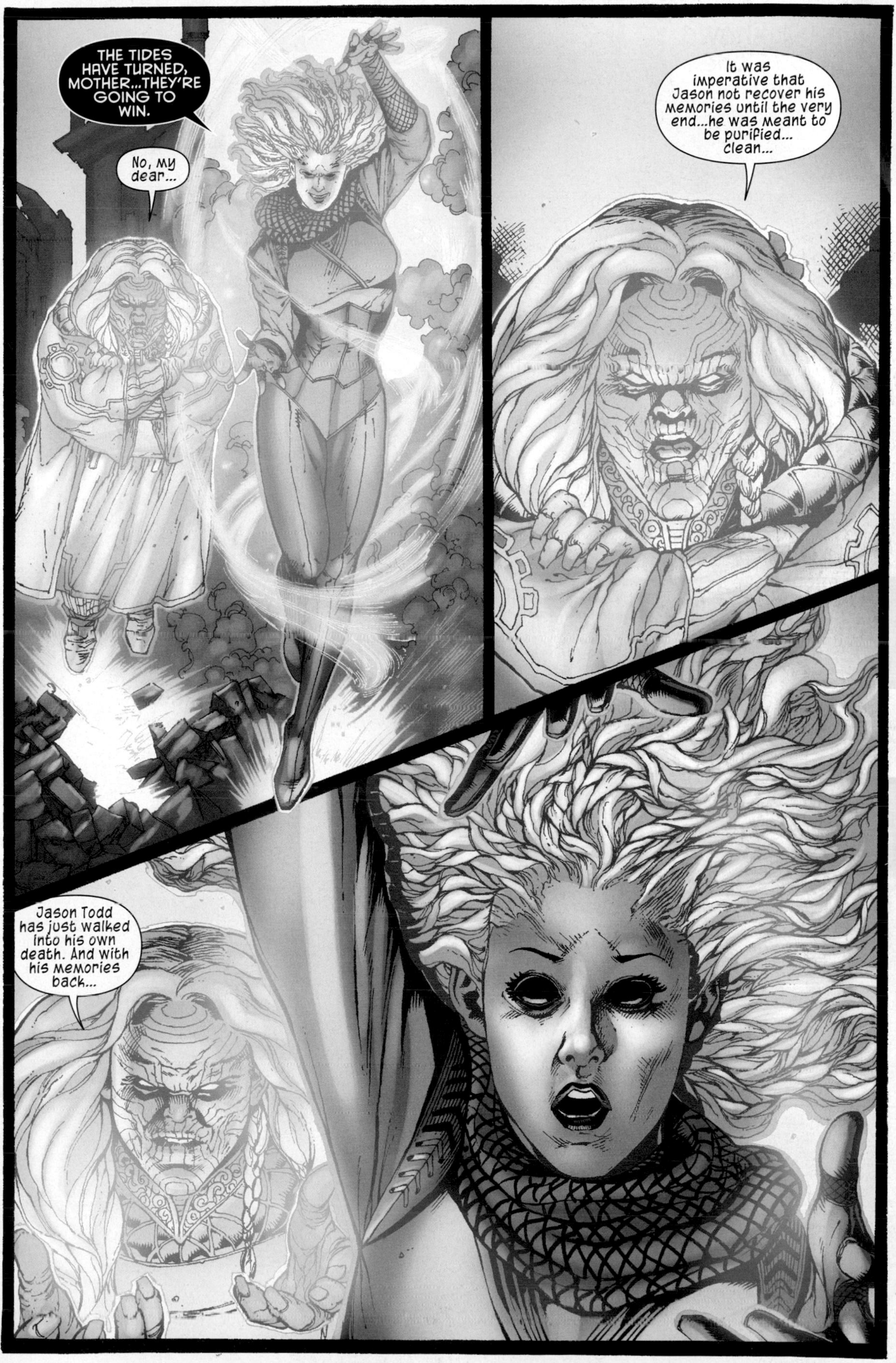
THE TIDES HAVE TURNED, MOTHER...THEY'RE GOING TO WIN.
No, my dear...
It was imperative that Jason not recover his memories until the very end...he was meant to be purified... clean...
Jason Todd has just walked into his own death. And with his memories back...

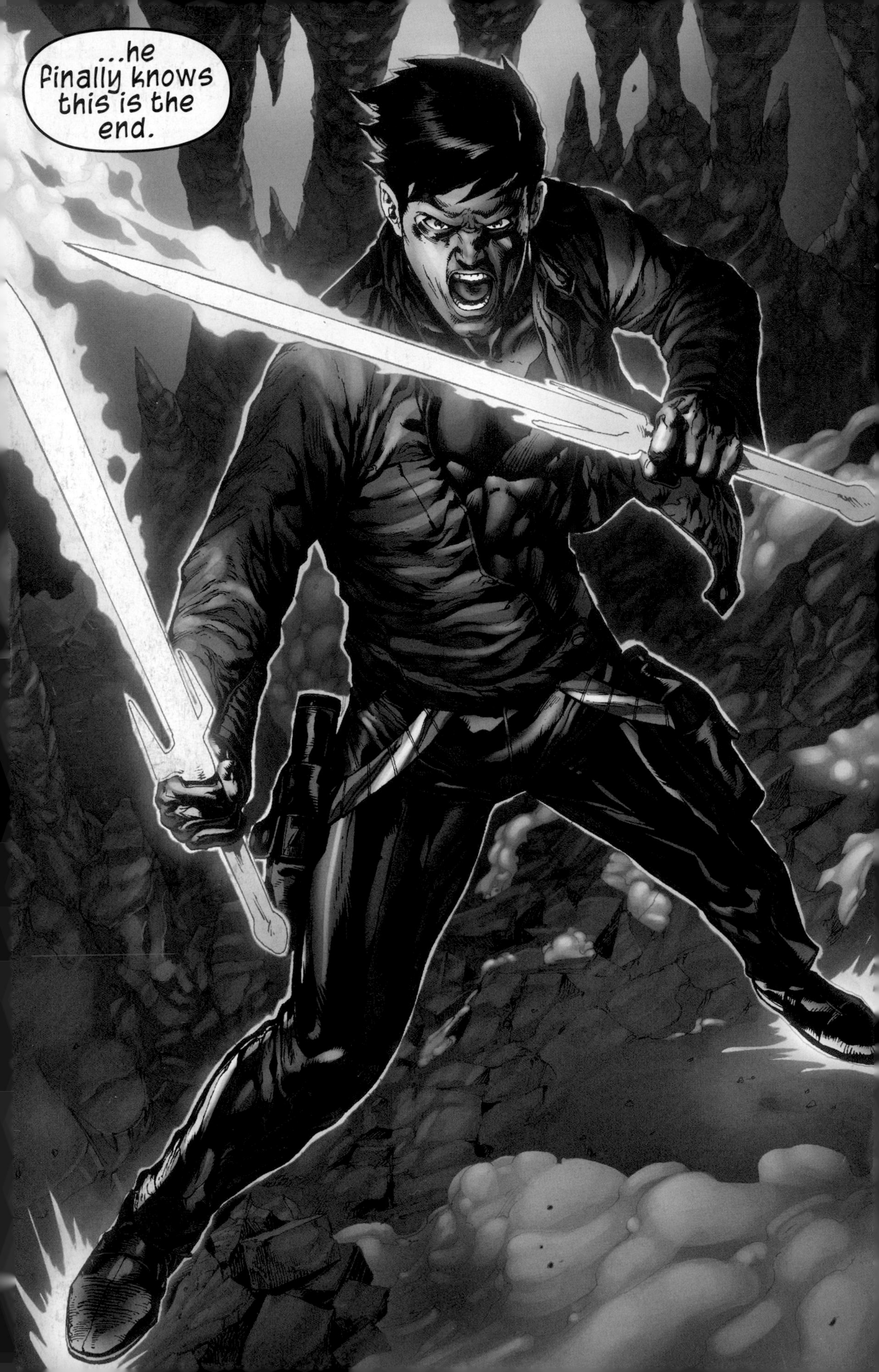
...he finally knows this is the end.